ELECTRICITY MATTERS

3RD EDITION

Englisch für elektrotechnische Berufe

von
Michael Benford
Ken Thomson
Wolf-Rainer Windisch

in Zusammenarbeit mit
der Verlagsredaktion

Verfasser:	Michael Benford Ken Thomson Wolf-Rainer Windisch
Berater:	Nils Krämer, Düsseldorf
Projektleitung:	Andreas Goebel
Verlagsredaktion:	Shaunessy Ashdown
Redaktionelle Mitarbeit:	Stefanie Heimann, Christine House, Simone Neumann Oliver Busch (Wörterverzeichnisse)
Bildredaktion:	Christiane Grosskopf, Gertha Maly
Illustration:	Sam Bryer (www.sambryerpaints.com) Oxford Designers & Illustrators
Gesamtgestaltung und technische Umsetzung:	vitaledesign, Berlin
Titelfoto:	Getty RF

Erhältlich sind auch:

Handreichungen für den Unterricht mit DVD-Extra und Audio-CD (ISBN: 978-3-06-450785-2)

Online-Ergänzungen unter www.cornelsen.de/matters

www.cornelsen.de

Die Links zu externen Webseiten Dritter, die in diesem Lehrwerk angegeben sind, wurden vor Drucklegung sorgfältig auf ihre Aktualität geprüft. Der Verlag übernimmt keine Gewähr für die Aktualität und den Inhalt dieser Seiten oder solcher, die mit ihnen verlinkt sind.

1. Auflage, 1. Druck 2013

Alle Drucke dieser Auflage sind inhaltlich unverändert und können im Unterricht nebeneinander verwendet werden.

Druck: H. Heenemann, Berlin

ISBN 978-3-06-450784-5

Inhalt gedruckt auf säurefreiem Papier aus nachhaltiger Forstwirtschaft.

VORWORT

Electricity Matters – 3rd Edition ist die völlige Neubearbeitung des bewährten Englisch-Lehrwerks für Lernende elektrotechnischer Berufe, die am Berufsschulunterricht oder an betrieblichen Fortbildungsmaßnahmen teilnehmen. Das Werk basiert auf den Lehrplänen der Bundesländer für Berufsschulen und bereitet auf die KMK-Zertifikatsprüfung Stufe II vor (Niveau B1 des Gemeinsamen Europäischen Referenzrahmens). Dies geschieht anhand prüfungsbezogener und mit einem KMK-Symbol gekennzeichneter Aufgaben, einer KMK-Seite pro Unit sowie einem *KMK mock exam* im Anhang.

Electricity Matters – 3rd Edition richtet sich an Lernende, deren Englischkenntnisse dem Niveau eines mittleren Bildungsabschlusses entsprechen. Darüber hinaus enthält jede Unit mit den *Extra materials* auch anspruchsvolleren Lernstoff für Lernende mit fortgeschrittenen Englischkenntnissen. Ein Grundwortschatz von ca. 650 Wörtern wird vorausgesetzt. Dieser ist in einem gesonderten Vokabelverzeichnis aufgeführt.

Electricity Matters – 3rd Edition besteht aus zwölf Units, von denen jede eine in sich abgeschlossene Handlung enthält. Es ist möglich, einzelne Units auszulassen, jedoch wird empfohlen, wann immer Zeit und Lehrpläne es ermöglichen, die gegebene Reihenfolge einzuhalten, da sich die Abfolge der Units im Wesentlichen an der Reihenfolge der Lernfelder für elektronische Berufe orientiert.

In berufsbezogenen, praxisnahen Situationen werden die Lernenden mit allen wesentlichen Aspekten des Englischen vertraut gemacht, die ihnen in ihrem beruflichen Alltag begegnen können. Ob es um Kontakte zu Kunden und Geschäftspartnern, den Umgang mit technischen Dokumenten, das Schreiben von E-Mails, die Kommunikation über Bauteile, Messungen oder Motoren geht – ***Electricity Matters – 3rd Edition*** bietet in jedem Fall das passende sprachliche Rüstzeug.

Alle Units zeichnen sich durch kleine Lernschritte aus, so dass auch Lernende, die nur eine Wochenstunde Englischunterricht haben, ihre Kenntnisse und Fähigkeiten sorgfältig und zielstrebig aufbauen können.

Electricity Matters – 3rd Edition bietet die Möglichkeit eines handlungsorientierten und praxisbezogenen Unterrichts. Die aus dem Berufsleben gegriffenen, häufig authentischen Materialien vermitteln den Lernenden praxisnah das wichtige Fachvokabular. Die Lernenden schulen aktiv ihre Sprechfertigkeit in Rollenspielen und in Partnerarbeit, wobei neben der beruflichen auch die soziale Komponente des Arbeitsalltags einbezogen wird.

Grammatik wird in jeder Unit punktuell wiederholt, wobei die Regeln auf das Wesentliche begrenzt sind und insbesondere der Festigung von Grundstrukturen dienen.

Electricity Matters – 3rd Edition vermittelt die englischsprachigen Grundpfeiler, auf denen sicheres Auftreten und korrektes Handeln im Berufsalltag basieren. Wenn die Lernenden sich dabei mit Vergnügen der englischen Sprache bedienen, hat dieses Werk sein Ziel erreicht.

2 Dialog bzw. Hörtext auf der Audio-CD

KMK Übungen zur Vorbereitung auf die KMK-Zertifikatsprüfung

Übungen für Lernende, die schon früher mit der vorherigen Aufgabe fertig sind.

WEBCODE EMU01 Die Webcodes weisen auf Zusatzmaterial zur selbstständigen Weiterarbeit hin und können unter **www.cornelsen.de/matters** abgerufen werden.

TABLE OF CONTENTS

UNIT 1

My company

- Describing jobs and companies
- Solving customers' problems
- Giving workplace tours

1 Warm-up

A Use the Language box to write a few sentences about your job and the company you work at. Then tell the rest of the class. Include the following points.

- name of your company
- location
- number of employees
- the type of work it does
- the type(s) of customers
- what you do there on a typical day
- what can happen if it is not done
- your own ideas

LANGUAGE

It's …	installation work …	install/check/test/replace …
called …	in houses	electrical components
located in …	in buildings	electrical circuits
	in factories	electrical fittings
It …	on building sites	materials
employs …		tools
installs …	van / mobile workshop	equipment
manufactures …		
exports …	customers:	projects/jobs:
repairs …	private	small
maintains …	commercial	medium-sized
carries out …	industrial	large/major

B Use words from the Language box to describe the jobs the people in the pictures are doing.

1

2

3

4

2 Company websites

A The company Ritter Starkstromtechnik has translated its website into English. Match the German headings with the English terms 1–8 on the website.

Elektrotechnik • Mechatronik • Notstromsysteme • Projektentwicklung • Schaltanlagenbau • Technische Gebäudeausrüstung • Telekommunikation • Trafoinstallation

B Unfortunately the headings and the texts have got mixed up. Match the texts A–H with the headings (1–8).

www.ritter.com

RITTER Starkstromtechnik

START NEWS COMPANY INSTALLATION AUTOMATION SWITCHGEAR SWITCH COMPONENTS JOB OPPORTUNITIES LEGAL NOTICE DEUTSCH

1 Technical building equipment	A Let us design the systems and machines you need to link computer technology and electronic, electrical and mechanical engineering.
2 Project development	B Let our engineers install the right equipment to step the voltage up or down for you, whenever and wherever you need it.
3 Mechatronics	C Whether it's a switch, a socket or a circuit, a motor, a machine or a magnet, we'll provide the know-how and service you need.
4 Transformer installation	D A power outage can bring production to a standstill and put human life at risk. Let us design a system so this will never happen at your company.
5 Telecommunications	E We'll install the technology needed to make your house, offices or factory comfortable and efficient.
6 Electrical engineering	F We'll make the state-of-the-art, fail-safe switching system you need to guarantee power to your low and medium-voltage equipment.
7 Switchgear manufacture	G A phone call, teleconference or video conference? Let us install the systems you need.
8 Emergency power systems	H Come to us with your ideas and let our experts plan, price and implement them for you.

C Fassen Sie die wichtigsten Inhalte der Website unter den entsprechenden Unterschriften in deutscher Sprache zusammen. KMK

D Go online and check out your company's website. Choose three or four headings to describe what it does and write a sentence under each heading. Present your results to the class.

E Complete the sentences with words from the box. They are all from the website above.

circuit • efficient • implement • outage • premises • socket • defective • step • state-of-the-art

We supply our customers with …[1] equipment and offer the best service on the market. It makes no difference if it's just a …[2] for a toaster, a 2,000 watt …[3] for a washing machine, a heavy-duty transformer to …[4] the voltage up or down for a whole neighbourhood or a fail-safe system for a hospital that works even if there is a power …[5]. We will provide the best possible service and …[6] our customers' instructions. Our technicians will arrive at our customers' …[7] on time and will install systems and equipment that are very …[8] and guarantee excellent value for money.

3 Contacting foreign suppliers

Ritter e-mails Stig Lindquist at COMSYS AB, a Swedish supplier of filter technology, to find a solution to a power supply problem.

Read the e-mail and say if statements 1–6 are true. Correct the false statements.

1 Stig works for Ritter Starkstromtechnik.
2 The problem with the power supply is in Germany.
3 Ritter Starkstromtechnik has a problem with its power supply.
4 When the lighting is switched on, the meat cutters cut out.
5 When the meat cutters are switched on, the lighting cuts out.
6 The power supply goes back to normal if some of the lights are switched off.

meat cutter

Neue E-Mail

Von: Markus.Prinz@ritter-starkstrom.de
Kopie:
Betreff: Power supply breakdown

Dear Mr Lindquist

We have found your company's website on the internet and believe that you may have the solution to a power supply problem that one of our customers is currently having at a large meat-processing plant in Dortmund, Germany.

When they switch on the electric meat cutters, the lighting cuts out sporadically in the cutting room and/or in the warehouse. When this happens, they have to completely disconnect all the lighting circuits and then switch them back on again to get them working again.

Please let us know if your company deals with this type of problem.

I look forward to hearing from you soon.

Markus Prinz
Graduate Engineer (FH)
RITTER Starkstromtechnik
Dortmund, Germany

4 Discussing problems

2 **Stig Lindquist phones Ritter Installation in Dortmund. Read/Listen to the telephone call and then choose the correct summary (a, b or c). Explain which facts are wrong in the other two summaries.**

Stig Good morning, Mr Prinz. It's Stig Lindquist from COMSYS AB in Sweden. Many thanks for your e-mail asking us to contact you. You say you're interested in one of our products to improve the power supply for a customer of yours. Could you describe the problem for me again in more detail?

Markus Yes, certainly. Our customer has a chain of supermarkets with a central meat-processing plant here in Dortmund. They've got three new heavy-duty commercial meat cutters and, as I said in my e-mail, the lighting sometimes cuts out when they switch on the cutters. They then have to disconnect all the lighting circuits and switch them back on again to get them working again. We've checked all the lighting circuits and they're fine, so we've also plotted the currents of the three phases in the power supply, and the graph shows that they become irregular when the cutters are used.

Stig I see. And what sort of motors do the meat cutters have?

Markus Each one has a three-phase AC motor with a frequency converter.

Stig Well, it sounds like the frequency converters are disturbing the power supply. I think you need one of our filters, but first of all I need to visit your customer to see for myself. When can I come?

Markus Well, as soon as possible because the supermarkets need their meat supplies.

Stig In that case I'll get on the first flight to Dortmund. I'll e-mail you the details as soon as I've booked.

Markus Excellent! I look forward to meeting you soon. Have a safe flight.

Stig Thanks. Goodbye.

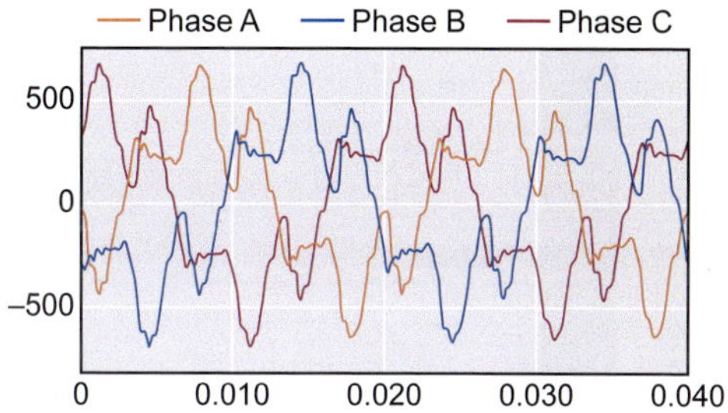

irregular phase currents during cutter operation

a Stig Lindquist would like to speak to Markus Prinz about a problem with the power supply to a supermarket in Dortmund, Germany. Each time someone switches on a meat cutter, the lights in the supermarket go out. The lighting circuits have all been checked and found to be in order. Tests have shown that the probable reason for the problem is a broken part in the meat cutter.

b Stig Lindquist would like to speak to Markus Prinz about a problem with the power supply at a meat-processing plant in Germany. Whenever the meat cutters are used, the lights all go out. The only way to get the lights back on is to disconnect all the lighting circuits and then switch them back on again. Tests have shown that the probable reason for the problem is the frequency converters in the meat cutters.

c Stig Lindquist would like to speak to Markus Prinz about a problem with the power supply at a meat-processing plant in Germany. When the meat cutters are used, this sometimes makes the lighting cut out. There is nothing wrong with the lighting circuits, but tests have shown that the power supply is irregular when the meat cutters are operated. This is probably due to the frequency converters in the meat cutters.

5 Working with words

Match these German words with their English equivalents in the dialogue.

1 verbessern
2 Stromzufuhr
3 Beleuchtung
4 ausfallen
5 einschalten
6 vom Netz trennen
7 Stromkreis
8 kontrollieren
9 Phase
10 Drehstrom
11 Frequenzumrichter
12 stören

GRAMMAR

Simple present

Aussagen

I *you* *we* *they*	*work*
he/she/it	*works*

Verneinungen

I *you* *we* *they*	*don't*	*work*
he/she/it	*doesn't*	

Fragen

do	*I* *you* *we* *they*	*work?*
does	*he/she/it*	

Present progressive

Aussagen

I	*'m*	*working*
you *we* *they*	*'re*	
he/she/it	*'s*	

Verneinungen

I	*'m not*	*working*
you *we* *they*	*aren't*	
he/she/it	*isn't*	

Fragen

am	*I*	*working?*
are	*you* *we* *they*	
is	*he/she/it*	

Siehe S. 144 für weitere Einzelheiten.

6 Practice: simple present or present progressive?

Complete the text with the correct verb forms.

It's 4 p.m. and Stig Lindquist is at Ritter Installation in Dortmund. Stig regularly (travel)[1] all over Europe for his Swedish employer. He (speak)[2] Swedish back home but today he (speak)[3] English with Markus Prinz. They (walk)[4] across the car park on their way to Markus's office.

Markus We (do)[5] a big job for a hospital near here at the moment, so most of our vans are on the road. Ah, look! See that car over there? The one that (just/come)[6] into the car park. It (belong)[7] to one of our electricians. He (drive)[8] home now after a long day.

Stig I see. Where (your company/do)[9] most of its work, Markus – on site or here in the workshop?

Markus 90 per cent of the time we (work)[10] on the customer's site.

7 Using organization charts

A Study Ritter's organization chart and complete the following sentences.

1. The company is owned by …
2. The person responsible for staff and training is called …
3. Markus Prinz is Head of …

4 The Head of Finance reports to …
5 Larissa Petrovna has a qualification in …
6 Ralph Benz supervises two …
7 Equipment and materials are stored in the …
8 When Ritter gets a contract to do work for a customer, it uses its own employees and/or …

B Find words in the organization chart to correspond to the following German expressions.

Anlagenbau • Einkauf • Fuhrpark • Geschäftsführung • Installationstechnik • Lager • Leittechnik • Nachunternehmer • Personalabteilung • Qualitätssicherung • Schutztechnik • Sicherheit

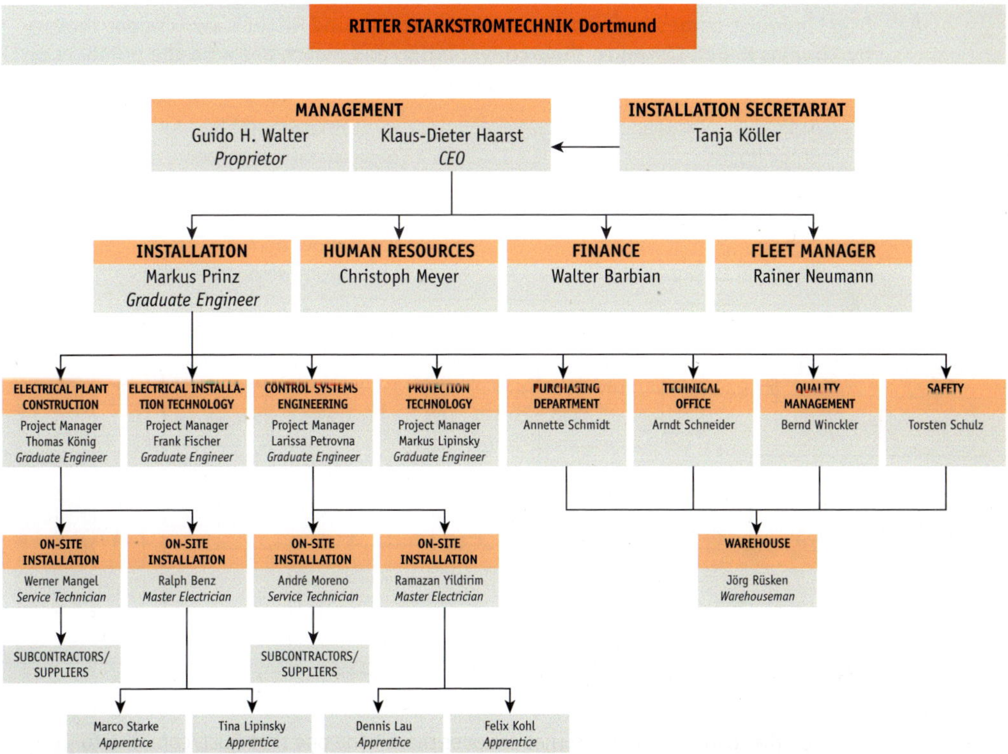

C Ritter möchte eine kurze englischsprachige Beschreibung des Dortmunder Installationsbetriebs ins Internet stellen. Benutzen Sie das Organigramm, um einen Text von 80–100 Wörtern zu erstellen, in dem die technischen Dienstleistungen des Dortmunder Werks beschrieben werden. KMK

8 Talking about your company

A With a partner, draw up an organization chart of your own company.

B Work in groups of two to four people. Use the phrases on p. 6 to write a description of your company and what you do there. Add other important points. Give a presentation to the class.

MATTERSTV

Putting your visitors in the picture

Check out video clip no. 1 to see how Ritter shows visitors around the factory. Use the clip as a model to make a similar video about your company.

9 A guided tour of Ritter's factory

3

A Stig Lindquist comes to Germany and is shown around Ritter's switchgear factory by Thomas Keller. Listen to their conversation and match a–l with the numbers on the diagram. The tour starts at number 1.

- **a** Assembly, Wiring and Training
- **b** Break Room
- **c** Conference Room
- **d** Copper Workshop
- **e** Design
- **f** Electrical Design
- **g** Final Assembly
- **h** Metal Workshop
- **i** Pre-assembly
- **j** Sales
- **k** Showroom
- **l** Storeroom

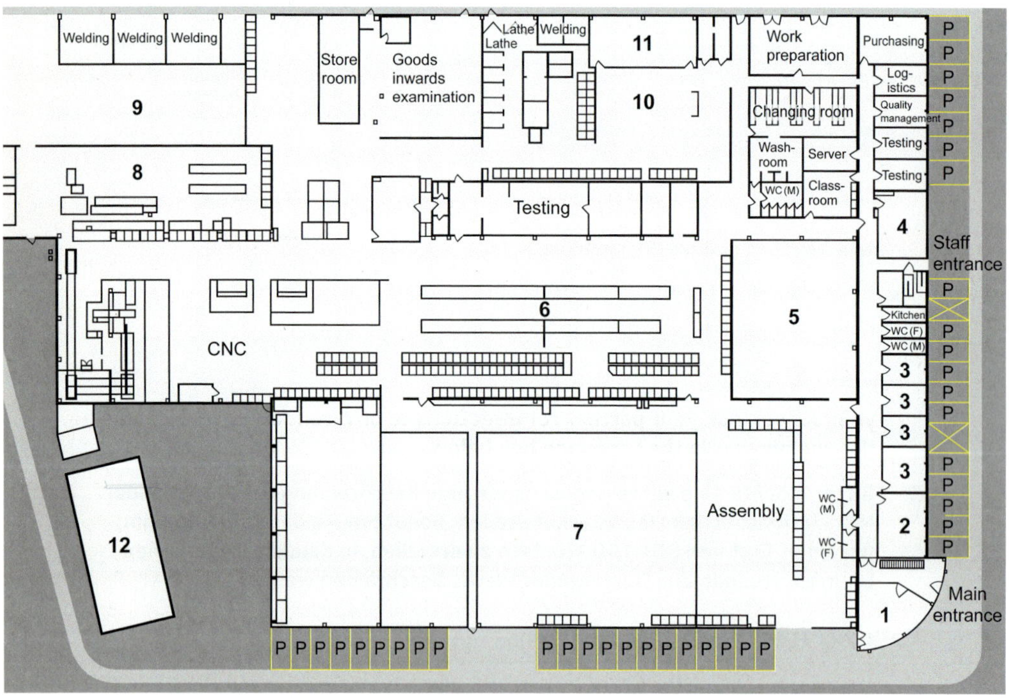

The Ritter switchgear factory

B Listen to the dialogue again and say if the following statements are true or false. Correct the false statements.

1. Thomas Keller and Stig Lindquist have met before.
2. Ritter only installs switchgear in commercial buildings.
3. Ritter only buys a few components from external companies.
4. Ritter is the only German firm selling switchgear.
5. Ritter's products are always made to customers' specifications.
6. The storeroom is for tools.
7. The pre-assembly and final assembly workshops are next to each other.
8. Ritter has a special machine which both bends and cuts metal.
9. Ritter trains apprentices.
10. Ritter's products are designed by an external company.

10 Showing visitors around the company

A An English-speaking visitor comes to the Ritter Switchgear factory and asks you to show him/her around. Take him/her on a tour of the factory starting at the entrance and finishing in the break room. Point out and describe three or four workshops and other places of interest on the way. Use the expressions in the following Language box.

LANGUAGE

Let's start by visiting the … department.

Here On the left/right	we have the … department.		
This is where	we design/make/assemble/store … … are designed/made/assembled/stored.		
We use a	bending machine punching machine	to make to manufacture	the panels. the components.

B With a partner, use a plan of your own company to help a visitor to find his or her way around.

C You are at the main entrance of the Ritter building, of your own company, or of your school. Ask your partner for directions to different areas of the building. Use the phrases in the Language box below.

LANGUAGE

Could you tell me the way to …, please?

Yes, certainly.
Go down the corridor until you get to …
Turn right/left at …
… the first/second/third door/hall on your right/left.
… the end of the corridor.

11 Hörverstehen

4

Im Rahmen der Projektwoche Ihrer Berufsschule besucht Ihre Klasse die Hannover Messe. Jede(r) Auszubildende soll ein Profil eines in Europa tätigen Elektrobetriebs erstellen. Sie besuchen den Stand eines großen amerikanischen Unternehmens und hören eine Präsentation in englischer Sprache über die Aktivitäten der Gesellschaft in Deutschland.

Kopieren Sie die Tabelle und füllen Sie sie während der Präsentation aus.

Name des Unternehmens	
Sitz	
Standort(e) in Europa	
Geschichte des Unternehmens	
Produkte	
Umsatz	
Zahl der Mitarbeiter	

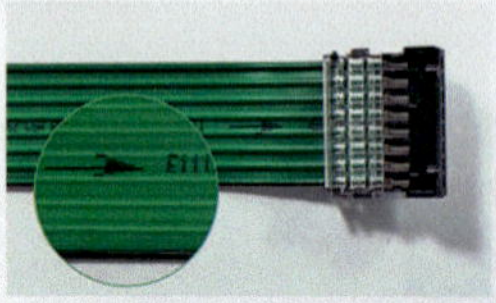

Achtpolige Flachleitung SmartWire-DT

Drehstrom-Ölschütz

Fließbandfertigung

Grobhandtaster

Speicherprogrammierbare Steuerung

12 Interaktion

Sie befinden sich auf dem Stand eines Unternehmens auf der Hannover Messe.

Erstellen Sie in Partnerarbeit einen Dialog aus folgenden Rollenkarten.

Jack/Jill Lawrence von Power Incorporated aus Delaware in den USA	**Eigener Name und Position in Ihrem Betrieb** die Person, die gerade Standdienst macht
Sie suchen englische Verkaufsliteratur von verschiedenen deutschen Firmen. Sie stellen Fragen zu: ▪ der Qualität der Produkte ▪ Lieferzeiten bzw. Installation bzw. Wartung ▪ Problemlösung/Troubleshooting ▪ Garantie Sie geben dem/der Mitarbeiter/-in Ihre Visitenkarte. Sie bitten um ein Angebot für … (Produkt/ Dienstleitung)	Sie nutzen diese Gelegenheit, Ihre Firma kurz zu präsentieren. Sie beschreiben: ▪ die Produkte Ihres Unternehmens ▪ die Dienstleistungen (z. B. Installation, Wartung, Reparatur) ▪ den/die Standort(e) Sie geben dem/der Besucher/-in: ▪ Verkaufsliteratur ▪ Ihre Visitenkarte

http://www.franklin-electrical.com

ABOUT US | SERVICES | CASE STUDIES | NEWS | LINKS | GALLERY | CONTACT US

We offer these contracting services:
Electrical design CAD
Electrical installation and refurbishment
Electrical maintenance
Inspections and reports
New stores and refits
Retail concessions at airports
PAT testing
Power quality analysis surveys
Project management

All our work meets the latest regulations and building code requirements.
Our health and safety advisers are CIBT-trained.

We supply and install:
Audio-visual systems
Back of house lighting
CCTV
Door entry/security systems
Electrical services in connection with mechanical supplies / HVAC
Emergency lighting
Energy-efficient and computer-controlled lighting systems / BMS
Fire alarm systems (PA/VA)
IT network data cabling (cat5e/cat6)
Mains distribution and sub mains distribution
Sales floor lighting
Small power

To read our customer reviews, click here.

Abbreviations: **BMS** Building Management System, a computer-based control system that controls and monitors a building's mechanical and electrical equipment; **CITB** Construction Industry Training Board, UK; **HVAC** Heating, Ventilation and Air Conditioning ; **PAT** Portable Appliance Testing; **PA/VA** Public Address / Voice Alarm systems

13 Understanding a company's service offerings

A Study Franklin's website and explain how we know that the company …

1. uses computers to design electrical systems.
2. will completely rewire a building.
3. is able to connect a building to the national grid.
4. will install lighting systems that do not use much electricity.
5. will install cameras to monitor movements in a building.

B Find the English-language website of a similar company and describe one of its major projects.

C Research PAT testing and PA/VA on the internet and explain when these services are necessary.

UNIT 2

My job and workplace

- Describing jobs
- Ordering and describing tools
- Discussing working conditions and tool defects

1 Warm-up

A Work with a partner. Match the job titles to the people (1–4).

panel building electrician • installation electrician • lineworker • electrical machine repairer

B Who says what about their jobs? Match the speech bubbles to the jobs.

My work involves installing, maintaining and testing wiring systems in houses and flats.

My work involves assembling and testing electrical panels for fitting in machinery.

In my job I install, inspect and repair machinery in a factory.

My work is about maintaining and repairing the grid system which delivers power across the country.

C Take turns to make more sentences about each job.

2 Talking about my job

A Four electricians from Europe and the US are talking about their jobs. Read their descriptions, then match the people to the jobs in exercise 1A.

B Answer the questions about the texts. There may be more than one answer to a question. Read the texts again to check your answers.

Who …

1 carries out routine maintenance?
2 works on site?
3 checks wiring systems?
4 works different hours on different days?
5 works regular hours?
6 occasionally works at unusual times?
7 is based in a workshop?
8 assembles electrical equipment?

My name's Martin O'Neil and I live in Seattle. During my training I specialized in building panels. I was interested in this because the panels are really complex. In my current job I follow wiring plans to assemble electronic control panels which use programmable logic controllers (PLCs). They're used to control things like heating, ventilation and air-conditioning systems in commercial buildings. We produce the panels in a workshop. I work 37 hours per week, from Monday to Friday. I like the regular hours because I have a few hobbies I like to do in the evenings.

I'm Sarah Clark and I come from Liverpool. In my job I'm responsible for inspecting, testing and installing wiring systems in houses and flats. There's lots of variety in my work, so I like it. And I don't have to go to the same office or workshop every day. I'm always out and about. One week I could be working on a new block of flats and the next week I might be installing wiring in a 300-year-old house! My work involves stripping out old wiring and replacing it. If I'm working on a new house which is just being built, I follow architects' drawings which show where I should install electrical equipment. I also bend and cut conduit and fix equipment to walls. I often work quite a lot of overtime, but my standard working week is 40 hours.

My name's Jarek and I come from Poland. In my job I install, maintain and test electrical equipment in a large industrial plant. I'm also responsible for making regular inspections of our equipment and machinery to ensure that it's working properly, and for locating and dealing with faults before they lead to breakdowns. The job also involves repairing electrical and electronic equipment if there is a breakdown. I often have to replace components such as switches, fuses and circuit breakers to stop equipment malfunctioning. One of my favourite and most important tasks is troubleshooting equipment like our production robots to find out why something isn't working properly. Our factory operates 24 hours a day, seven days a week. An electrician always has to be available to deal with problems, so the other electricians and I work shifts. For example, last weekend I worked nights.

I'm Jean-Luc and I'm from Calais in France. I work for the company which runs the national electricity grid and I'm a lineworker. Basically, my colleagues and I are responsible for maintaining the grid and keeping electricity flowing around the country. So our job's quite important! A lot of my work is about laying cables in the ground. For example, I replace cables that have been damaged. I also lay new cables for areas where there's no electricity and connect these to substations. I sometimes have to work at height on transmission towers. I was nervous about this at first but it's all just part of a day's work now. Even when I'm not at work I have to be on standby quite a lot. If there's an emergency, we have to go out and deal with it, even in the middle of the night. It's important that power outages are dealt with as quickly as possible, and that's our job. I really enjoy my work. I like working outdoors and having a change of scenery nearly every day.

C **Match the German words to the highlighted English terms in the texts on p. 17 which have a similar meaning.**

1 Schaltschrank
2 Hochspannungsmast
3 Industrieanlage
4 Netz
5 Panne
6 Stromausfall

D **Use the English words from exercise C to complete the sentences.**

1 When we're working up on a …, we have to wear special harnesses to keep us safe.
2 This … controls the building's air-conditioning system.
3 My company's … is so large that it employs 18 electricians to maintain its electrical systems.
4 We have a … at one of our substations. Could you go out and find out what the problem is?
5 It's a good thing I found this faulty fuse on the production line. It would have led to a … .
6 Basically, the power … is the backbone of the electricity system, so it's really important.

✈ **E** **Decide whose job each sentence is about: Martin's, Sarah's, Jarek's or Jean-Luc's.**

3 Writing your job profile

KMK

Ihre Firma eröffnet demnächst eine Filiale im Ausland. Ihr Chef bittet Sie deshalb um eine kurze Beschreibung Ihrer Tätigkeiten und Ihre Einstellung dazu. Schreiben Sie einen entsprechenden Text in Englisch. Der Text sollte enthalten:

- Ihre Berufsbezeichnung
- Die Art der Firma, in der Sie arbeiten
- Ihre Hauptaufgaben und Zuständigkeitsbereiche bei der Arbeit
- Ihre Arbeitszeiten

LANGUAGE

Describing your job

I work in a workshop / in the open / at height.
I install/test/replace/inspect/troubleshoot electrical systems/components.
I maintain/repair machines.
I diagnose problems/faults.
I advise customers/colleagues.
I follow wiring plans / technical drawings.
I work fixed hours / a 39-hour week / shifts / a bit of overtime.
I work/do a lot of overtime.
I'm often on call.

4 Discussing working conditions

A Form two groups for a class discussion.

Group A: Look at the information in the table and think of as many advantages of shorter working hours and longer holidays for companies and employees as you can. Prepare arguments for shorter hours and longer holidays.

Group B: Look at the information in the table and think of as many disadvantages of shorter working hours and longer holidays for companies and employees as you can. Prepare arguments against shorter hours and longer holidays.

Country	Annual working hours (average)	Annual paid holiday days (average)	Productivity ranking*
United States	1,966	10.2	1
Japan	1,889	17.5	4
United Kingdom	1,731	25	3
Germany	1,693	24–30	2

* 1 is the highest ranking; 4 is the lowest.

B Carry out the discussion. Use as many phrases as possible from the Language box below.

C Which view do you agree with personally? After the discussion, hold a classroom vote.

LANGUAGE

Offering an opinion
If you want my opinion …
If you ask me …
As far as I see it …

Disagreeing
I'm afraid I really can't agree.
I think you're wrong there.
I don't think that's right.
(**Not**: ~~I don't mean~~ that's right.)

Expressing doubt
I'm not so sure about that.
I would doubt that a bit.

Giving reasons
The main reason is …
You see, if … then …
Because …

Agreeing
I would agree with that.
Yes, I think that's right.
I think you're right there.

Making suggestions
I think it would be a good idea to …
Maybe we should …
How about -ing …?

Handing over to another speaker
What do you think?
What's your opinion?

Summarizing
OK, so we both/all agree that …

Interrupting
Sorry to interrupt you, but …

5 Talking about workbench tools

A What are these tools called? Match the names to the pictures.

Allen keys • box cutter • flashlight • flat-bladed screwdriver • folding rule • hacksaw • hammer • multimeter • needle nose pliers • Phillips screwdriver • pipe wrench • power drill • round nose pliers • side-cutting pliers • soldering iron • spanner • spirit level • vernier callipers • wire strippers

B **Make sentences with the phrases in the table.**

Example: *A multimeter is for testing electrical circuits.*

An Allen key A hacksaw A multimeter A pair of pliers A pair of vernier callipers A pair of wire strippers A power drill A screwdriver A soldering iron A spanner	is for	cutting gripping loosening making measuring joining stripping tightening turning	bolts. components. electrical circuits. holes. metal. nuts. objects. screws. wires.

C **Choose three of the tools in the box below and write sentences describing what they are used for.**

box cutter • flashlight • folding rule •
hammer • spirit level • water pump pliers

D **Work in a small group and discuss …**

- **which of the tools you use, how often and what for.**
- **which other tools and equipment you use and what for.**

6 Placing orders

A Sarah Clark is phoning TopTools to order a new multimeter.

Make a dialogue by putting these sentences in the right order. (Tip: Start with h.)

a	**Sarah**	Fine. Cash on delivery, then, please.
b	**TopTools**	How would you like to pay?
c	**Sarah**	OK. What other multimeters do you have then?
d	**TopTools**	I'm afraid we don't have the Existes 24-T in stock at the moment.
e	**Sarah**	OK. I'd like to order one then, please.
f	**TopTools**	Well, I could offer you the Existes 24-T Plus. Basically, it's the same as the 24-T but comes with a handle so you can carry it around easily.
g	**Sarah**	Can you send us an invoice for it?
h	**TopTools**	TopTools. Colin speaking. Can I help you?
i	**Sarah**	I'd like to order an Existes 24-T Bench Multimeter.
j	**TopTools**	The 24-T Plus is £54.90.
k	**Sarah**	How much does it cost?
l	**TopTools**	Of course. What would you like to order?
m	**Sarah**	Hello, I'd like to place an order with you.
n	**TopTools**	I'm sorry, but we only offer credit card payments or cash on delivery for new customers.

B **Arbeiten Sie mit einem Partner. Partner A blättert zu File 3 auf S. 127, Partner B zu File 6 auf S. 128.** KMK

MATTERSTV

The tools of the trade

Check out video no. 2 for a description of the tools and equipment in a fully equipped mobile workshop. Use the clip as a model to make a similar video about your workplace and the tools and equipment you use.

GRAMMAR

Simple past

Aussagen

I *you* *he/she/it* *we* *they*	***went*** *start**ed***

Verneinungen

I *you* *he/she/it* *we* *they*	***didn't***	*go* *start*

Fragen

did	*I* *you* *he/she/it* *we* *they*	*go?* *start?*

Siehe S. 144 für weitere Einzelheiten.
Eine Liste der unregelmäßigen Verben befindet sich auf S. 216.

7 Practice: simple past

Complete the social network posts by putting the verbs in brackets into the simple past.

Beatrice Zanchi When (you/choose)[1] to become an electrician?

David Brooks I (not know)[2] I (want)[3] to be an electrician until I (do)[4] a work experience placement for a company which (make)[5] electronic control panels. I (think)[6] the work was really interesting. So, when I (leave)[7] school I (know)[8] that I would become an electrician, and I (start)[9] my apprenticeship with the same company. Most of my training (be)[10] on the job, but I (attend)[11] college one day a week during the three years of my apprenticeship. When I (finish)[12] the apprenticeship, I (decide)[13] that I (not want)[14] to work in the workshop every day. So I (go)[15] to college in the evenings and (learn)[16] about maintaining electronic devices. I'm now a repair and maintenance electrician and I love my work.

8 Discussing problems with power tools

5

A Jörg is a trainee electrician who works for Fuller's Electrical Services in London. Listen as his supervisor Peter explains a job to him. Which order are the tools pictured on the following page mentioned in?

B Answer the questions about the dialogue.

1. Which task are Peter and Jörg to complete today?
2. Why does Peter say that the angle grinder would not be suitable for the job?
3. Why would the wall chaser be more suitable?
4. What will the chisel and mallet be used for?
5. What does Peter suggest the problem is with the wall chaser?
6. Why do they need to find out if the tool is under warranty?

C Work with a partner and make a dialogue.

Supervisor

Trainee

Supervisor: Erklären Sie die heutigen Aufgaben: Sagen Sie, dass er/sie einen 2 Meter langen Spalt in den Betonboden fräsen soll, um ein Kabel zu legen.

Trainee: Fragen Sie, ob Sie einen Winkelschleifer benutzen sollen.

Supervisor: Sagen Sie, dass der Mauerfräser ein besser geeignetes Gerät sei.

Trainee: Fragen Sie, ob Sie für den Mauerfräser ein Verlängerungskabel benutzen sollen.

Supervisor: Sagen Sie, dass es eine gute Idee sei, ein Verlängerungskabel zu nehmen.

Trainee: Schlagen Sie vor, Hammer und Meißel zu benutzen, um den Beton herauszuschlagen, nachdem er gefräst wurde.

Supervisor: Sie sind damit einverstanden, dass er/sie Hammer und Meißel benutzt.

Trainee: Sagen Sie, dass der Mauerfräser nicht richtig zu funktionieren scheint. Er macht ein lauteres Geräusch als üblich und es riecht verbrannt.

Supervisor: Sagen Sie, dass es sich anhört, als ob es ein Problem mit dem Motor gäbe.

Trainee: Fragen Sie, ob es sich lohnt, das Gerät zu reparieren.

Supervisor: Sagen Sie, dass Sie überprüfen wollen, ob das Gerät noch Garantie hat.

9 Leseverstehen

Sie haben ein neues Multimeter gekauft. Die folgende Gebrauchsanweisung ist auf Englisch geschrieben.

Überlegen Sie, welche der Aussagen 1 bis 4 richtig oder falsch sind. Beantworten Sie anschließend die Fragen 5 bis 7 auf Deutsch. Notieren Sie sich die Lösungen in Ihrem Heft.

The DigitalPlus Multimeter – better design, best quality!

Follow these suggestions about how to care for your multimeter and enjoy many years of use.

The meter should be kept dry at all times. Liquids can contain minerals which will corrode the delicate electric circuits. So wipe the meter dry of moisture as quickly as possible.

The meter should be stored and used in environments with normal temperatures. Use of the device in extreme temperatures can crack plastic components, deplete the battery and shorten the device's life.

Keep the meter in good condition by regularly wiping it clean with a damp cloth. The use of cleaning products including harsh solvents and strong detergents is to be avoided at all times. These will damage your device.

Do not open your device or attempt repairs on its internal components. This can cause the device to malfunction and may invalidate the warranty. If your meter is not working properly, return it along with your receipt of purchase and warranty to your retailer.

REPLACING THE FUSE

CAUTION: AVOID ELECTRIC SHOCK BY DISCONNECTING THE TEST PROBES BEFORE REMOVAL OF THE BATTERIES OR FUSE. REPLACE ONLY WITH SAME TYPE OF BATTERIES OR FUSE. THIS DEVICE DOES NOT CONTAIN USER-SERVICEABLE PARTS. SERVICE SHOULD BE CARRIED OUT BY QUALIFIED PERSONNEL ONLY.

Replace the fuse safely by following these steps. Your meter comes complete with a spare fuse, which is located at the back of the battery compartment.

1. Before disconnecting the test leads, turn off the power.
2. The battery compartment cover should now be opened.
3. Pull the green ribbon which will cause the fuse to eject.
4. Insert a replacement fuse on the ribbon ring. Use only a fuse of the following type/rating: 0.315A, 250V, 5 x 20 mm miniature fuse.
5. Snap the battery compartment cover closed.

1 Es ist wichtig, das Messgerät trocken zu halten.
2 Die Batterien im Multimeter sind hitzebeständig. Hohe Temperaturen verkürzen nicht ihre Lebensdauer.
3 Die Garantie erlischt, wenn Veränderungen am Multimeter vorgenommen werden.
4 Das Multimeter wird ohne Ersatzteile geliefert.
5 Wie sollte das Multimeter gesäubert werden?
6 Was ist zu tun, um einen Stromschlag zu vermeiden?
7 Wo befindet sich die Ersatzsicherung?

My dream job – and how I'm going to get it

Barry Sneddon lives in Barnsley, England and is in the third year of his electrotechnical apprenticeship. Here he tells us about his training and his hopes for the future.

I wasn't sure what I wanted to do when I left school. But when I told my careers adviser that my hobby was building model cars and that I found installing the electric motors and components really interesting, she suggested I apply for an apprenticeship to become an electrician.

I'm happy she did because I really like what I'm doing. I work for a company which maintains electrical systems in large office buildings. The work is really varied and, even though I haven't finished my apprenticeship yet, I'm given quite a lot of responsibility.

I go to college on day release every Thursday, which I really enjoy. Most of the other apprentices I know at college are around my age – 19 or 20 – but there are a few people who are quite a bit older. In the past, you couldn't become an apprentice if you were over 24, but these days, people of all ages can apply.

I'm going to be really well qualified when I finish my apprenticeship next year. I'll have a Level 3 Competence Qualification which shows that I have the right skills to do my job. I'll also get a Functional Skills Qualification in Maths and Physics which will show that I have the knowledge to be good at my job.

It was definitely the right choice to become an apprentice. I get paid €3.00 an hour and 20 days paid holiday a year. That means I can stand on my own two feet financially, as well as still have the time to do my hobby. That's still building electric model cars, by the way.

I hope to get taken on permanently by my company when I finish next year. That would be my dream job. I like it here and want to keep working in the same team. But even if that doesn't happen, I'm confident I can get a job quickly somewhere else. Electricians are in demand all over the UK, and there are always jobs for 'sparkies' like me!

10 Discussing apprenticeships

A **Work with a partner. Take turns outlining the key points made in the text in German.**

B **Compare the apprenticeship system in the UK with the system in your country. List the similarities and differences between the two systems.**

C **Work in a small group and discuss the questions.**

1. Which aspects of the way your apprenticeship is structured work well?
2. In what ways could the structure of your apprenticeship be improved? Make a list and report back to the class.

UNIT 3

House wiring, 1

- Working with customers
- Describing fittings, installations and EIB systems
- Comparing types of house wiring

1 Warm-up

A Work with a partner. Match the words in the vocabulary box with the numbers 1–12 in the diagram.

circuit breakers • conduit • consumer unit • earth terminal • electricity meter • flex • junction box • light switch • plug • RCD (Residual Current Device) • service entrance • socket

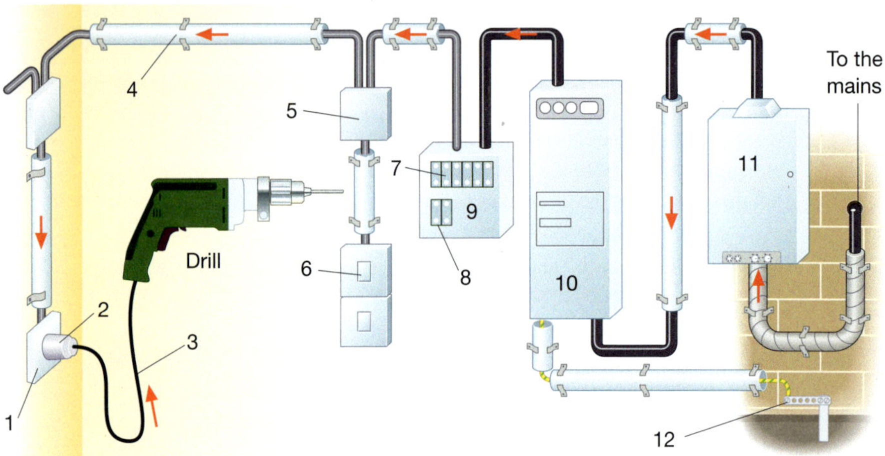

B Study the diagram again and match some of the English terms with their German translations.

- **a** FI-Schalter
- **b** Masseklemme
- **c** Netzkabel
- **d** Leitungsschutzschalter/Sicherungsautomat
- **e** Sicherungskasten/Unterverteiler
- **f** Steckdose
- **g** Stromzähler
- **h** Verteilerkasten

C Complete the list with the four missing components.

D Use the words *conduct, connect, disconnect, house, measure, protect from +-ing* and *switch off* to explain the function of each of the following components. Look at exercise 5B on p. 21 for help.

- **1** circuit breaker
- **2** consumer unit
- **3** earth terminal
- **4** electricity meter
- **5** junction box
- **6** RCD

2 Meeting customers

6

Trevor and Penny Bell are English website designers with an office in their old house in Essen. Their business is expanding so rapidly that they decide to buy new premises. They want the installation work to be state of the art, so they contact Ritter Installation GmbH & Co. KG in Dortmund and meet Thomas Keller to discuss what they need. The first part of the dialogue is printed on p. 147.

Trevor We'd like to discuss the installation work in our new premises. We're buying a three-storey building with offices and a showroom.

Penny Don't forget the flat at the top, Trevor! I call it our penthouse.

Trevor Yes, and there's the flat too, but we can talk about that later.

Thomas That's fine. Now what sort of installation system do you want – a conventional one or something more modern?

Trevor Well, I think we need something more modern. I've heard that today you can have what they call an 'intelligent building'.

Thomas Yes, exactly. And for that you'll need an EIB system, which you can program to operate all the consumers in the house.

Penny I'm sorry, but what do you mean by 'consumers'?

Thomas That means devices like the lights, blinds, heating system, air conditioning and so on. For example, you can press just one switch to turn off all the lights when you finish work in the evenings. You can also switch on the air conditioning or central heating before you come back from holiday.

Penny But how can you do that if you're not in the building?

Thomas You can do it with your smartphone or tablet computer. You have an app on your phone which you use to send commands to the actuators.

Penny Amazing! What's an actuator?

Thomas It's the switch which operates a consumer.

Penny Oh, I see.

Thomas You say it's a new building, is that right?

Trevor Yes, we now have planning permission, so we're starting next month.

Thomas Well, that's perfect for us because it's much easier to install the EIB system at the same time as the ordinary house wiring.

Trevor So what's the next step?

Thomas We'll need a plan of the building and all the rooms showing what consumers there are in each office.

Penny And the penthouse!

Trevor Yes, we can talk about the penthouse later. I'll make a plan for you and then we can talk again.

Thomas Great! And here's an interactive CD about EIB in English. It's a bit technical but it shows you the basic principles.

Are the following statements true, false or not mentioned in the dialogue? Correct the false statements.

1 Trevor and Penny have a new house.
2 There will be an apartment for Trevor and Penny.
3 An EIB system is a consumer.
4 EIB systems can also be used for cameras.
5 Intelligent buildings can be controlled remotely.
6 It's best to put in the ordinary house wiring first and then install the EIB system later.
7 Trevor gives Thomas a plan of the building.

TIP

Cables, flexes and wires

Im Englischen bedeutet *cable* fest installierte/s Kabel/Leitungen, z. B. auf oder unter Putz. *Flex* (auch *cord* oder *lead* genannt) bedeutet Netzkabel. *Flex* ist die Abkürzung von *flexible* – biegsam, elastisch. Draht heißt auf Englisch *wire* (oder *solid wire*) und Litze *stranded wire*. Vorsicht bei dem Wort Isolierung, denn es heißt auf Englisch *insulation*. Dementsprechend heißt isoliert *insulated* und unisoliert *uninsulated*. Wie heißen die abgebildeten Kabel auf Englisch?

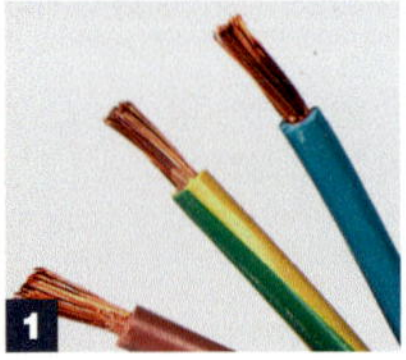

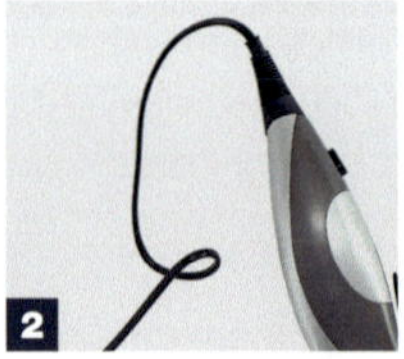

MATTERSTV

Basic house wiring

Check out video no. 3 to see how an installation board is used to practise basic electrical installation work. You can use the clip as a model to make a similar video about your own installation work, e.g. on site or on an installation board.

3 Describing modern electrical fittings

Jeff Taylor, a young trainee electrician from England, is helping Thomas Keller to install some two-way light switches. Look at the diagram below and then put Thomas's instructions in the right order. Hint: begin with b.

a Connect the conductors to the terminals of the light switch.
b Switch off the circuit breaker for this circuit, lock it and tag it.
c Cut away about 16 mm of insulation at the end of each of the three conductors.
d Cut the conductors to the right length.
e Push the switch into the mounting box in the recess in the wall and tighten the two big screws.
f Put on the plastic cover.
g Run the new cable through the conduit.
h Select the three conductors you will need for the light switch.

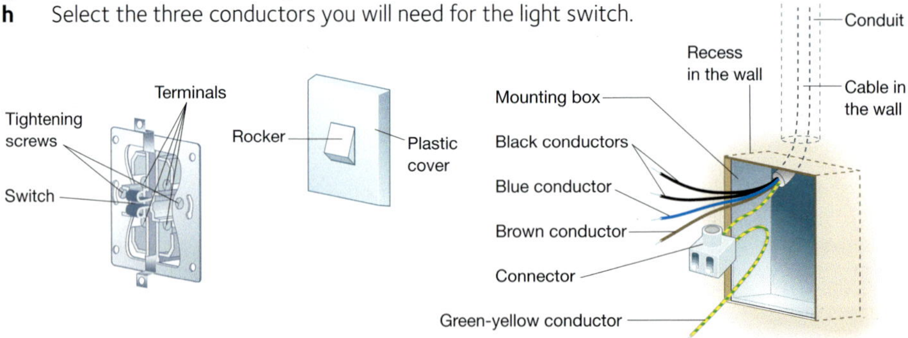

4 Comparing types of house wiring

A Study the diagram and explain …

- which appliance has its own circuit.
- which appliance is on a spur circuit.

Older British wiring

In older British houses there are often only two circuits – a 30-amp ring circuit to power electrical equipment (e.g. a dishwasher) and a 5-amp lighting circuit. Some appliances also have their own circuit or are connected to an existing circuit with a spur and a switched fused connection unit (e.g. for an electric shower). Each circuit has a circuit breaker in the consumer unit. In addition to this, British plugs have a 3, 5 or 13-amp cartridge fuse (*Patronensicherung*) which blows if overloaded.

30-amp ring circuit with 5-amp lighting circuit

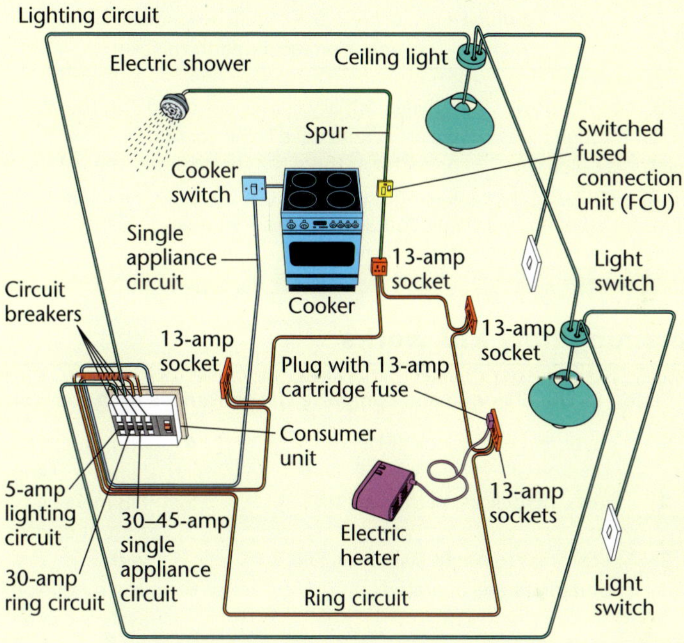

B Study the text and the diagram and write a comparison of the British and the German wiring systems. Use expressions in the Language box. Write 50–100 words.

LANGUAGE

In British/German houses, A British/German electrician In Britain/Germany, appliances British/German plugs	there is/isn't there are/aren't uses / doesn't use has / doesn't have have / don't have	a circuit breaker for … only two circuits. a …-amp … …-amp circuit breakers. a separate switch for the … one big circuit breaker for … cartridge fuses in …

C **With a partner, draw a diagram of the electrical installation system in your own flat/house. Label all the components in English and then give a short presentation to the class.**

D **Describe an electrical installation you have worked on recently. Write down what you did there (e.g. *First we ... Then we ... After that we ... Finally ...*).**

E **Ihre Berufsschulklasse bekommt den Auftrag, Informationen über verschiedene europäische Installationssysteme zu sammeln, um sie mit der heutigen deutschen Installationspraxis zu vergleichen. Benutzen Sie den Text und das Diagramm, um die wesentlichen Unterschiede darzustellen.** KMK

F **Use the words in the box to complete the text about electric circuits.**

cartridge • circuit breaker • circuits • conduits • consumer • current • protective earth • socket

The electricity to power a machine normally comes out of a ...[1] in the wall. The cables in the wall often run through pipes known as ...[2] and have three conductors. The green and yellow conductor is called the ...[3] conductor. If there is a short circuit, the ...[4] 'escapes' along this conductor and not, for example, through a person's body, so the person is safe. In the UK the plugs in the 30-amp ring circuit contain a ...[5] fuse, whereas in Germany there are separate ...[6] for each floor and for the bathroom and other equipment, too. If too much electricity passes through a wire, a ...[7] in the ...[8] unit switches off the supply.

5 Explaining how EIB works

7

A **Listen to the dialogue and complete the sentences with the words you hear.**

1. Trevor and Penny look at the explanation of ...
2. Trevor first clicks on the field for the ...
3. In contrast to a light switch, an EIB actuator can be operated ...
4. The direction of the motor for the blinds is changed by using a ...
5. EIB makes it possible to operate a lot of devices at the same time with ...
6. The function of any device in the system can be changed by using ...

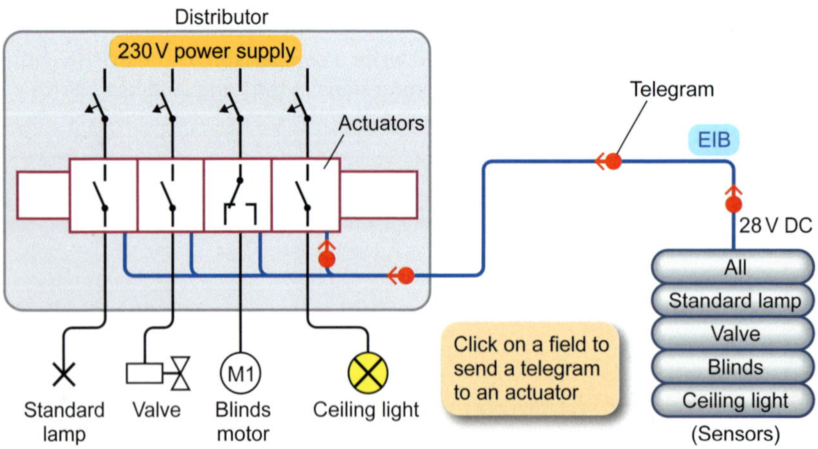

B **Use the diagram and your own knowledge to describe the features of the EIB system. Recommend situations in which it would or would not make sense to use it.**

6 Planning installations with customers

Thomas is talking to Trevor about how he and Penny would like to use EIB to program the lighting and security features of their new office building. Thomas marks what they want on a plan of the building, but he makes four mistakes.

8

A **Listen to their conversation and find the mistakes. Use the Language box if necessary.**

LANGUAGE

break area	*Pausenbereich*
entrance hall	*Eingangsbereich*
perimeter fence	*Umzäunung*
sliding gate	*Schiebetor*
stairs	*Treppenhaus*
storeroom	*Lagerraum*

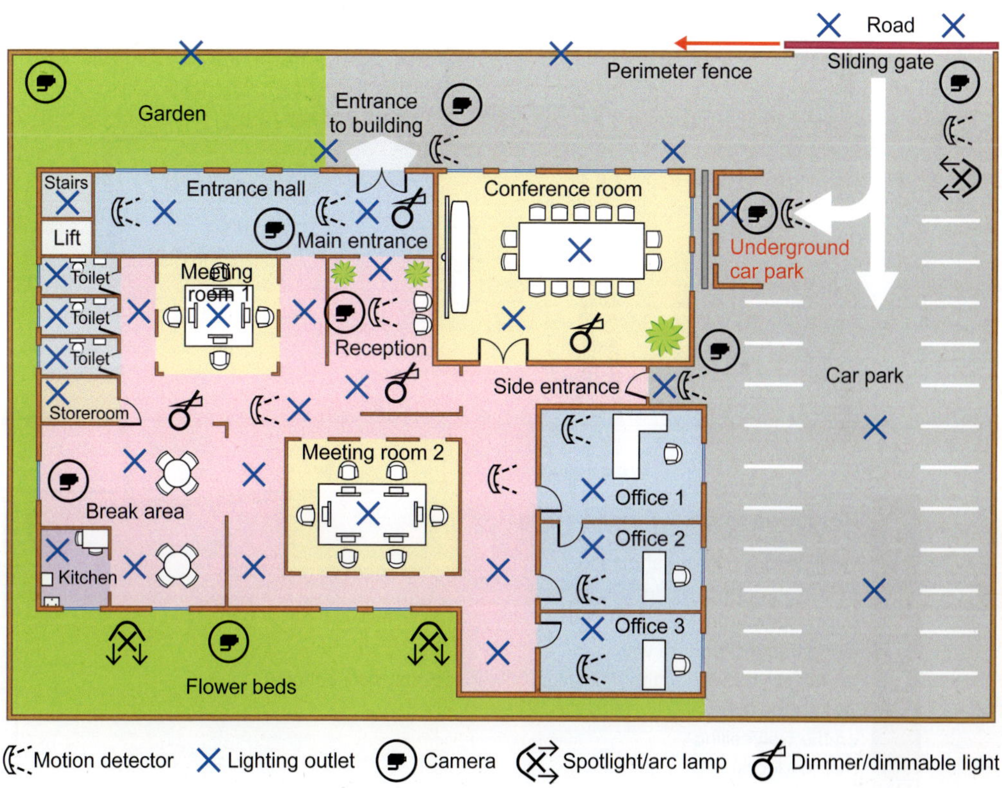

B Erstellen Sie in Partnerarbeit einen Dialog aus folgenden Rollenkarten. KMK

Ein/e Installateur/in bekommt den Auftrag von seinem/ihrem Arbeitgeber, das Ehepaar Bell zu besuchen, um die Installationsarbeiten für den Konferenzraum ihrer Firma zu besprechen.
Führen Sie mit Hilfe der zwei Rollenkarten das Gespräch und markieren Sie auf dem Plan des Konferenzraums, wo die Steckdosen, Lichtschalter und evtl. andere Betriebsmittel angebracht werden sollen.

Rolle A
Installateur/in (eigener Name)

- Vorstellung
- Grund Ihres Besuchs
- Sie fragen, wo die Teile montiert werden sollen.
- Sie machen entsprechende Vorschläge.
- Weitere Vorschläge nach Wahl
- Sie füllen den Plan gemeinsam mit Ihrem Gesprächspartner aus.
- Sie geben dem Gesprächspartner Ihre Visitenkarte, falls er/sie Sie kontaktieren möchte.
- Sie schließen das Gespräch höflich ab.

Rolle B
Auftraggeber (Trevor/Penny Bell)

- Vorstellung
- Sie benötigen im Konferenzraum:
  - eine hochfahrbare Roll-Leinwand (*retractable screen*)
  - einen Deckenbeamer (*video projector on the ceiling*)
  - Jalousien (*blinds*)
  - 8 Deckenlampen (*ceiling lights*)
  - 16 Steckdosen
  - 6 Lichtschalter
- Sie bitten den/die Installateur/in um Ratschläge für die Anbringung.
- Eigene Ideen nach Wahl
- Sie schließen das Gespräch höflich ab.

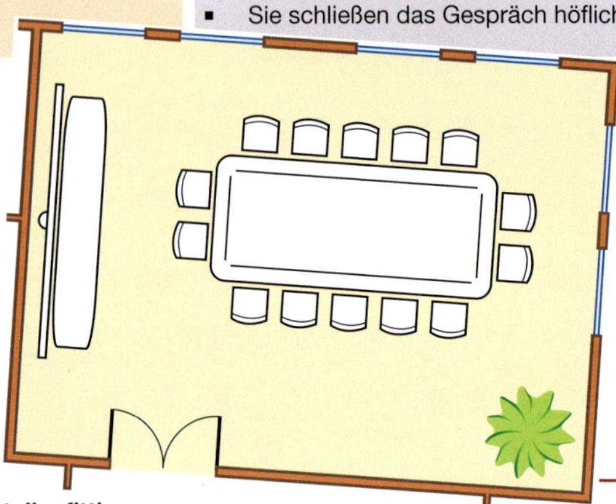

LANGUAGE

Describing where to install a fitting

We'll need … / There should be …
to the left/right of the (doors/screen)
over / under / next to / by / near
along the (top/bottom wall)
let into the surface of the table (e.g. power sockets, connections)
let into the floor
on the wall/ceiling
by the (doors)
between the windows
attached to the (wall/ceiling)
in the (top left-hand / bottom right-hand) corner

GRAMMAR

Conditional 1

If *you* ***touch*** *the live wire,*	*you'll* ***get*** *a shock.*
If *you* ***don't keep*** *to the safety rules,*	*you'll* ***hurt*** *yourself.*
If *you* ***give*** *bad service,*	*the customer* ***won't come*** *back.*
If *you* ***don't do*** *a good job,*	*the customer* ***won't pay****.*

If + Gegenwart	*will/won't* + Grundform

Siehe S. 142 für weitere Einzelheiten.

! 'If plus will makes me ill!'
If you ~~will~~ give bad service, …

7 Dangerous situations

Complete the warnings about what will happen by using the correct form of the verbs in brackets.

1 If the workman (touch) the overhead power cable with the ladder, he (get) a shock.

2 He (kill) himself if he (not be) careful.

3 The young man (have) a nasty accident if he (not tie) his hair back.

4 If he (drill) through the cable, the circuit breaker (trip).

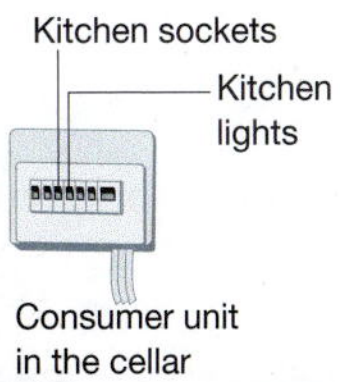

5 The circuit breaker in the cellar (not trip) fast enough to save the man if the radio (fall) into the water.

6 If the man (not take) his hand out of the water, he (electrocute) himself.

7 If Billy (turn) on the light, he (give) his father a dangerous electric shock.

8 The microwave (fall) onto his head if Billy (pull) the flex.

8 Produktion

Situation

Die Firma Ritter Starkstromtechnik GmbH & Co. KG erhält den Auftrag, das neue Bürogebäude von Bell Web Design zu verkabeln. Mr Bell möchte nun wissen, wann genau mit der Arbeit begonnen werden soll und wie lange sie dauern wird.

Aufgabe

Schreiben Sie im eigenen Namen als Projektmanager bei Ritter eine formgerechte E-Mail an Mr Bell (trevor.bell@bwd.com) unter Berücksichtigung folgender Punkte.

- Bezug auf Anruf von vor zwei Tagen
- Laut Baufirma ist das Gebäude bis spätestens 26. April rohbaufertig *(structurally complete)*.
- Anfang der Installationsarbeit am 6. Mai 20..
- Leider kein früherer Termin verfügbar
- Installationsarbeit wird ca. sechs Wochen in Anspruch nehmen, da ein EIB System installiert werden soll.
- Bitte um rechtzeitige Benachrichtigung, falls Erstellung des Rohbaus *(shell of the building)* sich verzögert.
- Bei evtl. Fragen Nachricht im Büro hinterlassen
- Höflicher Schluss

9 Hörverstehen

9

Sie sind zufällig im Büro, als ein wichtiger Geschäftspartner anruft, um Einzelheiten seines Besuchs Ihrer Firma mitzuteilen. Hören Sie sich das Gespräch an und füllen Sie eine Telefonnotiz für Ihren Arbeitgeber aus.

TELEFONNOTIZ

Anruf für: ____________

Anrufer (Name und Firma): ____

Telefonnummer: ____________

Grund des Anrufs: ____________

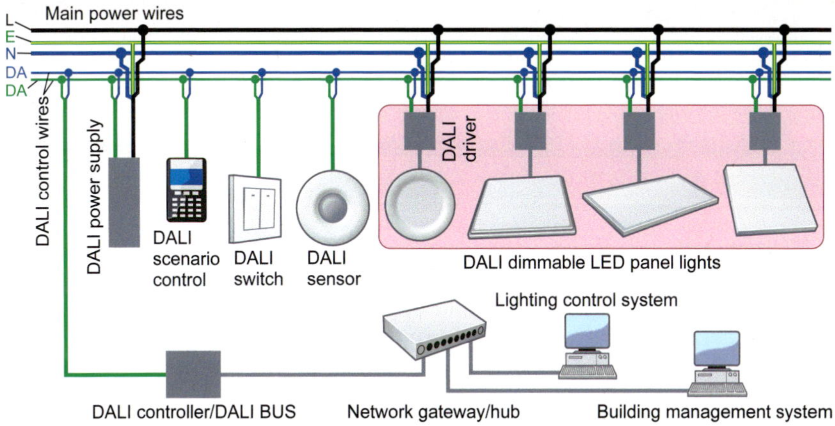

What is DALI?

The Pentagon is a six-million-square-foot building that has 250 lamp failures a day. So many failures that a full-time employee spends all his time just walking around looking for them.

If only the Pentagon had **DALI** (**D**igitally **A**ddressable **L**ighting **I**nterface)!

Remotely-controlled lighting systems are generally unidirectional. This means, for example, that when a command is sent via computer to a lamp or a ballast (a current-regulating device) to switch or dim the lamp, the computer does not receive confirmation that the command has actually been carried out. A physical check is the only reliable answer. A DALI system is bidirectional, so individual ballasts can send feedback to the computer via DALI controllers and indicate whether the command has been carried out.

DALI also allows ballasts/lamps to be controlled individually by a central computer and enables the creation of pre-defined lighting scenarios. In this way, one mouse click is enough to convert a multi-functional building into a conference venue in the morning and a concert hall in the evening. DALI can also be used to check and record the energy consumption of a particular light or lights. Thus, if DALI is programmed to lower the lighting at times of peak demand, major savings can be achieved.

A DALI system consists of a loop of up to 64 ballasts, each of which has an address and is linked to a central computer. Loops can be interlinked to create a network of loops within a building. A DALI system can be a retrofit, but it is best to install it from the start in a new building. It has a simple, two-wire control connection to each electrical fixture and is easy to install, e.g. by semi-skilled workers.

10 Summarizing information

A Complete the sentences using information from the text.

1 Every day in the Pentagon …
2 A lighting system which does not confirm that it has carried out a command is described as …
3 DALI-controlled lighting systems can be changed with one mouse click for a new situation by using …
4 At times of peak demand a lot of energy can be saved if DALI is used to …
5 It is best to install a DALI system while …
6 DALI installation work can be carried out by people who are only …

B Study the graphic and explain the following.

- what a DALI driver is
- the colour-coding of the 5 wires
- how the LEDs are controlled by the DALI system

UNIT 4

House wiring, 2

- Describing a wiring diagram
- Planning a room with a customer
- Explaining safety rules

1 Warm-up

A Use the Language box and your own ideas or experience to explain the following.

1 what every electrician must do before starting work on an electrical circuit
2 how he/she does this
3 what can happen if it is not done

LANGUAGE

make sure that …
check that …
disconnect …
lock and tag …
warn people that …
put a sign on …
damage …
overload …
get an electric shock
(seriously) injure …
be (seriously) injured
electrocute …
be electrocuted

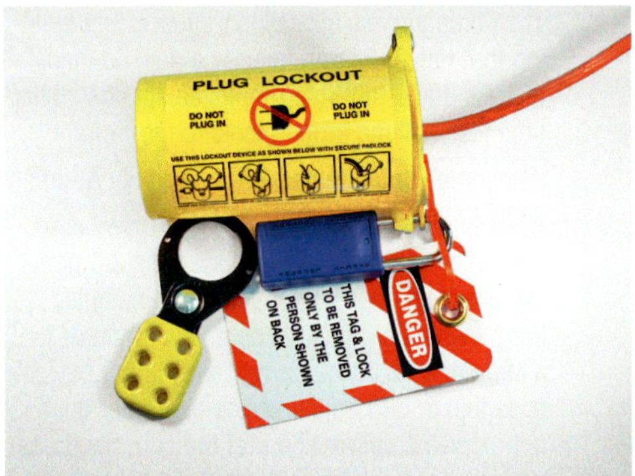

B Use the words in the box to label the safety devices.

blade fuse • cartridge fuse • circuit breaker • RCD

1

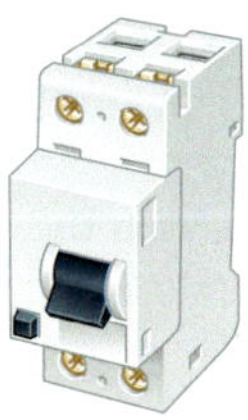

2

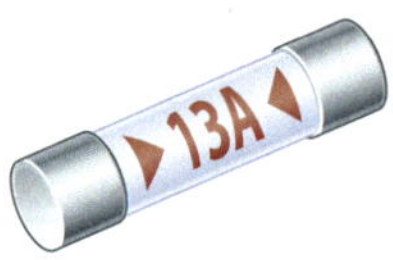

3

4

C Look at the illustrations and explain the following.

1 which safety device protects people
2 which safety devices protect circuits

D Explain in what sort of circuit you would expect to find each device.

2 Using electrical wiring symbols

A **The English terms in column C are mixed up. Match them with the symbols and German terms in columns A and B.**

	A	B	C		A	B	C
1		*Licht-anschluss*	400 V three-phase junction box	8		*Dimmer*	Lighting outlet
2		*Ausschalter*	Camera	9		*Spot*	Motion detector
3		*Wechsel-schalter*	Dimmer	10		*Taster*	One-way switch
4		*Serien-schalter*	Door opener	11		*Bewegungs-melder*	Push button
5		*geerdete Steckdose, Schutz-steckdose*	Double (triple, fourfold) socket	12		*Fernsehan-schlussdose*	Spotlight / arc lamp
6	 3/N/PE	*400 V Drehstrom-steckdose*	Double switch	13		*Türöffner*	TV socket
7	2 (3) (4) 	*Doppel-, Dreifach-, Vierfach-steckdose*	Earthed socket outlet	14		*Kamera*	Two-way switch

B **Work with a partner. Describe for each other where to put electrical fittings. Use the symbols in part A and the Language box to give your instructions.**

LANGUAGE

put/draw/include a … (e.g. socket) to the right/left of the …
on the top/bottom wall
on the left-hand/right-hand wall
in the bottom left-hand corner / top right-hand corner, etc.
next to / between / close to

Partner A: Turn to File 7 on page 128. **Partner B**: Turn to File 12 on page 130.

3 A wiring diagram for a penthouse kitchen

Thomas Keller from Ritter Installation is talking to Penny Bell about the wiring for the kitchen appliances and equipment in the penthouse at the top of the new office building.

A Can you name this kitchen equipment? Some of it will be mentioned in the dialogue.

10

B Listen to the dialogue and write a list of all the kitchen appliances and equipment Penny and Thomas talk about.

C Listen again. Copy the wiring diagram and mark the sockets and other fittings needed in the kitchen. The blue symbols are for the fittings that have already been discussed and marked on the diagram.

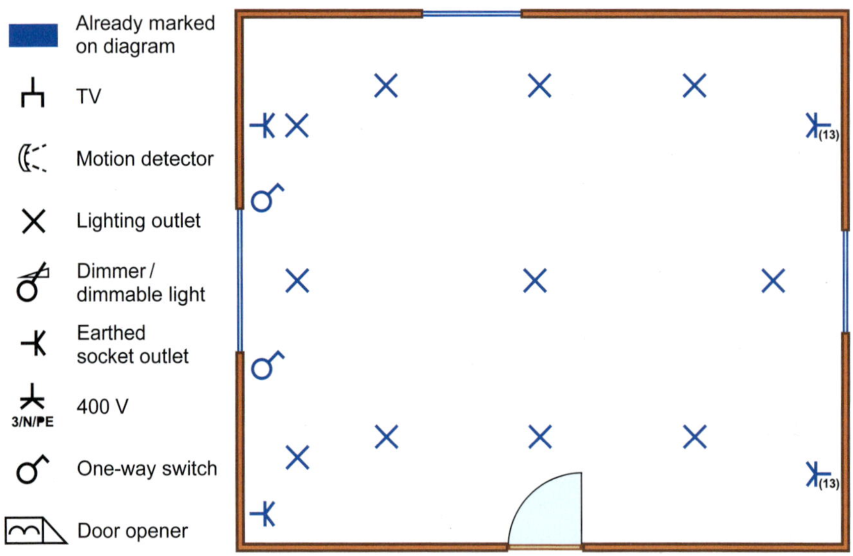

GRAMMAR

Conditional 2

If *I* ***was/were*** *you,* ***If*** *we* ***had*** *it there,* ***If*** *we* ***didn't have*** *a video intercom,*	***I'd put*** *the motion detector in the other corner.* *the fridge* ***would block*** *it.* *we* ***wouldn't see*** *the visitor's face.*

If + Vergangenheit	*would/wouldn't* + Grundform

Siehe S. 142–143 für weitere Einzelheiten.
Eine Liste der unregelmäßigen Verben befindet sich auf S. 216

! *If* plus *would* is no good!
If I ~~would~~ …

4 Practice: conditional 2

Thomas Keller is talking to Trevor Bell about the wiring in the kitchen. Use the conditional 2 grammar table to complete the dialogue with the correct verb forms.

Trevor How much …[1] (it/cost) if we …[2] (install) an EIB system later?

Thomas If you …[3] (do) that, it …[4] (be) a lot more expensive, Mr Bell. And remember that you'll have greater security with EIB. If you …[5] (not have) an EIB system, you …[6] (need) to switch off all the lights separately every night.

Trevor I see what you mean. Life …[7] (be) a lot easier if we …[8] (have) an EIB system now. If a burglar …[9] (break in), what …[10] (happen)?

Thomas If a burglar …[11] (stand) near a motion detector in the building, it …[12] (send) a signal to the police station or security company, and if they …[13] (receive) a signal, they …[14] (come) immediately.

5 What would happen if … ?

A Describe the following chain reaction using *if*-sentences.

If Thomas *used* the wrong cable, the installation *would melt.* → If the insulation *melted*, it *would trip* the circuit breaker. → If it *tripped* …

B Now make more sentences with these words.

Thomas / use / the wrong cable → the insulation / melt → it / trip / the circuit breaker → the circuit breaker / switch off / the circuit → the lights and sockets / not work → Penny and Trevor / be / annoyed → they / call / the company → Thomas / get / into trouble

C Work with a partner. Invent more 'chain reactions'.

Example: *If I didn't install an RCD in a bathroom circuit …*

6 Understanding technical texts

Read the text below, then complete the statements.

1 If five times the nominal current flows through a circuit …
2 The two different types of metal in a bimetallic strip …
3 The bimetallic strip breaks the circuit because …
4 A solenoid is …
5 A solenoid reacts more quickly …
6 To complete the circuit again you …

CIRCUIT BREAKERS

A circuit breaker breaks the circuit (trips) if the current flowing through it rises to an unacceptable level. This is usually between three and five times the current the circuit breaker is designed to take (nominal current).

Modern circuit breakers have a solenoid, a bimetallic strip or both.

Thermal-magnetic circuit breaker

In a thermal circuit breaker a bimetallic strip is made of two different types of metal which expand at different rates when heated. At room temperature the two strips of metal are both straight. If, however, a stronger current flows through them, heat is produced, and the two metal strips start to expand. As one of them expands more than the other, it trips the electrical contact and breaks the circuit.

In the circuit breaker shown in Figure 1 there is a bimetallic strip on the right (3) and a solenoid in the centre (2). A solenoid is an electromagnetic switch. This combination has the advantage that a sudden large current surge will trip the solenoid, which reacts quickly (e.g. in 20 milliseconds), and a smaller long-term overload will trip the bimetallic strip, which reacts more slowly but to a lower current. The circuit can be completed again by pushing the switch (1) up by hand.

Electrical Handbook

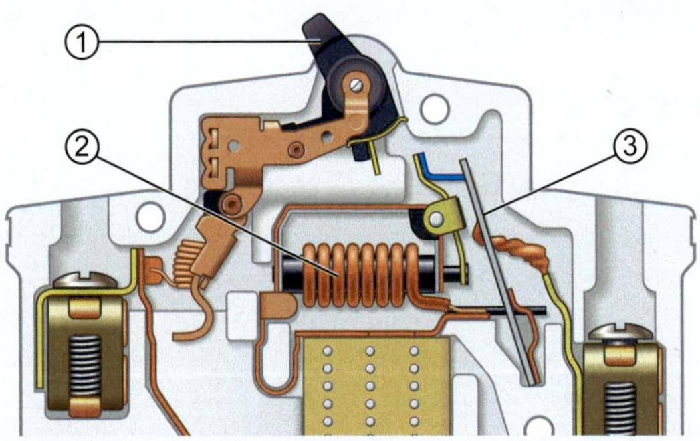

Figure 1: *Thermal-magnetic circuit breaker*

7 Working with words

Match a–e with 1–5. The expressions are all in the text.

1	break	a	the solenoid
2	produce	b	the switch
3	expand	c	when heated
4	trip	d	heat
5	push up	e	the circuit

8 Understanding technical texts

A Complete the text below with words from the diagram (Figure 2).

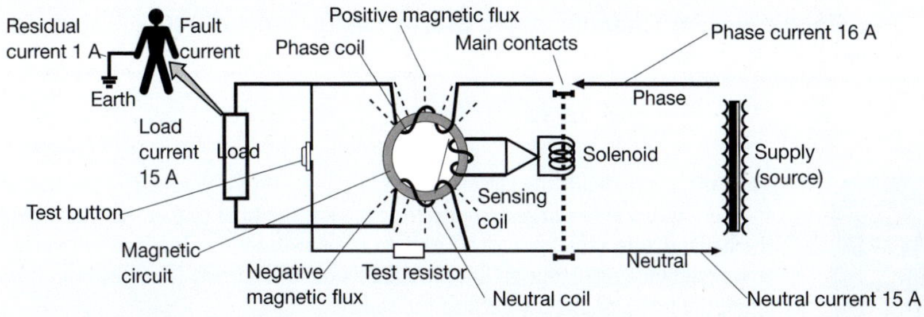

Figure 2: *How an RCD works*

Electrical Handbook

RESIDUAL CURRENT DEVICE (RCD)

In Figure 2 the …[1] current of 16 amps travels to the load in the left-hand part of the circuit and the …[2] current of 15 amps returns from it. As there is a …[3] current of 1 amp, the RCD switches off the circuit.

In a circuit without a fault, the current enters the phase …[4] on its way to the load and returns to the …[5] through the neutral coil. A magnetic …[6] is produced in both coils. However, as the coils are identical but wound in opposite directions, they cancel each other out because one is …[7] and the other …[8].

In the case of a fault, some current is lost to …[9], and the …[10] current returning to the supply is less than the …[11] current to the load. The …[12] flux in the neutral coil is therefore less than in the phase coil. This difference is picked up by a …[13] coil, which is connected to a …[14]. This disconnects the main …[15] and switches off the circuit.

B Study the diagram and text and then say whether the following statements are true or false. Correct the false statements.

1. The residual current is the difference between the phase and neutral currents.
2. The phase coil and the neutral coil are wound in the same direction.
3. The current from the supply first produces a negative magnetic flux, then a positive one.
4. There is no physical difference between the phase coil and the neutral coil.
5. The test button is connected to the solenoid.
6. The sensing coil is wound around the neutral coil.
7. The sensing coil triggers the test button.

C Explain the most important differences between a circuit breaker and an RCD in a few sentences. Give examples of when each device is used.

9 Understanding technical texts

A Ein Kollege hat den folgenden Text auf einer englischen Internetseite gefunden. Da er nicht ausreichend Englisch spricht, aber vergleichen will, ob die beschriebenen Sicherheitsstandards ähnlich wie in Deutschland sind, bittet er Sie, die wesentlichen Aussagen des Textes für ihn auf Deutsch zusammenzufassen. KMK

www.modern-safety-standards.com

Modern safety standards

In an electrical circuit the current from the power station flows along the **hot wire** (phase – *black, brown or grey conductor*) through the **load** (e.g. a light) and then along the **neutral wire** (*blue conductor*) back to the power source. The load in the circuit acts as a **resistance** and stops an uncontrolled amount of current (a *surge*) from flowing along the hot wire directly back to the source.

If there is a fault in the circuit, e.g. if the brown and blue conductors touch because the insulation has melted (*short circuit*), a massive amount of current suddenly flows through the circuit because there is almost no resistance in the circuit. This is a very dangerous situation because the extra energy takes the form of heat and can cause a fire.

For this reason a modern house wiring system includes safety devices to switch off the electricity supply if there is a surge in current.

There are basically two types of safety device in a modern home – **circuit breakers** to protect the circuit and **residual current devices** (RCDs) to protect people. A circuit breaker reacts if too much current flows through a circuit, whereas an RCD reacts if there is current leakage, e.g. in the case of a ground fault.

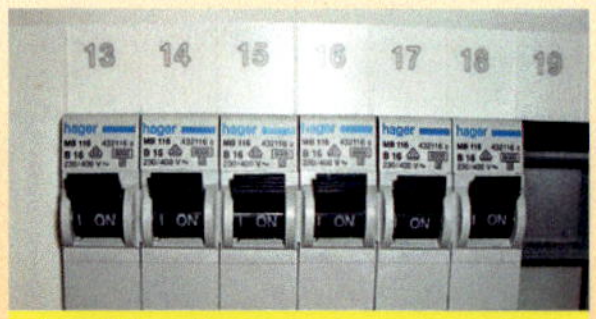

circuit breakers

In a modern house or flat there will normally be 10 – 20 circuit breakers and 1 or 2 RCDs, e.g. in the electrical circuit of a bathroom. Whereas a 16-amp circuit breaker will trip within 0.4 seconds if the current rises to 5 times the nominal value (e.g. $5 \times 16\,A = 80\,A$), an RCD will trip within 0.2 seconds if there is a fault current of only 30 mA.

RCD

B Read the text again and answer the questions.

1 What would happen if there was a short circuit in an electrical circuit without a safety device?

2 Which device in the circuit would react first to a fault current of 40 mA – a circuit breaker or an RCD?

3 Explain what would happen if someone in a bathroom without an RCD but with a circuit breaker in the circuit got an electric shock while under the shower or in the bath. Also explain what wouldn't happen.

10 Safety at work

A Hartvig Pekkala is a Finnish trainee electrician on work placement in Germany at Ritter Installation in Dortmund. When Hartvig and Thomas Keller are in the workshop, Hartvig sees a notice on the five safety rules. He asks Thomas to help him understand them. Complete their dialogue with German words from the notice.

5 Sicherheitsregeln
Vor Beginn der Arbeiten
- Freischalten
- Gegen Wiedereinschalten sichern
- Spannungsfreiheit feststellen
- Erden und kurzschließen
- Benachbarte, unter Spannung stehende Teile abdecken oder abschranken

Hartvig I'm not quite sure if I've understood this, Thomas. Does *'freischalten'*[1] mean 'switch off'?

Thomas Yes, that's right, but it means more than that. It means you must disconnect an electrical circuit or a piece of equipment before you work on it.

Hartvig Oh, I see. And what about '…'[2]? Has that got something to do with 'safety'?

Thomas Yes, but here it means 'protect' – protect the circuit against being turned on again.

Hartvig OK, I get it. Now what does '…'[3]. mean?

Thomas It means 'make certain'. We have to make sure the circuit isn't live. In German we say 'make certain it's free of electricity'. It's best to test it with a multimeter to make sure it's not connected to the mains.

Hartvig I'm sorry to bother you but there's just one more thing. Could you explain '…'[4]?

Thomas Certainly. It means 'earth and short-circuit'.

Hartvig I won't even try the last one but I think '…'[5] has got something to do with 'neighbours', hasn't it?

Thomas No, you've got the wrong end of the stick there, Hartvig. It means 'cover up or fence off nearby live components'.

Hartvig OK, I've made a note of that.

B Nach ihrem Gespräch über Sicherheit hält Thomas es für ratsam, Hartvig eine kurze Zusammenfassung der fünf Sicherheitsregeln auf Englisch zu geben. Schreiben Sie die Zusammenfassung mit Hilfe der Ausdrücke auf S. 36 und in der ‚Language'-Box unten. KMK

LANGUAGE

a multimeter reading	to disconnect
an electrical circuit	to lock and tag
electrical components	to short-circuit
electrical equipment	to switch off
live (e.g. a live conductor)	to tell your workmates
mustn't (*darf nicht*)	to test
to be careful not to (e.g. touch a live conductor)	to touch one conductor against another
	to turn back on again

C Write two or three sentences to describe the last time you used the five safety rules. Explain what could have happened if you hadn't used them.

11 Interaktion

Situation

Sie arbeiten bei einer Firma mit Niederlassungen in ganz Europa. Heute bekommen Sie den Auftrag, die Elektroinstallation im Keller eines Einfamilienhauses zu kontrollieren, weil jedes Mal, wenn der Wäschetrockner läuft, ein Brandgeruch entsteht, und der Trockner immer wieder ausgeht. Wenn Sie die Anschlussdose für den Trockner aufmachen, sehen Sie Folgendes (siehe Foto).

Aufgabe

Partner A: Sie sind ein/e ausländische/r Praktikant/in. Sie sollen sich sowohl den Vorgang als auch die fünf Sicherheitsregeln merken. Stellen Sie zu diesem Zweck sinnvolle Fragen auf Englisch. Nach diesem Gespräch schlagen Sie vor, was Sie dem Hausbesitzer raten würden, als Nächstes zu tun.

Partner B: Sie sind Elektroinstallateur/in. Erklären Sie Ihrem Partner auf Englisch, wie Sie unter Beachtung der fünf Sicherheitsregeln vorgehen, um die beschädigte Anschlussdose zu ersetzen. Beschreiben Sie die Vorgehensweise Schritt für Schritt.
Nach diesem Gespräch fragen Sie Ihrem Partner, was er dem Hausbesitzer raten würde, als Nächstes zu tun.

12 Produktion

Situation

Sie bekommen eine E-Mail von einem Auszubildenden bei der tschechischen Niederlassung Ihrer Firma. Er muss einen Herd anschließen und fragt Sie, wie er vorgehen soll. Er hat folgendes Bild der Mail beigefügt.

Aufgabe

Erklären Sie dem Auszubildenden auf Englisch, wie Sie unter Beachtung der fünf Sicherheitsregeln vorgehen, um den neuen Herd anzuschließen. Beschreiben Sie die Vorgehensweise Schritt für Schritt jeweils mit kurzer Begründung.

How dangerous is an electric shock?

Electricity can kill: most deaths result from a current entering the body and passing through the chest or the head. In all cases, the voltage (V) is less important than the strength of the current (A – amperage) and the duration (how long it flows through the body).

An electric shock of 1 mA isn't dangerous or painful to most people. You may feel a slight 'tingle', if anything. A 5 mA shock is unpleasant, but not usually dangerous.

With slightly higher currents, there is a danger that your muscles will 'freeze' and you won't be able to let go of the electricity source. This reaction greatly increases the duration of the shock and happens somewhere between 6 mA and 30 mA. Most adults can still let go at 15 mA AC (or 70 mA DC), and this value is known as the 'let go' or 'freezing' current. Higher currents than this are extremely painful and may cause death.

Currents of 1–4 amps disturb the rhythm of your heartbeat, causing ventricular fibrillation (uncoordinated heart function). Nerve damage is also likely. A shock of this strength may even stop your heart (cardiac arrest) and cause death.

A current of over 10 amps causes serious internal and external burns and will almost certainly cause death by cardiac arrest.

13 Understanding technical texts

Read the safety information above, then copy and complete the table.

	Strength of AC current	Reactions
1	1 mA	k
2	5 mA	
3	6–30 mA	
4	50–150 mA	
5	1.0–4 A	
6	>10 A	

a cardiac arrest possible
b cardiac arrest likely
c death likely
d death possible
e extreme pain
f freezing of muscles
g mild pain
h strong pain
i nerve damage
j severe burns
k tingling
l ventricular fibrillation

14 First aid

Explain what you should do if a colleague receives an electric shock.

Example: *1: Disconnect electricity source.*

UNIT 5

Installing a PLC

- Advising and corresponding with customers
- Arranging appointments
- Understanding instruction manuals

1 Warm-up

Work with a partner. Make a list of the processes a Programmable Logic Controller (PLC) can be used to control. Use the pictures to help you.

2 A new sliding door system

11

FruitFrais, a small-scale soft drinks manufacturer, wants to replace some of the doors at its factory in Strasbourg. Odette Alexander, a manager with the company, meets Matthias Marquardt, a salesperson for Schröder Automation GmbH, to discuss a new system.

Read or listen to their conversation and say whether the statements are true or false. Correct the false statements.

1. The door from the warehouse into the passage has to be shut before the door to the production area is opened.
2. The double-door system is needed to maintain the temperature in the production area.
3. The company wants automatic doors because the forklift driver is getting too old for the current system.
4. Matthias recommends a system which uses a PLC to signal to sensors when to open and close the doors.
5. Odette is concerned that the system will be too expensive.
6. Matthias says that the price of PLCs is going up.

Odette Right, here we are. This is the first door that we want to replace. As you can see, we currently use an old-fashioned, self-coiling door.

Matthias OK, I see. Can I just ask why you need these doors?

Odette Sure, let me show you. As you can see, we're standing in our warehouse area here. This is where we store the fruit we use in our drinks. We have to keep the temperature here at a constant 2 ° C so that the fruit stays fresh. Right, now we'll just go through the first door here. It takes a few moments. Right, now at the other end of this short passage is the other door we want to replace. So, we need to close the first door … before we open the next one. And you can see that we're now in our production area. The temperature here is quite a bit higher than next door basically because we do our production here. The machinery makes this room quite a bit warmer.

Matthias So, the double-door system is to help keep the temperature down in the warehouse.

Odette Exactly. Our forklift truck driver uses this passage to take fruit from the warehouse into the production area. The driver has to stop the forklift in front of the door, get out, press the button so that the door rolls up, drive through, stop, get out and press this button again to roll down the door. Then he has to drive along the passage …

Matthias And go through the whole thing again with the other door.

Odette Right. And he has to do this between twenty and thirty times a day, so in the end we spend quite a lot of time just opening and closing these doors.

Matthias OK. Well I can understand that you want to automate this process. I'd suggest that you think about installing two sets of sliding doors which open and close automatically.

Odette That sounds pretty complicated. How would it work?

Matthias Well, it's quite simple really. The motors which open and close the new doors would be controlled by a PLC unit which …

Odette PLC? What's that?

Matthias Sorry, that stands for Programmable Logic Controller. It's basically just a robust little computer which is dedicated to carrying out a particular automated task. We would fit sensors which would detect the forklift and signal this to the PLC, which would then open or close the doors.

Odette Yes, OK. But that all sounds like it could be more than we could afford.

Matthias I don't think you should worry too much about that. PLCs these days are cheaper than they used to be. I'm sure we can find you something that will fit your budget.

3 PLCs

A Ihr Kollege möchte mehr über PLCs erfahren und findet folgenden Artikel im Internet. Leider versteht er ihn nicht, weil er auf Englisch ist. Fassen Sie die wichtigsten Punkte des Artikels für Ihren Kollegen auf Deutsch zusammen. KMK

http://www.quickguide.com

Quick guide to industrial automation

PLC is for …
Programmable Logic Controller

PLCs are to be found everywhere these days. You can't go through an automatic door system in a shop or into a lift without encountering a PLC. These clever little devices also continue to be one of the central components of automation in industry. But what are they?

Well, basically a PLC is a small computer which can be programmed to issue commands to devices powered by electric motors, hydraulic or pneumatic cylinders, magnetic relays or solenoids so that they perform tasks automatically. This would include the sliding door in a shop or the automated production robot in a factory. The PLC is programmed with instructions which tell these devices what to do.

In order to issue the correct commands to the devices it controls, a PLC needs information and it gets this via the sensors that are linked up to it. Depending on what sort of information is required, a wide variety of sensors can be used with PLCs including, for instance, those which measure motion, speed, light or temperature. These sensors provide the input information which a PLC requires to provide output information. This input/output (I/O) information can be either digital or in analogue form.

B Work with a partner and answer the questions.

1 What sorts of sensors are mentioned in the text?
2 What other sorts of sensors do you know of? Make a list.

4 An e-mail from Schröder Automation

A Complete the e-mail which Matthias sends Odette with the words in the box.

activated • automated • cost-effectively • devices • expensive • installing • powerful • specifications • switch

B Think about the dialogue in exercise 2 again. Which additional technical suggestions does Matthias make in the e-mail?

Von: matthias.marquardt@gmail.com

Kopie:

Betreff: Thank you

Dear Odette

Thank you for inviting me to meet with you last week. I would now like to follow up on the suggestions which I made when we met.

I would like to recommend again the automatic aluminium sliding doors I described to you. The advantages of these are that they are less …[1] than other door materials. These sliding doors are also lighter which would mean that they could be driven by less …[2] and, therefore, cheaper motors.

I would also like to advise you to consider installing …[3] lighting in the passage between your warehouse and production area. I noticed that it is quite dark in the passage when the door to the warehouse is shut. We could achieve this …[4] by using the same PLC which controls the doors and by …[5] a relay which would …[6] the lights on and off automatically when one of the doors is opened or closed.

I would like to make one further suggestion. To help maintain a stable temperature in the warehouse area, we could fit a fan which would blow warmer air back into the production area when the door to that area is opened. Again, the fan would be …[7] by the PLC.

I am attaching a document containing technical …[8] about these suggestions, as well as the costs involved.

Please let me know if I can be of further assistance.

Best regards

Matthias Marquardt

5 A phone call from Odette

12

A **Listen as Odette phones Matthias to confirm his order. Which of the suggestions made by Matthias in the e-mail in exercise 4 does Odette accept? Which does she not accept?**

B **Matthias makes notes of what he agrees with Odette. He will give this list to the installation team. What four mistakes does he make?**

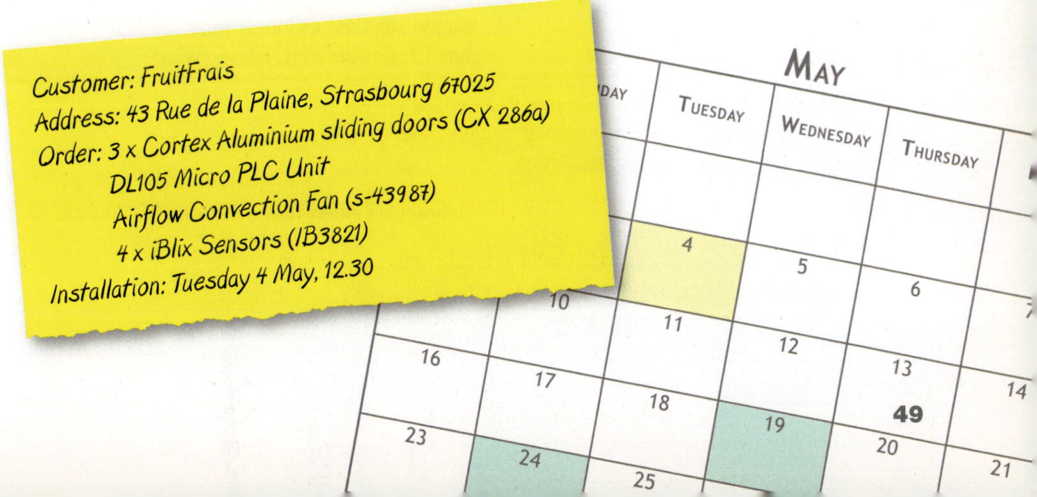

6 Arranging appointments and advising customers

LANGUAGE

Making suggestions
How about …?
My suggestion would be …

Rejecting a suggestion
Sorry, I don't think that's going to work.
I'm afraid I can't agree to that.

Accepting a suggestion
Good idea.
That sounds like a sensible/good idea.
I think we could say yes to that.

A Führen Sie das Rollenspiel in Partnerarbeit durch. KMK

Partner A

Partner B

A: Ein Kunde/Eine Kundin ruft Sie an. Beantworten Sie den Anruf, indem Sie Ihren eigenen Namen und den Firmennamen sagen.

B: Stellen Sie sich vor und bedanken Sie sich bei der Person am Telefon für die Informationen, die sie Ihnen zu den SPS-betriebenen Schiebetüren hat zukommen lassen.

A: Sagen Sie, dass Sie die Informationen gerne gesendet haben. Empfehlen Sie dem Kunden/der Kundin das gesamte System zu installieren, das Sie vorgeschlagen haben.

B: Sagen Sie, dass Sie nun endgültig beschlossen haben, SPS zu installieren und die Schiebetüren einzubauen.

A: Fragen Sie, ob der Kunde/die Kundin auch die Belüftungsanlage eingebaut haben möchte.

B: Lehnen Sie diesen Vorschlag ab. Sagen Sie, dass das Ihnen zu teuer ist. Sagen Sie, dass Sie gerne einen Termin machen möchten, um die Installation durchzuführen.

A: Fragen Sie, wann der Kunde/die Kundin Zeit für die Installation hat.

B: Sagen Sie, dass es Ihnen gegen Ende der Woche, die am 13. Juni anfängt, passen würde.

A: Schlagen Sie vor, dass Sie in drei Wochen, am Mittwoch, den 15. Juni vorbeikommen können, um die Installation durchzuführen.

B: Lehnen Sie einen Termin für den 15. Juni ab.

A: Sagen Sie, dass Sie am 16. und 17. Juni schon ausgebucht sind. Die Installation könnte am Montag, den 20. Juni stattfinden.

Sagen Sie, dass die Installation am Montag der darauffolgenden Woche stattfinden könnte. Fragen Sie, um wie viel Uhr begonnen werden kann.

Sagen Sie, dass Ihr Installationsteam am 20. Juni um 9:30 Uhr eintreffen wird.

Bestätigen Sie, dass es Ihnen am Montagmorgen um 9:30 Uhr passt. Bedanken Sie sich und verabschieden Sie sich.

Danken Sie Ihrem Kunden/Ihrer Kundin und verabschieden Sie sich.

B Make a list of the tools and components that you would need to take with you on the installation job.

GRAMMAR

Comparative and superlative forms of adjectives

Einsilbige Adjektive werden mit *–(e)r* und *–(e)st* gesteigert.	*These sliding doors are* ***lighter*** *than other models but they're not the* ***cheapest*** *available.*
Einzelkonsonanten werden nach einem kurzen Vokal verdoppelt.	*An extension module allows the PLC to carry out a* ***bigger*** *workload.*
Zweisilbige Adjektive mit den Endungen *–y*, *–er*, und *–le* werden ebenfalls mit *–(e)r* und *–(e)st* gesteigert.	*There are* ***easier*** *ways to do this. It would be* ***cleverer*** *to automate the process with a PLC. It's the* ***simplest*** *way.*
Alle anderen zwei- und mehrsilbigen Adjektive werden mit *more* und *most* gesteigert.	*This PLC is* ***more expensive*** *than other controllers on the market.*
Die Komparative und Superlative von einigen Adjektiven sind unregelmäßig.	*Please mount the unit 20cm* ***farther*** *away from the window. That's the* ***best*** *spot for it.*

Siehe S. 142 für weitere Einzelheiten.

7 Practice: comparative and superlative forms of adjectives

A Complete the sentences using the comparative or superlative forms of the adjectives in brackets.

1 We decided to invest in the … (up-to-date) PLC that we could afford.
2 As PLCs get … (cheap), more small companies use them to control their production processes.
3 Industrial PCs are … (expensive) than PLCs, which is the reason more companies still use PLCs.
4 The WV1 is certainly … (good) than the ZT8 because it has more process memory.
5 The installation was a bit … (easy) than I expected but programming the PLC was … (difficult).
6 Even the … (complex) industrial processes can be automated using PLCs.

B **Read the table comparing the three PLC models. Write as many sentences comparing them as possible. Use *long, high, wide, expensive, fast, slow* and *good.***

Model	UZ 382	UZx 31	UZTX 9
Price	$950	$1,200	$1,850
Operating speed	DC – 120 Mbps	DC – 150 Mbps	DC – 150 Mbps
No. USP ports	1	3	5
Length	45cm	30cm	22cm
Height	17cm	14cm	9cm
Width	12cm	10cm	7cm

8 Understanding instruction manuals

The team from Schröder Automation arrives at FreshFruit Fizz to carry out the installation.

A **Use the words in the box to complete the installation instructions.**

accommodate • bus • cable • clearance • cooled •
modules • panel • installation • vertically

Mounting your DL105 Micro PLC

- The PLC and expansion modules are designed to be … (1) by natural air convection. For effective cooling, a … (2) of at least 30mm must be provided above and below the PLC.
- If the PLC is being installed horizontally or … (3) on a … (4), you should allow 80mm for the minimum depth of the panel.
- If you intend to install additional … (5), you should allow a clearance of a minimum of 25mm on both sides of the unit to ensure sufficient space for the … (6) and later removal.
- Ensure that there is sufficient space in the mounting plan to … (7) the I/O wiring and communication … (8) connections.

B **Work with a partner. Take turns to explain in your own words what the highlighted terms in the text mean.**

C **Read the instructions for wiring the PLC unit on the next page and say if the statements (1–6) are true or false. Correct the false statements.**

1 Copper eye lugs should not be used when connecting the DL105.
2 The DL105 must be properly grounded in order to work properly.
3 Short wires should be avoided when planning the wiring route.
4 Where possible, DC and AC wiring should be run close together.
5 Input and output wiring should be run together wherever possible.
6 Individual wires should be kept as straight as possible.

Wiring

Warning

Always ensure that power to the DL105 is switched off when working on wiring. Death or serious personal injury may result from failure to do so!

Guidelines for wiring

1. The ground terminal on the DL105 base must be connected to a single point ground terminal. Use copper stranded wire to achieve a low impedance. Copper eye lugs should be attached by means of crimping and soldering to the ends of the stranded wire to ensure good surface contact.
2. There must be a single point ground (i.e. copper bus bar) for all devices in the panel requiring an Earth ground return. The single point of ground must be connected to the panel ground termination. The panel ground termination must be connected to Earth ground.
3. A good common ground reference (Earth ground) is essential for proper operation of the DL105. One side of all control and power circuits and the ground lead on flexible shielded cable must be properly connected to Earth ground. There are several methods of providing an adequate common ground reference, including:
   a) installing a ground rod as close to the panel as possible.
   b) connecting to incoming power system ground.
4. Isolation transformers are not normally necessary when installing a DL105, but may be helpful in eliminating/reducing suspected power problems.

Planning the wiring routes

The following guidelines provide information on how to wire the I/O connections to DL105 Micro PLCs.

1. Each terminal connection of the DL105 PLC can accept one 14 AWG wire or two 16 AWG size wires. Do not exceed this recommended capacity.
2. Always use a continuous length of wire.
3. Use the shortest possible wire length.
4. Use wire trays for routing where possible.
5. Do not run wires near high energy wiring.
6. Avoid running input wiring close to output wiring where possible.
7. To minimize voltage drops when wires have to run a long distance, consider using multiple wires for the return line.
8. Avoid running DC wiring in close proximity to AC wiring where possible.
9. Avoid bending wires too sharply.

D Find expressions in the text with the same meaning as the German expressions below. They are in the same order as they appear in the text.

1. Erdklemme, Masseklemme
2. Einfach-Erdungspunkt
3. Kupferlitze
4. Ösenanker
5. Masseanschluss
6. armiertes Kabel
7. Staberder
8. Trenntransformator
9. Kabelkanäle
10. Rücklaufleitung

9 Hörverstehen

13

Situation

Sie sind Auszubildende/r bei der Firma PLC System und Installation GmbH, einer Firma mit Hauptsitz in Großbritannien. Zurzeit sind Sie dort im Customer Service eingesetzt. Sie werden gebeten, Nachrichten auf dem Anrufbeantworter abzuhören und die wichtigen Informationen zu notieren.

Aufgabe

Übertragen Sie das Formular zweimal in Ihr Notizbuch. Hören Sie aufmerksam zu und füllen Sie das Formular aus. Sie hören beide Nachrichten zweimal.

Name und Sitz der Firma des Anrufers

Vor- und Zuname des Anrufers

Gewünschter Ansprechpartner

Name:

Abteilung:

Bestellung

Installationstermin

Rückruf unter

10 Produktion

Situation

Sie sind ein Kollege von Shiela Clark. Sie ist aus gesundheitlichen Gründen nicht zur Arbeit gekommen und kann die Nachrichten auf dem Anrufbeantworter nicht beantworten.

Aufgabe

Schreiben Sie eine E-Mail auf Englisch an Brian Anderson. Nehmen Sie folgende Punkte in Ihrer E-Mail auf.

- Sie haben gesehen, dass der XT9ZA anstelle des XT9 Micro PLC installiert werden soll.
- Donnerstag, der 14. Juli würde für die Installation gut passen.
- Das Installationsteam, das an dem Tag kommt, besteht aus Roger Nielsen und Karen Quigley.
- Die Fertigstellung der Installation dauert mehrere Stunden. Um zu vermeiden, dass das Team am 15. Juli zur Fertigstellung noch einmal kommen muss, sollte so früh wie möglich begonnen werden. Schlagen Sie vor, dass das Installationsteam um 6:00 Uhr anfängt.

Forum → Electrical Forum → PLCs → Help with ladder logic

Alec_Elec

We're going to be learning about ladder logic for PLCs next week in college. I don't know anything about it! Can anyone help me?

FuseBox

Sure! Let's start with the basics. Ladder logic is a common programming language used for PLCs. It's a graphic language and the name is based on the fact that programs in the language look like ladders, with two vertical 'rails' and a series of horizontal 'rungs' between them. Ladder logic programs are also called ladder diagrams and are similar to schematics for sets of relay circuits. This similarity is a big advantage of ladder logic. Basically, a wide variety of engineers, technicians and electricians can understand and use it without much additional training.

Alec_Elec

Thanks for the info. What's ladder logic used for?

FuseBox

Ladder logic is often used to program PLCs where sequential control of a real-time process or manufacturing operation is required. It's useful for simple but critical control systems, or for reworking old hardwired relay circuits. However, as PLCs become more sophisticated, ladder logic is used in more complex automated systems.

Alec_Elec

I've heard that ladder logic is quite easy to learn. Is that right?

FuseBox

Yes, basically. But there is a small problem with it. Ladder logic isn't really one language. It's more like a set of closely related programming languages. Normally, the ladder logic languages from two manufacturers will not be completely compatible. Even different models of programmable controllers within the same product family may have different ladder notifications so that programs cannot be seamlessly interchanged between models. The different versions of ladder logic can make programming a bit tricky for beginners.

11 Ladder logic

A Answer the questions about the online discussion in your own words.

1. How does ladder logic get its name?
2. Why can ladder logic be used easily by a wide range of jobs?
3. Which main use of ladder logic is mentioned in the text?
4. Why can ladder logic be difficult to learn at first?

B Which further questions about ladder logic would you have posted in the forum? Write them down, then find someone in your class who can answer them.

C Work in a small group. Make a list of the types of processes which ladder logic and PLCs can be used to control. Which of these have you experienced in your work? Tell your classmates about this.

UNIT 6

Energy and the environment

- Explaining installations and other processes
- Numerical expressions
- Explaining features of energy systems

1 Warm-up

Work with a partner.

A **Use the words in the box to name the forms of energy shown in the picture.**

biomass • fossil fuel • geothermal • hydro-electric • methane • nuclear • solar • tidal • wind

B **Which of these energy forms are 'conventional' and which are 'alternative'? Make two lists.**

C **Do you know which form of energy is used to generate the energy in your house? Would you prefer it was generated using another form of energy? If so, which?**

D **Work with a partner. Choose one of the energy forms and list its advantages and disadvantages. Tell the rest of the class what's on your list.**

2 Solar energy

A **Read the article on the website on the next page and decide which headline best summarizes what it says.**

1. PV systems still expensive but worth the investment
2. Solar thermal collectors remain most popular solar energy system
3. Solar thermal collectors or photovoltaic – Which solar energy choices are right for you?

http://www.energyadvice.net

I want to reduce my reliance on public utilities and cut environmental pollution with solar energy, but which system should I install?

How they work

The sun provides a free energy source, and solar thermal collectors are the most direct way of capturing its energy. The system works by trapping infrared radiation from the sun under the glass panels of an insulated collector housing and using it to heat a fluid (often water) which is then piped into your radiators.

PV systems work in a different way. They use silicon cells which convert sunlight into electricity. When light strikes the cells, electrons are released and start flowing as an electrical current.

Pros and cons

A lot can be said in favour of both systems. They're both durable and reliable. And they both help preserve the world's resources by using a source of energy which is renewable. On the downside, however, they're both fairly expensive to buy and install, though the cost of PV systems is falling slowly.

One problem with PV systems is that they don't generate electricity when the sun isn't shining. So on cloudy days or at night you'll still need to draw power from the electricity grid. Also, there's no efficient way of storing electricity generated by this system.

On the other hand, heat generated by solar thermal collectors can be stored and used at times when there's not enough sun.

Both systems can provide clean and efficient energy. You should speak to an energy adviser about which one will be best for you and your house.

B **Copy the table into your notebook. Read the text again and list the advantages and disadvantages of both systems.**

Solar thermal collectors		Photovoltaic cells	
advantages	disadvantages	advantages	disadvantages

C **Find the English equivalents of these words. They appear in the same order in the text.**

1 öffentliche Versorgungsbetriebe
2 Umweltverschmutzung
3 Energiequelle
4 Flüssigkeit
5 Heizkörper
6 langlebig
7 zuverlässig
8 erneuerbar

D Now use the English words from exercise C to complete the sentences.

1. It's cold in here so just let me turn on the … .
2. Wave or tidal power is one … which we could do more to exploit to cut our use of fossil fuels.
3. One problem with electricity from … is that you never really know how much of it has been generated using nuclear technology or alternative energy sources.
4. Another … used in solar thermal collectors is antifreeze solution.
5. Solar energy would not be a very … power source for me as I live in an area with little sun and a lot of rain.
6. PV systems are very tough and …, and usually need little repair work.
7. Nuclear energy may reduce … in the short term but if something goes wrong it has a catastrophic impact on the environment.
8. The government should do more to invest in … energy which doesn't pollute the environment.

E Go back to exercise C. Try to remember each English word without looking at the text or your answers. Do the same for exercise D.

3 Explaining PV system installations

14

Jean-Claude Bernard, a Belgian customer, has ordered a PV system from PowerTech GmbH, an alternative energy company in Aachen. Irene Riemar from PowerTech visits and explains the stages of the installation.

Listen to or read the dialogue. Which stages of the installation are shown in the photos/drawings and in which order are they mentioned?

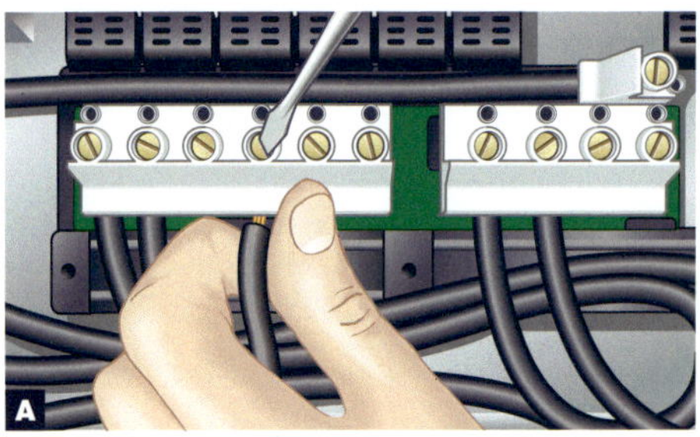

Jean-Claude So, work will begin on installing my PV system on Tuesday next week.

Irene That's right. If there are no problems with the installation, we should complete it by Thursday lunchtime.

Jean-Claude That's great. Could you tell me how you do the installation? My son has been asking me, and I want to be able to explain it to him when he gets home from school.

Irene Sure, no problem. Well, the first step to any PV installation is what we did the first time we visited you. We start by checking the orientation of the roof as well as its inclination. Basically, we need to find out if it is facing in the right direction and at the right angle. If it is, then the PV system can provide enough power to cover your household demand. As I've said, you have nothing to worry about regarding these factors. Your roof is more or less perfect.

Jean-Claude Yes, that is good. And what happens after that?

Irene Well, the second step in an installation is putting up the scaffolding. The scaffolding will be put up on Tuesday morning. It gives our installers a safe platform to work on, so it's important that it's done properly. Thirdly, we mark where the roof anchors are going to go. We just use chalk for this, so the next time it rains they will wash off.

Jean-Claude Oh, good.

Irene After that, the roof anchors are fixed onto your roof tiles. Once they're in place, the aluminium bars which make up the frame are screwed into place.

Jean-Claude And then comes the – what did you call it – PV array.

Irene Yes, that's right. After the frame is in place, the panels which make up the PV array are fitted onto it. The next step is to secure the cables from the panels onto the frame and to drill a small hole through your roof.

Jean-Claude A hole!

Irene Don't worry. We use a watertight sealant to ensure that rain doesn't get in.

Jean-Claude Thank goodness.

Irene In the meantime, our electrician will have installed the inverter in your house. Once that's done, we connect the DC wiring from the panel array to the inverter and then we're basically finished. We just have to throw the switch and power up the system.

Jean-Claude Excellent.

Irene The final stage of the installation is to monitor the system's efficiency in the first few weeks. We do this to make sure that everything is set just right. And then you have a fully functioning PV system for your home and guaranteed energy efficiency.

4 Describing processes

14

A Read or listen to the dialogue again and complete the sentences for describing processes.

1 We ... checking the orientation of the roof as well as its inclination.
2 The ... in an installation is erecting the scaffolding.
3 ..., we mark where the roof anchors are going to go.
4 ..., the roof anchors are fixed onto your roof tiles.
5 The ... is to secure the cables from the panels onto the frame.
6 The ... of the installation is to monitor the system's efficiency in the first few weeks.

B Führen Sie das Rollenspiel mit zwei Partnern durch. KMK

Partner A: Rollenkarte auf S. 127
Partner B: Rollenkarte auf S. 128
Partner C: Rollenkarte auf S. 130

C Work with a partner and choose three of the words. Take turns explaining what they mean to your partner without using the words themselves. Can your partner guess which words you are explaining?

1 orientation
2 inclination
3 household demand
4 scaffolding
5 roof anchors
6 PV array
7 Roof tiles
8 watertight sealant
9 inverter
10 energy efficiency

5 Numerical expressions

15

A Study the Language box below, then listen to the six numbers (a–f) being read. Write them down in your notebook.

B Work with a partner.

Partner A: Turn to File 1 on page 126.
Partner B: Turn to File 9 on page 129.

LANGUAGE

Numbers

0.739	nought point seven three nine (BE) zero point seven three nine (BE/AE)
3.754	three point seven five four
176	one/a hundred and seventy-six
4,765	four thousand seven hundred and sixty-five
1,000,000	one/a million
1,000,000,000	one/a billion (German: *Milliarde*)
1,000,000,000,000	one/a trillion (German: *Billion*)

LANGUAGE

Mathematical expressions

addition	+	plus
subtraction	−	minus
multiplication	x	times / multiplied by
division	÷	over / divided by
	=	is / is equal to / equals
	()	brackets

Exponents

10^2	ten squared
6^3	six cubed
13^7	thirteen to the power of seven
$4m^2$	four square metres
$8cm^3$	eight cubic centimetres

Fractions

$^1/_2$	(one/a) half
$^1/_3$	one/a third
$^1/_4$	one/a quarter
$^1/_6$	one/a sixth
$^5/_8$	five eighths

C Copy the table and complete it for your own home.

Complete this table to determine the number of solar modules you require in your home.

Method	Average home in the USA	Your home
How many kilowatt hours (kWh) do you use on average each month? Check your electricity bill!	600 kWh	
To arrive at the number of watt hours (Wh) you use a month, multiply this by 1,000.	600 x 1,000 = 600,000 Wh	
Now calculate the number of Wh you use on average a day by dividing by 30.	600,000 wh ÷ 30 days = 20,000 Wh per day	
Next, take away 6,400 Wh, the average saving made through energy efficiency.	20,000 Wh – 6,400 = 13,600 Wh per day	
How much of your home (as a percentage) do you want to power with the system? Multiply by this percentage.	100% x 13,600 =13,600 Wh per day	
Divide this by the maximum (June) insolation (7.5 kWh/m2/day).	13,600 Wh per day ÷ 7.5 kWh/m2/day = 1,813 watts	
Next multiply by 1.2 to cover system inefficiencies.	1,813 x 1.2 = 2,176 watts	
Now divide by the peak wattage of the module.	2,176 watts ÷ 120 peak watts per module = 18.13 modules	
Finally round up to a whole number.	19 modules	

6 Explaining how PV systems work

Irene from PowerTech is explaining to Jean-Claude how his new PV system generates electricity.

16

A Listen to the dialogue and label the schematic with the expressions in the box.

inverter • meter • national grid • PV array

B Now explain in your own words why the system requires two meters.

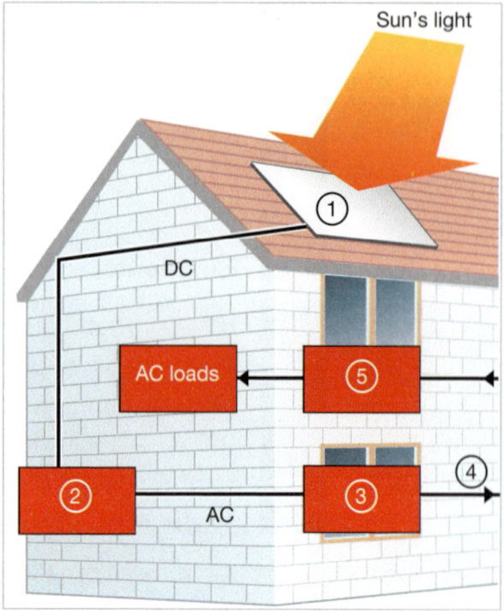

7 Explaining other domestic energy systems

Now Irene is visiting another customer in Holland. She explains how two other household energy systems work.

17

Look at the photos of the two systems and match the correct features to each. Listen to the dialogue to check your answers.

Vaillant/Honda Combined Heat and Power (CHP) unit

Honeywell wind turbine

1 An electrochemical process converts the hydrogen to electricity.
2 Electricity is generated with a rotation speed of as little as two mph.
3 Emissions are significantly reduced by the way the system operates.
4 It doesn't use the conventional generator which is standard with this sort of technology.
5 Fuel cell technology is used to generate heat and power at the same time.
6 Noise and vibration are significantly reduced.
7 Electric generation mechanism is housed in blade tips and frame.
8 Gas is converted into hydrogen by a proton exchange membrane.

GRAMMAR

Passive forms

		Form von *to be*	Partizip Perfekt (3. Verbform)	
Gegenwart	*Wind turbines*	***are***	***made***	*in the USA.*
Vergangenheit *(simple past)*	*In the past, little*	***was***	***done***	*for the environment.*
Unvollendete Vergangenheit *(present perfect)*	*This technology*	***has been***	***developed***	*recently.*
Modalverb	*This system*	***could be***	***installed***	*here.*
Zukunft	*The scaffolding*	***will be***	***put up***	*on Tuesday.*

Siehe S. 143 für weitere Einzelheiten.
Eine Liste der unregelmäßigen Verben befindet sich auf S. 216.

8 Practice: passive forms

A Complete the sentences with the correct passive form of the verbs in brackets. Sometimes more than one correct answer is possible.

1 Currently, most of the energy which … (waste) in the company is in the form of heating left on at night.
2 Look, this computer … (leave) on standby mode. That's just a waste of energy.
3 All lights … (turn off) by the last person to leave the office each evening.
4 The heating … (set) lower at 20 °C in the main building during the winter, leading to a savings of 16% on our heating bill.
5 Two windows in the sales office … (not close) last night. No wonder our heating costs are so high!
6 We hope that in part our energy saving targets for next year … (reach) by using low-wattage lights.
7 The fact that we spend so much on heat and light … (cause) in part by us not having guidelines about energy use for staff.
8 The company policy is that the energy-saving software in all PCs … (activate) at all times.
9 Solar thermal collectors … (soon be) installed here so that energy from the sun … (store) for when the sun doesn't shine.
10 We … (warn) about environmental disasters by scientists for many years but the warnings … (not take) seriously.

B Write passive sentences about your work: one in the present, one in the past, one in the present perfect, etc.

Example: *Where I work, many electronic control panels are assembled every day.*

9 Leseverstehen

Sie arbeiten im Ausland für einen Stromkonzern, wo in Sitzungen häufig von ‚*HVDC*' bzw. von ‚*DC*' und ‚*AC*' gesprochen wird. Um mitreden zu können, entscheiden Sie sich, über dieses Thema zu informieren und stoßen auf folgenden Artikel im Internet.

Beantworten Sie die Fragen zu dem Artikel auf Deutsch.

New generation DC may win next round in 'war of currents'

The story is well-enough-known. The contest over a century ago between AC or DC about which type of current would become the standard for delivering power to homes and businesses was won by AC. The basic reason for this was that AC was more suited to transporting electricity over long distances on large-scale grids than was DC.

Now, however, a high-voltage version of DC, known as HVDC, looks set to challenge AC's position as the standard for electricity grids. AC grids suffer quite dramatic losses in electricity over long distances. Over a distance of 1,000 miles, an AC grid will lose between 12% and 25% of the power it is transporting. But with an HVDC grid the losses are of a lower order: over the same distance they only amount to between 6% and 8%. The results of this greater efficiency in both cash and environmental terms should be immediately clear.

All this is being brought one step closer by the development of new technology which looks set to solve a major problem of HVDC systems. In the past, power surges on HVDC systems resulted in entire grids going down and far-reaching power outages. However, new HVDC breaker technology means that the section of a grid experiencing a surge can be quickly isolated, and the problem dealt with while the rest of the grid continues to operate normally.
Some experts believe that these developments clear the way for the harnessing of renewable sources of energy on a truly grand scale. According to Alan Peekson, energy technology analyst at the consultancy SynroCross, 'The new efficiencies over very long distances offered by HVDC could make the development of enormous wind farms in isolated, far-flung regions practicable for the first time. Basically, we could turn the Canadian tundra regions into wind farms which could power Canada and the United States.'

Energy technologists could start to consider power-generating schemes which have up until now seemed rather more like science fiction than potential reality.

'The idea of the wastes of the Sahara desert becoming a gigantic source of solar power for Africa, Europe and parts of Asia could now be realizable,' says Peekson.

In any case, thanks to HVDC we can now see a future for power beyond fossil fuels which we can look forward to with optimism.

1. Warum wird bei Energieübertragungen über weite Entfernungen Wechselstrom Gleichstrom gegenüber bevorzugt?
2. Welche statistischen Angaben werden im Artikel zur jeweiligen Effizienz von Wechselstrom und HGÜ gemacht?
3. Welches Hauptproblem hatten HGÜ-Netze in der Vergangenheit?
4. Welche Entwicklung könnte dieses Problem jetzt lösen? Wie?
5. Inwiefern vereinfacht die HGÜ das Nutzen von erneuerbaren Energiequellen?

Smart meter users 'need to see what they're saving'

Government plans for the installation of smart meters in homes across the UK by 2020 are coming in for simultaneous praise and criticism.

The government is planning the roll-out of smart meters to 26 million homes in an attempt to reduce the amount of CO_2 emitted by households. The move has been welcomed by Energy Check, the watchdog organization which promotes the interests of energy consumers.

William Linklater, a spokesperson for Energy Check, said, 'Smart meter technology certainly helps individual households to cut their energy consumption. Such widespread implementation will mean significant cuts in emissions and an overall benefit to the environment.'

The government points out a range of other benefits to energy consumers who will no longer have to pay estimated bills or stay at home waiting for their meter to be read.

However, according to Energy Check, government plans do not go far enough.

'Currently, energy companies will not be required to install energy monitors along with the new meters,' said Linklater.

'This will result in consumers being left in the dark about exactly how much energy they are using and where they could cut back. That's rather odd given that the point of the government's plans is to help them do just this.

'We are now calling on the government to include an integrated monitor with the meters which lets people see exactly where they stand.'

Energy Check says that a monitor could provide consumers with information about their current usage as well as their use of power in the past. This would allow them to identify times when they are consuming too much and take appropriate steps to cut back, claims the watchdog. They could also be provided with details of how much they have spent so far in the current month or year.

Linklater was dismissive of suggestions about providing this information to consumers online.

'If I have to go online to check up on my energy consumption, I'm not going to do this as regularly as I need to. Checking a monitor in my home would become another simple domestic task like making sure the windows are shut before going to bed. It would allow me to check my energy consumption as part of my domestic routine.

'We are now encouraging the government to think again and include monitors in their plans. That is the only way the roll-out of smart meters will be truly effective.'

10 Discussing energy-saving measures

A Answer the questions about the text.

1. What is the government in the UK planning to do by 2020?
2. What benefits of smart meters for consumers are mentioned in the article?
3. What objections does Energy Check have to providing information about energy consumption online?

B Work together in a small group. Note down how the members of your group answer the following questions. Then report the answers to the class.

1. What do you do to save energy?
2. What does your company do?
3. Does the German government do enough to encourage people to lower their consumption of energy? What additional steps could the government take to do this?

UNIT 7 Electrical components

- Explaining how to trace a fault
- Understanding technical advice
- Understanding a data sheet

1 Warm-up

A Identify the photos of the electrical components numbered 1–10. All the names are in the box.

capacitor • diode • full-wave bridge rectifier • glass fuse • integrated voltage stabilizer • mains input socket • resistor • transformer • transistor • tube

1

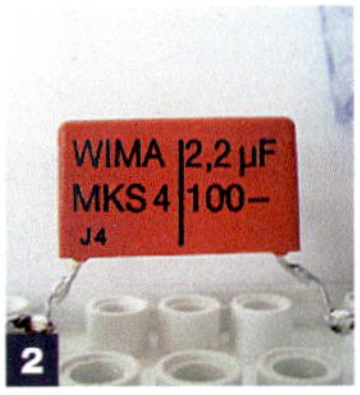

2

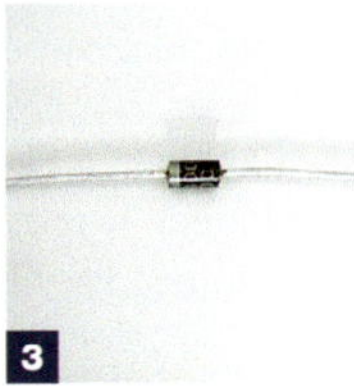

3

4

5

6

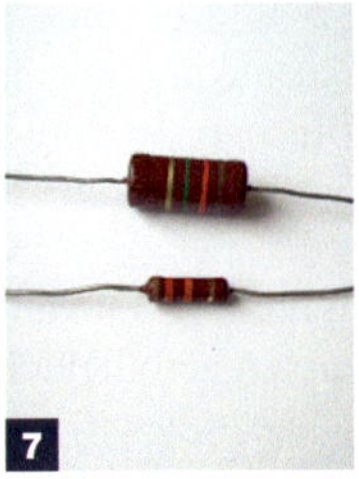

7

8

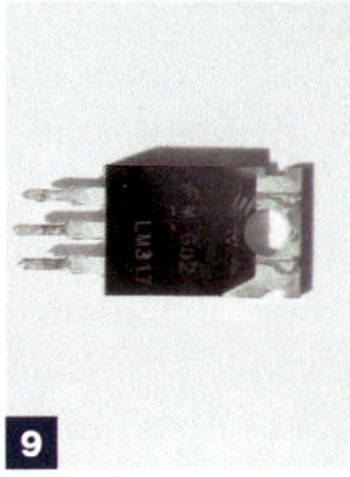

9

10

B Find the correct symbol (a–j) for each component.

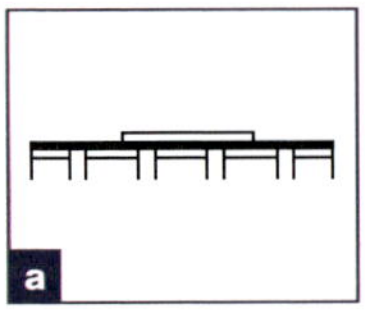

a

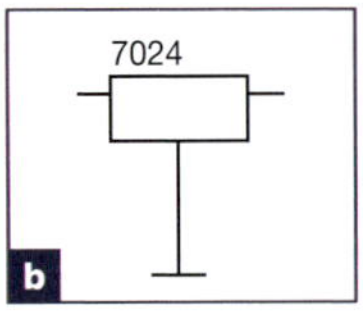

b

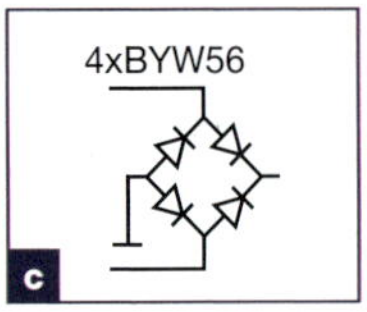

c

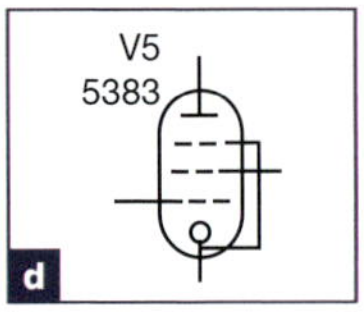

d

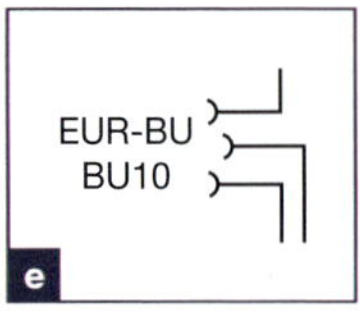

e

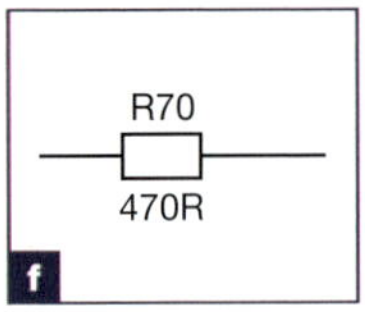

f

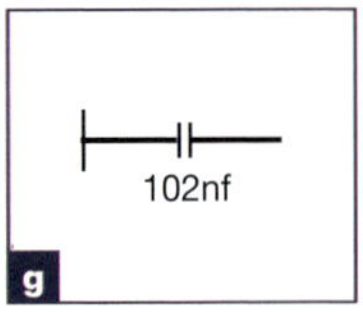

g

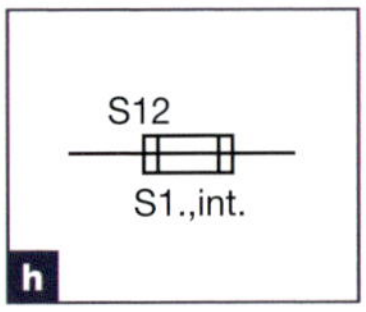

h

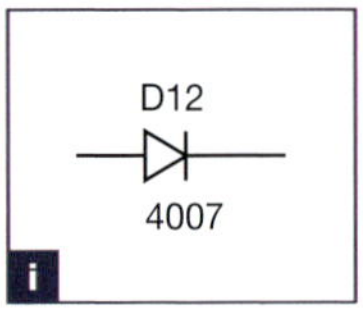

i

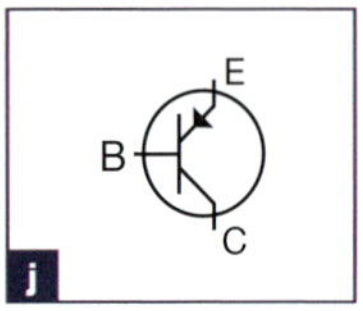

j

2 Radio ham saves rock star

18

A Armin Feiertag is a radio ham. His call sign is DC2GO. Listen to him talking to Randy Archer in Cleveland, Ohio and complete the sentences below.

Ham radio

Amateur radio is called ham radio, and an amateur radio enthusiast is called a radio ham. Radio hams are technical experts who use their knowledge to build and operate their radios and communicate with people all over the world. They are often the first and only people able to send messages to the outside world when all other means of communication fail, e.g. after an earthquake (Haiti) or a tsunami (Indonesia). Radio hams need a licence to operate and have to take an examination to obtain one.

1. Randy Archer's call sign is …
2. Armin is repairing …
3. Armin has so far replaced …
4. In Europe a GFCI is called …
5. Armin looks at the back of the device and checks the …
6. He takes off the back panel and carries out …
7. He's pleased when he finds the …
8. Armin uses a multimeter to measure the …
9. The reading on the multimeter is …
10. Either the … or the … is defective.

B Hören Sie den Dialog noch einmal und beantworten Sie die Fragen bzw. lösen Sie die Aufgaben auf Deutsch. KMK

1. Erstellen Sie eine Liste der von Armin und Randy erwähnten Bauteile und Werkzeuge.
2. Welche Reparaturen und Checks wurden von Armin vor dem Gespräch mit Randy durchgeführt?
3. Wie hat sich Armin vor einem Stromschlag geschützt, der tödlich hätte enden können?
4. Welche Prüfung führt Armin durch, ohne die Bauteile zu berühren?
5. Begründen Sie Randys Vorschlag, die Spannung an einem Bauteil zu messen.
6. Welche Bauteile wird Armin evtl. benötigen, um den Verstärker zu reparieren?

3 Discussion: tracing the fault, 1

Discuss this question in small groups.

According to the circuit diagram the amp has a 430V DC power supply when on standby, so Armin has to be careful. What would you do next if you were Armin?

Examples: *I'd first make sure that the amp was disconnected.*

I'd plug it into a circuit with …

I'd use a … to check the …

4 Identifying components

Work with a partner. Look at the circuit diagram (schematic) below and take it in turns to ask and answer questions about it. Each person should ask at least five questions using expressions from the Language box.

> **LANGUAGE**
>
> What's the component in square …?
> What is it attached to?
> Where is the …?
> How many … are there in the circuit?
> Where is it / are they?
> What is there between square … and square …?

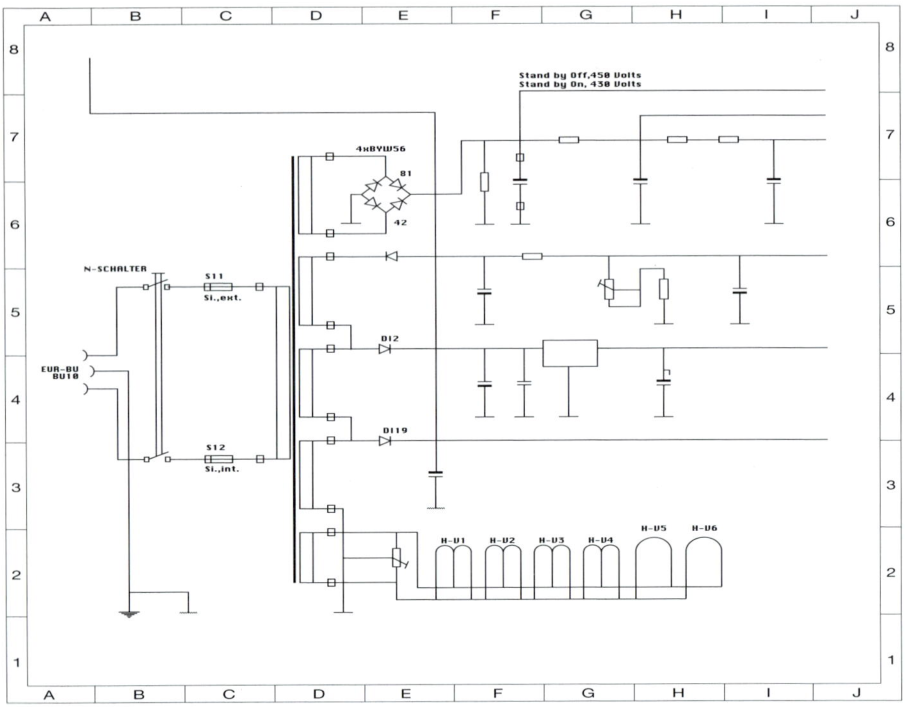

5 Tracing the fault, 2

A **Match 1–4 with a–d to find the possible causes of the fault in the guitar amplifier.**

1. A small metal object (e.g. a paper clip) has fallen into the amp …
2. There is a dry solder joint …
3. One of the wires to the circuit board was badly soldered …
4. The transformer is faulty …

a. so it came loose and short-circuited the diodes.
b. and is producing no voltage.
c. because the soldering iron used was at the wrong temperature.
d. and has caused a short circuit.

B **Decide which is the most probable cause.**

C **Tell a partner about a similar case of troubleshooting from your own experience.**

6 Technical advice

A Armin Feiertag ist Mitglied des englischsprachigen Internetforums *Electronics online* und schreibt auch einen deutschsprachigen Blog, in dem er über Lösungen technischer Probleme berichtet.

KMK

Fassen Sie die wichtigsten Aussagen von Armins Antwort an Don, einen amerikanischen Hobbyelektroniker, als Beitrag für seinen deutschsprachigen Blog zusammen.

http://forum.electronicsonline.com

ELECTRONICS ONLINE

The internet forum for electronics technology | http://forum.electronicsonline.com

Topic: Dead amplifier?

Posted by Don on 12/21/20... at 15.35

Hi there! Can anyone help me with some info on diodes and rectifiers? The full-wave bridge rectifier in my amplifier has an output of 0 volts! Does this mean I can throw away the amplifier now? Any help would be much appreciated. Cheers!
Don

Posted by Armin on 12/22/20... at 09.20

Hi Don,
I had a problem like that with an amplifier. Here's a link to the schematic so you can see what type of amplifier it was.
I opened up the amplifier and carried out a sensory check: no obvious problems. Next I plugged it in and saw that the tubes were illuminated. I used a DMM to check the voltage at the mains input and the rectifier. It was 230 V at the mains output but zero at the rectifier. This showed me that the fault was somewhere between the mains input and the smoothing circuit, so I took a closer look at the rectifier. I then noticed that the diodes were discoloured and one of the wires leading from the power supply to the circuit board had become loose and was touching the metal base, leaving a small black mark.
I disconnected the mains supply and unsoldered the transformer outlet to the rectifier. Then I reconnected the mains supply and checked the output of the transformer through this outlet. It was 308.5 V AC as expected.
Next I needed to check all four diodes, but to do this I had to take them out. After disconnecting the AC mains lead, I unsoldered them carefully using a soldering iron and a desoldering pump to suck off the solder, and tested them one by one with the multimeter. I set the multimeter to resistance mode and discovered that the diodes showed a high resistance in both directions and were consequently defective.
Now I knew I had to replace them, so I looked them up on the schematic and saw I needed four BYW 56 diodes. I found them on the internet and saw that a BYW 56 diode had a maximum forward current of 2 A and a maximum reverse voltage of 1,000 V. Using my ham radio contacts I found someone with suitable diodes nearby. I got the diodes, soldered them in, connected the wires of the power supply to the circuit board, plugged in the mains lead and checked the DC voltage again. It was 430 V!

B **Translate the highlighted words in the internet forum on the previous page into German. Make a list of the German words.**

C **Complete the following text with the highlighted words in the internet forum on the previous page. Use the German word list you wrote in B and try to remember the English words without looking at the forum again.**

Many electronic devices have an …[1] to make the sound louder. Some are battery operated and others are plugged into the …[2]. If a device breaks down, it's best not to work on it until it has been …[3] (otherwise you could get an electric shock). Then you can carry out a simple …[4] before taking it apart and replacing expensive electronic components like …[5]. Service personnel normally use a digital multimeter to measure the …[6] (V) or the …[7] (Ω) at test points inside the equipment. Sometimes the components are mounted on a printed …[8], and when a component has to be removed, the contacts must often be cleaned with a …[9]. In most cases it's best to …[10] a faulty component.

GRAMMAR

Present perfect

Aussagen

I *you* *we* *they*	**'ve**	***driven*** ***flown*** ***seen*** *start**ed***
he/ *she/it*	**'s**	

Verneinungen

I *you* *we* *they*	***haven't***	***driven*** ***flown*** ***seen*** *start**ed***
he/ *she/it*	***hasn't***	

Fragen

have	*I* *you* *we* *they*	***driven****?* ***flown****?* ***seen****?* *start**ed**?*
has	*he/* *she/it*	

Simple past

Aussagen

I *you* *he/she/it* *we* *they*	***drove*** ***flew*** ***saw*** *start**ed***

Verneinungen

I *you* *he/she/it* *we* *they*	***didn't***	*drive* *fly* *see* *start*

Fragen

did	*I* *you* *he/she/it* *we* *they*	*drive?* *fly?* *see?* *start?*

Siehe S. 143–144 für weitere Einzelheiten.
Eine Liste der unregelmäßigen Verben befindet sich auf S. 216.

7 Practice: present perfect

A **Decide whether these expressions of time are about *finished time* (simple past) or *unfinished time* (present perfect). None of them are about the future.**

today • last month • in 2010 • on my birthday • this year • on Tuesday • ever • 5 years ago • since 2009 • at Christmas • never • yesterday • in August • just • in the autumn • yet • at 8 o'clock • this week

B Complete these sentences using the present perfect or the simple past.

1. I (not repair) Tom's equipment yet.
2. He (buy) his guitar last year.
3. Tom (bring) out a new album this year.
4. He last (have) a big hit two years ago.
5. (you/hear) his new album yet?
6. His light show (break down) three times on his tour of Europe so far.
7. It (not break down) in 2011.
8. (your equipment / ever / break down)?
9. When (you/last/see) one of Tom's concerts?
10. I (not go) to his concert in Berlin last month.

C Work with a partner and follow the instructions below.

Partner A

1 Use the Language box to ask your partner a question beginning with *Have you ever …?*

Partner B

2 Answer the question with a short answer *(Yes, I have. / No, I haven't.).*

Partner A

3 If your partner gave a 'yes' answer, ask the follow-up question *When did you do that?*

If your partner gave a 'no' answer, go back to **1**.

Partner B

4 Answer the question using the simple past.

Partner A

5 Ask your partner another follow-up question starting with *How/Why/What did you …?*

Partner B

6 Give details of what you did. Then go back to **1** – you are now Partner A.

LANGUAGE

work on	equipment
take (took, taken) apart	an appliance
make (made, made) a mistake while working on	a machine
damage	a motor
short-circuit	a building site
	a tool

get (got, got/gotten)	an electric shock
	in trouble for making a mistake at work

Refer to Unit 4, pp. 36–38 for examples of equipment and/or use your own ideas.

8 Using a data sheet

19

A Nachdem er den Verstärker untersucht hat, lädt Armin das abgebildete Datenblatt aus dem Internet herunter und kontaktiert Randy Archer erneut, um die Reparatur mit ihm zu besprechen. Hören Sie das Gespräch und ergänzen Sie folgende Aussagen mit a, b oder c.

1 Der Gleichrichter im Verstärker liefert momentan eine Spannung von …
- **a** 308,5 V.
- **b** 0 V.
- **c** 4 V.

2 Armin braucht Dioden vom Typ …
- **a** BYW52.
- **b** BYW54.
- **c** BYW56.

3 Armin hat Dioden vom Typ …
- **a** BYW52.
- **b** BYW54.
- **c** BYW56.

4 Wenn Randy von ‚surge' spricht, meint er …
- **a** Durchlassstrom.
- **b** Spitzenstrom.
- **c** Wechselstrom.

5 Der wichtigste Unterschied zwischen den im Datenblatt aufgeführten Dioden liegt beim Wert des/r …
- **a** Durchlassstroms.
- **b** Stoßstrom-Grenzwerts.
- **c** Sperrspannung.

6 Die Dioden, die Armin sucht, haben einen …
- **a** Durchlassstrom von 50 A.
- **b** Sperrspannungswert von 1.000 V.
- **c** Stoßstrom-Grenzwert von 12 A.

B Erklären Sie folgende im Datenblatt enthaltene Angaben.

1 2 A
2 600 V
3 12 A
4 10 ms
5 1000 W
6 175 °C

19

C Entnehmen Sie dem Gespräch, wie Armin vorgehen wird, um den Verstärker zu reparieren. Schreiben Sie eine Zusammenfassung auf Deutsch.

BYW52 to BYW56

Semiconductors

Standard Avalanche Sinterglass Diode

Features

- Controlled avalanche characteristics
- Glass passivated junction
- Hermetically sealed package
- Low reverse current
- High surge current loading

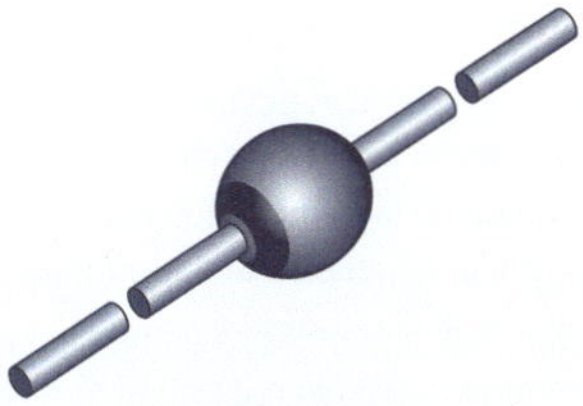

Applications

Rectification, general purpose

Mechanical Data

Case: Sintered glass case, SOD 57

Terminals: Plated axial leads, solderable per MIL-STD-750, Method 2026
Polarity: Color band denotes cathode end
Mounting Position: Any
Weight: 370 mg. (max. 500 mg)

Absolute Maximum Ratings

T_{amb} = 25 °C, unless otherwise specified

Parameter	Test condition	Sub type	Symbol	Value	Unit
Reverse voltage = Repetitive peak reverse voltage	see electrical characteristics	BYW52	$V_R = V_{RRM}$	200	V
	see electrical characteristics	BYW53	$V_R = V_{RRM}$	400	V
	see electrical characteristics	BYW54	$V_R = V_{RRM}$	600	V
	see electrical characteristics	BYW55	$V_R = V_{RRM}$	800	V
	see electrical characteristics	BYW56	$V_R = V_{RRM}$	1000	V
Peak forward surge current	t_p = 10 ms, half sinewave		I_{FSM}	50	A
Repetitive peak forward current			I_{FRM}	12	A
Average forward current	φ = 180°		I_{FAV}	2	A
Pulse avalanche peak power	t_p = 20 µs half sine wave, T_j = 175 °C		P_R	1000	W

9 Leseverstehen

In Ihrem Betrieb gibt es häufig Probleme durch Stromausfall. Sie sollen für Ihren Ausbildungsleiter eine Präsentation über ausfallsichere Stromversorgung machen und stoßen auf folgenden Artikel im Internet. Beantworten Sie die Fragen auf Deutsch.

Fault-tolerant power supplies

Why have redundant power supplies?

Imagine a 24VDC 10A power supply driving motors and sensors on a conveyor based production line. For two or three years everything works fine, then one Friday (always at the end of the month), the power supply fails causing the conveyor to stop. Even if a spare part is in stock, it could still result in 30 minutes of expensive lost production.

If two identical power supplies had been installed in a fault-tolerant, redundant mode, the remaining (good) unit would have continued to power the production line. The failed power supply could then be replaced at a more convenient time during routine maintenance.

The effectiveness of having a fault-tolerant power strategy was demonstrated after Hurricane Katrina hit the Gulf Coast in 2005. A television station interviewed the heads of two telecom carriers to find out when their telephone services would be operational again. The interview was very short – 'we never lost service' they replied.

Large industrial complexes have expensive and complex backup systems consisting of battery banks, generators and uninterruptible power supplies.

Frequently used terminology

Hot-swap

Some equipment is operated 24 hours a day, 7 days a week, allowing no time to bring the system down for maintenance. In this case the failed power supply must be 'swapped' out and a new one inserted without disruption to equipment operation.

DLP-PU block diagram

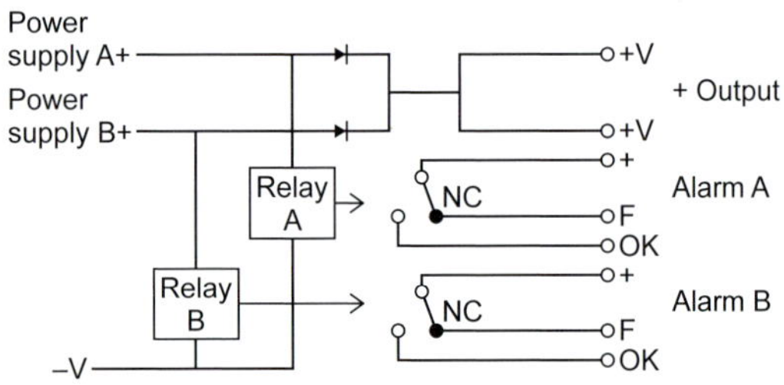

ORing diodes

In the rare event of a power supply failing with a shorted output, low-voltage-drop ORing diodes block that short from bringing down the system power. The diagram shows how a short circuit is flagged up by alarm relays to prevent a power failure from going unnoticed and bringing the whole system down.

1 Welche Produktionsart wird im ersten Beispiel beschrieben?
2 Warum ist in dem Beispiel eine schnelle Reparatur des Netzteils die schlechtere Lösung?
3 Welche Lösung wird stattdessen angeboten?
4 Welches positive Beispiel wird genannt?
5 Welche Lösungen für die ausfallsichere Stromversorgung findet man in großen Industrieanlagen?
6 Welcher Vorgang wird unter der Überschrift ‚Hot-swap' beschrieben?
7 Warum macht man einen ‚Hot-swap'?
8 Welche Funktion hat das ORing Modul?
9 Wozu dienen die Alarmrelais?

Why are tubes* still used?

High-power RF applications

Many radio stations still use big power tubes, especially for power levels above 10,000 watts and for frequencies above 50 MHz. High-power UHF TV stations and large FM broadcast stations are almost exclusively powered by tubes. The reason is cost and efficiency – only at low frequencies are transistors more efficient and less expensive than tubes.

Making a big solid-state transmitter requires wiring hundreds or thousands of power transistors. They also require large heat-sinks to keep them cool. An equivalent tube transmitter can use only one tube and can be cooled with air or water, thus making it smaller than the solid-state transmitter. The low cost of RF power generated by tubes has kept them economic.

Guitar amplifiers

Worldwide all-tube or hybrid tube-plus-transistor models make up 80% of the market for guitar amplifiers, which is thought to be worth at least $100 million.

Why tube amplifiers? It's the tone that musicians want. The amplifier and speaker become part of the musical instrument. The distortion and speaker characteristics of a tube amplifier, with an output transformer to match the speaker load, is unique and difficult to simulate with solid-state devices.

Even the wildest rock musicians seem to be very conservative about the equipment they use to make their music, and insist on vacuum tube technology.

*(vacuum) tube (US) = valve (GB)

10 Understanding the text

A Explain the advantages of valves over transistors (a) when used by radio stations, (b) when used in guitar amplifiers.

B Match the abbreviations in the text with the following definitions.

1. This is the number of million oscillations of electromagnetic waves per second.
2. This is the radio frequency range from 30 MHz (wavelength 10 m) to 300 MHz (wavelength 1 m).
3. This is the radio frequency range from 300 MHz (wavelength 1 m) to 3.0 GHz (wavelength 10 cm).
4. This means varying the frequency of a signal to communicate information.
5. This is the lengths of electromagnetic waves which are used for radio communication and generated by alternating current.

11 Mediation

You visit a German-language internet forum about electronics. Someone has posted a question about valves in guitar amplifiers. Summarize the text in German for your reply (approx. 100 words).

UNIT 8

Measuring and testing

- Giving and getting instructions
- Describing electrical components
- Understanding technical data

1 Warm-up

A Match the names with the instruments.

ammeter • capacitance meter • mains tester • multimeter • ohmmeter • oscilloscope • test light • voltmeter

1

2

3
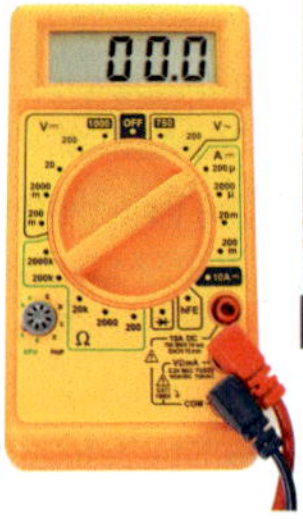

4
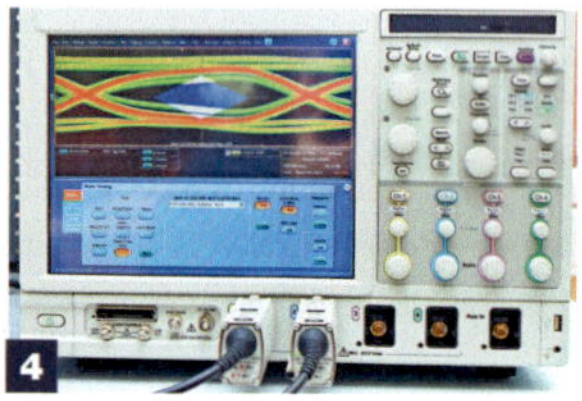

5

6

7

8
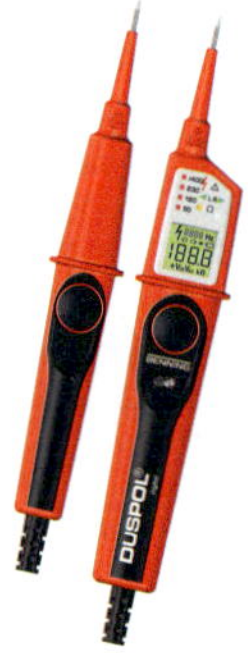

B Choose an instrument and explain what it is used for.

C Choose one of the instruments that you have used recently. What values did you measure and why?

D Work with a partner. Partner A: Turn to File 10 on p. 129 Partner B: Turn to File 19 on p. 133.

2 Working with multimeters (DMM)

Look at the DMM on the next page, then decide whether these statements are true or false. Correct the false statements.

1 This DMM can measure both alternating and direct current.
2 It can measure an AC voltage of up to 1,000 volts.
3 It can measure a DC voltage of up to 1,000 volts.
4 It can measure a resistance of 2,000,000 ohms.
5 It can measure a very strong current of up to 2,000 amps.
6 In AC mode it shows the maximum voltage.

3 Talking about voltages

Read the Language box, then work with your partner.

Partner A: Turn to File 15 on p. 131.

Partner B: Turn to File 17 on p. 132.

LANGUAGE

$\text{rms} = \dfrac{\text{Peak voltage (PV)}}{\sqrt{2}}$	The root mean square (rms) voltage equals the peak voltage over (divided by) the square root of two (root 2).
$\dfrac{17\ \text{V}}{\sqrt{2}} = ?$	What's the root mean square value of 17 volts?
$\dfrac{10{,}000\ \text{V}}{1.414} = 7{,}072.136\ \text{V}$	If the peak voltage is ten thousand volts, the root mean square voltage is ten thousand over (divided by) one point four one four, which equals seven thousand and seventy-two point one three six volts.

MATTERSTV

Making waves

Check out video no. 4 to see how waveforms can be visualized using an oscilloscope. Use the clip as a model to make a similar video of an oscilloscope showing sinusoidal, rectified and (if possible) faulty waveforms.

4 Working with oscilloscopes

A Match 1–5 to a–e to explain important features of an oscilloscope.

1. An oscilloscope draws a graph of …
2. The screen has eight squares on the vertical (Y) axis and …
3. It displays voltage and time …
4. The waveform shows how the voltage …
5. An oscilloscope gives an exact picture of a voltage and is …

- **a** alternates between positive and negative values.
- **b** an excellent tool for testing circuits and finding faults.
- **c** voltage against time – a V/t graph.
- **d** in the form of a wave.
- **e** ten squares on the horizontal (X) axis.

B Look at the oscilloscope and find the control (a–l) which matches each description (1–10).

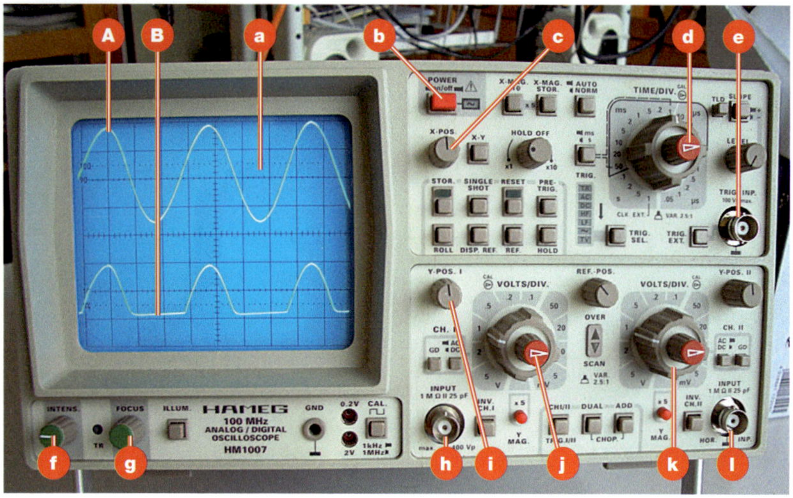

1. The three input sockets
2. The time per division control
3. The knob which adjusts the intensity (brightness) of the trace
4. The knob which focuses the trace
5. The knob which moves the waveform to the left and the right
6. The knob which moves the waveform up and down for voltage no. 1
7. The voltage per division control for voltage no. 1
8. The voltage per division control for voltage no. 2
9. The screen
10. The on/off button

C Choose three of the controls and explain how they work.

D Which of the graphs on the screen of the oscilloscope is (1) a sinusoidal waveform, (2) a rectified waveform?

E How many waveforms can this oscilloscope show at the same time?

F When did you or a colleague last use an oscilloscope or another measuring device? Write a brief description of how you used it and the values you tested.

5 Giving and getting instructions

20

A Today the apprentices at Elektro Schillinger have to make a battery charger using a circuit diagram. Dennis Lohmann is working with Martti Junkkari, an exchange student from Finland. Listen to the dialogue, then answer the questions.

1 What are the four stages of the task, as explained by Dennis?
2 Where will the apprentices get the components from?
3 What sorts of batteries will the device be able to charge?
4 What are the apprentices going to search for on the internet?

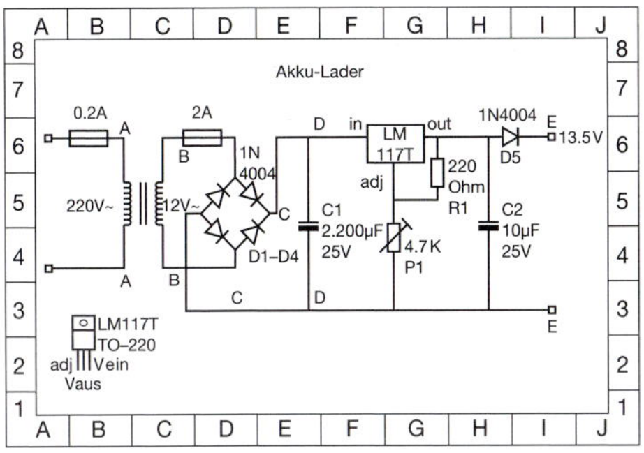

B Arbeiten Sie mit einem Partner. Partner A blättert zu File 2 auf S. 126, Partner B zu File 16 auf S. 131. KMK

C Listen and note how others complete the phrases in the Language boxes.

6 Understanding spoken technical details KMK

21

A Martti und Dennis arbeiten gemeinsam am Bau des Akku-Ladegeräts. Während des Gesprächs erstellt Martti eine Liste der benötigten Bauteile. Übertragen Sie ihre Liste in Ihr Arbeitsheft und ergänzen Sie sie um die Werte *(ratings)* und entsprechenden Einheiten oder die Bauteilnummern, während Sie das Gespräch hören. Sie hören es zweimal.

Martti Junkkari	Battery charger assignment – List of components required		
	Component	**Rating / Part No.**	**Unit**
1	fuse	*2*	*A (amp)*
2	fuse		
3	transformer		
4	diodes		
5	electrolytic capacitor		
6	electrolytic capacitor		
7	integrated voltage regulator		
8	resistor		
9	potentiometer		

B Hören Sie sich das Gespräch wieder an und ergänzen Sie die Aussagen mit Wörtern aus dem Dialog.

1. Martti and Dennis first make sure they have all the …
2. The fuses are pretty …
3. The fuses are much smaller than …
4. They need two …, two … and five …
5. To make sure the voltage regulator doesn't get too hot, they have a …
6. It's easy to identify resistors because they are …

C Beschreiben Sie ein Gerät, das Sie alleine oder mit anderen zusammen gebaut haben. Erstellen Sie zuerst eine Liste der verwendeten Bauteile und erklären Sie dann Schritt für Schritt, wie Sie vorgegangen sind.

7 Describing electrical components

A Choose the correct option to describe each component.

1. A **diode** is a device for …
   protecting a circuit. / storing an electric charge. / blocking or letting through current.
2. A **resistor** is a device for …
   limiting how much current flows. / converting AC into DC. / storing an electric charge.
3. A **fuse** is a device for …
   protecting a circuit. / increasing or decreasing voltage. / converting AC into DC.
4. A **capacitor** is a device for …
   increasing or decreasing voltage. / storing an electric charge. / protecting a circuit.
5. A **transformer** is a device for …
   protecting a circuit. / increasing or decreasing voltage. / storing an electric charge.
6. A **potentiometer** is a device for …
   storing an electric charge. / protecting a circuit. / varying electrical resistance.

B Work with a partner. Use the Language box to make definitions.

What's a mains tester?

A mains tester is an instrument for …

LANGUAGE

A mains tester An oscilloscope A DMM A test light A soldering iron A desoldering pump A rectifier A heat sink	is	a device an instrument a tool	for	conducting heat away. converting AC into DC. joining metals and wires using heat. showing voltage against time. removing solder. checking for a voltage of 230 V. checking for a low voltage. measuring amps, volts and ohms.

C Now define the following components in your own words.

1 RCD   2 battery   3 photovoltaic cell

8 Understanding technical data

A Martti writes up the experiment for his training officer in Finland. Read the report, then match the five oscilloscope readings (a–e) to the figures 1–5 which Martti refers to in her report.

Trainee: Martti Junkkari
Course: Electrical engineering
Assignment: Making a battery charger
Materials: Circuit diagram, components, printed circuit board
Tools: Soldering iron, pliers, digital multimeter, oscilloscope
Attachment: Circuit diagram of battery charger

Report

First a German trainee and I made a list of the components we needed. We were told to assemble the battery charger step by step and test each component separately before adding the next one.

We began by putting the transformer on the circuit board and testing its output voltage with a DMM. The reading was 12.09 V AC **(figure 1)**. Then we tested the output again with an oscilloscope. It showed us that the AC voltage had two peaks of +17 V and –17 V **(figure 2)**. The DMM had only shown us the rms value.

After that we added the full-wave bridge rectifier and checked the output with the oscilloscope. We saw a fully rectified waveform on the screen **(figure 3)**. It was a pulsating DC voltage with peaks of +15.6 V. The voltage was lower because of the voltage drop of 1.4 V across the two diodes.

We then smoothed the DC voltage by adding a capacitor to the circuit. With the oscilloscope we found out that the voltage was still +15.6 V DC. It was no longer a pulsating voltage but it had some ripple **(figure 4)**. We eliminated the ripple by adding the voltage stabilizer after the capacitor and checked the voltage again with the oscilloscope.

There was another voltage drop of about 2 V, but the waveform showed a constant DC voltage of 13.5 V **(figure 5)**. Finally, we added a diode to block a reverse voltage from the battery.

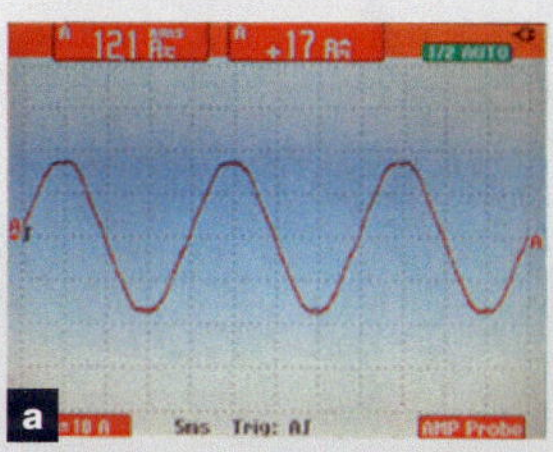

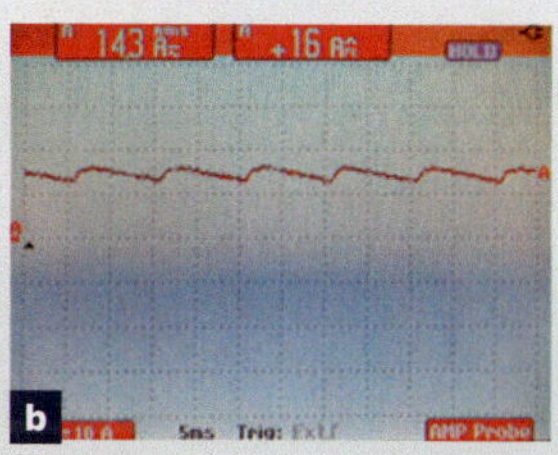

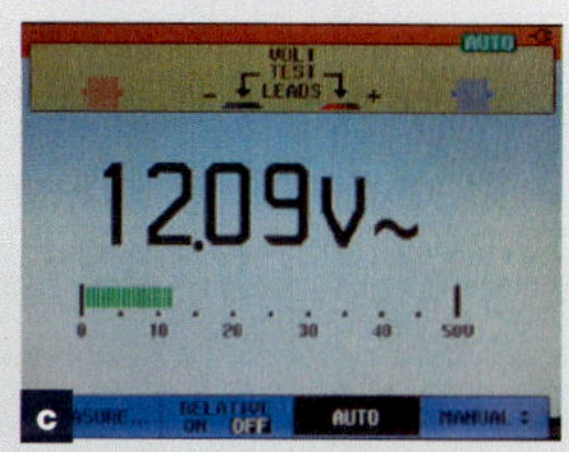

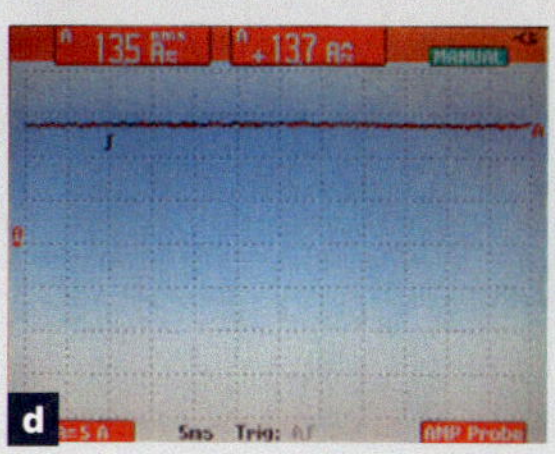

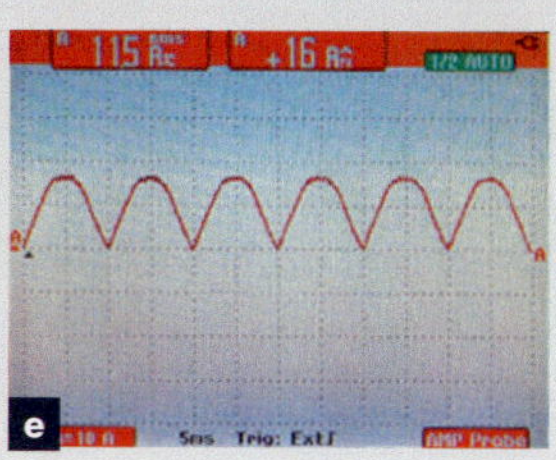

B Look at the readings (a–e) on the previous page.

1. Is the multimeter reading in picture c AC or DC? How can you tell?
2. Which component in the circuit changes the waveform from how it is in picture a to how it is in picture e?
3. Which component in the circuit changes the waveform from how it is in picture b to how it is in picture d?

C Ihr Ausbildungsleiter möchte kontrollieren, ob Marttis Bericht über den Bau des Akku-Laders inhaltlich stimmt. Da er aber nicht ausreichend Englisch spricht, bittet er Sie, die wesentlichen Aussagen des Berichts für ihn auf Deutsch zusammenzufassen. KMK

9 The assembled battery charger

Dennis and Martti have built the battery charger according to the circuit diagram. Look at the picture and identify the components of the battery charger (1–10). The names are all in the box. There are two words too many.

10 µF capacitor • transistor • 2,200 µF smoothing capacitor • 220 Ω resistor • 4 diodes (full-wave bridge rectifier) • 4.7 Ω potentiometer • valve • fuse • integrated voltage regulator • output diode • output terminals • transformer

GRAMMAR

Translating *können* and *müssen*

können: *can / could / to be able to*

	Aussagen	Verneinungen	Fragen
Gegenwart	ich kann ***I can***	ich kann nicht ***I can't***	kannst du ***can you***
Vergangenheit	ich konnte ***I could***	ich konnte nicht ***I couldn't***	konntest du ***could you***
Zukunft	ich werde … können ***I will be able to***	ich werde nicht … können ***I won't be able to***	wirst du … können ***will you be able to***

müssen: *must / had to / to have to*

	Aussagen	Verneinungen	Fragen
Gegenwart	ich muss ***I have to / I must***	ich muss nicht ***I don't have to***	musst du ***do you have to***
Vergangenheit	ich musste ***I had to***	ich musste nicht ***I didn't have to***	musstest du ***did you have to***
Zukunft	ich werde … müssen ***I'll have to***	ich werde nicht … müssen ***I won't have to***	wirst du … müssen ***will you have to***

!
ich muss nicht = ***I don't have to***
ich darf nicht = ***I mustn't***

10 Practice: translating *können* and *müssen*

Martti is talking to another apprentice electrician, Josh, from Cardiff, Wales. Use the Grammar box to complete the dialogue.

Josh Hi Martti. How are things?
Martti Great! I'm learning a lot at the company but they start early here.
Josh What time … *(musst ihr)*[1] start work in the mornings?
Martti At 7.30.
Josh 7.30! That's terrible. We … *(müssen nicht)*[2] start work so early at my company but we … *(dürfen nicht)*[3] be late! My boss goes crazy if we're late. Why didn't you phone yesterday?
Martti I … *(konnte nicht)*[4] phone because I didn't have a phone card. I've got one now so I … *(kann)*[5] phone any time I want.
Josh Good. It's my birthday in two weeks' time, and you and Sven are invited. … *(Könnt ihr)*[6] come? Don't worry. You … *(musst nicht)*[7] buy me a present. You … *(könntest)*[8] just give me a card!
Martti It's too early to say now but we … *(werden können)*[9] tell you next weekend, OK?
Josh All right. Sorry, but I … *(kann nicht)*[10] stay on the phone any longer. I really … *(muss)*[11] get back to work!
Martti OK. Bye.
Josh Bye.

11 Mediation

Ihr Kollege hat den Auftrag von einem Kunden bekommen, zwei Geräte zu bauen. Daraufhin hat er im Internet folgende Bauanleitung gefunden. Da er wenige Englischkenntnisse hat, bittet er Sie um Hilfe.

Fassen Sie nur die wesentlichen Aussagen der beiden Anleitungen auf Deutsch zusammen.

1 TV REMOTE CONTROL BLOCKER

You know the routine. You're watching your favourite programme when someone changes the channel on you. This small device solves that problem. Just point it at the TV to jam the remote!

The circuit is self-explanatory. IC 555 is wired as an astable multivibrator for a frequency of nearly 38 kHz. This is the frequency at which most of the modern TVs receive the IR beam. The transistor acts as a current source supplying roughly 25 mA to the infrared LEDs. To increase the range of the circuit simply decrease the value of the 180 ohm resistor to not less than 100 ohm.

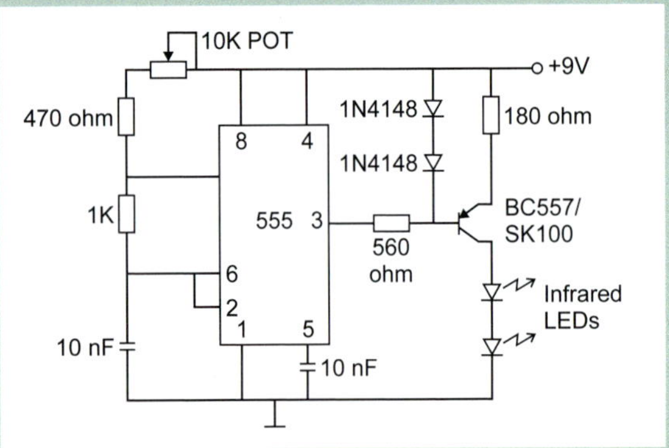

The 10 K potentiometer must be adjusted when the device is pointed at your TV to block the IR rays from the remote. This can be done by trial and error until the remote no longer responds.

2 POWER SUPPLY FAILURE ALARM

Most power supply failure indicator circuits need a separate power supply, which often simply isn't available. The alarm circuit presented here needs no additional supply source, so it can be used anywhere. It uses an electrolytic capacitor to store an adequate charge to feed power to the alarm circuit, which sounds an alarm for a reasonable duration if the electricity supply fails. I installed this at home after the freezer in my garage lost power and I didn't find out until I opened it two weeks later. You can imagine how bad the smell was.

This circuit can be used as an alarm for power supplies in the range of 5 V to 15 V.

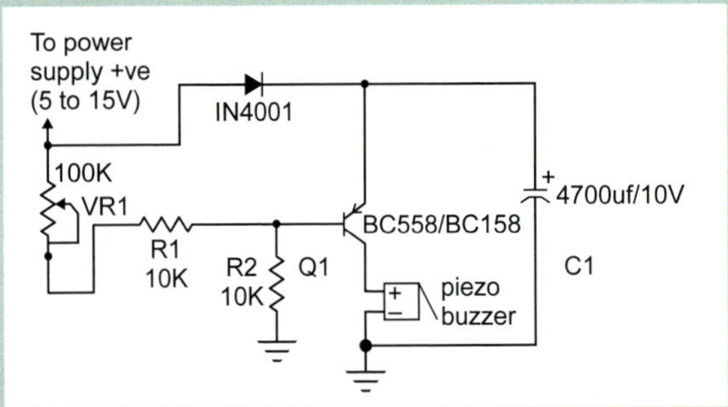

To calibrate the circuit, first connect the power supply (5 to 15 V), then vary the potentiometer VR 1 until the buzzer goes from on to off.

Whenever the supply fails, resistor R 2 pulls the base of the transistor low and saturates it, turning the buzzer ON.

LM117/217
LM 317

1.2 V TO 37 V VOLTAGE REGULATOR

- OUTPUT VOLTAGE RANGE: 1.2 TO 37 V
- OUTPUT CURRENT IN EXCESS OF 1.5 A
- FLOATING OPERATION FOR HIGH VOLTAGES
- COMPLETE SERIES OF PROTECTIONS: CURRENT LIMITING, THERMAL SHUTDOWN AND SOA (SAFE OPERATION AREA) CONTROL

DESCRIPTION

LM117/LM271/LM317 are monolithic integrated circuits in TO-220, TO-220FP, TO-3 and D^{2}PAK packages intended for use as positive adjustable voltage regulators.
They are designed to supply more than 1.5 A of load current with an output voltage adjustable over a 1.2 to 37 V range.
The nominal output voltage is selected by means of a resistive divide only, making the device exceptionally easy to use and eliminating the stocking of many fixed regulators.

TO-220

TO-220FP

TO-3

D2PAK

12 Understanding data sheets

A Study the data sheet, then answer the questions.

1. What are the maximum and minimum voltages produced by this regulator?
2. Is the maximum output current more or less than 1.5 amps?
3. How do you select the desired output voltage?
4. What do you have to mount the voltage regulator on? Why?
5. Why would the voltage regulator heat up?

B Fassen Sie die wichtigsten Inhalte des Datenblatts auf Deutsch zusammen.

C Fassen Sie ein weiteres Datenblatt Ihrer Wahl auf Deutsch zusammen.
Ein Datenblatt befindet sich auf S. 73.

UNIT 9

Electric motors

- Understanding technical instructions
- Troubleshooting on the telephone
- Understanding a trouble-shooting guide

1 Warm-up

A **What are the main types of electric motor?**

B **Which types of motor are used to power these applications and why?**

a washing machine

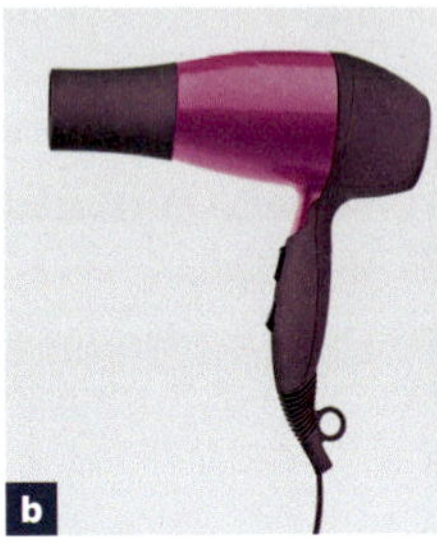

b hair dryer

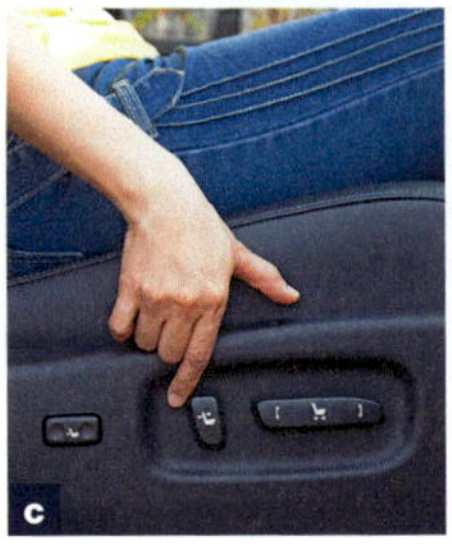

c car seat positioning device

d cordless drill

e electric fan

f conveyor belt

g food mixer

h lift

2 Electric motors and their components

A **Ein Freund von Ihnen möchte für die Schule etwas über Elektromotoren erfahren. Er findet folgende Webseite aber ist sich nicht sicher, worum genau es in dem Text geht. Helfen Sie ihm, indem Sie die Webseite lesen und den Inhalt auf Deutsch zusammenfassen.** KMK

Electric motors

The basics of how they work

Electric motors are fantastically versatile and can successfully perform a wide range of tasks. However, the science which lies behind these adaptable devices is really quite straightforward: like poles repel, while unlike poles attract. When electricity is made to flow through a conductor, it produces a magnetic field comprised of a north and a south pole. These poles result in the rotation of the motor. By means of this electromagnetic effect, electrical energy is transformed into mechanical power which can then be put to work carrying out various tasks.

Though there is a wide variety of different sorts of electric motor, these are the two most important types.

1 Three-phase AC motor

A 3-phase AC motor is one which is designed to take full advantage of the three-phase AC power used in many industrial applications.

A motor like this consists of two main parts: the stator and the rotor. Due to the fact that it is made up of a circular network of bars that look similar to a cage, the rotor is often referred to as the 'squirrel cage'. The stator is comprised of three pairs of coils which are spaced evenly around the rotor. Each of these pairs of coils is hooked up to one of the three phases of power. Since they are all out of phase with one another, they create a magnetic field which rotates at a constant rate around the stator. This, in turn, causes the rotor to spin and results in mechanical power.

2 Universal motor

Universal motors can be powered either with AC or DC current. The stator field in universal motors is created using an electromagnet. This is due to the fact that every half-cycle of the AC current the field has to reverse its polarity.

Among the advantages of universal motors are the practical characteristics they share with DC motors (these include high starting torque, high operating speeds and compact design) along with the fact that they can be run by an AC power supply. This makes them suitable for powering household appliances which demand high-speed operation such as hair dryers and food mixers.

B Match the motors to the appropriate section of the text (1 or 2). Then label the specific parts of the motors using the words in the box.

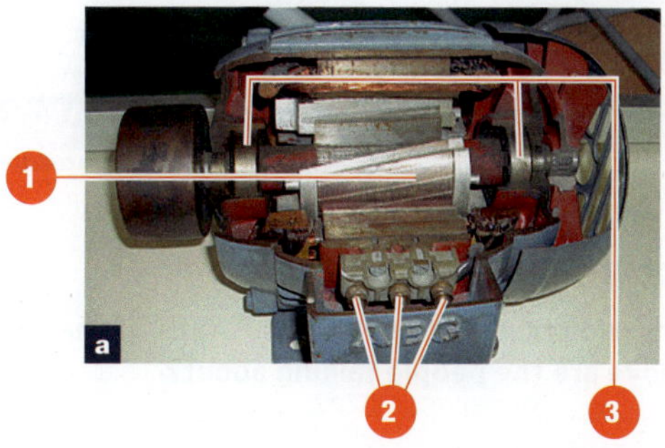

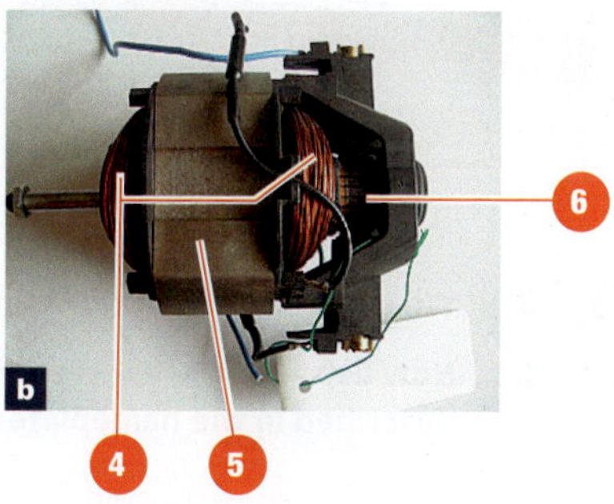

stator • bearings • terminals • commutator • coil • rotor

C **Find the English translations of the following words in the text on p. 87. They are in the same order here.**

1 (sich) abstoßen
2 (sich) anziehen
3 Spulen
4 (sich) drehen
5 umkehren
6 Polarität
7 Drehmoment
8 Hochgeschwindigkeits-

3 Electric motor nameplates

A **Look at the electric motor nameplates (a–c). What information is given for each motor regarding the following characteristics (1–6)?**

1 frequency
2 rated full-load speed
3 insulation class and rated ambient temperature
4 rated horsepower
5 voltage
6 amperage

a

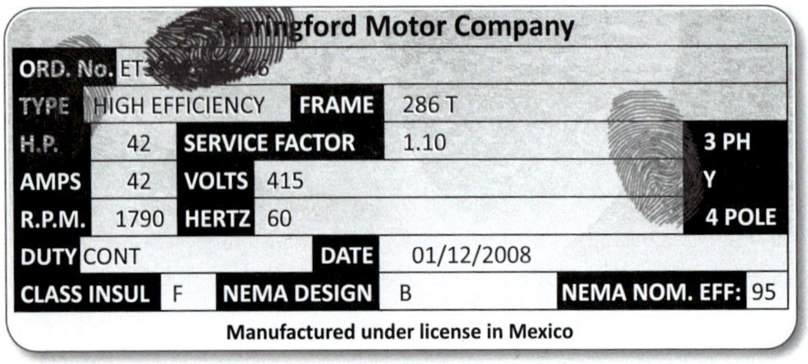

b

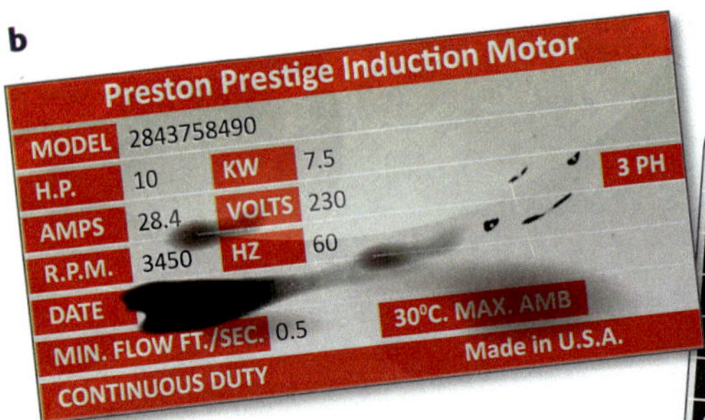

c

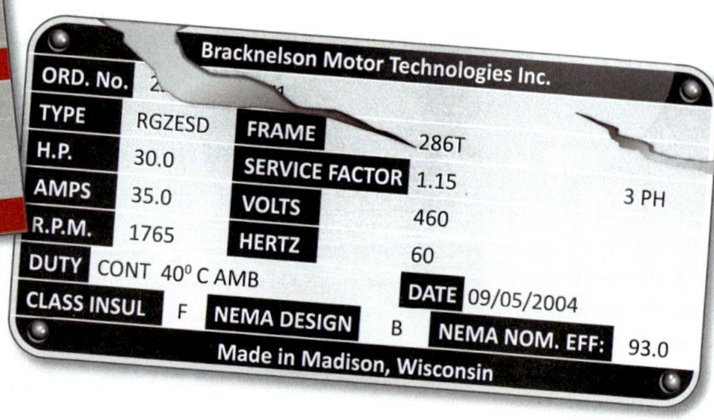

B **What other information can be found on the nameplates and where?**

22

C **Now listen to the excerpts from two phone conversations. Which of the engines described in the nameplates above are the people talking about?**

4 Understanding technical instructions

Ihr Ausbildungsleiter bittet Sie, eine Zusammenfassung darüber zu schreiben, wie man Elektromotoren überprüft, um sich auf die praktische Umsetzung vorzubereiten. Sie finden folgenden Artikel darüber im Internet.

A Lesen Sie den Artikel und geben Sie an, ob die Aussagen (1–6) wahr oder falsch sind. Beantworten Sie die Fragen (7–9). KMK

Testing electric motors

Testing electric motors is an easy job. Motor testing is also a task which can be done quickly. So, before grabbing your multimeter, read our step-by-step guide to find out how it's done effectively and safely.

Before you get started, make sure that the power wires are disconnected from the motor. It can't be said often enough: Safety comes first when working with any electrical device, and electric shocks can kill!
Next, think about how you are going to get the best possible access to the motor to carry out the test. If you can remove the motor from the appliance it powers without too much difficulty, you should probably do this. This will make testing easier and potentially more exact. However, it may still be possible to carry out the test with the motor in place.
Now your multimeter comes into play. To test continuity, set it on the RX1 scale to measure resistance. Next, attach one of the multimeter's probes to the motor's common lead, which is usually white. Then, attach the other probe to each of the other wires on the motor in turn. The probe will be checking to see if it can measure the multimeter's input signal at the output. A low or moderate reading (in ohms) means the component is functioning acceptably. However, if the reading is high, then the motor is probably faulty. You could then consider whether or not to repair it. However, this can be time-consuming and, given that most motors are inexpensive to buy, you may consider simply replacing the faulty motor. If you choose to do the latter, ensure that the replacement is of the same type, power rating and size as the motor you plan to replace.

1 Die Überprüfung von Elektromotoren ist unkompliziert und dauert nicht lange.
2 Obwohl es gefährlich ist, sollte der Motor während der Überprüfung mit der Stromquelle verbunden bleiben.
3 Es ist immer erforderlich den Motor von dem Gerät zu entfernen, um ihn zu überprüfen.
4 Es ist wichtig, dass man systematisch jedes Kabel des Motors zusammen mit der Zuleitung überprüft.
5 Wenn ein niedriger bis mittlerer Ohm-Messwert am Multimeter abzulesen ist, muss der Motor ausgetauscht werden.
6 Aufgrund der niedrigen Preise von Elektromotoren ist es häufig sinnvoller, sie auszutauschen, als sie zu reparieren.
7 Warum kann es besser sein, den Motor von dem Gerät, das er antreibt, zu entfernen, bevor man ihn überprüft?
8 Wie sollte das Multimeter am Motor angeschlossen werden?
9 Welche Faktoren sollte man beachten, wenn man den Motor austauscht?

B Correct the statements (1–6) which are false.

5 Asking the right questions when troubleshooting

23

Jan Aaronovitch, who works for Novak SA, a light engineering company in Poland, is having problems with the electric motor which powers one of the lathes he is responsible for.

A Read or listen as he calls the technical support service his company uses and answer the questions.

Stefan Guten Tag. Elektro Bauer GmbH. Stefan Döring am Apparat.
Jan Hello, Stefan. It's Jan Aaronowicz from Nowak here.
Stefan Jan. Hi. What can I do for you today?
Jan Stefan, I'm having some problems with a DC motor which runs one of my lathes. I was hoping you could help.
Stefan I'm always happy to try. What sort of problems are you having?
Jan Well, the motor is starting OK. And it also runs OK at first. But then it cuts out after a few minutes of operation.
Stefan Ah, that's interesting. Do you mind if I ask a few questions about the problem? Your answers will help me to get to the bottom of it.
Jan No, of course not.
Stefan Great, thanks. How long have you been having these problems?
Jan Just for the last couple of days. I think they started on Monday.
Stefan OK. How often has this problem occurred since then?
Jan Well, a few times. I think the motor cut out four times yesterday and twice this morning.
Stefan And you're only just calling now?
Jan Yes. I'm afraid I've been busy with other things.
Stefan OK. Does the motor vibrate while it's operating?
Jan Yes, it does rattle a bit more than usual, I must say. But it actually rattles anyway.
Stefan Ah, does it? Does the motor make a humming sound during operation?
Jan Yes. But that goes with the vibration, I think.
Stefan Yes, perhaps. Is the motor housing hot to the touch?
Jan Hmm. No, not particularly. I wouldn't say I've noticed that. Are you able to say what's wrong with the motor?
Stefan It could be a few things. I'm going to get one of our technicians to come out to you and take a look. Can I just ask: How old is the motor?
Jan Let me see. It says on the name plate that it was built in 1992.
Stefan Ah, OK. Well, it is getting on a bit, isn't it? It could be that it's just wearing out and is not really worth repairing. If that's the case, we would probably recommend you just replace it.
Jan Really?
Stefan Sure. You might be advised to do that anyway. It would probably be better just to invest in a new three-phase induction motor. Apart from being quieter and easier to maintain, three-phase motors also tend to be more efficient when it comes to their consumption of power. That's the reason we generally recommend that ...

1 What problem does Jan say he is having with the motor?
2 How often has the problem occurred?
3 What does Stefan finally recommend Jan think about doing?

24

B Listen again and complete the questions from the dialogue.

1 What … problems are you having?
2 How long … these problems?
3 How often has the problem … since then?
4 Does the motor … while it's operating?
5 Does the motor make a … sound during operation?
6 Is the motor housing hot …?

C With a partner, role-play the following phone call between a service technician and a customer. Use questions from exercise 6A.

Techniker/in

Kunde/Kundin

Techniker/in: Gehen Sie ans Telefon, indem Sie sich mit Ihrem eigenen Namen und dem Firmennamen melden.

Kunde/Kundin: Erklären Sie, dass Sie ein Problem mit einem Elektromotor haben. Sagen Sie, dass Sie Hilfe benötigen.

Techniker/in: Sagen Sie, dass Sie gerne helfen. Fragen Sie, was das Problem ist.

Kunde/Kundin: Sagen Sie, dass Sie den Eindruck haben, dass der Motor nicht so schnell läuft wie sonst.

Techniker/in: Fragen Sie, seit wann der Kunde/die Kundin das Problem hat.

Kunde/Kundin: Sagen Sie, dass das Problem gestern Nachmittag aufgetreten ist.

Techniker/in: Fragen Sie, ob der Motor vibriert, wenn er läuft.

Kunde/Kundin: Sagen Sie, dass er nicht mehr vibriert als sonst.

Techniker/in: Fragen Sie, ob der Motor ein summendes Geräusch von sich gibt.

Kunde/Kundin: Sagen Sie, dass er ein leises Summen von sich gibt.

Techniker/in: Fragen Sie, ob er sich warm anfühlt.

Kunde/Kundin: Sagen Sie, dass er warm ist. Fragen Sie, was es sein könnte.

Techniker/in: Sagen Sie, dass es sich so anhört, als würde ein Problem mit den Lagern vorliegt und dass Sie einen Techniker vorbeischicken, der es sich anschaut.

D Tell your partner about the last time you had a problem with a machine or tool. What was the problem? Were you able to fix it?

6 Understanding a troubleshooting guide

A Match the German expressions to English words in the troubleshooting guide.

durchgebrannt • Auslastungsgrad • lose • Schutzschalter • Lager

B Answer the questions in German.

1. Welche Schritte sollten unternommen werden, wenn der Motor nicht startet?
2. Was sollte unternommen werden, wenn die Sicherung oder der Schutzschalter ausgelöst werden?
3. Welches Problem würde gelöst werden, wenn man die Sicherung auswechselt oder den Schalter zurückstellt?
4. Was sollte unternommen werden, wenn die Lager verschlissen wirken?
5. Welcher Fehler würde den Motor in die falsche Richtung laufen lassen?

Motor troubleshooting guide

Note that troubleshooting of your motor should only be carried out by staff who are fully-qualified and equipped with the correct tools.

Problem	Probable cause	Steps to take
Motor will not start	Fuses are blown	Replace with fuses of correct type and rating.
	Incorrect power supply	Confirm that power is in accordance with specifications supplied on motor name plate and load factor.
	Improper line connections	Check connections against diagram which motor comes supplied with.
	Open winding or control switch circuit	This is indicated by omission of a humming sound when the switch is closed. Confirm that there are no loose wiring connections. Ensure also that control contacts are closed.
Motor runs, but then fails to re-start	Fuse or circuit breaker has been tripped	Replace fuse or reset breaker.
	Controller could be faulty	Confirm that voltage is coming out of the controller.
Motor takes too long to accelerate	Bearings may be worn or otherwise faulty	Check bearings for wear and tear. Worn bearings should be replaced.
Motor runs in the wrong direction	Wiring is incorrect	Swap the motor leads.

GRAMMAR

Adjectives and adverbs

Adjektive werden benutzt, um Personen oder Sachen näher zu beschreiben.	*Replacing the electric motor was an* ***easy*** *job.* *We should do a* ***quick*** *test of the wiring first.*
Adverbien haben in der Regel eine andere Form als Adjektive. Oft wird die Endung *-ly* an das Adjektiv angefügt.	*We need the motor to be fixed* ***quickly****.* *Can it be fixed* ***easily****?*
Adverbien beziehen sich auf Verben (a) oder Adjektive (b).	**a** *Now that it's repaired, the motor should work* ***effectively****.* **b** *It's* ***really*** *important to check the polarity of the motor properly.*
Das Adverb von *good* lautet *well*.	*The motor isn't running very* ***well****.*

Siehe S. 142 für weitere Einzelheiten.

7 Practice: adjectives and adverbs

Complete the text using the correct form of the words in brackets.

Eight rules for helping customers on the phone

1 Customers don't … (usual) understand language which is too technical, so keep things simple.
2 It pays to deal with customers … (patient). Take time to answer their questions.
3 Even if something is … (obvious) to you, it might not be to a customer. Spend time explaining things!
4 Even if a customer doesn't treat you … (good), you must be … (polite)! Always talk to customers … (polite)!
5 Don't confuse customers by using a lot of … (high) … (technical) language.
6 Use your time on the phone with customers … (effective) by asking them the right questions.
7 Making sure that a customer knows you care about their problem is an … (important) part of your job as a service technician.
8 If a repair is going to be … (significant) more … (expensive) than replacing a component or device, let a customer know. Customers value … (honest) advice.

8 Discussion

Work with a partner. What other tips would you give to technicians who give advice to customers over the telephone? Make a list, then tell the class.

9 Interaktion

Benutzen Sie die Rollenkarten, um ein Telefongespräch zwischen einem Kunden und einem Elektriker als Rollenspiel durchzuführen.

Prüfling A

Sie sind Techniker/in in der Produktion bei einer kleinen Leichtmaschinenbaufirma. Der Motor von einer Ihrer Produktionsmaschinen ist leistungsschwächer geworden. Rufen Sie die Kundenbetreuung an und fragen Sie um Rat. Bereiten Sie sich auf das Gespräch mit folgenden Punkten vor.

- Der Motor läuft nicht so schnell wie vorher. Das verlangsamt die Leistung der Maschine, die er antreibt.
- Der besagte Motor ist ein Gleichstrommodell, das 1996 hergestellt wurde.
- Der Motor summt und startet manchmal nicht. Er vibriert leicht und fühlt sich ziemlich warm an.
- Ihre Firma würde das Ersetzen des Motors in Erwägung ziehen, wenn das Ersatzteil eine langfristige Geldersparnis darstellt.
- Geben Sie Ihre E-Mail-Adresse an, wenn Sie danach gefragt werden: bothingwood@lexitec.com

Prüfling B

Sie sind Techniker bei der Kundenbetreuung einer Elektrofirma für industrielle Komponenten. Sie erhalten den Anruf eines Kunden, der Probleme mit einem Motor hat. Bereiten Sie sich auf das Gespräch mit folgenden Punkten vor.

- Finden Sie heraus, um welche Art Motor es sich handelt und wann er produziert wurde.
- Fragen Sie, welche Probleme der Kunde/die Kundin mit dem Motor hat.
- Empfehlen Sie, dass der Kunde/die Kundin es in Erwägung ziehen sollte, den Motor gegen einen neuen Drehstrommotor auszutauschen. Sagen Sie, dass Sie ihm/ihr gerne eine E-Mail schicken, in der Sie ihm/ihr genau auflisten, was die Vorteile von einem solchen Modell wären.
- Fragen Sie den Kunden/die Kundin nach seiner/ihrer E-Mail-Adresse und bedanken Sie sich für den Anruf.

10 Produktion

Herr Rowe ist ein Kunde, den Sie betreuen. Er besitzt momentan einen Gleichstrommotor. Sie haben ihm angeboten, einen Drehstrommotor zu installieren. Daraufhin hat er Sie in einer E-Mail nach den Vorteilen dieses Motors gefragt.

Schreiben Sie Herrn Rowe eine Antwort und verwenden Sie folgende Punkte.

Drehstrommotoren ...

- sind leiser als Gleichstrommotoren.
- benötigen weniger Wartung.
- sind in Hinblick auf den Stromverbrauch effizienter.
- werden auf lange Sicht zu Stromersparnissen führen.

Electric motors ready to go

a ...

As long ago as the early 1970s, experts started speculating seriously about the possibility of powering cars with electricity. But the electric car seemed more like science fiction than a real transport alternative until recent years. Now, however, improvements in electric motor technology mean that electric cars can accelerate almost as fast as petrol-powered models as well as reach similar top speeds. The result is increasing numbers of electric cars on European roads.

b ...

Electric cars, in fact, come in a number of configurations ranging from 'hybrid' models which combine an electric motor with a conventional engine through to 'pure' electric cars which are powered solely by electricity. Whatever the configuration, the advantages of these cars are clear. They reduce emissions and noise pollution. They're also easier and cheaper to maintain than conventional cars.

c ...

However, a couple of interrelated problems stand in the way of greater increases in the number of electric cars on the roads. The first of these is battery capacity. Currently, batteries are large, heavy and rather expensive. They tend not to take the car very far either: average battery driving distances range from 50 to 100 km.
The second problem is related to this. Currently there are not many recharging stations at which motorists can plug in their vehicles and recharge their batteries. This could change soon, at least in Europe where the EU has agreed a standardized recharging plug for electric cars and is actively encouraging the development of large numbers of recharging stations. That's good news for electric motorists who want to use their cars for more than just trips round town. However, there is another small difficulty with the batteries used to power electric cars: they take an average of four hours to recharge.

d ...

That probably won't remain the case for long, though. Recent experience in developing in other types of batteries – for instance, those designed for laptops or smartphones – shows that it doesn't take too long before battery capacity is increased at the same time that size is reduced. Once that happens there'll be nothing left in the way of full-scale development of the market for electric cars. And the petrol-powered car will finally become a thing of the past.

11 Electric cars

A Match the subheadings (1–3) to the most appropriate sections of the article (a–d), then write a subheading for the remaining section of the article.

1. The pros of electric cars
2. A good reason to be optimistic about car batteries
3. Current limitations of electric cars

B Work in a small group and discuss the questions.

1. Would replacing petrol with electricity as a source of fuel end all the problems caused by cars? Which problems would still remain?
2. What steps could be taken to reduce these remaining problems? Make a list.

UNIT 10

International contacts

- Expressing opinions in meetings
- Meeting customers at trade fairs
- Describing plugs and sockets

1 Warm-up

A Look at the cartoon and answer the questions.

1 What does the cartoon show?
2 What point do you think the cartoonist is making?

B Work with a partner and write a caption for the cartoon. Read your caption to your classmates. Vote on which pair has written the best caption.

C Work with a partner. Make a list of the most important things you should remember to take with you if you have to travel to another country to do a job for your company.

D How important are the items on your list? Rank them in order of importance.

2 A checklist for business trips

Emsket SA is based in Stockholm, Sweden, and does a lot of business in other European countries.

24

A Listen as Mark Blomkvist leads a meeting with other installation team members at Emsket to discuss trips to other countries. How many of the items from your list in exercise 1 C/D are mentioned during the meeting?

24

B Complete the sentences from the dialogue with words from the box. Listen again to check your answers.

ask • come • concerned • mean • opinion • reckon

1. Conrad, would you like to … in here?
2. As far as I'm …, things like passport and tickets are really obvious.
3. Do you know what I …?
4. Well, in my …, Conrad is right.
5. They also forget to take the right tools with them quite a lot, so I … we should mention that as well.
6. If you … me, the list should also include taking a company credit card to cover expenses while on trips.

C Refer back to the list you made in exercise 1 C/D. Discuss with your partner if there are any other work-related items you should add to the list.

D You've packed all the items on your list, but at the airport you're told your case is too heavy. You have to leave some items behind.

Your partner and you should team up with another pair to discuss which items should be left behind. Use phrases from the Language box.

LANGUAGE

Meetings

Giving opinions
As far as I'm concerned, …
In my opinion, …
If you ask me, …
I reckon that …

Checking that people understand
Do you know what I mean?
Do you know what I'm saying?

Inviting other people's ideas
Sarah, would you like to come in here?
Tom, any ideas from you?

See pp. 139–140 for additional phrases.

E Schreiben Sie eine E-Mail, in der Sie Kollegen die Checkliste erklären. Weisen Sie darauf hin, dass sich die Checkliste im Anhang der E-Mail befindet. Machen Sie insbesondere auf die Punkte der Checkliste aufmerksam, die sich auf die Arbeit beziehen. KMK

3 Meeting customers at trade fairs

A What trade fairs are represented by the following logos? What other trade fairs do you know of? Which of these are important for your company?

light+building CABEX ie

B A customer wants to enquire about a product at a trade fair and has the following conversation with a company representative. Read the Tip box, then rewrite the dialogue to make it polite.

Company representative	Hello, I want to introduce myself. I'm Norbert Schmidt from Axo Elektrotechnik. This is our new product. I want to tell you about it.
Customer	It looks good. Have you got a brochure with some details?
Company representative	No. Do you want a leaflet with some general information, though? If you want, I can send you the details later.
Customer	OK. Take my business card.
Company representative	Good. You'll get an e-mail with the details at the end of the week.
Customer	Alright.
Company representative	Here's my card. If you want more information, I'll give it to you.
Customer	OK.
Company representative	Bye.
Customer	Goodbye.

✈ **C Write some impolite statements of your own. Swap papers with a partner and rewrite his/her statements to make them polite.**

TIP

Politeness

English native speakers generally feel it's important to express themselves politely. There are a few words that they use to do this. Here's a quick guide.
Rather than saying *I want to …*, say *I'd like to …* .
I'd like to show you our new product.
Also, it's probably more polite to say *Can I give you our new brochure?* than *Here's our new brochure*.
Similarly, *Could you give me …?* is probably better than *Do you have …?* or *Have you got?*
Also, remember to say *please*.
Note also that short, abrupt answers to questions can also sound impolite. So it's more polite to say *No, sorry* or *No, I'm afraid not* than just *No*.

D Work in pairs.

Partner A: Turn to File 11 on p. 129.
Partner B: Turn to File 18 on p. 132.

4 International standards

International standards protect consumers and make it much easier for companies from different countries to do business with each other.

A Read the website and answer the questions.

1. What makes international standards important, according to the website?
2. What attitude do most people have to standards, according to the text?
3. Which organizations responsible for creating standards are mentioned in the text? What are they responsible for?
4. Why are businesses willing to work with standards created by the ISO?
5. What big development in standardization has the IEC been responsible for?
6. What challenges are faced these days by the IEC in its work?

http://www.all-about-standards.com

Where do international standards come from?

Safety standards exist to protect life and property, while trade standards make business between countries possible. We all take these standards as given. But where do they come from and how are they made? Read our quick guide to find out more.

International Organization for Standardization

The ISO, which was set up in 1947, is the main organization with the job of creating international standards. The standards which are agreed by the ISO have always been created by consensus. That's because businesses in various countries recognize the enormous benefits of having standards to work with. The voluntary nature of ISO standards is one of their great strengths. Businesses – and consumers – accept the standards because they're not created by rigid external directives. Rather the standards result from discussion and compromise.

International Electrotechnical Commission

Since its creation in 1906, the IEC has harmonized the rules for the wiring of buildings at a global level. The industry it works in moves fast, and this has been a challenge, particularly in recent years. The commission constantly has to work hard to keep up with rapid developments in computer technology.

International Telecommunications Union

The ITU is one of the oldest organizations that deals with international standards. Founded in 1865, it works to ensure the compatibility of telecommunication systems between different countries. The ITU, along with the ISO and the IEC, sees the convergence of technologies such as telephony, computers and TV as a major challenge. It warns of an 'electronic jungle' if the rapid advances in technology are not harmonized through international standardization.

B **Choose the best meaning (a–l) for each word (1–6) from the website on p. 99.**

1	take as given	**a**	important	**g**	instructions
2	voluntary	**b**	automatic	**h**	receive as a gift
3	rigid	**c**	fast	**i**	uncompromising
4	directives	**d**	standards	**j**	technical specifications
5	rules	**e**	impressive	**k**	done from free choice
6	rapid	**f**	regulations	**l**	accept something without thinking about it

✈ **C** **Write meanings for the following words: *consensus, enormous, challenge.***

5 Discussion: international standards

A **Look at the photos. Which areas/industries regulated by international standards do they show? What other areas that are regulated in a similar way by international standards can you think of?**

B **Choose three of these areas to examine in more detail. Why are international standards important in these fields? Write brief notes in English about your opinions. Give examples from your own experience.**

C **Work in groups. Think of something which is not regulated by standards where you would like to see new standards applied. Make arguments in favour of this.**

6 Defining words

Work with a partner. Pick a word from the box without saying which one you have picked. Use phrases in the table on the next page to make a definition of the word. Your partner should guess which word you are defining.

electrician • engineer • multimeter • plug • programmer • solar cell • standard • trainee

It's	someone something	who which	connects converts designs learns measures repairs serves writes	a piece of electrical equipment to the electricity supply. as an official unit of measurement. electrical equipment. instructions for computers. light and heat energy into electricity. machines. a trade from someone who is already qualified.

GRAMMAR

Relative clauses

Relativpronomen leiten Relativsätze ein.	*The staff **who/that run the ITU** are based in Geneva.* *The IEC, **which creates standards for the electrotechnical industries**, was founded in 1906.*
Notwendige Relativsätze, die für das Verständnis des Satzes unbedingt erforderlich sind, stehen ohne Komma. In notwendigen Relativsätzen kann das Relativpronomen wegfallen, wenn es Objekt ist, d.h. wenn im Relativsatz ein Subjekt steht.	*Actions **which are taken by the ISO** make trade between countries easier.* *The measuring tool **(which/that) I bought for the workshop** has inches and centimetres.*
Nicht notwendige Relativsätze geben lediglich Zusatzinformationen und werden durch Kommas getrennt.	*The ISO, **which was set up in 1947**, is the main organization with the job of creating international standards.*

Siehe S. 144 für weitere Einzelheiten.

7 Practice: relative clauses

Write these sentences in English with the help of a dictionary. Use relative pronouns where necessary.

1. Die Firma, bei der ich mich für eine Stelle beworben habe, hat ihren Firmensitz in Essen.
2. Es gab verschiedene Probleme mit der Elektroinstallation, die darin resultierten, dass wir das Gebäude neu verkabeln mussten.
3. Der Kunde, der uns im Internet gefunden hat, ist mit unserer Arbeit sehr zufrieden.
4. Die Standards, die durch die IEC geschaffen wurden, haben einen tagtäglichen Einfluss auf unsere Arbeit als Elektriker.
5. Das Multimeter, das anscheinend einen Wackelkontakt hat, war so günstig, dass eine Reparatur keinen Sinn macht.
6. Der Kollege, der mit dem Kunden gesprochen hat, sagte, dass er sein Haus von uns neu verkabelt haben möchte.

8 Electricity around the world

A Sie finden diese Diskussion im Internet, während Sie sich auf einen Urlaub in Amerika vorbereiten. Lesen Sie den Text und beantworten Sie die Fragen auf Deutsch. KMK

1. Welches Problem hatte Eurotourist?
2. Was hat das Problem laut Sparky98 verursacht?
3. Welche elektrische Spannung wird in den USA benutzt?
4. Was machen Adapterstecker laut Sparky98 nicht?
5. Inwiefern unterscheidet sich der Smartphone-Adapter?
6. Wie viele verschiedene Arten von Steckern gibt es auf der Welt?
7. Wie wird Europlug im Text beschrieben?

Eurotourist

My wife and I made a trip to Germany last month. We bought a plug adaptor which worked fine with my smartphone. But when my wife plugged in her hair dryer, it blew up!
I took this photo of the event. ;-)

Can anyone tell me why this happened?

Sparky98

Oh, poor wifey! :-D
Your problem was the mains voltage, which varies around the world, along with the frequency. Europe and many other countries use 220 to 240 volts at 50 hertz frequency. But the US and Japan as well as most South American countries use 100 to 127 volts at 60 hertz.
Plug adaptors let you connect your electric appliance with the local mains socket but they're only half the story because they don't help with any voltage disparity. Your hair dryer was designed for use in the US and that's why it went up in smoke when plugged into the mains in Germany.

Eurotourist

Thanks. But why did this not happen to my smartphone?

Sparky98

Your smartphone recharger differs from the hair dryer because it contains a switched-mode power supply which converts electrical power safely. This can be done with smartphones and even tablet computers but would be too expensive for appliances which are more power-hungry.

---

steve_in_miami

@Sparky98 – I'm planning a round-the-world trip in the summer. Could you give me any information about different plug types?

Sparky98

Sure. Well, many countries have not adopted the US standard but have developed their own types of plug and wall outlet. There are no fewer than 13 varieties internationally. Here's a quick description of some of them.
You'll know that in the US and Central America ungrounded plugs with two flat parallel prongs are standard. But in Germany the plugs are round with two round pins and two grounding contacts on the top and the bottom. A plug with three round pins which are in line is almost exclusively in use in Italy. The UK and China actually use the same plug type with three rectangular pins which form a triangle. In Japan the plugs have two flat parallel prongs and a round grounding pin. A plug with three round pins arranged in a triangle is used almost exclusively in India and Sri Lanka. Then there's the Europlug which has two round pins and is ungrounded. It's used in many European countries but not in Britain or Ireland. In Brazil and Switzerland the standard plug has three round pins which are offset. So you're going to need a lot of adaptors, Steve_in_Miami!

B **Read the discussion thread again and look at the pictures below. In which order are the different plugs mentioned? In which countries is each type used?**

C **Work with a partner. Take turns describing the plugs. Which plug is your partner describing?**

D **Match each word (1–8) from the text to its definition (a–j). The words (1–8) appear in the same order in the text.**

1 mains
2 appliance
3 (voltage) disparity
4 differ
5 adopt
6 pin
7 exclusively
8 offset

a difference
b short piece of metal
c not be the same
d very expensive
e limited to a certain group
f device for a specific task
g not in one line
h letter to apply for a job
i AC electricity supply in the house
j take on

E **Write meanings for the following words: *adaptor, power hungry.***

9 Leseverstehen

Ihr Chef bittet Sie für jedes Mitglied des Installationsteams einen Steckdosenadapter für die Dienstreisen ins Ausland zu kaufen. Sie finden folgenden Adapter im Internet. Lesen Sie die Produktbeschreibung und die Kundenbewertungen und beantworten Sie die Fragen auf Deutsch.

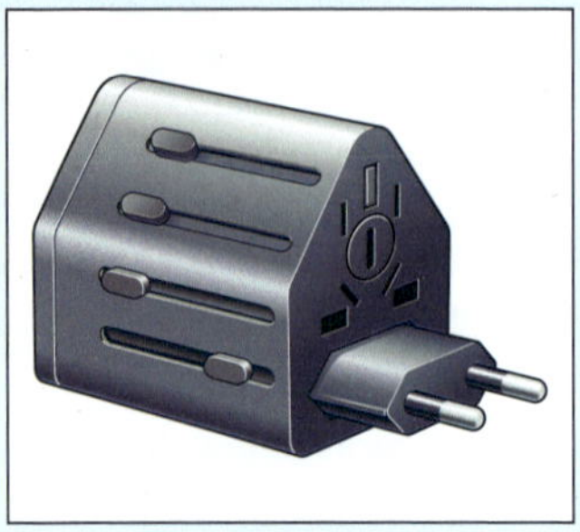

The **Maybridge Travel Pal** is a take-anywhere power adaptor which is small enough to fit in your pocket and can be used in over 150 countries. It has a robust, practical design which ensures that it is simple to use and contains everything you need in one unit. And, due to the slide-out, slide-in plug design, you won't lose any important parts. The Travel Pal adapts power outlets for common devices such as laptops and tablet PCs. Safe operation is ensured by an integrated fuse and a safety release button.

The Maybridge Travel Pal does not convert or reduce electrical voltage and is suitable for use with most consumer electronics ranging from 110 volts to Mac 275 watts, to 200 volts to Mac 550 watts. Measuring 1.9 x 2 x 2.5 inches, the device weighs 600 grams. The product is backed by Maybridge's two-year warranty. It should be noted that the product is not designed to be used with high-watt devices such as irons and hairdryers: users should check electronic device specifications before use.

Price: **€29.99**

ADD TO CART

User reviews

Barry Boston ★★★★★

I bought the Travel Pal two years ago and, I have to say, it's pretty good. I haven't been to a country where I couldn't plug the thing in yet, so top marks there. However, on the downside a couple of points should be made. The first is that the Travel Pal isn't as compact as some of the other multi-plug adaptors out there. When you're trying to keep luggage to a minimum on trips, that can be a bit of a pain. The other thing is, it's not as robust as it looks. A mate of mine dropped his on a carpeted hotel room floor and broke the casing. He found out that no refund was possible for this under the terms of the product warranty. So you do have to be careful with it.

Sue Lewis ★★★★★

Travel Pal! Yeah, well, with friends like this, who needs enemies? I made the mistake of buying the Maybridge Travel Pal and wish I hadn't. Why? Because the 'clever' slide-out plug adaptors just keep on sliding and the thing falls apart in the bottom of your rucksack.

1. In wie vielen Ländern kann das Produkt benutzt werden?
2. Welcher Designaspekt sorgt dafür, dass keine Teile verloren gehen?
3. Welche Geräte kann man damit benutzen?
4. Welche Geräte sollte man nicht damit benutzen?
5. Was sollten Kunden überprüfen, bevor sie ein Gerät mit dem Adapter benutzen?
6. Welche Probleme hatten die Käufer, die die Kundenrezensionen geschrieben haben, mit dem Adapter?

10 Cross-cultural understanding

A Complete the quiz to find out how good your cross-cultural knowledge is. Then get the answers from your teacher and discuss with a partner which answers surprised you.

1 The main aim of meetings in Spain is to ...

a discuss issues at length.
b give information about decisions which have already been made.
c reach a consensus.

2 You notice that a Japanese colleague who is junior to your boss looks down when answering a question from him. He/she ...

a is showing your boss respect.
b is embarrassed by not being sure of the answer.
c is flirting.

3 You give a gift to a South Korean client. He/she refuses to accept it. You should ...

a say sorry for embarrassing the client.
b say that it is not a problem that he/she does not have a gift for you.
c continue offering the gift until it is accepted.

4 During a presentation, a group of Japanese business people sit with their arms folded and their eyes closed. They're ...

a not looking at the speaker so as not to embarrass him/her.
b listening carefully.
c just plain bored.

5 You meet a group of Saudi visitors to your company in the toilets. They're washing their feet because ...

a they're preparing to pray.
b they think German streets and floors are very dirty.
c they have sweaty feet, and it's important to them that they don't smell.

6 An Italian business partner arrives half an hour late for a meeting because ...

a Being 30 minutes late is considered polite in Italy.
b he/she wants to make you feel uneasy before your meeting.
c being right on time is not considered important in Italy.

B Work in a small group. Use the Internet to find more information about people from other cultures. Use the information to write a quiz, then swap your quiz with another group and see how highly you score.

UNIT 11

An installation abroad

- Discussing plans for an installation abroad
- Giving presentations
- Mediating between colleagues and customers

1 Warm-up

A **Work in a small group. You are going on an installation outside of Europe. What practical arrangements will you and your company need to make for your trip? Make a list.**

Well, I'll need to book on a flight for the trip.

Yes, and a place to stay.

B **Tell your group what countries you would most like to visit for your work.**

2 Discussing plans for an installation abroad

25

A Sie fliegen nach Indien, um dort eine Installation durchzuführen. Die Person, die für die Organisation der Reise verantwortlich ist, hinterlässt eine Nachricht auf Ihrem Anrufbeantworter, um die Reiseinformationen zu bestätigen. **KMK**

Hören Sie sich die Nachricht auf dem Anrufbeantworter an und beantworten Sie die Fragen auf Deutsch. Sie hören die Nachricht zweimal.

1 An welchem Datum geht der Flug?
2 Mit welcher Fluggesellschaft fliegen Sie und was ist die Flugnummer?
3 Wie lange dauert der Zwischenstopp in Abu Dhabi?
4 Wie lautet die Flugnummer des zweiten Fluges von Abu Dhabi aus?
5 Um wie viel Uhr landet das Flugzeug in Neu Delhi?
6 Was müssen Sie nicht mitnehmen?
7 Woran erinnert Sie Mike Oliver?

B **Think back to the list you made in exercise 1A. Which items on your list were mentioned in the answerphone message? Which items were not mentioned? Was anything mentioned which you did not think of?**

C **Work with a partner. What are the German translations of the following words from the answerphone message?**

1 check in
2 departure time
3 stopover
4 scheduled time
5 destination
6 pick up
7 travel documents
8 receipts

3 At the airport

A In which parts of the airport would these things be said to passengers? Sometimes there may be more than one answer.

1 Could you please take your jacket off and put it in the tray?
2 Do you have anything to declare? Any alcohol? Cigarettes? Any goods for sale?
3 What is the purpose of your visit?
4 The departures area is down there to the right. Just follow the signs.
5 Passengers in rows 17 to 35 may now board the plane.
6 May I see your passport, please?
7 How many pieces of luggage do you have for the hold?
8 Here's your boarding card. You need to go straight to security now.

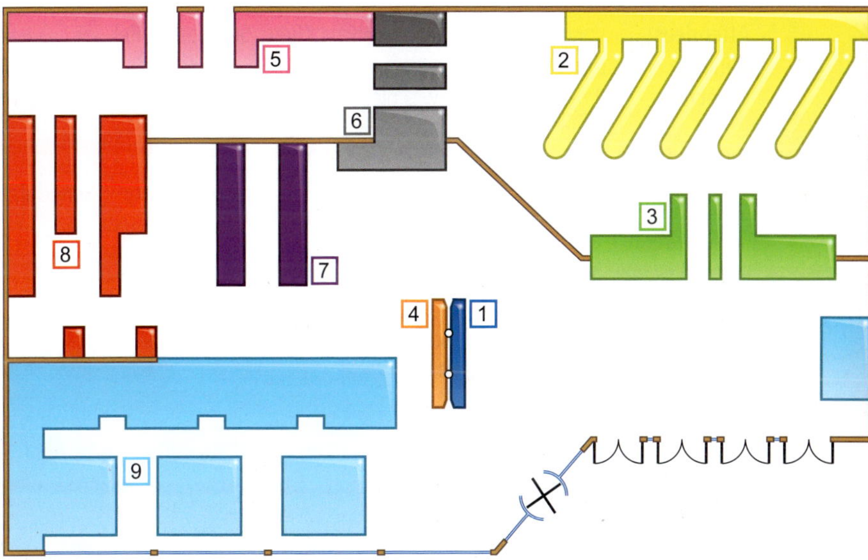

1 Arrivals board
2 Baggage reclaim
3 Customs
4 Departures board
5 Gates
6 Immigration
7 Passenger check-in
8 Security check
9 Shopping and restaurants

B Look at the airport plan with a partner. What way do passengers go through the airport to their aeroplanes?

26

C Sebastian is an electrician travelling to China for an installation. Listen to a conversation between him and the clerk at the check-in counter. Which of these problems does Sebastian have?

1 His flight is over-booked, and he will have to wait for the next flight.
2 The flight is delayed.
3 It is not possible to take two pieces of hand luggage.
4 His luggage is too heavy.
5 He can't get a seat near the toilets.
6 There are no window seats left.

D **Work with a partner. Which of the problems 1–6 in exercise C can a traveller avoid and how? Make a list of other problems a travelling electrician can have and how these can be avoided. Don't think only of the check-in desk. Use the plan of the airport on p. 107 to help you think of as many complications as possible.**

4 Understanding meeting agendas and minutes

Agenda – Chengdu Packaging Company Project Meeting

Date/time Monday, 13 May 20.., 09:00–13:00
Chair Marie Schultz (Project Manager)
Attendees Vong Heng, Petra Heinrich, Paula Berg, Sebastian Eiffel
Minutes Doreen Nadel
Objectives Project status review – please be prepared to report on each phase of the project.

Project phase	Responsibility	Schedule
Preparation • Site preparation (i) Preparation of site flooring (ii) Clearance of way for delivery • Clarifying installation procedures for local subcontractors	VH, PB	6–9 May
Delivery • Shipping • On-site delivery	PH, SE	18 April–15 May
Installation • Installation of PT 169 • Quality control of electrical subcontractors	VH, PH, SE	16–22 May
Commissioning • Test runs • Acceptance test	VH, PH, SE	29–30 May
Training • Identifying key Chengdu Packaging Company staff for training • Settings and production modes • Troubleshooting	PH, SE	3–7 June

A Pactec, eine deutsche Firma, die Verpackungsmaschinen herstellt, beliefert eine neue Verpackungsmaschine an die Chengdu Packaging Company in Chengdu, China. **KMK**

Lesen Sie die Tagesordnung für das Projekt-Meeting und finden Sie heraus, ob die Aussagen (1–4) wahr oder falsch sind. Beantworten Sie die Frage (5) auf Deutsch.

1 Es werden sechs Personen am Meeting teilnehmen.
2 Die Vorbereitung des Firmengebäudes wird in der Woche nach dem Meeting stattfinden.
3 Die Maschine wird sofort nach der Installation in Betrieb genommen.
4 Alle Mitarbeiter von Chengdu werden in der Benutzung der Maschine geschult.
5 Welche Vorbereitungen wurden in dem Firmengebäude getroffen?

B **Read the following extracts from the minutes of the meeting.**

1 Which points are reports of past events and which are decisions taken during the meeting?
2 Which project phase does each extract refer to?
3 Find two problems the team has to deal with.

a

Vong Heng wants an inspection of the operational machine to be carried out by an independent expert. It is not clear who would pay for this as the project is already over Chengdu Packaging Company's planned budget.

b

The foundations of the area where the machine will be located have now been reinforced and the floor levelled off.

c

The PT 169 is being shipped Hamburg to Chengdu and is scheduled to arrive in Chengdu on 17 May, two days behind schedule.

d

In addition to seminars and hands-on practice, Pactec shall supply instruction materials for a successful knowledge transfer.

C **Match each word (1–5) to a definition (a–f).**

1 agenda
2 minutes
3 chair
4 objective
5 attendees

a The people who go to a meeting
b A written record of what was discussed in a meeting
c The aim or goal of a meeting
d A plan of what will be discussed in a meeting
e The place where the meeting will be held
f The person who leads the meeting

D **List five topics you have had meetings about at work. Also include informal meetings. Compare lists with a partner.**

GRAMMAR

Talking about the future

Spontane Entscheidungen, Versprechen und allgemeine Aussagen	***I'll send*** *you an e-mail later with the details. You****'ll be*** *responsible for collecting the receipts for anything you buy during the trip.*
Verabredungen oder feste Pläne	*A driver* ***is picking*** *you* ***up*** *at the airport.*
Zukünftige Absichten	*He****'s going to drive*** *you around during your stay.*
Fahr- und Zeitpläne	*Your flight* ***departs*** *at 4.30 p.m. on the 25th.*

5 Practice: talking about the future

A Choose the best future forms to complete the conversation.

Paula Sebastian, where is our machine now? (Will it be / Is it)[1] delivered on time?

Sebastian The machine is at the port of Shanghai right now, waiting to be loaded onto a river barge. The port supervisor promises that (will happen / happens)[2] today. Then the machine (will float / floats)[3] down Yangtze until it reaches Chongqing. Finally, it (will get / gets)[4] loaded onto a special truck and driven here to the factory. I think it (will arrive / is arriving / arrives)[5] by May 15.

Paula Just in time! OK. But before that (we'll meet / we're meeting)[6] the key staff here and talking them through the installation. I'd like you to discuss how (we're going to handle / we handle)[7] setting up components such as the external sensors and the PLC control console. OK?

Sebastian No problem. (I'll prepare / I'm going to prepare / I prepare)[8] a quick presentation tomorrow.

Paula Great. Well, I've got another meeting now. Oh dear, I'm afraid (I'm being / I'm going to be)[9] late. (I'll see / I'm seeing / I see)[10] you later.

Sebastian See you later, Paula.

B Write four sentences about yourself and your plans. Each sentence should contain one of the future forms.

C Work with a partner. Tell your partner about your plans for the next few weeks. Try to use the future forms correctly.

D Ask your partner for more information about one of his/her plans.

6 Giving presentations

27

Sebastian gives a presentation at Chengdu Packaging to inform the team about how the system's sensors and PLC will be set up.

A Listen to the presentation and answer the following questions.

1. What parts of the system have not yet been set up in the factory?
2. In what order will these components be connected to the machine?
3. What components will be able to be tested before the test run?
4. Does Sebastian warn the team that the installation will be 'complex', or does he assure them that it will be 'straightforward'?

B Complete these sentences with the words Sebastian uses in his presentation.

1. I'm … to be talking to you this morning about the procedure for setting up the PT169's sensors and PLC.
2. I want … now at how we will mount these.
3. If anyone has any questions, … answer them at the end of my presentation
4. To …, I'd like to talk about the reasons for the separate packaging of the sensors and PLC unit.
5. Let's … how we will go about this.
6. Now I … the testing procedure.
7. I want … that installing the PT169 is really quite straightforward.
8. If there are any questions, I'd … to answer them now.

C Now decide which of the phrases are used in a presentation to do the following things.

1. explaining what you plan to talk about
2. inviting input from the audience
3. indicating that you're moving to a new subject

D Prepare a presentation about safety procedures that you have to follow at work, then give it to the class. Use the Tip box to help you.

TIP

If you have to give a presentation, there are a few things you can do to make sure it goes well.

- Think about the tone you'll use during the presentation. Will it be formal or less formal? Write a presentation which will suit your audience.
- Find out how much time you'll have to speak and write a presentation that fits your time slot.
- Practise your presentation. Ideally, you should be able to talk without reading.
- Use phrases from exercise 6B–C.
- Summarize your text into notes you can use when giving your presentation.

7 Talking about commissioning the machine

During the preparation for commissioning the PT 169 Mr Tong, the factory director, asks Paula Berg to explain how the work is progressing.

A Read the dialogue, then answer the questions below.

Mr Tong Hello, Ms Berg? I'm the factory director, Mr Tong.
Paula Hello, Mr Tong. Yes, I'm Paula Berg. It's nice to meet you.
Mr Tong Yes, likewise. Ms Berg, I was wondering if you could tell me what stage you're at and if you're ready to begin commissioning.
Paula Yes, of course. Well, let me just tell you what we've been doing this morning and what the next stages are before we start commissioning. Basically, the machine is now connected to the mains supply and all wired up. We've also fitted all the external sensors and the PLC control console and wired these up. I was really quite impressed by the electrical subcontractors you brought in to help us with this.
Mr Tong Good. So it's ready to run?
Paula Well, not quite. There are a few things we still have to connect and test. For instance, we have to connect the inlet and return lines of the cooling water to the cooling system. Then we have to test that the system is pumping water effectively.
Mr Tong Can I ask why that's important? It's just that I have some very important people coming in here to see the machine in operation tomorrow and I need to know that it will be working.
Paula Don't worry, Mr Tong. We'll have the PT 169 ready for the test run tomorrow morning. But we do have to ensure that it doesn't overheat when we switch it on. That's why we need to set up and test the cooling system properly.
Mr Tong What else do you still have to do?
Paula The pneumatics lines still have to be connected to the compressed air supply. But that won't take too long. Then we have to run a check on all the safety systems to make sure everything's running properly. Then we're ready to switch on.
Mr Tong And then we can do the test run tomorrow. Very good. Can we move straight on to the acceptance test after that?
Paula Yes, if there are no problems during the test run, we can do that.
Mr Tong And then we can do the handover.
Paula Well, not quite. We generally ask you to sign off on the installation and commissioning once we've completed the training.
Mr Tong Ah, yes. I suppose that makes sense. But I wanted to ask if there's any way we can reduce the training from four days to two. I really want to avoid too much production downtime and would like to see the machine and my staff fully operational as soon as possible.
Paula I'm afraid that really won't be possible. We may be able to manage the training in three days but not in two. We need the time to guarantee full knowledge transfer to the staff who will be operating the machine. That's the only way to get it running safely and at an optimal level.

1. Why is it so important for Mr Tong that the test run takes place on time?
2. When will Mr Tong and his colleagues take full responsibility for the machine?
3. Why does Mr Tong want to shorten the length of the training?

B **Work with a partner. Match the German words to English terms in the dialogue, where they appear in the same order. Explain in your own words what the terms mean.**

1 Zulieferer
2 Testlauf
3 Annahmeprüfung
4 Übergabe
5 abzeichnen
6 Wissensweitergabe

C **Discuss what you think the difference is between the test run and the acceptance test.**

8 Mediating between colleagues and customers

Two electricians – one senior and one junior – are on an installation project in India where they are installing packaging machinery. The senior electrician isn't confident in English, so the junior offers to mediate between him and the manager of the factory where they are carrying out the installation.

Join with two partners and role-play the situation three times, so that everyone takes a turn playing the junior electrician.

Senior electrician	Junior electrician	Manager
Guten Tag. Mein Name ist Simone/ Simon Schmidt, von der Firma Verpackungssysteme Strauss GmbH. Das ist mein/e Assistent/in Martina/Martin Glück. Wir sind hier, um die elektrische Installation abzuschließen.	?	
		Hello, welcome to our company. My name is Aarya/Aarav Majumdar. Please tell me what the electrical installation involves.
	?	
Die Installation wurde zum größten Teil bereits in unserer Firma gemacht. Unsere Aufgabe ist, die Technik zu überprüfen und optimal einzustellen.	?	
		I think this pre-installation method is very good and I'm happy you're using it. What will the testing process involve exactly?
	?	
Wir werden zunächst die Kühlungs- und Pneumatik-Systeme einstellen und überprüfen. Danach werden wir die Sicherheitssysteme überprüfen und den Testlauf durchführen. Anschließend kann die Übergabe erfolgen.	?	
		That all sounds good. Will you be training our staff so that they can maintain the equipment as well and know what to do in the event of a breakdown?
	?	
Ja, natürlich. Es ist unsere Firmenpolitik, technisches Wissen an die Kunden weiterzugeben, damit sie den Herstellungsprozess eigenständig am Laufen halten können.	?	
		Very good! Well, we're very pleased to be co-operating with your company on this upgrade of our production line. We're most satisfied with the work that you are doing.
	?	
Wir bedanken uns ebenfalls für die gute Zusammenarbeit.	?	

9 Produktion

Situation

Sie machen ein Praktikum bei der britischen Firma, von der Ihre Firma ein Subunternehmen ist. Sie und Ihr Team wurden gebeten, eine Maschine in Saudi-Arabien zu installieren.

Aufgabe

Schreiben Sie eine E-Mail auf Englisch an Ruth Stivek, die Verantwortliche für die Organisation der Reise. Bitten Sie sie, Buchungen für Sie und Ihre Kollegen vorzunehmen. Ihre E-Mail sollte alle der folgenden Punkte beinhalten.

1 Mitglieder des Installationsteams

- Sie selbst
- Brian Norton
- Karen White

2 Reisedaten

- 19.–26. Juli

3 Reise

- Sie würden gerne an dem Flughafen, der der Stadt Ahsa am nächsten ist, landen.
- Wenn es nicht möglich ist einen Flug zu buchen, der am 19. Juli vormittags (Ortszeit) ankommt, würden Sie gerne schon am 18. Juli nachmittags fliegen.

4 Unterkunft

- Wenn möglich, würden Sie gerne in einem Hotel im Westen von Ahsa unterkommen, in der Nähe der Fabrik, bei der Sie arbeiten.
- Außerdem hätten Sie gerne ein Raucherzimmer für ein Team-Mitglied, wenn das möglich ist.

5 Autovermietung

- Sie würden gerne ein Auto am Flughafen abholen und für die Dauer Ihres Aufenthalts behalten. Das Auto muss groß genug sein, um das Werkzeug und die Ausrüstung, die Sie mitbringen, zu transportieren.

Doing business in China: the things you need to know

Saying hello

As a European, you probably greet someone by shaking their hand firmly for a few seconds. But be prepared for a Chinese handshake to be rather less firm and, at around 10 seconds, somewhat longer. A Chinese person may, however, not offer their hand but bow slightly instead. They may also show respect by lowering their eyes. It's worth keeping in mind that making direct eye contact can be seen as disrespectful in China.

Chinese names

The first important point for Westerners to note here is that surnames and 'first' names are reversed in China. Take Diao Han as an example. Han is actually the given or 'first' name while Diao is the family name. It's Mr Diao, then, and very definitely not Mr Han. Remember also that first names are only used by close friends or family, so use the formal address at all times.

Business meetings

Meetings with Chinese people can be very formal affairs. In advance of any meeting, you'll receive a list of all those who will attend. You should be sure to send the same information to your Chinese counterparts.

When you arrive for a meeting, you'll generally find your Chinese partners already in the meeting room. Take care to follow the strict seating arrangements. The most senior people from each side sit opposite each other while other team members sit across from their counterparts in descending order of importance.

Expect some small talk right at the beginning. Expect also quite a formal speech of introduction from your senior Chinese host. Your senior team member should make similar introductory remarks which should be directly addressed to the senior host.

'Face'

'Face' – or the good reputation that somebody enjoys – is very important to Chinese people. Causing someone to lose face through something you say or do is likely to bring your relationship, and any business that may have resulted from it, to a swift end. Take care then not to make fun of or embarrass Chinese business contacts. And you should certainly avoid criticizing someone directly, especially if others are present.

Directness and talking about problems

Direct, negative responses to questions are felt to be rather impolite in China. Take care not to answer with a direct 'No'. Use answers such as 'I'll examine that', 'I'll think that over' or 'Perhaps' instead. Be aware that when Chinese business partners say there are no longer any problems, there probably still are!

10 Doing cross-cultural business

A **After reading the text, give at least five examples of ways in which it would be possible to accidentally upset a Chinese customer.**

B **Which country would you like to visit? Research the culture of the country on the internet, then write some tips for other people who want to visit the country. Be careful not to include things which are just stereotypes.**

UNIT 12

Applying for a job

- Evaluating job advertisements
- Writing your CV and cover letter
- Interviewing for jobs

1 Warm-up

A **Write down why you would or would not like a permanent job at the company where you are doing your apprenticeship now. You have four minutes for this task.**

B **Turn to your neighbour and discuss your reasons with each other. Find the points on which you agree. Again, you have just four minutes.**

C **Share your ideas with the rest of the class.**

2 CVs for international purposes

Philipp Wahler is a trainee electrician in Schweinfurt. He has prepared a CV in English so that he can apply for jobs outside of Germany.

A **Work with a partner. Look at Philipp's CV on the opposite page. How is it different to a CV in German?**

1. What isn't included?
2. What extra information does it contain?
3. What is in a different order?

CULTURE

Der englische Lebenslauf:
CV (britisches Englisch) / *résumé* (amerikanisches Englisch)

Im englischsprachigen Raum ist der Lebenslauf die wichtigste Komponente einer Bewerbung. Manchmal wird ein Begleitschreiben gar nicht verlangt.
Wichtige Unterschiede zwischen *CV*/*résumé* und deutschem Lebenslauf:

- maximal zwei DIN A4 Seiten (Schriftgröße 12) lang
- umgekehrte chronologische Reihenfolge
- sämtliche Kontaktmöglichkeiten angeben (Anschrift, Festnetz- und Handy-Nr., Fax-Nr., E-Mail-Adresse)
- wichtige Infos für die jeweilige Bewerbung unter Überschriften angeben (siehe Beispiele)
- ggf. weitere Überschriften hinzufügen
- Folgendes wird weggelassen: Foto, Geburtsort, Unterschrift, Datum, Konfession, Angaben zu Eltern und ihren Berufen, Angaben über Geschwister

Philipp Wahler
[1]Siedlerweg 26, 97422 Schweinfurt, Germany
Landline: [2]+49 9721 79664 · Mobile: +49 179 4327791 · Fax: +49 9721 79665
E-mail: philipp.wahler@profimail.de[3]

[4]PROFILE
Trainee [5]electrician in final year of 3-year course seeking post abroad with opportunities for development. Able to work independently and in a team. Mobile and flexible.

[6]KEY SKILLS
Installation work, incl. consumer unit
Cable trunking and tray work
[7]Good spoken and written English

EDUCATION AND TRAINING

Since 2013	[8]3-year traineeship at Buderus Medical Care AG and Dr. Georg Schäfer Vocational Training College in Schweinfurt, Germany.
June 2012	German Class 10 school leaving certificate
2002–2012	[9]Primary and secondary education in Schweinfurt

WORK EXPERIENCE

Since 2013	Experience of installing, maintaining and repairing electrical systems (household and industrial wiring) and motors
2012	5-day placement at Elektro Wilhelm (local electrical contractor) doing maintenance and repairs of household wiring 3-day placement at SKF Gebäudetechnik GmbH (energy-efficient building technology)

[10]FURTHER SKILLS
Knowledge of CAD and technical drawing
Familiar with word-processing and spreadsheet programs
Full driving licence
First aid certificate
Lifesaving certificate

[11]HOBBIES AND INTERESTS
Voluntary member of local fire and rescue service
Captain of local soccer team
Active member of church community service group

PERSONAL DETAILS

Date of birth:	06 [12]April 1997
Nationality:	German
Marital status:	Single
Driving licence:	Full driving licence

REFERENCES
Available on request

Die hochgestellten Zahlen 1–12 beziehen sich auf die Tipps auf S. 121.

B Match the information with the headings. There are two facts for each heading.

PROFILE
KEY SKILLS
EDUCATION AND TRAINING
WORK EXPERIENCE
FURTHER SKILLS
HOBBIES AND INTERESTS

Goods vehicle licence
Fluent spoken and written Turkish
Construction site work in commercial premises and private houses
Licensed electrician with experience working in Arab countries
Trainee electronic technician with basic English
Member of church choir
Single and three-phase power distribution
June 20.. German higher education entrance qualifications
Regular holiday jobs as electrician's mate
Webmaster for homepage of local rock band
Primary school in Romania
Installation work, incl. steel and PVC conduit

C Find the English equivalent (a–j) for each German expression (1–10).

1 Allgemeine Hochschulreife (Abitur)
2 Ausbildung, Lehre
3 Azubi, Lehrling
4 Berufsschule, Berufskolleg, Gewerbliche Schule
5 Fachhochschulreife
6 Führerschein Klasse 3
7 Mittlere Reife
8 Sekundarstufe 1 und 2
9 Wehrdienst
10 Zivildienst

a secondary education
b military service
c traineeship, apprenticeship
d German school leaving certificate (year 10)
e community service
f vocational college (GB), vocational school (US)
g trainee, apprentice
h category B (car) driving licence
i German university entrance qualification
j German higher education entrance qualification

3 Your strong points

Make a list of your own skills and strong points under the headings in exercise 2B. You can invent more headings if necessary.

TIP

Work in groups of 3–4 and list each other's strong points. Add what strong points your boss thinks you have.
Think of the following fields:

- any skills relevant to work
- 'soft' skills (e.g. communication skills, friendly personality, diplomatic manner, leadership experience, captain of football team, trip organizer, etc.)
- community work experience (e.g. social, voluntary or charity work)
- sporting achievements (e.g. prizes, awards, member of winning team)
- performing arts (e.g. playing music, acting, painting, sculpture, writing, dancing)

4 Evaluating job advertisements

A Read the job advertisement and explain …

1. where the job is.
2. how much you can earn.
3. how long you can work for the company.
4. the opportunities for overtime.

B Describe the sort of person the employer is looking for in a few sentences.

C Compare the skills required with your own skills and explain if you could do the job or not.

D Explain how to apply for the job.

E List reasons why you would or would not apply for the job.

POWERSERVE.ORG · Global recruitment

INSTALLATION ELECTRICIAN

Pay rate: £16/hour minimum
Location: Colchester, Essex, UK
Job type: 2 to 4-month contract, renewable, some overtime available
Starting date: ASAP
Contact: Mike Soames, Powerserve Global Recruitment, PO Box 999, London SW1 4HX, United Kingdom
Job reference: IECEU

JOB DESCRIPTION
Our client is an electrical contractor working on schools, colleges, leisure centres, libraries and office buildings. The duties will include installation, maintenance, conduit, cable trunking, tray work, light fittings, fuse boards and electrical refurbishment.

WHO SHOULD APPLY?
You are a qualified electrician interested in working on commercial or industrial electrical systems. You are hard-working with a professional attitude and good communication skills.

Register online and upload your CV HERE

F Find the translation of the following English words, which appear in the same order in the advertisement.

1. verlängerbar
2. Elektroinstallationsfirma
3. Aufgaben
4. Leerrohr
5. Leitungsführungskanal
6. Renovierung

G Discuss your reasons from exercise E with your neighbour and report back to the class.

5 Writing skills summaries

As part of his application, Philipp has to write a 75–80-word summary of his skills.

Use the information in Philipp's CV on p. 117 (work experience, relevant skills, extra-curricular activities) to write the summary.

Example: *In the course of my 3-year traineeship in Germany, I have gained experience of …*

6 Phillip's cover letter

Read Philipp's cover letter and find the following information. Write down the line number(s).

1. when he can start
2. his skills
3. his training
4. what job he is applying for
5. what he is sending with the letter

Siedlerweg 26
97422 Schweinfurt
Germany
Tel. +49 9721 79664
Mobile: +49 179 4327791
E-mail: philipp.wahler@profimail.de

7 May 20..

Ms Lisa Mallory
Tekskil Recruitment Group
180 Market Street
Merrylands NSW 2160
Australia

Dear Ms Mallory

Vacancy for Switchboard/Panel Wirer dated 19 April 20.. Ref. SBPW2000

With reference to your advertisement on the internet, I wish to apply for the above-mentioned post.

By June of this year I will have completed a three-year apprenticeship at Buderus Medical Care AG with theoretical instruction at Dr. Georg Schäfer Vocational Training College in Schweinfurt, Germany. I will then be a licensed electrician.

In the course of my apprenticeship I have gained experience of household and industrial electrical installation, including all the usual safety features and also maintenance and repair work. I have learned to work reliably and independently in environments ranging from hospital operating theatres to building sites.

My CV is enclosed for your information, and I am available for interview at short notice.

As I have a good command of spoken and written English, and will soon have the qualifications you specify, I would be grateful if you would consider me for this post.

Yours sincerely

Philipp Wahler

Enc

7 Applying for jobs

Look at the advertisement for an installation electrician on p. 119 and apply for the job.

A Write your CV, using the information in the tips below. The numbers refer to the CV on p. 117.

TIP

Tipps für den englischen Lebenslauf

1. Geben Sie möglichst viele Kontaktinformationen an, damit Sie leicht zu erreichen sind.
2. Das Pluszeichen ersetzt den Auslandscode 00.
3. Die Überschrift ‚Curriculum Vitae' entfällt, denn jeder weiß, was es für ein Dokument ist und man gewinnt dadurch mehr Platz.
4. Hier erfährt der Arbeitgeber auf einen Blick, wer der Bewerber ist und was er will.
5. Weitere Berufsbezeichnungen:
   Elektroniker – *electronic technician*
   Energieelektroniker – *energy electronics technician*
   Kommunikationselektroniker – *communications electronics technician*
   Energie- und Gebäudetechniker – *energy and building services technician*
6. Geben Sie an, über welche Fertigkeiten Sie verfügen, die für die ausgeschriebene Stelle relevant sind.
7. Die Beherrschung einer Fremdsprache wird mit *fluent*, *good* und *basic* beschrieben.
8. Alle deutschen Begriffe sind ins Englische zu übersetzen.
9. Eine knappe Bezeichnung der schulischen Laufbahn genügt bei der Bewerbung für eine handwerkliche Tätigkeit.
10. Alle weiteren für das Arbeiten im Ausland relevanten Fähigkeiten sind hier zu erwähnen.
11. Alle außerschulischen Aktivitäten, die Aufschluss über die Persönlichkeit des Bewerbers geben, sind hier zu erwähnen.
12. Schreiben Sie den Monat immer voll aus: June 2013 statt 06.2013.

B Write a 75–80-word summary of your skills. Use the list you made in exercise 3 on p. 118 as a starting point.

C Write a cover letter. It should reply specifically to the advertisement on p. 119. Before writing, look again at the example letter on p. 120 and complete the tips below.

TIP

Tipps für das englische Bewerbungsschreiben

1. Schreiben Sie Ihre Adresse … auf dem Blatt.
2. Vergessen Sie nicht, sämtliche … anzugeben.
3. Die Betreffzeile kommt … der Anrede und wird … .
4. Wenn Sie eine bestimmte Person anschreiben, lautet die Schlussformel: Yours …
5. Der Name wird unter der … ausgeschrieben.
6. Wenn Sie eine Anlage (z. B. Ihren Lebenslauf) mit dem Brief schicken, vermerken Sie unten: … .

TOP TEN INTERVIEW QUESTIONS

We asked 100 personnel managers about their favourite interview questions. Here are the ten most popular.

1. Please take us through your CV.
2. Are you a team player?
3. Do you have any hobbies?
4. What are your strengths?
5. What are your weaknesses?
6. Why did you decide to become a …?
7. Why do you want this job?
8. Why should we employ you and not someone else?
9. What are your plans for the future?
10. Do you have any questions you'd like to ask?

8 Interviewing for jobs

28

A **Maik Gärtner interessiert sich für den Job in Großbritannien und bewirbt sich. Er kommt in die engere Wahl und wird für ein Vorstellungsgespräch nach Colchester eingeladen. Das Gespräch wird von der Sekretärin der Personalleiterin protokolliert. Übertragen Sie den Protokollbogen in Ihr Heft und füllen Sie ihn während des Gesprächs aus.** KMK

Applicant's name: *Maik Gärtner*
Current employer:
Type of installation work done so far:
Team player? Examples:
Strength(s):
Weakness(es):
Reason for becoming an electrician:
Reason for wanting this job:
Applicant's question(s):

B **Work in groups of three.**

Partner A: Turn to File 5 on p. 127.
Partner B: Turn to File 14 on p. 130.
Partner C: Turn to File 20 on p. 133.

9 Managing your online reputation

A **Sie wollen sich demnächst bewerben und finden den Artikel auf S. 123 im Internet. Fassen Sie die wichtigsten Inhalte des Textes auf Deutsch zusammen.** KMK

B **Form two groups, employers and employees, and write down the advantages and disadvantages of finding out about job applicants by using social networks. When you have completed your lists, have a debate with the other group. Make sure you disagree with each other. Use the Language box on p. 19.**

ONLINE PRIVACY

What do you do if an employer wants access to your Facebook account?

A number of young people have told us that employers and college admission officers are asking them to log onto Facebook during their interview and show the photos they have uploaded and the messages they have posted. In one case, the HR officer at a prison even wanted to see who the candidate's friends were. At some schools, team coaches are now making young athletes 'friend' them in order to monitor their lifestyle. As if this weren't enough, schools and companies even hire services to do this dirty work for them.

Facebook says that no one should ever be made to share passwords or give access to an account or do anything at all which might endanger the security of an account or invade a friend's private sphere. Facebook describes such practices as a violation of its statement of rights. They also state that employers must have policies in place to ensure that private information remains confidential and that recruitment staff are held responsible for protecting any personal information they gather.

GRAMMAR

-ing forms and infinitives (with *to*)

Verben + *-ing*-Form	Verben + Infinitiv	Verben + *-ing*-Form oder Infinitiv	Präposition + *-ing*-Form
enjoy	*agree*	*begin*	*to be afraid of*
involve	*choose*	*continue*	*to be guilty of*
mind	*decide*	*hate*	*to be interested in*
miss	*expect*	*like*	*to be proud of*
recommend	*hope*	*love*	*to be responsible for*
stop	*learn*	*prefer*	*to be worried about*
suggest	*want*	*start*	*to look forward to*

Siehe S. 143 für weitere Einzelheiten.

10 Practice: *-ing* forms and infinitives

Use the table to complete the sentences with the correct form(s) of the verbs in brackets.

Interviewer Why did you choose (become)[1] an electrician, Tim?

Electrician I enjoy (wire)[2] circuits and I'm very interested in (experiment)[3] with electrical components.

Interviewer I see. When did you start (work)[4] as an electrician?

Electrician At the age of 16 after leaving school. I wanted (do)[5] something technical, so I talked to my father and he suggested (contact)[6] a local electrical contractor. They took me on as an apprentice and I agreed (start)[7] work straight away. It was great!

Interviewer What are your plans for the future, Tim? What are you looking forward to (do)[8]?

Electrician Well, I hope (find)[9] a job where I can continue (develop)[10] professionally. I really want (learn)[11] (do)[12] a lot more things, like telecommunications engineering.

WORK IN THE USA

Major US electrical contractor has opportunities for qualified electricians on sites all over the USA. If you are young, flexible and highly motivated, send your résumé to Don Jones at d.jones@yournextjob.org. Short-listed candidates will be contacted for an interview.

11 Interaktion

Rolle A – Personalvermittler/in

Sie arbeiten bei einer Personalvermittlung für technische Fachkräfte. Heute führen Sie Gespräche mit Kandidaten/-innen, die sich auf eine Stelle als Elektriker/in in der amerikanischen Baubranche beworben haben. Die von Ihnen vertretene Firma hat überall in den USA Baustellen und verkabelt Privathäuser, Bürogebäude, Datenzentren und Industrieanlagen.

Sie sind kein/e Spezialist/in für den Elektroberuf, müssen aber herausfinden, ob der/die Kandidat/in geeignet ist. Stellen Sie Fragen zu folgenden Themen.

- Warum ausgerechnet diese Stelle?
- Hobbys
- Stärken und Schwächen
- eigene Fragen

Rolle B – Personalvermittler/in

Sie arbeiten bei einer Personalvermittlung für technische Fachkräfte. Heute führen Sie Gespräche mit Kandidaten/-innen, die sich auf eine Stelle als Elektriker/in in der amerikanischen Baubranche beworben haben. Die von Ihnen vertretene Firma hat überall in den USA Baustellen und verkabelt Privathäuser, Bürogebäude, Datenzentren und Industrieanlagen. Sie sind Experte/-in für Elektrotechnik und sollen herausfinden, ob der/die Kandidat/in über die benötigten Fertigkeiten verfügt. Stellen Sie Fragen zu folgenden Themen.

- Gründe für Entscheidung, Elektriker zu werden
- Beschreibung der Ausbildung
- bisherige Erfahrung
- relevante Fertigkeiten

Rolle C – Kandidat/in

Sie haben eine Stellenanzeige für Elektriker/innen in der amerikanischen Baubranche gesehen und sich gleich beworben. Bereiten Sie sich auf das Vorstellungsgespräch mit Hilfe folgender Informationen vor.

Profil:
- Sie sind ein selbständiger (*independent*) Mensch.
- Sie reisen gern und wollten schon immer die USA besuchen.
- Sie erledigen Ihre Aufgaben ohne viel Hilfe.
- Sie sind manchmal ungeduldig.

Ausbildung:
- Sie haben eine dreijährige Lehre bei Elektro Kaiser gerade abgeschlossen.
- Sie hatten auch Teilzeitunterricht am Berufskolleg [Name].
- Sie haben vorwiegend alte Häuser verkabelt und Heizanlagen repariert.

Hobbys:
- Es macht Ihnen Spaß, alte Radios und Tonbandgeräte zu reparieren.
- Sie sind Mitglied im Kanuverein und bringen Kindern das Kanufahren bei.

Berufserfahrung:
- Sie haben im vergangen Sommer als Hilfsarbeiter/in für die Elektriker auf einer Baustelle gejobbt. Sie haben für sie Werkzeug geholt und aufgeräumt.

Eigene Frage:
- Besteht die Möglichkeit, in [Lieblingsstaat, z. B. Kalifornien] zu arbeiten?

DOs and DON'Ts for JOB INTERVIEWS

As you come into the room, you have a price tag hanging around your neck and the employer is picking you up, shaking you, looking at you from all angles, wondering, 'Is he/she really worth that much?'

DO

- Look professional – not trendy.
- Wear neutral tones (darker is more impressive), nothing loud or shiny.
- Make sure your clothes are perfectly clean. They needn't be expensive but they must be in perfect condition.
- Wear a good-quality shirt/blouse in a colour that suits your skin.
- Wear sensible shoes.
- Men: wear good socks. (You can wear your Mickey Mouse socks later, when you've got the job.) Women: if you wear a skirt, choose light-coloured tights. (Dark tights are evening wear.)
- Men: shave well in advance so your skin has time to settle. Women: wear only a little make-up to bring out your best features.

DON'T

- Don't put your hands in your pockets.
- Men: don't have long hair – get it cut a week before your interview.
- Men: don't use strong aftershave – the interviewer may hate it! Women: don't use perfume.
- Turn off your mobile phone.
- Don't wear lots of jewellery. This is seen as a sign of insecurity. Don't wear that chunky gold necklace or bracelet you wear at the disco. Wear a maximum of one ring on each hand. Men: don't wear big chunky watches. You are not James Bond.

ON THE GREAT DAY

- Telephone to confirm that you're coming. Do this the day before if the interview is in the morning.
- Don't eat strong-smelling foods before the interview. You can smell garlic for at least 24 hours.
- Travel to the location of the interview well ahead of time and wait in a nearby car park or café. Allow plenty of time for traffic and parking. Arrive at the interview five to ten minutes early.
- Give your coat (and umbrella) in at reception.
- Ask to use the bathroom and then: check your hair; women: check your make-up; clean your glasses; re-polish your shoes; wash your hands in warm water; dry them thoroughly; check your nails are clean; check your clothing a final time.

12 Understanding the text

According to the text, what is the job candidate in the cartoon doing wrong?

13 Research

With a partner, go online and search for videos using "blue collar interview attire". You will find a number of videos explaining what to wear at an interview. Make notes on what you find. Now do the same again with "white collar interview attire". What differences do you see? Report your findings to the class.

1 Unit 6, exercise 5B

Partner A

1 Read these mathematical expressions to your partner. Check that he/she has written them down correctly.

a $15 \times 15 \times 15 = 15^3$
b $569 - 81 = 488$
c $3{,}927 \times 84 = 398{,}868$
d $0.3 \div 0.07 = 4.28$
e $7 + (45 \div 8) = 12.62$
f 4 kilovolts = 4,000 volts
g 2 gigawatts = 2,000,000,000 watts
h $\frac{1}{4} + \frac{1}{2} = \frac{3}{4}$

2 Write down the mathematical expressions that your partner reads to you.

2 Unit 8, exercise 5B

Partner A

Rolle A – Auszubildende/r

Sie sind Azubi in einer Firma. Heute bekommen Sie einen *shadow* (Arbeitsbegleiter/in) aus dem Ausland, der Sie eine Woche lang bei Ihrer Arbeit begleiten soll. Momentan sind Sie mit dem Bau des oben abgebildeten Ladegeräts beschäftigt, das Sie anschließend mit einem Oszilloskop testen sollen. Beantworten Sie die Fragen Ihres ‚shadow', d.h. u.a.

- Benennen Sie die Bauteile.
- Erklären Sie die jeweilige Funktion der Bauteile.
- Erklären Sie die Vorteile des Oszilloskops als Testgerät.
- Zeigen Sie mit Hilfe des Schaltplans, wo Sie das Oszilloskop ansetzen werden (Stellen A, B und C).
- Fügen Sie ggf. weitere Infos hinzu.

LANGUAGE

Giving information/confirmation
We have to …
The boss wants us to …
Exactly. / No, he/she/it doesn't.
Yes, that's right. / No, I'm afraid not.
Yes, we do. / No, we don't.
Yes, it is. / No, it isn't. It's a/an …

3 Unit 2, exercise 6B

Partner A

Sie wollen einen Akkubohrer bestellen. Sie möchten, dass er so schnell wie möglich geliefert wird und so wenig wie möglich kostet. Sie haben keine Kreditkarte und wollen deswegen eine Rechnung zugeschickt bekommen.

- Rufen Sie Stevenson Tool Supplies an und erkundigen Sie sich nach ihren günstigsten Bohrmaschinen.
- Wählen Sie ein Gerät, das Ihre Ansprüche erfüllt.
- Geben Sie für Lieferung und Abrechnung Ihre Adresse an. Benutzen Sie dafür den Namen und die Anschrift Ihrer Firma.

4 Unit 6, exercise 4B

Partner A

Sie und ein Kollege treffen sich mit einem Kunden, um zu erklären, wie eine Photovoltaikanlage installiert wird. Bereiten Sie Stellungnahmen zu folgenden Punkten vor.

- die Ausrichtung und Neigung des Daches feststellen – wann das erledigt wird und warum es wichtig ist
- Deckenanker und Aluminiumstäbe – was das jeweils ist und wie sie angebracht werden
- die Gleichstromverkabelung des Photovoltaikgenerators mit dem Wechselrichter verbinden

5 Unit 12, Exercise 8B

Partner A

You are a headhunter, interviewing candidates for jobs in the construction industry in various parts of Europe. You don't know much about electrical engineering, but you want to find out what kind of person the candidate is.

- Ask the candidate about his/her reasons for becoming an electrician.
- Ask about his/her strengths and weaknesses.
- Ask what he/she does in his/her free time.
- Ask if he/she has any questions he/she would like to ask.
- Answer the candidate's question about the rest of the interview process. Explain that you will contact him/her within three weeks and there may be a second interview.

6 Unit 2, exercise 6B

Partner B

Sie sind Verkäufer/in bei Stevenson Tool Supplies. Beantworten Sie die Fragen des Anrufers anhand der unten stehenden Informationen. Vergessen Sie nicht, die Adresse des Kunden zu notieren.

Serial no.	Manufacturer	Price	Currently in stock
RST2	Daxei	€ 93.00	3
DC887E	Tretnorm	€ 125.00	0
PZL 6	Hynari	€ 155.00	6
TZ 89	Grossner	€ 174.00	1

Payment terms: Payment on invoice only possible on orders of more than €100.00. On orders of less than this, payment is by credit card or cash on delivery.

7 Unit 4, exercise 2B

Partner A

1. **Describe the position of the electrical fittings on your plan to your partner. He/she must write them on his/her plan without looking at yours!**
2. **Listen to Partner B's instructions and mark the positions of the electrical fittings on your plan.**
3. **Swap plans with your partner and check how well you followed your partner's instructions.**

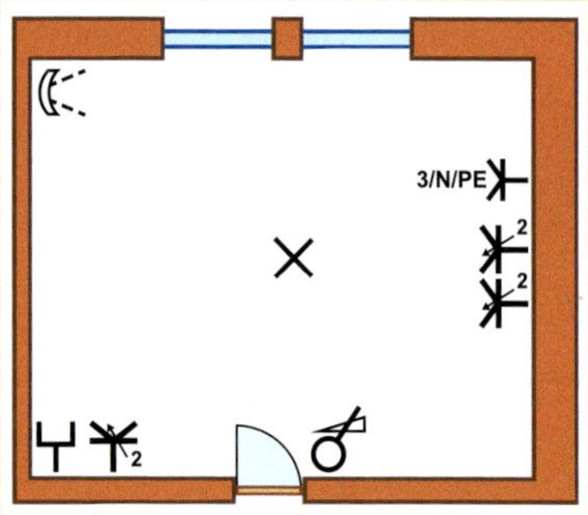

8 Unit 6, exercise 4B

Partner B

Sie treffen zusammen mit einem Kollegen einen Kunden, um zu erklären, wie eine Photovoltaikanlage installiert wird. Bereiten Sie Stellungnahmen zu folgenden Punkten vor.

- das Baugerüst – warum es wichtig ist und wann es aufgestellt wird
- ein Loch durch das Dach bohren – warum das notwendig ist
- die Kontrolle der Anlageneffizienz – wann sie stattfindet

9 Unit 6, exercise 5B

Partner B

1 **Write down the mathematical expressions that your partner reads to you.**

2 **Read these mathematical expressions to your partner. Check that he/she has written them down correctly.**

i $3 \times 3 \times 3 \times 3 \times 3 = 3^5$
j $728 - 54 = 674$
k $7{,}932 \times 66 = 523{,}512$
l $0.86 \div 7 = 0.122$
m $13 + (5 \div 8) = 13.62$
n 14 megaohms = 14,000,000 ohms
o 6 terabits = 6,000,000,000,000 bits
p $\frac{1}{2} - \frac{1}{3} = \frac{1}{6}$

10 Unit 8, exercise 1D

Partner A

1 **Write down the values that your partner reads to you, then ask your partner to check your answers.**

2 **Read out these values to your partner.**

a 90 µs
b 23,000 V
c 150 µF
d 10,000 W
e 50.5 Hz

11 Unit 10, exercise 3D

Partner A

You are representing your company at the InterElectric trade show. A visitor to your stand approaches you.

- Greet the visitor politely and introduce yourself.
- Offer the customer a coffee.
- Explain which products or services your company offers.
- Offer the visitor a brochure.
- Ask if the customer would like to watch a video about your products.
- Give the visitor your business card and say that you would be pleased to answer further questions once the trade show is over.

12 Unit 4, exercise 2B

Partner B

1. **Listen to Partner A's instructions and mark the positions of the electrical fittings on your plan.**
2. **Describe the position of the electrical fittings on your plan to Partner A. He/She must write them on his/her plan without looking at yours!**
3. **Swap plans with your partner and check how well you followed your partner's instructions.**

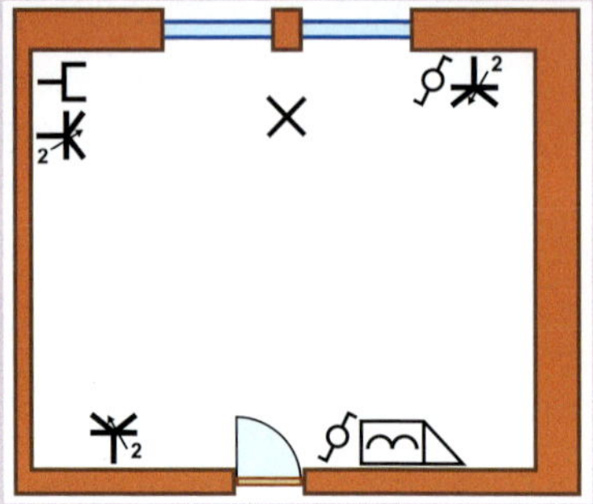

13 Unit 6, exercise 4B

Partner C

Sie sind Kunde und treffen sich mit den beiden Elektroinstallateuren, die eine neue Photovoltaikanlage auf Ihrem Dach installieren sollen. Bereiten Sie Fragen zu folgenden Punkten vor.

- den besten Teil des Daches für die Photovoltaikanlage aussuchen
- wie die Anlage auf dem Dach befestigt wird
- wie das Kabel vom Dach in das Haus kommt
- wie die Photovoltaikanlage mit dem Haus verkabelt wird

14 Unit 12, Exercise 8B

Partner B

You are interviewing candidates for jobs in the construction industry in various parts of Europe. You are an electrical engineering expert, and you want to find out whether the candidate has the right technical skills.

- Ask about his/her training.
- Ask about his/her experience so far, e.g. work placements.
- Ask whether he/she has any other relevant skills.
- Answer the candidate's question about training. Explain that he/she would work together with an experienced employee until he/she was ready to work independently.

15 Unit 8, exercise 3

Partner A

1 Ask your partner to solve the following problems. Then check your partner's answers against the answer in brackets.

Begin like this:

What's the root mean square / peak voltage if …?

1	PV = 60 V	(Answer: rms = 42.4328147 V)
2	rms = 290.5 V	(Answer: PV = 410.767 V)
3	PV = 3,000 V	(Answer: rms = 2121.64074 V)
4	rms = 282,885.43 V	(Answer: PV = 399,999.998 V ≈ 400,000 V)

2 Write down the problems that your partner reads out.

Use a calculator to work out the answers ($\sqrt{2} \approx 1.414$).
Read out the answers to your partner.

16 Unit 8, exercise 5B

Partner B

Rolle B – Shadow

Sie machen ein Praktikum im Ausland. Am ersten Tag bekommen Sie die Gelegenheit als *shadow* (Arbeitsbegleiter/in) einen/eine heimische/n Auszubildende/n bei der Arbeit zu beobachten. Momentan ist sie/er mit dem Bau des auf S. 79 abgebildeten Ladegeräts beschäftigt, das anschließend mit einem Oszilloskop getestet werden soll. Sie begleiten sie/ihn und möchten Folgendes wissen.

- was Ihr Gesprächspartner momentan für eine Aufgabe hat
- die Namen von 4 oder 5 Bauteilen im Schaltplan
- wie das Gerät getestet werden soll
- was für Akkus damit geladen werden können
- ob man eine Autobatterie damit laden kann
- ggf. weitere Fragen

LANGUAGE

Asking for information/ confirmation

Could you explain …?
I'm not quite sure …
Does the boss want us to …?
Does that mean …?
Do we have to …?
What's the component in square G5?
Is that a/an …?

17 Unit 8, exercise 3

Partner B

1 **Write down the problems that your partner reads out.**

Use a calculator to work out the answers ($\sqrt{2} \approx 1.414$).
Read out the answers to your partner.

2 **Ask your partner to solve the following problems. Then check your partner's answers against the answer in brackets.**

Begin like this:

What's the root mean square / peak voltage if …?

1 PV = 95 V (Answer: rms = 67.18529 V)
2 rms = 400 V (Answer: PV = 565.6 V)
3 PV = 30000 V (Answer: rms = 21,216.4074 V)
4 rms = 424,328.14 V (Answer: PV = 599,999.99 V ≈ 600,000 V)

18 Unit 10, exercise 3D

Partner B

You are visiting the InterElectric trade show and notice a company you would like to know more about. You approach one of the representatives working at the company's stand.

- Greet the representative politely and introduce yourself.
- Accept the offer of a cup of coffee.
- Explain that you are interested in finding out more about the products or services offered by the company.
- Ask if the representative can give you a brochure.
- Decline the offer of watching a video about the company's products.
- Accept the representative's business card and offer your own card. Say that you will get in touch after the trade show if you have any further questions.

19 Unit 8, exercise 1D

Partner B

1 Read out these values to your partner.

- **f** 2.3 Ω
- **g** 90 ms
- **h** 0.5 A
- **i** 5 μH
- **j** 45,000 kWh

2 Write down the values that your partner reads to you, then ask your partner to check your answers.

20 Unit 12, Exercise 8B

Partner C

You have answered an advertisement for electricians to work in the construction industry in various parts of Europe. Read the information below before the interview.

Profile:

- You have always wanted to travel.
- You are an independent person: you always get the job done and you don't need a lot of supervision.
- Your weakness: sometimes you are impatient.

Training:

- Give true information about yourself.

Hobbies:

- Give true information about yourself.

Work experience:

- Give true information about yourself.

Questions:

- Ask what kind of training you would receive, if you get the job.
- Ask what the next step of the interview procedure will be.

Schriftliche Prüfung

Zeit: **90 Minuten**
Hilfsmittel: **allgemeines zweisprachiges Wörterbuch**
Maximale Punktzahl: **100 Punkte**

Im Rahmen der schriftlichen Prüfung werden die Aufgabenanteile für die drei Kompetenzbereiche wie folgt gewichtet:

- **Rezeption 40 %**
- **Produktion 30 %**
- **Mediation 30 %.**

Im Folgenden werden vier Aufgaben vorgelegt, die Sie bearbeiten sollen. Die erste und die zweite Aufgabe beziehen sich auf Ihre Fähigkeit, englische Texte (gesprochene und geschriebene) zu verstehen = **Rezeption**. Bei der dritten Aufgabe wird von Ihnen erwartet, dass Sie Texte von der deutschen oder englischen in die jeweils andere Sprache übertragen = **Mediation**. In der vierten Aufgabe sollen Sie ein Schriftstück erstellen = **Produktion** eines englischen Textes.

Die Prüfung beginnt mit der Hörverständnisaufgabe. Alle weiteren Aufgaben können in beliebiger Reihenfolge bearbeitet werden.

Rezeption I: Hörverstehen

29

Situation

Sie sind Auszubildende/r bei der Firma Schattauer Installationstechnik, deren Dienstleistungsprogramm u. a. das Einrichten von Datenzentren umfasst. Heute erhalten Sie einen Anruf von einem englischsprachigen Kunden.

Aufgabe

Übertragen Sie das Formular in Ihr Notizbuch. Füllen Sie es für die Verkaufsabteilung aus, während Sie das Gespräch zweimal anhören.

Erstgespräch mit potenziellem Kunden

1. Name des Kunden
2. Firma des Kunden
3. Projektstandort
4. Sicherheitsvorkehrungen benötigt? (ja/nein)
5. Welche Sicherheitsvorkehrungen?
6. EIB empfohlen? (ja/nein)
7. Kontaktdaten des Kunden
8. Weiteres Vorgehen

Rezeption II: Leseverstehen

Situation

Sie arbeiten bei einer Bühnentechnikfirma, die an mehreren Orten in Europa eine Reihe von Festivals veranstalten soll. Hierfür braucht Ihr Unternehmen einen möglichst umweltfreundlichen Stromgenerator. Sie finden auf der Website der britischen Firma Firefly Solar Generators Limited folgende Produktbeschreibung.

Aufgabe

Lesen Sie die Informationen und beantworten Sie untenstehende Fragen in Stichworten auf Deutsch.

The Hybrid Power Solution

Firefly solves the problem of temporary power. Combining existing diesel generators with battery storage systems has a number of benefits including:

Reduced operating costs
Hybrid power can reduce fuel consumption by up to 30 % and reduce maintenance of the diesel generator by 50 %.

Lower environmental impact
A hybrid system can reduce carbon emissions by up to 30 % compared to using a diesel generator. Local residents and staff can also benefit from silent operation and no exhaust fumes.

Cygnus Hybrid Power Generator (HPG) 12–24 kVA

Product Overview
Firefly is proud to announce the latest member of the family. Cygnus HPG is an extremely versatile power solution for a wide range of temporary applications including live events, broadcast, construction and disaster response. The HPG can deliver single or 3 phase 415 V, with integral transfer switching that moves between external and inverter power – avoiding the need to run twin diesel sets for UPS. With significant storage the intermittent nature of renewable energy sources is no longer a concern. Auxiliary control function is determined by flexible user defined parameters, such as maximum battery discharge and load.

Product Features
- Up to 24 kVA 240 V 50 Hz continuous output
- 72 kVA peak output (5 seconds)
- 48 kWh usable stored energy
- IP 44 rated
- Rental specification
- Backup or stand-alone operation
- Remote generator start
- Lifting ring & forklift pockets
- Compact design
- Pure sine wave output
- One piece lift canopy
- Easy access for maintenance
- Buzz bar for hard wiring
- RCD/MCB protection

Options
- Power storage extender pack (12 kWh)
- Solar prep
- Remote monitoring kit
- Road tow
- Harsh environment kit (hot)
- Harsh environment kit (cold)
- 110 V/60 Hz inverter

Benefits
- Reduce carbon emissions by up to 30 %
- Reduce fuel consumption by up to 30 %
- Reduce maintenance costs by 50 %
- Truly silent – zero noise
- Zero emissions in stand-alone mode
- 2-year standard warranty

1 Wann ist es sinnvoll, den hier beschriebenen Generator einzusetzen?
2 Warum wird der Generator als Hybrid bezeichnet?
3 Um wie viel ist der hier beschriebene Generator sparsamer als ein herkömmlicher?
4 Warum wird der Einsatz eines solchen Generators von Bevölkerung und Personal begrüßt?
5 Welche Leistungen hat ein Cygnus HPG?
6 Warum ist es beim Cygnus HPG nicht notwendig, zwei Dieselmotoren zu haben, um unterbrechungsfreie Stromversorgung (UPS) zu gewährleisten?
7 Welche Parameter kann der Benutzer dieses Geräts selber einstellen?
8 Welche Sicherheitsvorkehrungen hat das Gerät?
9 Erläutern Sie drei der aufgeführten Produkteigenschaften unter der Überschrift ‚Product Features'.
10 Woher weiß man, dass das Gerät auch unter extremen Witterungsverhältnissen eingesetzt werden kann?

Produktion

Situation
Ihre Firma, Bühnentechnik Funlight GmbH in Freiburg, interessiert sich für den Stromgenerator der britischen Firma Firefly Solar Generators Limited.

Aufgabe
Schreiben Sie im eigenen Namen als Projektleiter eine E-Mail-Anfrage an info@fireflysolar.co.uk unter Berücksichtigung folgender Punkte:

- Sie haben die Website der britischen Firma im Internet gesehen.
- Kurzbeschreibung Ihrer Firma
  - mittelständisches Unternehmen in Deutschland
  - Versorgung von kleinen und großen Festivals mit Bühnentechnik
  - überall in Europa tätig
- Interesse an Cygnus HPG Generator
- Bitte um nähere Beschreibung des Geräts.
- Bitte um Preisangabe bei Vermietung und Kauf.
- Lieferzeit?
- Lieferbedingungen?
- Bei einem günstigen Mietangebot wird Ihr Unternehmen ein Gerät für eine Woche mieten und evtl. bei Entsprechung Ihrer Erwartungen anschließend kaufen.
- Höfliche Schlussformel

Mediation

Situation
Sie arbeiten für eine Firma, die auf Event Management und Bühnentechnik spezialisiert ist und danach strebt, ihren Kunden besonders umweltfreundliche Lösungen anzubieten. Ihr Geschäftsführer bittet Sie, über die britische Firma Firefly Solar Generators Limited Auskünfte einzuholen und insbesondere herauszufinden, ob deren Aggregate für größere Events geeignet sind. Sie finden auf Fireflys Website unten stehenden Bericht über ein Festival in den Niederlanden, das die britische Firma mit Strom versorgt hat.

Aufgabe
Übertragen Sie die wichtigsten Inhalte des Berichts ins Deutsche.

Lowlands Festival – solar powered eco-houses

PROJECT SUMMARY
Essent Energy, the largest producer of renewable power in the Benelux countries, needed an environmentally friendly and sustainable means of powering the Lowlands interactive experience festival – the largest in the Netherlands.
Firefly Solar Generators Limited, UK installed a 15 kVa solar unit which provided enough power for the whole event.

BACKGROUND
Lowlands is an annual music festival located in the Netherlands. The festival is one of the biggest in the country with over 60,000 visitors, 200 acts and more than ten stages every year. Lowlands festival started in 1967 and has since hosted some of the world's most famous alternative acts and musicians. Lowlands not only provides music but also a wide variety of acts, including stand-up comedy, film, visual arts, literature and theatre.

Flat pack houses with Fold Arrays

Essent Energy is the leading producer of sustainable energy in the Netherlands and always uses the most affordable, reliable and sustainable means possible. It looks for solutions that are better for people, the environment and society as a whole.

TASK & SOLUTION
Essent Energy were unable to locate a suitable supplier in the Netherlands or elsewhere in mainland Europe, so they contacted Firefly, UK to enquire about a renewable energy solution to power a large, interactive exhibition.

Firefly quickly decided that its 'Fold Array' was ideal for this project, and designed a sustainable power distribution system combining three of its Orion generators and a number of Fold Arrays. The Fold Arrays were adapted to be mounted on the roofs of the flat pack houses built by Essent for their interactive experience.

RESULTS
Lowland's 60,000 festival attendees saved a total of 37,821 kg of CO_2 demonstrating how the green festival movement is now spreading across international borders and how willing and enthusiastic the public are to take responsibility and make a difference.

Mündliche Prüfung

Die Prüfung ist eine Gruppenprüfung, bei der Sie Gespräche persönlichen und fachlichen Inhalts in der Fremdsprache führen sollen. Es wird von Ihnen erwartet, dass Sie der vorgegebenen Situation entsprechend sprachlich agieren und reagieren. Es kommt dabei vor allem darauf an, dass Sie sich spontan äußern, dass Sie versuchen, sich verständlich zu machen, und dass Sie gut zuhören.

Die Prüfung besteht aus zwei Teilen und dauert insgesamt ca. 20 Minuten. Sie erhalten eine angemessene Vorbereitungszeit, wenn die Aufgabe dies verlangt.

Im **ersten Teil** der mündlichen Prüfung werden Sie gebeten, sich zu persönlichen oder beruflichen Themen zu äußern.

Im **zweiten Teil** sollen Sie zusammen mit einem anderen Kandidaten ein Rollenspiel durchführen. Dazu erhalten Sie vom Prüfer Rollenkarten, auf denen eine Situation beschrieben ist, die Sie vorspielen sollen.

Hilfsmittel: allgemeines zweisprachiges Wörterbuch

Mündliche Prüfung Teil I

Erzählen Sie uns etwas über ...

- sich selbst und Ihre Familie.
- die Firma, in der Sie Ihre Ausbildung machen.
- Ihre Berufsschule.
- Ihre Hobbys.
- Ihre Pläne für die Zukunft.
- wo sie beruflich gerne in fünf Jahren wären.

Mündliche Prüfung Teil II

Situation

Es ist Winter. Ihre Chefin teilt Ihnen und Ihrem Partner mit, dass Sie morgen früh nach Schottland fliegen müssen, um dort dringende Reparaturen am Stromgenerator eines entlegenen Hotels im schottischen Hochland bei Inverness vorzunehmen. Ihre Firma hatte vor einigen Jahren einen Generator dort installiert, und jetzt setzt er unter extremen Witterungsverhältnissen gelegentlich aus. Ein Mietwagen wird morgen für Sie am Flughafen Edinburgh bereit stehen.

Aufgabe

Besprechen Sie mit Ihrem Partner ...

- welche Dokumente Sie für Ihre Reise nach Schottland benötigen.
- welche Werkzeuge Sie auf jeden Fall mitnehmen werden.
- welche Werkzeuge Sie evtl. nachschicken lassen werden.
- was Sie sonst noch alles an Kleidung u. Toilettenartikeln mitnehmen werden.
- weitere Angaben nach Wahl.

Scottish Highlands

Useful phrases

Your company and your job

Describing your company

The company's located in …	*Das Unternehmen hat seinen Sitz in …*
It employs … people.	*Es hat … Beschäftigte.*
It installs …	*Es installiert …*
It manufactures …	*Es fertigt …*
It exports …	*Es exportiert …*
It maintains …	*Es hält … instand.*
It carries out …	*Es führt … aus.*

Describing your job

I work in a workshop / in the open / at height.	*Ich arbeite in einer Werkstatt / im Freien / in [luftigen] Höhen.*
I install/test/replace/inspect … electrical systems/ components.	*Ich installiere/teste/ersetze/kontrolliere elektrische Systeme/Komponenten.*
I troubleshoot electrical systems.	*Ich behebe Fehler in elektrischen Systemen.*
I maintain/repair machines.	*Ich warte/repariere Maschinen.*
I diagnose problems/faults.	*Ich stelle Probleme/Fehler fest.*
I advise customers/colleagues.	*Ich berate Kunden/Kollegen.*
I follow wiring plans / technical drawings.	*Ich halte mich an die Anschlusspläne / technischen Zeichnungen.*
I work fixed hours / a 39-hour week / shifts.	*Ich habe feste Arbeitszeiten / eine 39-Stundenwoche / arbeite Schicht.*
I do a lot of overtime.	*Ich mache viele Überstunden.*
I'm often on call.	*Ich bin häufig im Bereitschaftsdienst.*

Showing visitors around your company

Let's start by visiting …	*Lassen Sie uns mit dem Besuch der/des … beginnen.*
Here we have the … department.	*Hier haben wir die Abteilung …*
On the left/right, you can see …	*Zu Ihrer Linken/Rechten sehen Sie …*
This is where we design/store/ make/assemble …	*Hier entwerfen/lagern wir … / stellen wir … her. / bauen wir … zusammen.*

Asking for and giving directions within a company

Could you tell me the way to …, please?	*Könnten Sie mir bitte sagen, wie ich nach / zu/r/m … komme?*
Yes, certainly.	*ja, selbstverständlich.*
Go down the corridor until you get to …	*Gehen Sie den Flur entlang, bis Sie zu/r/m … kommen.*
Turn left at the first/second/third/last door on your right.	*Nehmen Sie die erste/zweite/dritte/letzte Tür rechts.*
Turn right at the end of the corridor.	*Biegen Sie am Ende des Flures rechts ab.*

Meetings

Asking for and giving an opinion

What do you think?	*Was meinen Sie?*
What's your opinon?	*Welcher Meinung sind Sie?*
(Sarah,) would you like to come in here?	*(Sarah,) möchten Sie an dieser Stelle etwas sagen?*
(Tom,) any ideas from you?	*(Tom,) haben Sie eine Idee?*
I think/reckon that …	*Ich denke/gehe davon aus, dass …*
In my opinion, …	*Meiner Meinung nach …*
If you ask me, …	*Wenn Sie mich fragen, …*
As far as I see / I'm concerned, …	*So, wie ich das sehe / Was mich anbelangt, …*

Useful phrases

Checking that people understand

- Do you know what I mean? — *Wissen Sie, was ich meine?*
- Do you know what I'm saying? — *Verstehen Sie, was ich sagen will?*

Checking back if you don't understand

- Excuse me. Could you repeat that, please? — *Entschuldigung, könnten Sie das bitte wiederholen?*
- Could you say that again, please? — *Könnten Sie das bitte noch einmal sagen?*
- I didn't quite catch what you said. — *Ich habe das, was Sie gesagt haben, nicht ganz verstanden.*
- If I understood you correctly, … — *Wenn ich Sie richtig verstehe, …*

Agreeing and disagreeing

- I would agree with that. — *Dem würde ich zustimmen.*
- Yes, I think that's right. — *Ja, ich glaube, das stimmt.*
- I think you're right there. — *Ich denke, Sie haben in diesem Punkt Recht.*
- I'm afraid I really can't agree. — *Tut mir leid, aber dem kann ich nicht zustimmen.*
- I don't think that's right. — *Ich glaube nicht, dass dies richtig ist.*

Expressing doubt and giving reasons

- I'm not so sure about that. — *Ich bin mir hierüber nicht so sicher.*
- I would doubt that a bit. — *Ich habe da so meine Zweifel.*
- The main reason is … — *Der Hauptgrund liegt in …*
- This is because … — *Dem ist so, weil/da …*

Making suggestions

- I think it would be a good idea to … — *Ich denke, es wäre gut, … zu …*
- Maybe we should … — *Vielleicht sollten wir …*
- How about + -ing? — *Wie wäre es mit …?*
- My suggestion would be to … — *Mein Vorschlag wäre …*

Accepting and rejecting suggestions

- Good idea. — *Gute Idee.*
- That sounds like a sensible idea. — *Das klingt vernünftig.*
- I think I could say yes to that. — *Ich denke, ich kann dem zustimmen.*
- Sorry, I don't think that's going to work. — *Tut mir leid, ich glaube, das funktioniert nicht.*
- I'm afraid we can't agree to that. — *Ich bedaure, aber dem können wir nicht zustimmen.*

Interrupting someone at a meeting

- Sorry to interrupt you, but … — *Entschuldigen Sie bitte, dass ich Sie unterbreche, aber …*
- Could I just say something, please? — *Könnte ich bitte kurz etwas sagen?*
- Do you mind if I just add something here? — *Haben Sie etwas dagegen, wenn ich hier etwas hinzufüge?*

Summarizing the main points of a meeting

- OK, so we both/all agree to … — *Wir beide/alle sind uns darin einig, dass …*
- Let me just sum up what we have agreed. — *Lassen Sie mich kurz zusammenfassen, was wir soeben beschlossen haben.*
- Before we finish, I would just like to summarize the main points we agreed on. — *Bevor wir zum Ende kommen, möchte ich kurz die wichtigsten Punkte zusammenfassen, auf die wir uns geeinigt haben.*

Useful phrases

Safety at work

Describing safety measures

Make sure that …	*Stellen Sie sicher, dass …*
Check that …	*Überprüfen Sie, ob …*
Disconnect …	*Lösen/Unterbrechen Sie die Verbindung … / Ziehen Sie den Stecker …*
Lock and tag …	*wörtlich: verriegeln und kennzeichnen …; hier: gegen wiedereinschalten sichern …*
Warn people that …	*Warnen Sie die Leute vor …*
Put a sign on …	*Bringen Sie ein Schild an der/am … an.*
Be careful not to …	*Achten Sie darauf, … nicht zu (tun).*
You mustn't …	*Sie dürfen nicht …*
Always ensure that …	*Stellen Sie immer sicher, dass …*

Explaining potential risks

You could get an electric shock / be seriously injured / be electrocuted.	*Sie könnten einen Stromschlag bekommen / sich schwer verletzen / durch einen Stromschlag umkommen.*
You could electrocute / seriously injure …	*Sie könnten … durch einen Stromschlag töten / schwer verletzen.*
Death or serious injury may result from failure to …	*Das Unterlassen von … könnte den Tod oder schwere Verletzungen zur Folge haben.*

Installations and processes

Describing where to put electrical fittings

Put/Place a(n) …	*Setzen/Stellen Sie ein/e/n …*
to the right/left of …	*rechts/links von …*
on the top / bottom / right-hand / left-hand wall	*auf der Wand ganz oben / unten/rechts/links*
in the bottom left-hand / top right-hand corner	*in der Ecke links unten / rechts oben*
next to / between / close to	*neben/zwischen/nahe*

Explaining processes

The first step in any installation is to …	*Der erste Schritt jeder Installation ist …*
We start by + -ing …	*Wir beginnen mit der/dem …*
The second step is to …	*Der zweite Schritt ist …*
After that / Then / Next we …	*Im Anschluss / Dann / Als nächstes … wir …*
Once that is done, we …	*Sobald dies getan ist, … wir …*
The final stage of the installation is to …	*Der letzte Schritt der Installation ist …*

Troubleshooting

Asking the right questions

What sort of problems are you having?	*Welche Art der Probleme haben Sie?*
Do you mind if I ask you a few questions about …?	*Darf ich Ihnen bzgl. … ein paar Fragen stellen?*
How long have you been having these problems?	*Wie lang haben Sie diese Probleme bereits?*
How often has the problem occurred?	*Wie häufig ist das Problem aufgetreten?*
Does the … rattle / vibrate / make a humming sound / get hot / …?	*Klappert/Vibriert/Brummt der/die/das …? / Wird der/die/das … heiß?*
How old is the …?	*Wie alt ist der/die/das …?*

Suggesting possible solutions

It could be that the … is wearing out.	*Es könnte am Verschleiß des/der … liegen.*
It is not really worth repairing it.	*Eine Reparatur lohnt kaum noch.*
We recommend you replace it.	*Wir empfehlen Ihnen, es zu ersetzen.*
In this case, we generally recommend you …	*In diesem Fall empfehlen wir Ihnen allgemein …*
It might be advisable to …	*Es mag ratsam sein, … zu …*
It would probably be a good idea / better to invest in a(n) …	*Es ist wohl eine gute Idee / besser, in eine/n … zu investieren.*

Adjectives and adverbs

1 Repairing the washing machine is an **easy** job.
2 I need it to be fixed **quickly**.
3 It's **really** inconvenient not having a washing machine.
4 Can it be fixed **easily**?
5 I don't speak German very **well**.

- Man benutzt Adjektive, um Personen oder Sachen näher zu beschreiben (1).
- Adverbien beziehen sich auf Verben (2, 4, 5) oder Adjektive (3).
- Adverbien haben in der Regel eine andere Form als Adjektive. Man fügt normalerweise die Endung *–ly* an das Adjektiv an (2, 3). Endet das Adjektiv auf *–y*, wird die Endung zu *–ily* (4).
- Das Adverb von *good* lautet *well* (5).

Übung auf S. 93

Comparative and superlative forms of adjectives

1 It's the **simplest** and **cheapest** network, but not the **best**.
2 It's **more expensive than** the other networks.
3 You spend **less** money on hardware.
4 It isn't **as easy** to manage **as** the other networks.

- Unregelmäßig sind: *good–better–best, bad–worse–worst, little* (wenig) *–less–least, far–farther/further–farthest/furthest* (1, 3).
- Vergleiche bildet man mit *than* und *(not) as … as* (2, 4).

Übung auf S. 51

Conditional 1

1 **If** we rewire the whole house, it**'ll** be much safer for you.
2 We**'ll** need to put in a new circuit **if** you want an electric cooker.

- Ein *if*-Satz des Typs 1 drückt eine Bedingung aus, die der Sprecher für durchaus möglich oder wahrscheinlich hält. Der damit verbundene Hauptsatz drückt eine Vorhersage aus, die je nach Situation als Warnung, Versprechen o. ä. zu verstehen ist.
- Steht der *if*-Nebensatz an erster Stelle, wird er vom Hauptsatz durch ein Komma getrennt (1).

Übung auf S. 33

Conditional 2

1 I **wouldn't** do that **if** I **was/were** you.
2 **If** you had more money, **would** you buy a bigger house?
3 **If** the motor **was/were** smaller, it **wouldn't** be able to power the machine.

- Durch die Wahl eines *if*-Satzes des Typs 2 gibt der Sprecher seinem Gesprächspartner einen Ratschlag oder teilt ihm mit, dass er die Erfüllung der Bedingung für unmöglich (1), unwahrscheinlich (Spekulationen, Theorien) (2) oder nicht wünschenswert (3) hält.

- Steht der *if*-Nebensatz an erster Stelle, wird er durch ein Komma vom Hauptsatz abgetrennt (2, 3).

Übung auf S. 39

–ing-forms and infinitives

1 I enjoy **driving**.
2 I expect **to drive**.
3 I love **driving**. / I love **to drive**.
4 I'm interested in **driving**.

- Auf eine Gruppe von Verben folgt immer die *–ing*-Form (1).
- Auf eine zweite Gruppe von Verben folgt immer ein Infinitiv (2).
- Auf eine dritte Gruppe von Verben kann sowohl die *–ing*-Form als auch ein Infinitiv folgen (3).
- Nach einer Präposition kommt immer die *–ing*-Form (4).

Übung auf S. 123

Passive forms

1 The roof anchors **are fixed** onto the roof.
2 The scaffolding **was put up** on Tuesday morning.
3 Fossil fuels **have** already **been depleted**.
4 Two solar systems **could be installed** in your house.
5 The meters **will be installed** by us as part of our service.

- Das Passiv wird oft verwendet, wenn man auf eher unpersönliche Art und Weise über Fakten, Vorgänge und Zahlen berichtet.
- Das Passiv wird mit der entsprechenden Form von *be* + Partizip Perfekt (3. Verbform) gebildet. Wie im Aktiv können alle Zeiten gebildet werden.
- Passivsätze mit modalen Hilfsverben werden mit einem modalen Hilfsverb + *be* + Partizip Perfekt (3. Verbform) gebildet (4).
- ‚Von' und ‚durch' werden in Passivsätzen durch *by* ausgedrückt (5).

Übung auf S. 63

Present perfect

1 He**'s worked** here for six months.
2 They **haven't found** the cause of the problem yet.
3 I**'ve talked** to her twice today.
4 **Have** you **been** able to repair the motor?

- Mit dem *present perfect* sagt man, dass (nicht: wann!) etwas geschehen ist. Man drückt damit auch aus, seit wann oder wie lange ein Zustand schon andauert.
- Signalwörter (Zeitadverbien): *for two years, this week, since 1998, already ,yet*; sie benennen einen Zeitraum, auf den sich der Satz bezieht und der bis in die Gegenwart reicht.

Übung auf S. 70

Present progressive

1 One of our customers **is** currently **having** a problem with the power supply.
2 The converters **are disturbing** the power supply.

- Das *present progressive* wird gebraucht, wenn man gerade ablaufende oder noch nicht abgeschlossene Handlungen beschreibt.
- Signalwörter: *at the moment, (right) now, just, currently*.

Übung auf S. 10

Relative clauses

1 Trading standards are doorways **which/that enable goods to enter other countries**.
2 The ISO is the body **(which/that) creates international standards**.
3 Manufacturers are the ones **who have to follow these regulations**.
4 The IEC, **which was created in 1906**, has harmonized the rules worldwide.

- Relativpronomen leiten Relativsätze ein.
- Es gibt den notwendigen und den nicht notwendigen Relativsatz. Notwendige Relativsätze sind für das Verständnis des Satzes unbedingt erforderlich (1, 2, 3) und stehen ohne Komma. Nicht notwendige geben lediglich Zusatzinformationen und werden durch Kommata getrennt (4).
- In notwendigen Relativsätzen kann das Relativpronomen wegfallen, wenn es Objekt ist, d. h. wenn im Relativsatz ein Subjekt steht (2).

Übung auf S. 101

Simple past

1 Last week I **did** a job in a block of flats.
2 I **didn't get** home until 10 a.m.
3 What time **did** you **start** work?
4 My first day at work **was** a disaster.

- Das *simple past* verwendet man, um zu sagen, wann etwas geschehen ist (1, 2, 3), oder um über Vergangenes zu berichten.
- Signalwörter: *yesterday, last week, two days ago, in 1998, When …?*

Übung auf S. 22, 70

Simple present

1 The lighting sometimes **cuts** out.
2 It **doesn't work** when they switch on the cutters.

- Das *simple present* wird für wiederholte, oft regelmäßige Handlungen in der Gegenwart verwendet.
- Signalwörter: *regularly, sometimes, often, always, normally*.
- Manche Verben, die keine Handlung, sondern einen Zustand ausdrücken (*need, like, want, hate, love, know, believe*), stehen (fast) ausschließlich im *simple present*.

Übung auf S. 10

Unit 1, exercise 4: Discussing problems

2

FRAU KÖLLER Ritter Starkstromtechnik, Köller. Was kann ich für Sie tun?
STIG Hello. Do you speak English?
KÖLLER Yes, I do. How can I help?
STIG It's Stig Lindquist from COMSYS AB in Sweden. I'd like to speak to Markus Prinz, please.
KÖLLER Certainly, Mr Lindquist. I'll put you through.
MARKUS Prinz.

Remaining transcript on pp. 8–9

Unit 1, exercise 9: A guided tour of Ritter's factory

3

THOMAS Ah, good morning, Mr Lindquist. My name's Thomas Keller. Welcome to the Ritter switchgear factory.
STIG Good morning, and thanks for taking the time to show me round your factory. By the way, please call me Stig.
THOMAS Fine. Please call me Thomas. Let's start in the showroom here by the main entrance. Please come this way, Stig. Here you can see some examples of our products. We install switchgear in places like shops, hospitals, supermarkets, factories, office buildings, apartment blocks and so on.
STIG Do you make all your own parts?
THOMAS Most of them. We have our own copper and metal workshops here on site, but we get the computer control systems from an external supplier. Let's walk down the corridor past the big conference room on our right. After the conference room you can see our sales offices. We have four of them here. Competition is tough, but we offer a top quality high-tech product at a good price. Let's walk a little further down the corridor past the staff entrance to the electrical design department. This is where we make sure the customer gets the equipment he wants.
STIG Do you make equipment to customers' specifications?
THOMAS Yes, sometimes, but often the customer wants one of our standard models. Let's go into the factory now, shall we? Here on our left is the storeroom. We keep our components here. Let's walk on to the first big workshop on our left after the store room. This is the pre-assembly workshop, and over there behind the pre-assembly workshop on the other side of the wall is the final assembly workshop.
STIG Does that mean they assemble the main parts here and complete the switchgear units over there?
THOMAS Exactly. Our next stop is the copper workshop, so we now have to walk past the testing section on our right to the end of the building. Now we're in the copper workshop. We have a special machine here to bend the copper for the switchgear.
STIG I see. And what about the metal panels? Do you make them yourselves?
THOMAS Yes, we do. We make them in the next workshop, which is the metal workshop. It's next door to the copper workshop just over here. Here in the metal workshop we have another special machine to cut the metal, and you can also see three welding bays over there by the wall, which is where we join the panels.
STIG Very impressive! I thought you would buy these parts from an external supplier.
THOMAS No, we make them ourselves, so we can guarantee the quality of the product. OK, let's now walk back the way we came to the last workshop I want to show you. We first have to walk by the testing section. Over there on our left you can see the lathes and some more welding equipment, and now we're in the assembly, wiring and training workshop.

STIG Assembly, wiring and *training*. Does that mean you train your apprentices here?

THOMAS Yes, we have a master electrician who shows them how to do basic installation work. Over there, for example, you can see two practice installation boards on the wall. The apprentices use them to practise wiring. Our last stop is the break room, where we can sit down and talk to some of the apprentices.

STIG Great idea! By the way, do you have a design department?

THOMAS Yes, the design department is in a separate building outside the factory. I can show it to you later. Now what would you like, tea or coffee?

4

Unit 1, exercise 11: KMK Hörverstehen

CHUCK Good morning, everybody, and thank you for taking the time to come to this presentation. My name's Chuck Henderson. I work for Eaton Industries in Cleveland, Ohio and I'm here to tell you all about our corporation's activities in Germany.
Many of you will remember the famous German Moeller Group which was founded in Cologne in 1899. In the 1920s Hein Moeller introduced assembly line production. Today, the Moeller Group has its headquarters in Bonn and is fully owned by Eaton Industries. It's a great example of a successful German-American partnership.
The Moeller Group first became famous for its contactors. For those of you who are not experts, a contactor is an electrically controlled switch. Way back in the 1910s, Moeller was the first ever European manufacturer to make a three-phase *oil* contactor. It was a breakthrough discovery, and there were many more to come. Today we still sell a lot more than just contactors. Our range includes switchgear devices, foot and palm switches – you know those big red emergency on-off switches you see everywhere? – and programmable logic controllers. In addition to this, we have a wide range of relays and ground fault circuit interrupters – I believe you call them RCDs over here in Europe. In 2008 the Moeller Group, which by then was 100% owned by Eaton, brought out the first digital RCD and also introduced its SmartWire-DT system, which is an 8-pole flat cable which makes interconnecting all the electronic devices in a system a piece of cake. A piece of cake? Sorry, I should have said that the system makes interconnecting devices child's play. Anyone can do it.
Our turnover in Germany is now over a billion euros a year and we have a workforce of 8,600. Oh, and one more thing. We also sponsor a handball club called VfL Gummersbach. They're a great team!
Thanks for coming to the presentation. If you have any questions, please don't hesitate to ask them, and remember to visit our website.

5

Unit 2, exercise 8: Discussing problems with power tools

PETER Right, Jörg. Here we are. This is where we'll be working today.

JÖRG OK. What did you say we're going to be doing?

PETER Well, we're going to be laying a cable in some concrete flooring. To lay the cable, we'll need to cut a trench about four metres long in the concrete. Now, I've got the cable we're going to be laying here. But what tools do you think we're going to need for the job?

JÖRG How about this? The electric drill. We'll need that to cut into the concrete, right?

PETER Well, like I said, we'll be cutting a trench into the concrete floor, so I reckon something else would be better.

JÖRG What about the angle grinder? We could cut long lines in the concrete with that.

PETER Yeah, that's right. But the problem with using that might be that the lines we cut wouldn't be parallel with each other. Now, *this* would be a better tool because the cutting blades are positioned parallel to each other. It would allow us to cut a neat trench into the floor.

JÖRG Eh, sorry. What is that?

PETER It's a wall chaser. Look. See the way the blades are parallel with one another?

JÖRG Yes.

PETER That makes it the ideal tool for this job. Now, we'll need something else to knock out the concrete between the lines we cut. What would you use for that?

JÖRG I think I'd use a chisel and a mallet.

PETER Exactly! Good. OK, so we'll take this lot with us and I'll show you where we're doing the job. You take the chisel and the mallet and that extension cable. I'll take the wall chaser and the cable we're going to lay.
OK, here we are. So, the cable we're going to lay has to run from under this junction box here and over to the other side of this room. It's currently not being used but it's going to be turned into a storage area. Now, you can see that I marked the measurements on the floor when I was here yesterday afternoon so we can see exactly where we have to cut.

JÖRG Great. Can I do it?

PETER Well, sure. But I want to cut the first bit so that you can see what to do. OK, so, I'll just plug the wall chaser into the extension cable … and then line it up with the markings I've made here … and then press down this trigger with my finger and … Wait a minute. That doesn't sound good. It sounds like there's something wrong with the motor, and the blades are hardly rotating.

JÖRG Yes, and there's the smell of smoke.

PETER Well, we can't use this. That's a bit annoying. We need to run back to the office and pick up another wall chaser.

JÖRG OK. Will we put this one into our workshop for one of the lads to repair?

PETER We have to look and see if it's still under warranty. If it is, we can't try to repair it ourselves or else the warranty will be void. If it's not in warranty anymore, it's not really likely that a repair will be worthwhile. We'll probably just buy a new wall chaser and throw this one away.

JÖRG Really? Ah, OK.

6

Unit 3, exercise 2: Meeting customers

TREVOR Hello.

THOMAS Guten Tag. Mein Name ist Thomas Keller von der Firma Ritter in Dortmund. Sind Sie Mr Bell?

TREVOR I'm sorry, I don't speak much German …

THOMAS That's OK, sir. My name's Thomas Keller from Ritter in Dortmund. Are you Mr Bell?

TREVOR Yes, I am. Pleased to meet you.

THOMAS Pleased to meet you. *(They shake hands.)* You phoned us yesterday to discuss the installation work in your office building.

TREVOR Yes, that's right. Come in please. This is my wife, Penny.

THOMAS Pleased to meet you, Mrs Bell.

PENNY Pleased to meet you.

Remaining transcript on p. 27

Unit 3, exercise 5: Explaining how EIB works

7

PENNY I'm still not quite sure what EIB really is, Trevor.

TREVOR Me neither. But I've got the interactive CD on the screen now, so let's have a look at the explanation of the distributor.

PENNY Alright.

TREVOR So it says, 'Click on a field to send a telegram to an actuator'. Let's see what will happen if we click on the 'ceiling light' field. Look, the EIB system sends a telegram to the actuator and the light goes on.

PENNY But surely you could just do that with a light switch!

TREVOR Yes, but remember what the electrician said. You can't operate a light switch remotely. You can do this by sending a telegram to the EIB actuator of a light switch by smartphone. Anyway, let's try the blinds motor. So now the motor's turning to lower the blinds. Let's just click it again. Ah yes! Now the motor's turning the other way to raise the blinds again. You can see on the circuit diagram that it's a two-way switch.

PENNY I still don't see why it's so much better.

TREVOR Well, look at the top field – 'All'. If I click on it, all the devices will come on – look! Now you can't do that with a normal on-off switch, can you? Just imagine how useful this will be if we install it everywhere. With one click you can switch everything off at night, or prepare the showroom for a presentation. That means you could lower the blinds, switch on the video projector, dim the lights and adjust the temperature of the room before you start your presentation – all with one flick of a switch or command from a smartphone. And you can also change the function of a switch later if you want. Hm, I wonder how you do that.

PENNY It says here, 'The system is controlled using software installed on a laptop. You can use this software to change the function of any device in the system. If, for example, the switch next to your bed only switches off the light, you can reprogram it so it switches off the light, lowers the temperature at night and turns on the light over the front door.'

TREVOR Wow!

PENNY Well why didn't they say that in the first place? EIB is brilliant! And I thought it was just an expensive switch!

Unit 3, exercise 6: Planning installations with customers

8

THOMAS Mr Bell, shall we now finish off planning the electrical installation work for the ground floor?

TREVOR Yes, let's do that. I see you've already marked a lot of lighting outlets on the plan, and they're fine. I don't think we can have too many of them because lighting is so important in an office. So let's now take a look at the security features on the ground floor, shall we?

THOMAS Yes, and I'll mark them on the plan. So shall we start with the sliding gate?

TREVOR Yes, we'll need a camera and a motion detector there, I think.

THOMAS And what about lighting, especially at night?

TREVOR Good idea. We can put a spotlight there too, linked to the camera, so it comes on at night if someone walks or drives in. Can you program it to do that?

THOMAS No problem, Mr Bell. What about the underground car park? You'll need another camera and motion detector there to record all movements in and out, won't you?

TREVOR Yes, but I don't think we'll need to link it to the spotlight.

THOMAS No, that won't be necessary.

TREVOR OK, so let's say a visitor comes in through the gate and walks to the entrance of the building. I'd like a motion detector and a camera at the entrance to show the receptionist that someone's coming and another motion detector and camera in the entrance hall.

THOMAS OK, I've marked that and I've added another motion detector by the lifts and stairs, so you know if there are people walking through the entrance hall. We can link that motion detector to the camera near the main entrance.

TREVOR Ah, yes. I hadn't thought of that.

THOMAS Shall we now mark in any other cameras and motion detectors needed?

TREVOR Yes, so where else do we need them?

THOMAS I suggest you have a camera and motion detector inside the building in reception, by the side door, over the flower beds here and in the break area.

TREVOR Hm, I don't think we can have a camera and motion detector there because the employees won't want to think Big Brother is watching them!

THOMAS OK, fine. Now what about motion detectors on their own? Do we need any more of them?

TREVOR Well, I would say we need one between the two meeting rooms, one outside the three offices and one in each of the three offices.

THOMAS Right, I've marked that. Now how about dimmers?

TREVOR Yes, I'd like five dimmers in all. One in the entrance hall, one in the conference room, one in reception, one outside the storeroom and one by the offices.

THOMAS Why do you want one outside the storeroom *and* outside the offices? The lighting in the corridors will be linked, and we can dim it all with one dimmer.

TREVOR OK, fine. Cut the dimmer outside the storeroom.

THOMAS Right. Anything else?

TREVOR Yes, just one more thing. I'm going to plant some special flowers in the flower beds, so I want two spotlights over them.

THOMAS Fine, we'll do that. No problem at all, Mr Bell.

9

Unit 3, exercise 9: KMK Hörverstehen

YOU Ritter Installation, Keller. Was kann ich für Sie tun?

STIG Good morning. Could I speak to Markus Prinz, please?

YOU I'm sorry, Markus Prinz is out of the office at the moment. Can I take a message?

STIG Yes, would you tell him Stig Lindquist from COMSYS AB in Sweden called?

YOU Sure, I'd be happy to. Could you just spell your name for me, please?

STIG Yes, certainly. My first name's Stig spelt S–T–I–G and my surname's L–I–N–D–Q–U–I–S–T. My company's called COMSYS AB – spelt C–O–M–S–Y–S A–B, and we're located in Sweden.

YOU OK, Stig Lindquist from COMSYS AB in Sweden. Is there a phone number he can reach you on, Mr Lindquist?

STIG Yes, my phone number's 0046 84 75 73 59.

YOU 0046 84 75 73 59.

STIG Yes. That's my office number. If I'm not in, he can leave a message with my secretary.

YOU OK, I've got that. What message would you like me to give Mr Prinz?

STIG Would you tell him that I'll be flying in to Düsseldorf Airport next Thursday, arriving at 10.15 a.m.

YOU Düsseldorf ... Thursday ... 10.15 a.m.

STIG And please tell him that I would like to go straight from the airport to the meat-processing plant in Dortmund to examine the filters we've installed there.

YOU … examine the filters at the meat-processing plant in Dortmund. Right, I've got that. Was there anything else, Mr Lindquist?
STIG Yes, please tell him I would also like to visit the switchgear factory again.
YOU You've visited us before, have you?
STIG Yes, and I'd like to visit again because I may have a customer for your latest product.
YOU Oh, that sounds good. Thank you for that.
STIG Sure, no problem. I'll be staying for three days, so that should give us time to arrange a visit.
YOU Right, I've got all that. Is there anything else I can do for you, Mr Lindquist?
STIG That's all, thanks.
YOU And I'll pass your message on to Mr Prinz as soon as he's back in the office. Thanks for calling, and for recommending us to the customer.
STIG Yes, I hope that works out. Well, you have a good day.
YOU You too.
STIG Bye-bye.
YOU Bye.

10

Unit 4, exercise 3B: A wiring diagram for a penthouse kitchen

THOMAS Right, so let's start with the electric cooker. Where would you like it?
PENNY I want all the cooking equipment along the top wall. I want an eye-level oven to the right of the window and the ceramic hob to the left of it.
THOMAS Oven to the right of the window, which means a 400 volt junction box, hob to the left of it … I've got that. And what about the rest of that wall? What else do you want along it?
PENNY I'd like to plug in a toaster in the left-hand corner and perhaps a mixer there, too. And then between the toaster and the ceramic hob I'd like a microwave.
THOMAS So we want a double socket in the left-hand corner, a single socket for the microwave and another single socket for the hob. Will you want a cooker hood with an extractor fan over the hob to extract the cooking fumes?
PENNY Oh yes, of course!
THOMAS So that's a double, a single and a double socket to the left of the window. Anything else to the *right* of the window apart from the eye-level oven?
PENNY Yes, I'd like an eye-level grill to the right of the eye-level oven and also a coffee machine in the right-hand corner.
THOMAS So that's another socket to the right of the oven for the grill and one more to the right of that for the coffee machine. OK. Is that everything along the top wall?
PENNY Yes, I think so.
THOMAS Good. Let's look at the left-hand wall now. We've already got a few things there. Anything else?
PENNY Yes, I also want a socket for cable TV.
THOMAS Alright. Where would you like the cable TV socket?
PENNY In the top left-hand corner near the end of the wall.
THOMAS So that's a cable TV socket in the top left-hand corner near the end of the wall on the left. And we'll also need a single socket to plug in the TV next to the cable TV socket.
PENNY Oh yes, of course. I was forgetting.
THOMAS Now, your husband said he wanted a motion detector in every room, so where shall we put it in the kitchen?

PENNY How about in the bottom left-hand corner over the fridge? It would be out of the way there.

THOMAS Well, if we had it there, the high fridge/freezer would perhaps block it. If I were you, I'd put it in the top left-hand corner over the cable TV socket. It'll have a clear view of the door and windows if we put it there.

PENNY Oh, yes, you're right.

THOMAS Good. Now we only have to talk about the light switches. How about to the left of the door as you walk in?

PENNY Yes, that's a good place.

THOMAS I suggest you have three light switches and a dimmer, too. Will there be a buzzer to buzz people in who ring at your door from downstairs?

PENNY Yes, and it's going to be a video intercom.

THOMAS Video intercom, three light switches and a dimmer to the left of the kitchen door ... right, I've marked all that. So all in all we have ... 17 sockets, five light switches, one dimmer, one video intercom, one TV socket and 11 lighting outlets.

Unit 5, exercise 5: A phone call from Odette

12

MATTHIAS Hallo, Matthias Marquardt. Was kann ich für Sie tun?

ODETTE Hello Matthias. It's Odette Alexander from FruitsFrais.

MATTHIAS Hi, Odette. How are you?

ODETTE Fine, thanks. Listen, I just wanted to say thanks for your e-mail and to confirm what we want to do.

MATTHIAS OK.

ODETTE So, obviously we'd like to go ahead and order the two aluminium sliding doors along with the PLC. I think it's the solution we're looking for.

MATTHIAS That's great, Odette. What about my suggestion about installing automated lighting?

ODETTE Yes, I think that sounds like a good idea. And it's not too expensive, so we'd like to go for that as well.

MATTHIAS Fine. How did you feel about our suggestion that you should install a fan?

ODETTE Well, I can see what you mean about it helping to control the warehouse temperature, but that's going to be just a bit too expensive for us.

MATTHIAS OK.

ODETTE But apart from that, everything that you proposed is fine. We just have to arrange when you could install the new doors and PLC system.

MATTHIAS Yes, sometime in around three weeks would be possible. Let me just check our schedule ... Yes, one of our installation teams is going to be near you doing a job on Tuesday, the fourth of May, and we'll be finished the same day. Would it be possible for us to come to you first thing on Wednesday morning?

ODETTE Let me see. No, I'm afraid not. We're going to be finishing off a large special order on that morning. Doing the installation then would slow us down too much.

MATTHIAS Right. Well, would we be able to start work in the afternoon? We could then finish the job the next morning.

ODETTE Yes, OK. That sounds like it could work. We'll have finished off the order by around 1 p.m. at the latest. Would you be able to start at half one?

MATTHIAS Yes, that'll be fine. We'll come to FruitFrais, 43 Rue de la Plaine, Strasbourg 67025.

ODETTE Yes, splendid. Well, I look forward to meeting your team on the fifth, then. Thanks, Matthias.

MATTHIAS It's my pleasure.

Unit 5, exercise 9: KMK Hörverstehen

13

ANSWERPHONE You have two messages. Message one. Monday, July 4th, 8.25 a.m.

BRIAN Hello. This is Brian Anderson from Five Star Computers in Dublin, Ireland. I was hoping to speak to Sheila Clark in the Sales department but ... OK ... she doesn't seem to be about just now. I just want to confirm an order with her. I've already done it by e-mail but I thought it would be better if I also called in person.
I discussed the XT9 Micro PLC with Sheila last week and just wanted to confirm now that we have decided against this model and would like to order the XT9ZA instead.
I'd also like to suggest a date that will work from our point of view with the installation. Would it be possible for you to install the PLC on Thursday, 14th July? We're going to be stopping production on that day to carry out maintenance on some of our production equipment so, if that day would work for you, it would certainly also be ideal for us.
Anyway, I'd be grateful if this message could be passed onto Sheila. Oh, and I'll be out of the office in the next few days so she can reach me on my mobile number. That's 0173 453 467 654. I repeat 0173 453 467 654.
Thanks. Bye.

ANSWERPHONE Message two. Monday, July 4th, 8.45 a.m.

GERTRUDE Hello, this is Gertrude Feroni. I'll spell my surname for you: F–E–R–O–N–I. Feroni. I work for the company Manchester Foods in Manchester, England. We've received a very interesting e-mail from Sheila Clark in Sales. She's made us an offer to install a PLC on our production line, and we would like to go ahead with this. It's the PLC model number 44A.
We would like you to install it as soon as possible. Would tomorrow be possible? I suppose you're booked up, but it would be great if you could install tomorrow. Hopefully you have the PLC 44A in stock already. If not, please order it right away.
Could you have Ms Clark call me back, please? My number is 052 899 2525. That's 052 899 2525.
Thank you. Bye

Unit 6, exercise 5: Numerical expressions

15

a 43 (forty-three)
b 14.3 (fourteen point three)
c 5,376 (five thousand three hundred and seventy-six)
d 76,927 (seventy-six thousand nine hundred and twenty-seven)
e 59,473.48 (fifty-nine thousand four hundred and seventy-three point four eight)
f 476,902.08 (four hundred and seventy-six thousand nine hundred and two point oh eight)

Unit 6, exercise 6: Explaining how PV systems work

16

JEAN-CLAUDE Well, thanks for running through the steps of the installation for me.

IRENE No problem at all.

JEAN-CLAUDE Would it be possible just to go over how the system will generate electricity again?

IRENE Yes, sure. Look, I have a diagram here which will help explain. So, on the roof you can see the PV array. Direct current is produced by this and is changed into alternating current by an inverter. Then the electricity you produce is fed straight into the national grid.

JEAN-CLAUDE Oh, yes.

IRENE The electricity you produce is bought by your electricity provider. Then you take electricity from the national grid in the normal way for all your household appliances.

JEAN-CLAUDE And that's why the system requires two meters?

IRENE Right. The power you sell to the grid is measured by one, and the power you buy from the grid is measured by the other.

JEAN-CLAUDE OK. Remind me. Do I need to get the electricity company to install the meters?

IRENE No, you don't. The meters will be installed by us as part of our service.

Unit 6, exercise 7: Explaining other domestic energy systems

17

CUSTOMER So, you're saying that a solar system is really not going to work here.

IRENE I'm afraid not. Your house roof doesn't face in the right direction. You simply wouldn't have enough sunlight to make the investment in the system worthwhile.

CUSTOMER Well, that is disappointing.

IRENE Don't worry, though. I have a couple of suggestions which you may like to think about.

CUSTOMER Oh, OK. Go on.

IRENE Well, you might not get much sunlight here, but you do get plenty of wind. You could think about installing a domestic wind turbine like the Honeywell.

CUSTOMER I'm not sure I'd want one of these noisy things anywhere near my house.

IRENE Yes, but the technology has been developed dramatically in recent years. A turbine like the Honeywell, for example, operates really quite quietly. In traditional wind power systems, the wind is used to turn a generator which produces the electricity. Not only is this quite inefficient, it's also noisy. The Honeywell uses a system where the electricity is generated at the tip of the rotating blades. So it's quieter and more efficient. Basically, electricity is generated by a rotation speed of as little as two miles per hour. I think a system like this could be installed quite successfully here.

CUSTOMER Well, that does sound interesting. Is it expensive?

IRENE Well, yes, I'm afraid it is quite expensive. But you might also like to think about one of the new types of electrochemical CHP units.

CUSTOMER What's a CHP unit?

IRENE Oh, sorry. CHP stands for Combined Heat and Power. It's a power unit which uses gas to produce both heat and electricity, which is very efficient. Electrochemical CHPs don't actually burn the gas so there's a significant cut in emissions. Instead the gas is converted into hydrogen and then, by means of an electrochemical process, the hydrogen becomes electricity.

CUSTOMER Yes, that is interesting. I'll have to think about it.

Unit 7, exercise 2: Radio ham saves rock star

18

ARMIN CQ CQ, this is DC2GO in Freiburg, Germany. Anybody there?

RANDY This is Victor Oscar 22 Foxtrot in Cleveland, Ohio. I can hear you loud and clear.

ARMIN Hi Randy. Good to hear from you. Have you got a moment to spare?

RANDY Hi Armin. Yes, I'll be glad to help. Fire away.

ARMIN I'm looking at a guitar amp here in my radio shack right now. It belongs to Tom Vincent, the rock guitarist. He has a gig tonight here in Freiburg, but his amp isn't working. It went dead during the sound check about two hours ago. Since then I've replaced the glass fuse, which was blown, and checked the mains lead, which was fine. Anyway, I've just switched the amp back on, but it still hasn't started working again. Any ideas?

RANDY I hope your shack has a ground fault circuit interrupter, Armin. If not, you could electrocute yourself!

ARMIN Don't worry! We call that type of circuit breaker an RCD over here. I have one in the circuit.

RANDY That's good to hear. OK, so have the mains and standby control lights come on?

ARMIN Yes, they have.

RANDY So now look at the back of the amp and check to see if the tubes have come on. They should be illuminated.

ARMIN OK, here we go ... Yes, the tubes have come on.

RANDY Well, that's good because that shows they haven't blown. Disconnect the AC mains lead and remove the back panel of the amplifier.

ARMIN OK ... I've removed the back panel and can see inside the amp.

RANDY Now you need to carry out a sensory check. Can you see charred wires anywhere? Is there a smell of burning?

ARMIN No, nothing at all but, hey, what's this? It's the schematic of the amp! I think we're in luck.

RANDY Yes, that's very helpful. Find the transformer and check out the output voltages.

ARMIN Just a moment ... according to the schematic, the transformer has five output voltages. Three rectified low voltage outputs for the semi-conductors, one to heat the tubes and one high-voltage output to a bridge rectifier.

RANDY Well, I guess the high voltage rectifier provides the DC output to power the tubes, so the DC output is what we need to check first. Do you have a multimeter there, Armin?

ARMIN Yes, I do.

RANDY In that case I suggest you measure the output voltage of the rectifier. I think I know what it's going to be ...
(A few minutes later)

ARMIN OK, I've measured the output voltage of the rectifier and it's zero!

RANDY Just as I thought. So now we know where the fault is, but we still need to know if the transformer's not supplying the voltage to the rectifier or if the rectifier's not changing AC into DC.

ARMIN Exactly. So I'll either need a new transformer or some diodes for a new rectifier. I'll get started on that now. Thanks for your help, Randy.

RANDY You're welcome, Armin. Take care.

Unit 7, exercise 8A, C: Using a data sheet

19

ARMIN CQ CQ, this Kilo Sierra 90 Mike in Freiburg, Germany. Are you there, Randy?

RANDY Victor Oscar 22 Foxtrot in Cleveland, Ohio. Hi, Armin. I'm receiving you loud and clear. How's the repair job going?

ARMIN I'm making progress, Randy.

RANDY That's good to hear. So do you have to replace the transformer or the rectifier?

ARMIN The transformer's fine. It's producing an output voltage of 308.5 volts to the rectifier but the output voltage of the rectifier is zero.

RANDY Just as I thought!

ARMIN Yes, so now I have to replace the rectifier. For that I need four BYW56s, according to the schematic. I already have four BYW52s here in my radio shack, so do you think I could use them instead?

RANDY You have to be very careful with diodes, Armin! You could blow the amp again with the wrong ones. Do you have the data sheet there?

ARMIN Yes, I've downloaded it from the internet.

RANDY Great! Let's look at some of the most important data on it, to see if you can use what you have there. First of all, we need to know the average forward current.

ARMIN It's 2 amps for both the BYW52 and the BYW56.

RANDY OK, so that means the BYW52 will provide the right current but what we really need to know is what will happen if there's a surge.

ARMIN A surge?

RANDY I mean if the current suddenly increases massively. A surge is like an electrical tsunami. If the load shoots up unexpectedly, will the diodes handle it or blow?

ARMIN So where do I find that out?

RANDY First, tell me what the value for the peak forward surge current is.

ARMIN It's 50 amps for both. It also says tp = 10 ms half sine wave for both. Is that important?

RANDY Yes, that means that both diodes can handle a peak forward current of 50 amps for a maximum time of ten milliseconds – meaning 'for half a sine wave' – because the power supply to the rectifier is alternating current.

ARMIN Ah yes, 308.5 volts AC.

RANDY Well, there's no difference so far, so let's look at the repetitive peak reverse voltage. What are the values?

ARMIN It's 200 volts for the BYW52 and 1,000 volts for the BYW56.

RANDY Well, I think we have our answer to your question, Armin. If you use BYW52s, they won't be able to handle a reverse voltage of 1,000 volts. You need diodes that can handle 1,000 volts!

ARMIN OK, thanks a lot. I'll call some of the local radio hams and get four BYW56s.

RANDY Yes, but it doesn't have to be BYW56s. You can also use other diodes with similar maximum ratings. As long as the average forward current is 2 amps and the repetitive peak reverse voltage is 1,000 volts, you'll have what you need.

ARMIN Good. Thanks for all your help, Randy.

RANDY You're welcome, Armin, and good luck!

Unit 8, exercise 5: Giving and getting instructions

20

MARTTI Could you explain something to me, Dennis? I think I've understood but I'm not quite sure. Does Herr Böhm want us to make what it says in this circuit diagram?

DENNIS Yes, that's right. It's a battery charger. We have to get all the components we need, assemble them on a circuit board and test the battery charger at different points and explain how it works.

MARTTI I see. Will we have to buy the parts?

DENNIS No, we won't. We have them all here in our store.

MARTTI Oh, I see. I'm not quite sure what sort of battery we will be able to charge with it. Will it be a car battery?

DENNIS No, look here ... The voltage regulator in the circuit only supplies a low amperage, and you need about 10 amps for a car battery.

MARTTI I see. But there's an adjustable voltage regulator in the circuit. Does that mean it can recharge different types of batteries?

DENNIS Yes, but only low-power batteries. This type of circuit can't charge a car battery.

MARTTI And do we have to test the battery charger on a rechargeable battery?

DENNIS We can if we want, of course, but we don't have to. Herr Böhm's more interested in the readings we get when we test the circuit. Let's go to the store with a list of all the parts we need and then look up the voltage regulator on the internet.

Unit 8, exercise 6: Understanding spoken technical details

21

MARTTI I think I've got all the components we need now.

DENNIS Good, but we'd better check to make sure. We mustn't forget anything otherwise it won't work! You tell me what we need and I'll make sure we've got it.

MARTTI OK. We need a 2-amp fuse and a 0.2-amp fuse and a …

DENNIS Just a moment – not too fast! They're pretty small … Right, we've got them. Now what's the next part?

MARTTI A transformer with a 12 V output.

DENNIS We've certainly got the transformer. It's so big you can't miss it! How about diodes? How many of them have we got?

MARTTI We've got five diodes all the same. They're 1N4004 diodes.

DENNIS One, two three four, five – OK, we've got them. Now have we got more than one of anything else?

MARTTI Yes, we've got two electrolytic capacitors.

DENNIS Both the same?

MARTTI No. One's a 2,200 µF / 25 V electrolytic capacitor.

DENNIS Just a minute. I'm just checking what it says on them. The writing's very small. What's the other one?

MARTTI The other one's a 10 µF / 25 V electrolytic capacitor.

DENNIS Yes, we've got both. One's a lot bigger than the other one. Anything else?

MARTTI We've got three more things on our list. There's the LM117 adjustable integrated voltage regulator …

DENNIS Here it is, and it's got a heat sink to stop it from getting too hot.

MARTTI Ah yes. I see. OK, the next component is a 220 Ω resistor.

DENNIS Another very small part, but they're colour-coded to make it a bit easier to identify them. Right, we've got it. And the last part?

MARTTI The last part is a 4.7 kΩ potentiometer.

DENNIS OK, we've got that, too. Now we can get started.

Unit 9, exercise 3C: Electric motor nameplates

22

Conversation 1

CUSTOMER As I said, the engine has been making a strange noise and running a bit hot for the last couple of days.

SERVICE AGENT And just to confirm: You did say it's a three-phase induction.

CUSTOMER Yes, that's right.

SERVICE AGENT OK. Could you give me the date of manufacture, please?

CUSTOMER Sure, I'll take a look. Oh, wait. The date's been a bit blotted out on the name plate. I can't really read it.

SERVICE AGENT No problem. Just give me the serial number and …

Conversation 2

SERVICE ENGINEER 1 Anyway, I'm with the customer now and am taking a look at the motor. The thing is, I haven't seen one just like this before. I was hoping I could ask you a few questions about it before I get started.

SERVICE ENGINEER 2 Sure, Mike. What's the model number?

SERVICE ENGINEER 1 Well, that's the thing. I can't really read it.

SERVICE ENGINEER 2 Oh, right. Well give me a few more details about the name plate then.

SERVICE ENGINEER 1 Well, it's a three-phase, obviously.

SERVICE ENGINEER 2 Yeah, obviously. But what kind of frame does it have?

SERVICE ENGINEER 1 Ehhh … hold on … 286 T.

SERVICE ENGINEER 2 And continuous duty, yeah?

SERVICE ENGINEER 1 That's right.

SERVICE ENGINEER 2 And NEMA B, right?

SERVICE ENGINEER 1 Yeah.

SERVICE ENGINEER 2 What about its revs per minute.

SERVICE ENGINEER 1 Ehhh … one, seven, sixty-five.

SERVICE ENGINEER 2 Ah, OK. 30 horse power?

SERVICE ENGINEER 1 Yeah.

SERVICE ENGINEER 2 Well, in that case, I suppose you must be dealing with a …

24

Unit 10, exercise 2A–B: A checklist for business trips

MARK OK. Everybody's here. Right, let's get started then. As you know, the aim of today's meeting is to brainstorm a checklist of the things that our people should take with them when they're travelling abroad. The idea is to avoid the problems which arise when people forget things. So, let me just make a suggestion to get us started. In my opinion, the first two things on the list should be passport and travel documents. Ah, Conrad. I see you have something to say. Would you like to come in here?

CONRAD Yes, thanks. Well, as far as I'm concerned, things like passport and tickets are really obvious. I mean, they're so obvious, they don't need to be on a list. It would be more appropriate to have the documentation relating to the job you're travelling to do at the top of the list. This would save us having to e-mail these to our installation people when they forget them. Do you know what I mean?

MARK OK, yes. That's a point. Eva. What do you think?

EVA Well, in my opinion, Conrad is right. The list shouldn't be too long and should only contain really important items. We haven't had any cases where staff have forgotten their plane tickets. But they do routinely forget job-related paperwork. They also forget to take the right tools with them quite a lot, so I reckon we should mention that as well.

CONRAD Yes, that's right. If you ask me, the list should also include taking a company credit card to cover expenses while on trips. We have had several cases where these have not been taken. It wastes a lot of time both for us at headquarters and for staff who are out on the road.

MARK Right. These all seem like pretty sound suggestions. These items should definitely be on the list. I do still think that we should mention passport and tickets though.

25 Unit 11, exercise 2A: Discussing plans for an installation abroad

MIKE Hello there. Mike Oliver here. I was hoping to speak to you about the arrangements for your trip to India on 25 September. I'll send you an e-mail later with the details. But here they are anyway in the meantime.

So, your flight departs at 4.30 p.m. on the 25th from London Heathrow. Don't forget to check in at least one hour before your departure time. You'll be flying with India Airways and your flight number is IA 3487. Now, unfortunately I couldn't get you on a direct flight so you have a two-hour stopover in Abu Dhabi. You'll also be making the next leg of your journey with India Airways, this time on flight number IA 4539.

Your scheduled time of arrival at your destination is 7.15 a.m. local time. A driver provided by the customer is picking you up at the airport. He'll take you to your hotel – that's the Palace International. He's going to drive your around during your stay so you won't need to take your driving licence. But please do remember to take your passport and the travel documents which I'll be sending to you by next Monday at the latest. Oh, and please also remember that you'll be responsible for collecting the receipts for anything you buy during the trip using the company credit card.

OK. That's it just now. If you have any questions, just give me a call.

26 Unit 11, exercise 3C: At the airport

CHECK-IN CLERK Good morning, sir.

SEBASTIAN Good morning.

CHECK-IN CLERK Can I have your passport and ticket, please?

SEBASTIAN Yes, sure. Here we are.

CHECK-IN CLERK OK. So, you're flying to China?

SEBASTIAN That's right.

CHECK-IN CLERK I'm afraid I have to tell you that your flight is going to be a little late in leaving. Sorry about that. We expect it to depart around forty minutes later than scheduled.

SEBASTIAN Oh, dear. Well, never mind. At least I'll have a chance to buy some magazines.

CHECK-IN CLERK OK, now how many pieces of luggage are you taking with you?

SEBASTIAN Well, I have these two bags for the hold and then I'd like to take these two small bags with me on the plane.

CHECK-IN CLERK Oh, I'm sorry, sir. I'm afraid it's only possible to take one piece of hand luggage onto the aircraft.

SEBASTIAN Ah, OK, I see. Oh dear. Hm, what can I do? I certainly don't want to leave a bag here. I guess I should have checked the baggage limits on your website. I know what I can do. I just need to take something out of this bag and then put the bag in my case ... OK.

CHECK-IN CLERK Right, would you like to put your bag on the scale, please?

SEBASTIAN OK, there we go.

CHECK-IN CLERK Thank you. 16 kilograms. That's fine.

SEBASTIAN Would it be possible for me to have a window seat?

CHECK-IN CLERK Let me just check. The flight is almost full so it might not be possible. No, I'm afraid we don't have any window seats left.

SEBASTIAN Ah, OK.

CHECK-IN CLERK Sorry about that. Here's your boarding card. Your flight departs from gate 19c. Please be at the departure gate no later than 30 minutes before the flight departs.

Unit 11, exercise 6A–C: Giving presentations

27

SEBASTIAN Good morning, everybody. My name's Sebastian Eiffel, and I work for Pactec. I'm going to be talking to you this morning about the procedure for setting up the PT 169s sensors and PLC. Now, most of the machine's set-up takes place in our factory in Germany. You really can more or less plug-and-play the PT169 straight out of the box. But the external sensors and the PLC control console come separately packaged. I want to look now at how we will mount these. If anyone has any questions, I'll be happy to answer them at the end of my presentation.

To begin with, I'd like to talk about the reasons for the separate packaging of the sensors and PLC unit. Basically, these are delicate components which require extra protection during shipping. We feel that we can best achieve this by packaging them separately and mounting them on site. I want to emphasize that we won't need to mount all of the machine's sensors. Those which are located internally are mounted before the machine leaves our factory and can stay in place during shipping because of the extra protection their position gives them.

Let's move on to how we will go about this. The sensors will be mounted first. The PT 169 will be fully wired on arrival so once the sensors have been screwed in place they just need to be connected to the machine. The next step will be to mount the PLC control console and connect it.

Now I want to turn to the testing procedure. We will carry out a test to ensure that the sensors are mounted at the correct angles and are properly wired up. Now, monitoring sensor performance is something we'll do when we're carrying out the test run. However, the PLC software contains a test module which allows us to run a preliminary sensor test.

Though it may appear quite complex, I want to conclude by saying that installing the PT 169 is really quite straightforward, and we shouldn't expect any difficulties. So, I'm looking forward to working with you to get the machine up and running. If there are any questions, I'd be happy to answer them now.

Unit 12, exercise 8: Interviewing for jobs

28

JESSICA Hello Maik. My name's Jessica Teesdale. Pleased to meet you.

MAIK Pleased to meet you.

JESSICA Please take a seat.

MAIK Thanks.

JESSICA Now as I said on the telephone I'm looking for electricians to work for a contractor operating globally, starting here in Colchester, so let's first take a look at your CV, shall we? Please take me through it.

MAIK Yes, certainly. At the moment I'm just finishing a three-year training course at an electrical contractor's called Elektro Wilhelm in Frankfurt. I've worked in private houses, shops, hospitals and on building sites doing electrical installation, maintenance and repair work and I must say that I like working on big projects, like factories or industrial sites.

JESSICA Hm, why's that?

MAIK It's good to work with other people, have a target and get the work done on time. I also like to work outside in the fresh air.

JESSICA Right. Now would you like to say a few words about your hobbies and interests?

MAIK As you can see from my CV, I like playing football and I train twice a week and I'm a member of the Federal Agency for Technical Relief – what we call the THW – I'm in the Electric Supply group and I've learned a lot about what to do in an emergency.

JESSICA I see. So would you describe yourself as a team player?
MAIK Yes, I'd say that. I'm in a team at the THW, I enjoy working with other people and I play in a football team.
JESSICA Right. Do you have any other hobbies?
MAIK Yes, do. I like building computers and robots.
JESSICA Good. Now what are your strengths?
MAIK I'm hard-working, punctual and reliable. If I need help, I ask for it and I'm happy to help other people, too.
JESSICA And your weaknesses?
MAIK I don't have much experience because as an apprentice you have to do the routine work under supervision. I need more experience, really.
JESSICA I see. Now why did you train to become an electrician?
MAIK It's in the family. My dad's an electrician, so I know what it means to be one.
JESSICA What made you apply for this job in particular?
MAIK I want experience with a big company outside Germany because my apprenticeship is only the beginning. My brother worked in Ireland for two years and he learned a lot, so I want to do the same sort of thing. I've always wanted to work in the UK, and this is my chance.
JESSICA And why should we employ you and not someone else?
MAIK I expect to get a good final grade at the end of my apprenticeship and I really want to work somewhere very different.
JESSICA All right. And what are your plans for the future?
MAIK I want to set up my own business. I'll need to be a master electrician, but first I want to see the world.
JESSICA I see. Do you have any questions you'd like to ask?
MAIK Yes, please. What age are the other employees at the company in the UK, and what other countries could I perhaps work in?

KMK mock exam, exercise 1: Hörverstehen

29

APPRENTICE Schattauer Installationstechnik, Klopp. Was kann ich für Sie tun?
CALLER Good morning. I hope you speak English because I don't speak much German.
APPRENTICE No problem, sir. How can I help you?
CALLER Well, my name's Jess Johnson and my company is Data Solutions Incorporated. We're building a data centre near Freiburg, Germany next year. We've been given your company's name by a German business partner who tells us that you do electrical installation work in high-security buildings.
APPRENTICE That's exactly right, Mr Johnson. We're specialists in this field. Could you give me some more details of what your company needs?
CALLER Well, our data centre is going to be built next year, and we'll need a lot of security features. For example, we'll need an electronic alarm system that can be activated easily when the building is empty – at night or at weekends, for example.
APPRENTICE We can do that for you, Mr Johnson. What other security features will you need?
CALLER Well, apart from a burglar alarm, we'll need access control, so we can log the movements of all employees and visitors entering the building and moving from place to place inside it. Our data is so sensitive and so attractive to data thieves that we must know who enters the building and where they go. Can you do that, too?
APPRENTICE Oh yes, we can. We do a lot of work for banks over here and we install access control using the EIB system.
CALLER EIB? Never heard of it. How does it work?

APPRENTICE Well, basically, every electrical device in the building has an actuator, which can be controlled digitally. In that way we can install and link all the actuators needed in the ceilings and walls and so on with a minimum of work. You then only need a laptop or a smartphone to program the system. And you can do that from anywhere in the world. Would you like us to send you some sales literature, Mr Johnson?

CALLER Sure, that would be great. And I'll be in Germany next week to talk to the architect, so let's set up a meeting.

APPRENTICE I'll do that for you, Mr Johnson. May I have your e-mail address and cell phone number, please?

CALLER Yes, my e-mail's jess.johnson@dsi.org. I'll spell that for you. J–E–S–S dot J–O–H–N–S–O–N at D–S–I dot O–R–G. Have you got that?

APPRENTICE Yes, and your cell phone number, please?

CALLER It's 001 707 499 3877.

APPRENTICE 001 707 499 3877. OK, I've got everything I need for the time being. We'll e-mail you some brochures on EIB straight away. And I'll arrange that meeting.

CALLER Wonderful.

APPRENTICE Thanks for calling, Mr Johnson.

CALLER Bye-bye.

APPRENTICE Bye.

Basic word list

Dieses Liste enthält Grundwörter, die in *Electricity Matters – 3rd Edition* als bekannt vorausgesetzt werden.

A
able, to be ~ können, in der Lage sein
about über, etwa
above über, oben(stehend), oben genannt
absolutely absolut, völlig
accept annehmen, akzeptieren
across (quer) über
active aktiv(iert)
activity Tätigkeit, Aktivität
add zusammenzählen, hinzufügen
address Adresse; adressieren
advert(isement) Werbung, Anzeige
afraid, I'm ~ leider
after (all) schließlich (doch)
afternoon Nachmittag
again wieder
age Alter
agree zustimmen, vereinbaren
aim Ziel, Absicht
air Luft
airport Flughafen
all alle(s)
allow erlauben, gestatten, (zu)lassen
almost fast, beinahe
alone allein(e)
along entlang
already schon, bereits
also auch, außerdem
although obwohl
altogether insgesamt
always immer
a.m. vormittags, morgens (vor 12 Uhr)
among zwischen, unter
amount Menge, Betrag
angry wütend, verärgert
another noch eine/r/s
answer Antwort, Lösung; (be)antworten
any irgendetwas, -welche, jede
anybody jemand, jede/r
anyone jemand, jede/r
anything etwas, alles
anyway jedenfalls, sowieso
anywhere irgendwo(hin)
apart from abgesehen von, außer
area Gebiet, Bereich
arrange arrangieren, vereinbaren
arrival Ankunft
arrive ankommen
ask fragen, bitten
assistant Assistent/in
away weg, entfernt

B
back Rückseite, Rücken; zurück
bad schlecht, schlimm
badly sehr
bag Tasche, Tüte, Beutel
basic grundsätzlich, einfach
basically grundsätzlich, im Grunde
because weil
become werden
before vor(her)
begin anfangen, beginnen
beginning Anfang
behind hinter, hinten
believe glauben
belong gehören
below unter, unten(stehend)
beneath unter(halb), unten
beside neben
best beste, am besten
better besser
between zwischen
big groß
bit Stück
board Brett, Tafel
body Körper
book Buch; buchen, reservieren
boring langweilig
bored gelangweilt
born geboren
boss Chef/in
both beide
bottle Flasche
bottom Unterseite, Unterteil, Boden, Ende
box Kasten, Kästchen, Kiste, Schachtel
bracket Klammer
breakfast Frühstück
bring bringen, holen
broad breit
broken kaputt
busy beschäftigt, besetzt
button Taste, Knopf
buy kaufen
bye tschüs

C
call Anruf; (an)rufen
caller Anrufer/in
camera Fotoapparat
can dürfen, können
cannot nicht können
car Auto
car park Parkplatz, Parkhaus
care, take ~ of sich kümmern um
careful(ly) vorsichtig, sorgfältig
case Fall
cash Bargeld
chain Kette
chair Stuhl
change (Ver-)Änderung; (aus)wechseln, (sich) ändern
cheap billig, günstig
check überprüfen, kontrollieren
cheque Scheck
choice Wahl, Auswahl
choose (aus)wählen
Christmas Weihnachten
city (Groß-)Stadt
class Klasse
clean sauber; reinigen, säubern
clear klar, deutlich
clever klug, intelligent
clock Uhr
close schließen, zumachen
close (to) nahe (bei)
clothes Kleidung, Kleider
clue Hinweis, Tipp
coffee Kaffee
colour Farbe
come kommen, geliefert werden
comma Komma
common üblich, gemeinsam, verbreitet
commonly häufig, gewöhnlich, üblicherweise
complete vollständig; vervollständigen
completely völlig
contact Kontakt, Verbindung
control Kontrolle; kontrollieren, regeln, steuern, überwachen
copy Exemplar, Kopie; abschreiben, kopieren
corner Ecke
correct richtig, genau; korrigieren
cost Kosten; kosten
could konnte/n, könnte/n
count zählen
country Land, Staat
couple Paar
course Kurs, Lehrgang, Gang
create (er)schaffen, erstellen
creative kreativ, schöpferisch
cross (an)kreuzen
culture Kultur

D
damage Schaden; beschädigen
danger Gefahr
dangerous gefährlich
dark Dunkelheit, dunkel
data Daten
date Datum, Termin
date of birth Geburtsdatum
day Tag
dear liebe/r
death Tod
decide entscheiden, beschließen
definite(ly) (ganz) sicher, bestimmt
delete löschen
describe beschreiben
description Beschreibung, Schilderung
desk (Schreib-)Tisch, Arbeitsplatz
details Einzelheiten, Angaben
dialogue Gespräch, Dialog
diary (Termin-)Kalender
dictionary Wörterbuch
die sterben
difference Unterschied
different unterschiedlich, verschieden
difficult schwer, schwierig
difficulty Schwierigkeit
dinner (Abend-)Essen
direct direkt, gerade
direction Richtung
disadvantage Nachteil, Schaden
dislike nicht mögen
do tun, machen
door Tür
draw zeichnen
drink Getränk; trinken
driver Fahrer/in
during während

E
each jede/r/s
early früh
east (nach) Osten, Ost-
Easter Ostern
easy, easily leicht, einfach
education Erziehung, (Aus-, Schul-) Bildung
educational Bildungs-
either entweder
electricity Elektrizität, Strom
else andere/r/s
empty leer
end Ende, Schluss; (be)enden
ending Ende
energy Energie
enjoy genießen, gefallen, gern tun
enough ausreichend, genug
enter eintreten, betreten, eingeben
entrance Eingang, Einfahrt
equal gleich
especially besonders

Basic word list

even sogar (noch)
evening Abend
ever je(mals)
every jede/r/s
everybody jede/r
everyone jede/r, alle
everything alles
exactly exakt, genau
example Beispiel
excellent hervorragend, ausgezeichnet
excited aufgeregt, begeistert
exciting aufregend, spannend
exercise book (Schul-)Heft
exercise Übung
expensive teuer
experience Erfahrung
expert Fachmann/-frau
express ausdrücken
extra zusätzlich
eye Auge

F

fact Tatsache
factory Fabrik
fairly ziemlich
false falsch
family Familie
far weit (entfernt)
fast schnell
feel (sich) fühlen, meinen, glauben
feeling Gefühl
(a) few ein paar, wenig/e
fight Kampf; (be)kämpfen
file Ordner, Datei
final letzte/r/s
finally schließlich, endlich
financial finanziell
find finden, suchen
find out herausfinden
fine gut, schön
finish (be)enden, abschließen, fertig werden
firm Firma
first(ly) erst; zuerst
fix festlegen, reparieren
flat Wohnung; flach
flight Flug
floor Etage, Stockwerk; (Fuß-)Boden
fly fliegen
follow (be)folgen
(the) following der/die/das Folgende
food Essen, Nahrung
foreign ausländisch, Auslands-, fremd
forget vergessen
form Form, Formular
forward nach vorne
free frei; gratis, kostenlos
friend Freund/in
friendly freund(schaft)lich
front Vorderseite
front, in ~ of vor
full voll
fully völlig
funny komisch, merkwürdig
future Zukunft; (zu)künftig

G

gap Lücke
garage Garage
gate Tor
general allgemein, generell, normal
generally im Allgemeinen, normalerweise
get holen, bekommen, werden
give geben
glad froh
go gehen, fahren
go ahead anfangen, weitermachen
go for sth sich bemühen um, gefallen
go on weitermachen, fortfahren
go out ausgehen
good gut
goodbye auf Wiedersehen
great groß(artig)
greatly in hohem Maße
greet (be)grüßen
greeting Gruß(formel), Begrüßung
ground Boden, Grund
group Gruppe; gruppieren
grow wachsen, werden
guess Annahme; raten, schätzen
guest Gast

H

half Hälfte; halb
hall Diele, Saal, Halle
handle umgehen mit, bearbeiten, erledigen, fertig werden mit
happen passieren, geschehen
happy glücklich, zufrieden
health Gesundheit
hear hören
heart Herz
heavy schwer
height Höhe, Größe
help Hilfe; helfen
helpful hilfreich, nützlich
here hier
high; highly hoch; äußerst
history Geschichte
holiday Ferien, Urlaub, Feiertag
home Zuhause, Heim; nach Hause
hope Hoffnung; hoffen
hopefully hoffentlich
hot heiß
hour Stunde
house Haus
how wie
however doch, jedoch
huge riesig
human menschlich
hurry sich beeilen

I

idea Vorstellung, Idee
identity Identität
if wenn, falls, ob
illness Krankheit
image Bild
important wichtig
impossible unmöglich
individual einzeln, individuell
informal ungezwungen, inoffiziell, informell
inform informieren, unterrichten
information Auskunft, Information(en), Angaben
inside innerhalb, drinnen
instead stattdessen
instead of statt
instruction Anweisung, Anleitung
interest Interesse; interessieren
interested interessiert
interesting interessant
introduce (sich) vorstellen, (miteinander) bekannt machen, einführen
introduction Einleitung, Einführung, Vorstellung

J

job Arbeit(sstelle), Aufgabe
join beitreten, verbinden
just einfach, nur, genau

K

keep (be)halten, weiterhin tun
key Schlüssel, Taste; Haupt-
kind freundlich; Art, Sorte
know kennen, wissen
knowledge Wissen, Kenntnis(se)

L

language Sprache
large groß
last dauern; letzte/r/s
late spät
later später
latest neueste/r/s
lead führen
learn lernen, erfahren
least, at ~ wenigstens
leave lassen, verlassen, ab-/wegfahren
left links; übrig
length Länge
less weniger, abzüglich
let erlauben, (zu)lassen
letter Buchstabe, Brief
level Ebene, Niveau
lie Lüge; lügen
life Leben
lift Fahrstuhl, Aufzug
light Licht, Leuchte; hell, leicht
like mögen; (ähnlich) wie
line Linie, Leitung, Zeile
list Liste; auflisten, notieren
listen zuhören
little klein, wenig
live wohnen, leben
local örtlich, lokal
log in/on einloggen
log off/out ausloggen
long lang
look Blick, Aussehen; (aus)sehen, blicken
look after sich kümmern um
look for suchen nach
look forward to sth sich auf etw freuen
lose verlieren
lots of/a lot of viel, viele
love Liebe; lieben, sehr gern mögen
lovely schön, hübsch, reizend
low niedrig
lunch Mittagessen

M

magazine Zeitschrift
main Haupt-, wichtigste/r/s
make machen
manage leiten, verwalten, regeln, (es) schaffen
manager Manager/in, leitende/r Angestellte
many viele
mark Note
match zuordnen, (zusammen) passen
may dürfen, können, mögen
maybe vielleicht
meal Essen, Mahlzeit
mean bedeuten, meinen, heißen
media Medien
medium mittlere; Medium, Mittel
meet (zusammen)treffen, begegnen
meeting Sitzung, Besprechung, Treffen
memory Gedächtnis, Speicher
message Meldung, Nachricht, Mitteilung, Botschaft
metal Metall
middle Mitte
might könnte(n) (vielleicht)
miss verpassen, vermissen
missing fehlende/r/s
mistake Fehler, Irrtum
mobile (phone) Mobiltelefon, Handy
money Geld
month Monat
monthly monatlich

more mehr
morning Morgen
most der/die/das meiste, die meisten
move (sich) bewegen, umziehen
movement Bewegung
much viel
must müssen

N
name Name; nennen, benennen
national national, staatlich
nationality Staatsangehörigkeit
near in der Nähe von
nearly beinahe, fast
need Bedarf, Bedürfnis; brauchen, benötigen
negative verneinend, negativ
neither … nor weder … noch
never nie(mals)
new neu
news Neuigkeit(en), Nachricht(en)
next nächste/r/s; danach
night Nacht
noon Mittag
normal(ly) normal(erweise)
north (nach) Norden, Nord-
note Notiz, Anmerkung; beachten, notieren
nothing nichts
now nun, jetzt
nowadays heutzutage
number Nummer, Zahl

O
object Gegenstand
of course natürlich, selbstverständlich
offer Angebot; anbieten, bieten
office Büro
often oft, häufig
oil Öl
old alt
once einmal, einst; sobald
only nur, einzig
open öffnen, eröffnen; offen, geöffnet
opposite Gegenteil; gegensätzlich, gegenüber
option Möglichkeit, Option
or oder
order bestellen, ordern
ordinary gewöhnlich, normal
organization Organisation
organize organisieren
original original, ursprünglich; Original(-)
other andere/r/s
ought to sollen
outside außerhalb (von)
over über
own eigene/r/s; besitzen

P
page Seite
pain Schmerz
pair Paar
paper Papier, Zeitung
part Teil, Bauteil
pass (a test) (eine Prüfung) bestehen
passport Pass
pay Lohn, Bezahlung; zahlen, bezahlen
pen Stift
per cent Prozent
perfect vollkommen, perfekt
perfectly völlig
perhaps vielleicht, eventuell
period Zeit(raum)
personal persönlich
phone Telefon; anrufen
photo(graphy) Foto(grafie)
phrase Redewendung, Satz(teil)
picture Bild
piece Stück, Teil
place Stelle, Platz; setzen, stellen
plain einfach
plan Plan; planen
plane Flugzeug
plastic Plastik, Kunststoff
pleasant angenehm, nett
plenty viel, reichlich
p.m. nachmittags, abends (nach 12 Uhr)
point Punkt; Komma
point to zeigen auf
poor arm, schlecht, mangelhaft
popular beliebt, populär
position Stellung, Lage, Position
positive positiv, bejahend
possibility Möglichkeit
possible möglich
possibly möglicherweise
power Kraft, Strom; antreiben
powerful mächtig, stark
practical praktisch
practice Praxis, Training
practise (ein)üben
prefer vorziehen, bevorzugen, lieber mögen
present Gegenwart; Geschenk; vorstellen, präsentieren
press drücken
price Preis
print Druck; drucken, ausdrucken
printer Drucker/in
printout (Computer-)Ausdruck
private privat, persönlich
probably wahrscheinlich
produce produzieren, herstellen
product Produkt, Erzeugnis
program(me) Programm, Sendung
properly richtig
proud stolz
provide liefern, bieten, zur Verfügung stellen
public öffentlich; Öffentlichkeit
push schieben, drücken
put setzen, stellen, legen

Q
quality Eigenschaft, Qualität
(a) quarter past/to Viertel nach/vor
question Frage
quick(ly) schnell
quiet ruhig
quite ziemlich, ganz

R
rarely selten
rather ziemlich, lieber
reach erreichen, greifen
read lesen
reader Leser/in, Lektüre
ready bereit, fertig
real echt, wirklich
really wirklich, eigentlich, tatsächlich
reason Vernunft, Grund
recent aktuell, neu
recently neulich, vor kurzem
record Aufzeichnung, Beleg
regular(ly) regelmäßig
relative Verwandte/r, relativ
relatively relativ, verhältnismäßig
remain (ver)bleiben
remember sich erinnern, daran denken
repair reparieren
repeat wiederholen
reserve reservieren
respect Respekt, Achtung; (be)achten, respektieren
restart neu starten
return zurückkehren, zurückgeben
rich reich
right rechts, richtig
risk Risiko; riskieren
road (Land-)Straße
role Rolle
role play Rollenspiel
room Zimmer, Raum
round Runde; rund
rude unhöflich, unverschämt
rule Regel, Vorschrift
run laufen (lassen); betreiben, leiten

S
sad traurig
safe(ly) sicher
same gleiche/r/s, der-, die-, dasselbe
save retten, sichern, sparen
say sagen
school Schule
screen Bildschirm
search Suche; (durch)suchen
second zweite/r/s, Sekunde
secondary school weiterführende Schule
secondly zweitens
secretary Sekretär/in
see sehen, besuchen, verstehen
seem (er)scheinen
sell (sich) verkaufen
send senden, schicken
sentence Satz
service Dienst, Dienstleistung, Service
set setzen, stellen
several etliche, einige, mehrere
shall sollen, werden
shelf Regal
shop Laden, Geschäft; einkaufen
short kurz, klein, knapp
should solle/n, sollte/n
show zeigen
show sb around jdn herumführen
shut schließen
side Seite
sign Zeichen, Anzeichen, Schild
simple einfach
since da, weil, seit
single einzig, einzeln
sit sitzen, sich hinsetzen
site Website
size Größe
skill Fähigkeit, Fertigkeit
slow langsam
small klein
smile lächeln
so also, damit, deshalb, so
some einige, etwas
someone jemand
something etwas
sometimes manchmal
somewhere irgendwo(hin)
soon bald
sorry traurig; Verzeihung
sound Klang, Geräusch; klingen, sich anhören
south (nach) Süden, Süd-
space Raum, Platz, Abstand
speak sprechen, reden
special besondere/r/s
specially speziell, extra, besonders
speed Geschwindigkeit
spell buchstabieren, schreiben
spelling Rechtschreibung, Schreibweise
spend (Geld) ausgeben, (Zeit) verbringen
stand stehen, aushalten
standard Standard; normal, üblich
start Beginn; anfangen, starten
state (Bundes-)Staat
statement Aussage, Erklärung, Feststellung

stay Aufenthalt; bleiben
step Schritt, Stufe
still still, trotzdem, (immer) noch
stop (an)halten, aufhören (mit)
street Straße
strength Kraft, Stärke
strong stark, heftig
student Student/in, Lernende/r
study lernen, studieren, untersuchen, betrachten
stuff Material, Stoff, Zeug
subject (Schul-)Fach, Thema
success Erfolg
successful erfolgreich
such as wie zum Beispiel
sure sicher
surname Nachname, Familienname
surprise Überraschung; überraschen

T
table Tisch, Tabelle
take nehmen, bringen, dauern
take off ausziehen, abnehmen, abheben
take part teilnehmen, mitmachen
talk Gespräch, Vortrag; sprechen, reden
tall groß, hoch
task Aufgabe
teach unterrichten, lehren
teacher Lehrer/in
team Mannschaft
technology Technik, Technologie
telephone (call) Telefon(anruf)
television Fernsehen, Fernseher
tell sagen, erzählen
test untersuchen, prüfen
than als
thank danken
thank you danke
thanks Dank; danke
then dann
there da, dort(hin)
these diese
thin dünn
thing Sache, Ding, Gegenstand
think denken, meinen, finden, glauben
those jene
though obwohl, allerdings, jedoch
through durch
throughout überall (in), die ganze Zeit hindurch
throw werfen
tick (off) mit einem Häkchen versehen, abhaken
ticket Karte, Fahrschein
tidy aufgeräumt, ordentlich; aufräumen
time Zeit, Mal
timetable Fahrplan, Stundenplan
tip Hinweis, Tipp
today heute
together zusammen
tomorrow morgen
tonight heute Abend/Nacht
too zu, auch
top Spitze, Gipfel; Spitzen-
topic Thema
total (Gesamt-)Summe; gesamte/r/s, Gesamt-
touch anfassen, berühren
town Stadt
toy Spielzeug
traffic Verkehr
train Zug
trainee Auszubildende/r, Praktikant/in
travel Reisen; reisen, fahren
trip Ausflug, Reise, Besuch
trouble Mühe, Umstände, Problem(e), Ärger
true wahr, richtig
try versuchen, probieren
turn (sich) drehen, wenden, werden
twice zweimal
type Art, Sorte, Typ; tippen, Schreibmaschine schreiben
typical typisch

U
unable unfähig, nicht in der Lage
under unter
understand verstehen, begreifen
unfriendly unfreundlich
university Universität
unless es sei denn, außer wenn
unlike anders als, im Gegensatz zu
until bis
use Gebrauch; gebrauchen, benutzen, verwenden
useful nützlich
user Anwender/in, Benutzer/in
usual gewöhnlich, normal, üblich
usually gewöhnlich, normalerweise, meistens

V
vary variieren, schwanken
verb Verb
visit Besuch; besuchen, besichtigen
visitor Besucher/in, Gast

W
wait warten
wall Wand, Mauer
want wollen
wash waschen
watch Armbanduhr
water Wasser
way Weg, Methode, Art (und Weise)
weather Wetter
week Woche
weekend Wochenende
weekly wöchentlich
welcome Willkommen; willkommen heißen
well gesund, gut; also
west (nach) Westen, West-
whatever was auch immer
wheel Rad
when wenn, als, wann
whenever immer wenn
where wo(hin)
whether ob
which welche
while während
who(m) wen, wem
whole ganz
why warum
wide breit, weit
will Wille; werde(n), wollen
window Fenster
wish Wunsch; wünschen
with mit, bei
within innerhalb (von), in
without ohne
woman Frau
wonderful wunderbar
wood Holz
word Wort
work Arbeit; funktionieren, arbeiten
worker Arbeiter/in
world Welt
world-famous weltberühmt
worldwide weltweit
worried besorgt, beunruhigt
worse schlechter, schlimmer
worst schlechteste/r/s, schlimmste/r/s
would würde/n
write schreiben
wrong falsch

Y
year Jahr
yesterday gestern
young jung

Chronological word list

Dieses Wörterverzeichnis enthält alle neuen Wörter aus *Electricity Matters – 3rd Edition* in der Reihenfolge ihres Erscheinens (Seitenzahlen sind angegeben). Nicht angeführt sind die Wörter aus dem Grundwortschatz (vgl. *Basic word list*). Wörter aus den Hörverständnisübungen sind mit einem **T** *(Transkript)* und Wörter aus den *Partner files* mit einem **P** gekennzeichnet. Die Zahl am linken Rand gibt die Seitenzahl an.

Abkürzungen	*AE* = amerikanisches Englisch	*jdm* = jemandem	*pl* = plural noun
	BE = britisches Englisch	*jdn* = jemanden	*sb* = somebody
	etw = etwas	*jds* = jemandes	*sth* = something

UNIT 1

6	to **solve** [sɒlv]	lösen
	customer ['kʌstəmə]	Kunde, Kundin
	workplace ['wɜ:kpleɪs]	Arbeitsplatz
	tour [tʊə]	Rundgang
	location [ləʊ'keɪʃn]	Standort
	to **be located in ...** [bi ləʊ'keɪtɪd ɪn]	in ... sein/liegen
	to **employ** [ɪm'plɔɪ]	beschäftigen, an-/einstellen
	to **install** [ɪn'stɔ:l]	installieren, einbauen
	to **manufacture** [ˌmænju'fæktʃə]	herstellen, fertigen
	to **maintain** [meɪn'teɪn]	warten, instandhalten
	to **carry sth out** [ˌkæri 'aʊt]	etw ausführen, etw durchführen
	building ['bɪldɪŋ]	Gebäude
	building site ['bɪldɪŋ saɪt]	Baustelle
	van [væn]	Lieferwagen
	mobile ['məʊbaɪl]	mobil, beweglich, fahrbar
	workshop ['wɜ:kʃɒp]	Werkstatt
	commercial [kə'mɜ:ʃl]	Gewerbe-, gewerblich
	industrial [ɪn'dʌstriəl]	Industrie-, industriell
	to **replace** [rɪ'pleɪs]	ersetzen, austauschen
	electrical [ɪ'lektrɪkl]	elektrisch
	component [kəm'pəʊnənt]	Bauteil
	circuit ['sɜ:kɪt]	Stromkreis, Schaltkreis
	electrical fittings pl [ɪˌlektrɪkl 'fɪtɪŋz]	Elektroinstallation, elektrische Betriebsmittel
	tool [tu:l]	Werkzeug, Instrument, Gerät
	equipment [ɪ'kwɪpmənt]	Ausstattung, Ausrüstung, Geräte
	project [prə'dʒekt]	Projekt, Auftrag
	major ['meɪdʒə]	groß, bedeutend
	to **translate** [træns'leɪt]	übersetzen
	term [tɜ:m]	Begriff
	heading ['hedɪŋ]	Überschrift
7	**unfortunately** [ʌn'fɔ:tʃənətli]	leider
	to **get mixed up** [get ˌmɪkst 'ʌp]	durcheinander geraten
	technical ['teknɪkl]	technisch, Fach-
	technical building equipment [ˌteknɪkl 'bɪldɪŋ ɪkwɪpmənt]	technische Gebäudeausrüstung
	development [dɪ'veləpmənt]	Entwicklung
	mechatronics *pl* [mekə'trɒnɪks]	Mechatronik
	transformer [træns'fɔ:mə]	Transformator, Trafo
	telecommunications [ˌtelikəˌmju:nɪ'keɪʃnz]	Telekommunikation
	electrical engineering [ɪˌlektrɪkl ˌendʒɪ'nɪərɪŋ]	Elektrotechnik
	switchgear ['swɪtʃgɪə]	Schaltanlage
	manufacture [ˌmænju'fæktʃə]	Herstellung, Fertigung, Bau
	emergency [ɪ'mɜ:dʒənsi]	Notfall, Not-
	emergency power system [ɪˌmɜ:dʒənsi 'paʊə sɪstəm]	Notstromsystem
	to **design** [dɪ'zaɪn]	entwerfen, konstruieren
	machine [mə'ʃi:n]	Gerät, Maschine
	to **link (up)** [lɪŋk]	verbinden, anschließen
	electronic [ˌɪlek'trɒnɪk]	elektronisch
	electronic engineering [ɪlekˌtrɒnɪk endʒɪ'nɪərɪŋ]	Elektronik, Elektrotechnik
	mechanical [mɪ'kænɪkl]	mechanisch
	mechanical engineering [mɪˌkænɪkl endʒɪ'nɪərɪŋ]	Maschinenbau
	engineer [ˌendʒɪ'nɪə]	Ingenieur/in
	voltage ['vəʊltɪdʒ]	Spannung
	to **step up** [ˌstep 'ʌp]	(Spannung) erhöhen, hochtransformieren
	to **step down** [ˌstep 'daʊn]	(Spannung) senken, heruntertransformieren

	whenever [wen'evə]	wann (auch) immer, immer wenn, jedesmal wenn
	wherever [weər'evə]	wo (auch) immer
	switch [swɪtʃ]	Schalter
	socket ['sɒkɪt]	Steckdose
	power outage ['paʊər aʊtɪdʒ]	Stromausfall
	standstill ['stændstɪl]	Stillstand
	to **put sth at risk** [ˌpʊt ət 'rɪsk]	etw gefährden
	comfortable ['kʌmftəbl]	angenehm, komfortabel
	efficient [ɪ'fɪʃnt]	effizient, leistungsfähig, wirtschaftlich
	state of the art [ˌsteɪt əv ði 'ɑːt]	auf dem neuesten Stand der Technik, neueste/r/s
	market ['mɑːkɪt]	Markt
	fail-safe ['feɪlseɪf]	ausfallsicher, betriebssicher
	switching system ['swɪtʃɪŋ sɪstəm]	Schaltanlage, Schaltsystem
	to **guarantee** [ˌgærən'tiː]	garantieren
	low voltage [ˌləʊ 'vəʊltɪdʒ]	Niederspannung
	medium voltage [ˌmiːdiəm 'vəʊltɪdʒ]	Mittelspannung
	teleconference ['teləkɒnfərəns]	Konferenzschaltung
	to **price sth** [praɪs]	einen Preis festsetzen
	to **implement** ['ɪmplɪmənt]	(Ideen etc.) umsetzen
	result [rɪ'zʌlt]	Ergebnis
	premises *pl* ['premɪsɪz]	Räumlichkeiten, (Betriebs-)Gelände
	defective [dɪ'fektɪv]	schadhaft, defekt
	to **supply (sb with sth)** [sə'plaɪ]	(jdm etw) liefern, (jdn mit etw) versorgen
	washing machine ['wɒʃɪŋ məʃiːn]	Waschmaschine
	heavy-duty [ˌhevi 'djuːti]	Hochleistungs-
	neighbourhood ['neɪbəhʊd]	Stadtteil, Wohngegend
	hospital ['hɒspɪtl]	Krankenhaus
	instruction [ɪn'strʌkʃn]	Anweisung
	technician [tek'nɪʃn]	Techniker/in
	on time [ɒn 'taɪm]	pünktlich
	value for money [ˌvæljuː fə 'mʌni]	Preis-Leistungs-Verhältnis
8	to **contact sb** ['kɒntækt]	sich an jdn wenden, mit jdm Kontakt aufnehmen
	supplier [sə'plaɪə]	Lieferant
	solution (to sth) [sə'luːʃn]	Lösung (für etw)
	power supply ['paʊə səplaɪ]	Stromversorgung, Stromzufuhr
	lighting ['laɪtɪŋ]	Beleuchtung, Licht
	to **switch on/off** [ˌswɪtʃ 'ɒn/ɒf]	ein-/ausschalten
	meat [miːt]	Fleisch
	meat cutter ['miːt kʌtə]	Fleischwolf, Fleischkutter
	to **cut out** [ˌkʌt 'aʊt]	ausgehen, (sich) abschalten
	currently ['kʌrəntli]	im Moment, momentan, aktuell
	plant [plɑːnt]	Werk, Betrieb, Anlage
	meat processing ['miːt prəʊsesɪŋ]	Fleischverarbeitung
	sporadic(ally) [spə'rædɪk]	sporadisch, vereinzelt
	cutting room ['kʌtɪŋ ruːm]	*(Fleischverarbeitung:)* Zerlegeraum
	warehouse ['weəhaʊs]	Lager(halle)
	to **disconnect** [ˌdɪskə'nekt]	vom Netz trennen
	to **deal with sth** ['diːl wɪð]	etw bearbeiten, etw erledigen, sich um etw kümmern
	graduate engineer [ˌgrædʒuət endʒɪ'nɪə]	Diplom-Ingenieur/in
	to **discuss** [dɪ'skʌs]	besprechen, erörtern, diskutieren
	summary ['sʌməri]	Zusammenfassung
	to **explain** [ɪk'spleɪn]	erläutern, erklären
	certainly ['sɜːtnli]	gewiss, natürlich, selbstverständlich
T	to **put sb through** [ˌpʊt 'θruː]	jdn durchstellen, verbinden
	to **improve** [ɪm'pruːv]	verbessern
	in detail [ɪn 'diːteɪl]	genau, im Detail, detailliert
9	**chain** [tʃeɪn]	Kette
	to **plot** [plɒt]	aufzeichnen, grafisch darstellen, plotten
	current ['kʌrənt]	Strom
	phase [feɪz]	Phase
	graph [grɑːf]	Kurve, Diagramm
	irregular [ɪ'regjələ]	unregelmäßig
	sort [sɔːt]	Art
	AC (alternating current) [ˌeɪ 'siː/ˌɔːltəneɪtɪŋ 'kʌrənt]	Wechselstrom
	three-phase AC [θriː ˌfeɪz eɪ 'siː]	Drehstrom
	frequency ['friːkwənsi]	Frequenz
	frequency converter ['friːkwənsi kənvɜːtə]	Frequenzumrichter

	to **disturb** [dɪ'stɜ:b]	stören
	to **see for oneself** [ˌsi: fə wʌn'self]	sich selbst ein Bild machen
	supplies *pl* [sə'plaɪz]	Vorräte, Nachschub, Lieferungen
	flight [flaɪt]	Flug
	phase current ['feɪz kʌrənt]	Phasenstrom
	in order [ɪn 'ɔ:də]	in Ordnung
	probable ['prɒbəbl]	wahrscheinlich
	broken ['brəʊkən]	defekt, kaputt
	to **operate sth** ['ɒpəreɪt]	etw betreiben, etw bedienen, etw steuern
	to **be due to sth** [bi 'dju: tə]	auf etw zurückzuführen sein, an etw liegen
	equivalent [ɪ'kwɪvələnt]	Entsprechung, Übersetzung
10	**employer** [ɪm'plɔɪə]	Arbeitgeber/in
	electrician [ɪˌlek'trɪʃn]	Elektriker/in
	on site [ɒn 'saɪt]	vor Ort
	site [saɪt]	Ort, Standort, Anlage
	organization chart [ˌɔ:gənaɪ'zeɪʃn tʃɑ:t]	Organigramm
	responsible [rɪ'spɒnsəbl]	verantwortlich, zuständig
	staff [stɑ:f]	Personal
	training ['treɪnɪŋ]	Ausbildung, Schulung
	head [hed]	Leiter/in, Chef/in
11	**Finance (Department)** ['faɪnæns]	Rechnungswesen, Finanzressort
	Head of Finance [ˌhed əf 'faɪnæns]	Leiter/in Finanzen
	to **report to sb** [rɪ'pɔ:t tə]	jdm unterstellt sein
	qualification [ˌkwɒlɪfɪ'keɪʃn]	Abschluss, Qualifikation
	to **supervise sb** ['su:pəvaɪz]	jdm vorgesetzt sein
	to **store** [stɔ:]	lagern, speichern
	contract ['kɒntrækt]	Vertrag
	employee [ɪm'plɔɪi:]	Beschäftigte/r, Angestellte/r
	to **correspond to sth** [ˌkɒrɪ'spɒnd tə]	einer Sache entsprechen
	management ['mænɪdʒmənt]	Geschäftsführung
	proprietor [prə'praɪətə]	Eigentümer/in
	CEO (Chief Executive Officer) [ˌsi: i: 'əʊ/ˌtʃi:f ɪg'zekjətɪv ɒfɪsə]	Geschäftsführer/in, Vorstandsvorsitzende/r
	secretariat [ˌsekrə'teəriət]	Sekretariat
	Human Resources (HR) [ˌhju:mən rɪ'sɔ:sɪz]	Personal(abteilung)
	fleet [fli:t]	Fuhrpark
	plant construction ['plɑ:nt kənstrʌkʃn]	Anlagenbau
	installation technology [ˌɪnstə'leɪʃn teknɒlədʒi]	Installationstechnik
	control systems technology [kənˌtrəʊl sɪstəmz tek'nɒlədʒi]	Steuer-/Regel-/Leittechnik
	protection [prə'tekʃn]	Schutz
	department [dɪ'pɑ:tmənt]	Abteilung
	Purchasing (Department) ['pɜ:tʃəsɪŋ]	Einkauf(sabteilung)
	quality management ['kwɒləti mænɪdʒmənt]	Qualitätssicherung
	safety ['seɪfti]	Sicherheit
	master electrician [ˌmɑ:stər ɪlek'trɪʃn]	Elektromeister/in
	warehouseman ['weəhaʊsmən]	Lagerist, Lagerverwalter
	subcontractor [ˌsʌbkən'træktə]	Nachunternehmer, Subunternehmer
	apprentice [ə'prentɪs]	Lehrling, Auszubildende/r
	to **draw sth up** [ˌdrɔ: 'ʌp]	etw erstellen
	presentation [ˌprezn'teɪʃn]	Präsentation
12	to **put sb in the picture** [ˌpʊt ɪn ðə 'pɪktʃə]	jdn informieren, jdn ins Bild setzen
	to **show sb around** [ˌʃəʊ ə'raʊnd]	jdn herumführen, jdm etw zeigen
	model ['mɒdl]	Vorlage
	similar ['sɪmələ]	ähnlich
	guided tour [ˌgaɪdɪd 'tʊə]	Führung
	conversation [ˌkɒnvə'seɪʃn]	Gespräch, Unterhaltung
	assembly [ə'sembli]	Montage
	wiring ['waɪərɪŋ]	Verdrahtung, Beschaltung, Elektroinstallation
	break [breɪk]	Pause
	conference room ['kɒnfərəns ru:m]	Tagungsraum, Besprechungsraum
	copper ['kɒpə]	Kupfer
	design [dɪ'zaɪn]	Konstruktion
	electrical design [ɪˌlektrɪkl dɪ'zaɪn]	Elektroplanung
	final ['faɪnl]	letzte/r/s, End-
	final assembly [ˌfaɪnl ə'sembli]	Endmontage
	pre-assembly [ˌpri: ə'sembli]	Vormontage
	Sales (Department) ['seɪlz]	Verkauf(sabteilung), Vertrieb

	showroom ['ʃəʊru:m]	Ausstellungsraum
	storeroom ['stɔ:ru:m]	Lagerraum
	welding ['weldɪŋ]	Schweißen
	goods *pl* [gʊdz]	Ware(n), Güter
	goods inwards examination [ˌgʊdz 'ɪnwədz ɪgzæmɪneɪʃn]	Wareneingangskontrolle
	lathe [leɪð]	Drehbank, Drehmaschine
	testing ['testɪŋ]	Prüfung
	entrance ['entrəns]	Eingang, Einfahrt
T	**this way** ['ðɪs weɪ]	hier entlang
	apartment block [ə'pɑ:tmənt blɒk]	Mietshaus, Wohnblock
	control system [kən'trəʊl sɪstəm]	Steuerung, Steuer-/Regelsystem
	external [ɪk'stɜ:nl]	extern, von außen
	corridor ['kɒrɪdɔ:]	Flur, Gang
	past sth [pɑ:st]	an etw vorbei
	competition [ˌkɒmpə'tɪʃn]	Konkurrenz
	tough [tʌf]	hart
	to **make sure** [ˌmeɪk 'ʃʊə]	sicherstellen, gewährleisten
	specifications *pl* [ˌspesɪfɪ'keɪʃnz]	Spezifikationen, technische Daten
	to **assemble** [ə'sembl]	montieren, zusammenbauen
	unit ['ju:nɪt]	Gerät, Einheit
	stop [stɒp]	Halt
	section ['sekʃn]	Abteilung, Abschnitt
	to **bend** [bend]	biegen
	panel ['pænl]	Blech, Tafel, Schalttafel
	next door to [ˌnekst 'dɔ: tə]	neben
	welding bay ['weldɪŋ beɪ]	Schweißplatz
	wall [wɔ:l]	Wand
	impressive [ɪm'presɪv]	beeindruckend
	to **train sb** [treɪn]	jdn ausbilden, jdn schulen
	installation board [ˌɪnstə'leɪʃn bɔ:d]	Installationsplatte
	by the way [baɪ ðə 'weɪ]	übrigens
	separate ['seprət]	getrennt, eigen
13	to **point out** [ˌpɔɪnt 'aʊt]	hinweisen auf
	expression [ɪk'spreʃn]	Ausdruck
	bending machine ['bendɪŋ məʃi:n]	Biegemaschine
	punching machine ['pʌntʃɪŋ məʃi:n]	Stanzmaschine
	to **find one's way around** [ˌfaɪnd wʌnz ˌweɪ ə'raʊnd]	sich zurechtfinden
	to **ask for directions** [ˌɑ:sk fə də'rekʃnz]	nach dem Weg fragen
	to **turn left/right** [ˌtɜ:n 'left/'raɪt]	links/rechts abbiegen
	hall [hɔ:l]	Saal, Halle, Flur
14	**corporation** [ˌkɔ:pə'reɪʃn]	Unternehmen, Konzern T
	to **found** [faʊnd]	gründen
	assembly line [ə'sembli laɪn]	Fließband, Montageband
	headquarters *pl* [ˌhed'kwɔ:təz]	Firmensitz, Zentrale
	fully ['fʊli]	vollständig
	partnership ['pɑ:tnəʃɪp]	Partnerschaft
	contactor ['kəntæktə]	Schütz, Schaltschütz
	to **control** [kən'trəʊl]	steuern, regeln
	way back [weɪ 'bæk]	damals
	the first ever [ðə ˌfɜ:st 'evə]	der/die/das allererste
	three-phase oil contactor [θri: ˌfeɪz 'ɔɪl kəntæktə]	Drehstrom-Ölschütz
	breakthrough ['breɪkθru:]	bahnbrechend
	discovery [dɪ'skʌvəri]	Entdeckung
	range [reɪndʒ]	Angebot(spalette), Sortiment
	to **include** [ɪn'klu:d]	einschließen, einbeziehen
	device [dɪ'vaɪs]	Gerät, Apparat
	palm switch ['pɑ:m swɪtʃ]	Handballenschalter, Grobhandtaster
	programmable logic controller (PLC) [ˌprəʊgræməbl ˌlɒdʒɪk kən'trəʊlə]	speicherprogrammierbare Steuerung (SPS)
	in addition [ɪn ə'dɪʃn]	außerdem
	wide [waɪd]	groß, breit, weit
	relay ['ri:leɪ]	Relais
	ground fault circuit interrupter [ˌgraʊnd fɔ:lt 'sɜ:kɪt ɪntərʌptə]	Fehlerstromschutzschalter
	pole [pəʊl]	Pol
	cable ['keɪbl]	(fest installiertes) Kabel, Leitung
	flat cable [ˌflæt 'keɪbl]	Flachkabel
	to **interconnect** [ˌɪntəkə'nekt]	miteinander verbinden
	cake [keɪk]	Torte, Kuchen
	a piece of cake [ə ˌpi:s əv 'keɪk]	ein Kinderspiel
	turnover ['tɜ:nəʊvə]	Umsatz
	billion ['bɪliən]	Milliarde
	workforce ['wɜ:kfɔ:s]	Belegschaft, Arbeitskräfte, Mitarbeiter
	to **hesitate** ['hezɪteɪt]	zögern
15	**contracting services** *pl* ['kɒntræktɪŋ sɜ:vɪsɪz]	Dienstleistungen

Chronological word list

refurbishment [riːˈfɜːbɪʃmənt]	Instandsetzung, Sanierung, Modernisierung, Renovierung
maintenance [ˈmeɪntənəns]	Wartung, Instandhaltung
portable [ˈpɔːtəbl]	tragbar
appliance [əˈplaɪəns]	(Elektro-/Haushalts-) Gerät
inspection [ɪnˈspekʃn]	Prüfung, Kontrolle, Abnahme
report [rɪˈpɔːt]	Bericht, Prüfbericht
analysis [əˈnæləsɪs]	Analyse
survey [ˈsɜːveɪ]	Studie
store [stɔː]	Geschäft, Laden
refit [ˌriːˈfɪt]	Überholung, Instandsetzung, Umbau
retail [ˈriːteɪl]	Einzelhandel
concession [kənˈseʃn]	Lizenz, Konzession
regulation [ˌregjuˈleɪʃn]	Vorschrift, Regelung
requirement [rɪˈkwaɪəmənt]	Vorschrift, Anforderung
internal [ɪnˈtɜːnl]	intern
health [helθ]	Gesundheit
health and safety [ˌhelθ ənd ˈseɪfti]	Arbeitssicherheit
adviser [ədˈvaɪzə]	Berater/in
supply [səˈplaɪ]	Lieferung, Bereitstellung
mains *pl* [meɪnz]	(Versorgungs-)Netz, Stromnetz, Netzstrom
mains distribution [ˈmeɪnz dɪstrɪbjuːʃn]	Hauptverteiler
sub mains distribution [ˌsʌb ˈmeɪnz dɪstrɪbjuːʃn]	Unterverteiler
sales floor [ˈseɪlz flɔː]	Verkaufsraum, -fläche
back of house [ˌbæk əv ˈhaʊs]	Verwaltungsbereich, Back of House
scheme [skiːm]	Programm, Plan
lighting scheme [ˈlaɪtɪŋ skiːm]	Beleuchtungskonzept
small power [ˌsmɔːl ˈpaʊə]	Kleinleistung
addressable [əˈdresəbl]	individuell identifizierbar, adressierbar
in connection with [ɪn kəˈnekʃn wɪth]	in Zusammenhang mit, bezüglich
network [ˈnetwɜːk]	Netz, Netzwerk
data *pl* [ˈdeɪtə]	Daten
cabling [ˈkeɪblɪŋ]	Leitungen, Verkabelung
audio-visual [ˌɔːdiəʊ ˈvɪʒuəl]	audiovisuell
door entry system [ˈdɔːr entri sɪstəm]	Zugangskontrollsystem, Personalschleuse
CCTV [ˌsiː siː tiː ˈviː]	Videoüberwachung
review [rɪˈvjuː]	Rezension, Kritik
client [ˈklaɪənt]	Kunde/Kundin
to **view sth** [vjuː]	sich etw ansehen
latest [ˈleɪtɪst]	neueste/r/s
case study [ˈkeɪs stʌdi]	Fallbeispiel, Fallstudie
abbreviation [əˌbriːviˈeɪʃn]	Abkürzung
construction industry [kənˈstrʌkʃn ɪndəstri]	Baugewerbe
board [bɔːd]	Gremium, Kommission, Amt
to **monitor** [ˈmɒnɪtə]	überwachen
public address system [ˌpʌblɪk əˈdres sɪstəm]	Beschallungsanlage
voice alarm system [ˈvɔɪs əlɑːm sɪstəm]	elektroakustisches Notfallwarnsystem
heating [ˈhiːtɪŋ]	Heizung
ventilation [ˌventɪˈleɪʃn]	Belüftung
air conditioning [ˈeə kəndɪʃnɪŋ]	Klimatisierung, Klimaanlage
offering [ˈɒfərɪŋ]	Angebot
to **rewire** [ˌriːˈwaɪə]	neu verkabeln, eine neue Elektoinstallation einbauen
to **connect** [kəˈnekt]	verbinden
(national) grid [grɪd]	Stromnetz
movement [ˈmuːvmənt]	Bewegung
to **check sth out** [ˌtʃek ˈaʊt]	sich etw ansehen
to **research sth** [rɪˈsɜːtʃ]	etw recherchieren, über eine Sache Nachforschungen anstellen
necessary [ˈnesəsəri]	nötig, notwendig, erforderlich

UNIT 2

16	**condition** [kənˈdɪʃn]	Bedingung
	working conditions *pl* [ˌwɜːkɪŋ kənˈdɪʃnz]	Arbeitsbedingungen
	defect [ˈdɪfekt]	Schaden, Defekt
	job title [ˈdʒɒb taɪtl]	Berufsbezeichnung, Stellenbezeichnung
	(electrical) panel [ˈpænl]	Schalttafel, Schaltschrank, Schaltpult, Steuerpult
	panel building electrician [ˌpænl bɪldɪŋ ≈ɪlekˈtrɪʃn]	Schalttafelbauer, Schaltschrankbauer
	installation electrician [ˌɪnstəˈleɪʃn ≈ɪlektrɪʃn]	Elektroinstallateur/in
	lineworker [ˈlaɪnwɜːkə]	*Elektriker/in, der/die am öffentlichen Stromnetz arbeitet*

	electrical machine repairer [ɪˌlektrɪkl mə'ʃiːn rɪpeərə]	Elektriker/in für Maschinen/Motoren
	to **involve** [ɪn'vɒlv]	beinhalten, mit sich bringen, einbeziehen
	wiring system ['waɪərɪŋ sɪstəm]	Leitungsnetz, Elektroinstallation
	flat *BE* [flæt]	Wohnung
	fitting ['fɪtɪŋ]	Einbau
	machinery [mə'ʃiːnəri]	Maschinen, Maschinenanlagen
	to **inspect** [ɪn'spekt]	überprüfen
	to **take turns** [ˌteɪk 'tɜːnz]	sich abwechseln
	hours *pl* ['aʊəz]	Arbeitszeit(en)
	occasional(ly) [ə'keɪʒənəl]	gelegentlich
	unusual [ʌn'juːʒʊəl]	ungewöhnlich, unüblich
	to **be based in** [bi 'beɪst ɪn]	seinen Sitz in … haben, in … wohnen
17	to **specialize in sth** ['speʃəlaɪz ɪn]	sich auf etw spezialisieren
	to **build** [bɪld]	bauen
	complex ['kɒmpleks]	komplex, aufwändig
	current ['kʌrənt]	aktuell, gegenwärtig
	wiring plan ['waɪərɪŋ plæn]	Anschlussplan, Verdrahtungsplan
	control panel [kən'trəʊl pænl]	Steuerkonsole, Schaltschrank
	variety [və'raɪəti]	Abwechslung, Vielfalt
	to **be out and about** [bi ˌaʊt ənd ə'baʊt]	unterwegs sein
	block of flats *BE* [ˌblɒk əv 'flæts]	Mietshaus, Wohnblock
	to **strip sth out** [ˌstrɪp 'aʊt]	etw herausreißen
	architect ['ɑːkɪtekt]	Architekt/in
	drawing ['drɔːɪŋ]	Zeichnung
	conduit ['kɒndjuɪt]	Rohrleitung, Kabelkanal, Leerrohr
	to **fix** [fɪks]	einbauen, installieren
	to **work overtime** [ˌwɜːk 'əʊvətaɪm]	Überstunden machen
	standard ['stændəd]	Norm, normal
	industrial plant [ɪnˌdʌstriəl 'plɑːnt]	Industrieanlage, Werk
	to **ensure** [ɪn'ʃʊə]	sicherstellen, gewährleisten
	to **locate** [ləʊ'keɪt]	aufspüren, ausfindig machen
	fault [fɔːlt]	Fehler, Defekt
	breakdown ['breɪkdaʊn]	Panne
	fuse [fjuːz]	Sicherung
	circuit breaker ['sɜːkɪt breɪkə]	Leistungsschutzschalter, Sicherungsautomat
	to **malfunction** [ˌmæl'fʌŋkʃn]	ausfallen, nicht richtig funktionieren
	favourite ['feɪvərɪt]	Lieblings-
	to **troubleshoot sth** ['trʌblʃuːt]	die Fehler bei etw suchen, die Störung von etw beheben
	production robot [prə'dʌkʃn rəʊbɒt]	Fertigungsroboter
	to **operate** ['ɒpəreɪt]	in Betrieb sein, laufen, funktionieren
	available [ə'veɪləbl]	verfügbar, erhältlich
	shift [ʃɪft]	Schicht
	to **run sth** [rʌn]	etw betreiben
	colleague ['kɒliːg]	Kollege, Kollegin
	to **flow** [fləʊ]	fließen
	to **lay cables** [ˌleɪ 'keɪblz]	Kabel verlegen
	ground [graʊnd]	Erde, Erdboden
	substation ['sʌbsteɪʃn]	Umspannwerk, Transformatorenstation
	height [haɪt]	Höhe
	transmission tower [træns'mɪʃn taʊə]	Hochspannungsmast
	nervous ['nɜːvəs]	aufgeregt, nervös
	at first [ət 'fɜːst]	zunächst, zuerst
	on standby [ɒn 'stændbaɪ]	auf Abruf
	in the middle of sth [ɪn ðə 'mɪdl əv]	mitten in etw
	outdoors [ˌaʊt'dɔːz]	draußen, im Freien
	scenery ['siːnəri]	Kulisse, Landschaft
	change of scenery [ˌtʃeɪndʒ əf 'siːnəri]	Tapetenwechsel
18	to **highlight** ['haɪlaɪt]	hervorheben, markieren
	meaning ['miːnɪŋ]	Bedeutung
	harness ['hɑːnɪs]	Klettergurt
	faulty ['fɔːlti]	defekt, fehlerhaft, schadhaft
	production line [prə'dʌkʃn laɪn]	Fertigungsstraße
	backbone ['bækbəʊn]	Rückgrat
	in the open [ɪn ði 'əʊpən]	im Freien
	to **diagnose sth** ['daɪəgnəʊz]	etw untersuchen, etw prüfen
	to **advise sb** [əd'vaɪz]	jdn beraten
	fixed hours [ˌfɪkst 'aʊəz]	feste Arbeitszeiten
	on call [ɒn 'kɔːl]	in Bereitschaft
19	to **prepare** [prɪ'peə]	(sich) vorbereiten, erstellen
	annual ['ænjuəl]	jährlich

	paid holidays *pl* [ˌpeɪd ˈhɒlədeɪz]	(bezahlte) Urlaubstage
	average [ˈævərɪdʒ]	Durchschnitt, durchschnittlich
	productivity [ˌprɒdʌkˈtɪvəti]	Produktivität
	ranking [ˈræŋkɪŋ]	Rangliste, Platz
	vote [vəʊt]	Abstimmung
	opinion [əˈpɪniən]	Meinung, Ansicht
	to **disagree** [ˌdɪsəˈgriː]	anderer Meinung sein
	doubt [daʊt]	Zweifel
	to **doubt** [daʊt]	bezweifeln
	to **give reasons for sth** [ˌgɪv ˈriːznz fə]	etw begründen
	suggestion [səˈdʒestʃən]	Vorschlag
	to **hand over** [ˌhænd ˈəʊvə]	übergeben
	to **summarize** [ˈsʌməraɪz]	zusammenfassen
	to **interrupt** [ˌɪntəˈrʌpt]	(jdn) unterbrechen
20	**workbench** [ˈwɜːkbentʃ]	Werkbank
	Allen key [ˈælən kiː]	Inbusschlüssel, Innensechskantschlüssel
	pipe wrench [ˈpaɪp rentʃ]	Wasserpumpenzange
	power drill [ˈpaʊə drɪl]	Bohrmaschine
	folding rule [ˈfəʊldɪŋ ruːl]	Zollstock
	hacksaw [ˈhæksɔː]	Bügelsäge
	multimeter [ˈmʌltimiːtə]	Mehrfachmessgerät
	Phillips screwdriver [ˌfɪlɪps ˈskruːdraɪvə]	Kreuzschlitzschraubenzieher/-dreher
	pliers *pl* [ˈplaɪəz]	Zange
	round nose pliers *pl* [ˌraʊnd nəʊz ˈplaɪəz]	Rundzange
	flat-bladed screwdriver [ˌflæt bleɪdɪd ˈskruːdraɪvə]	Schlitzschraubenzieher/-dreher
	side-cutting pliers *pl* [ˈsaɪdkʌtɪŋ plaɪəz]	Seitenschneider
	soldering iron [ˈsəʊldərɪŋ aɪən]	Lötkolben
	spanner [ˈspænə]	Schraubenschlüssel
	needle nose pliers *pl* [ˈniːdl nəʊz plaɪəz]	Spitzzange
	vernier calliper [ˈvɜːniə kælɪpə]	Messschieber
	wire strippers *pl* [ˈwaɪə strɪpəz]	Abisolierzange
	box cutter [ˈbɒks kʌtə]	Teppichmesser
	flashlight [ˈflæʃlaɪt]	Taschenlampe
	spirit level [ˈspɪrɪt levl]	Wasserwaage
21	to **grip** [grɪp]	greifen, packen
	to **measure** [ˈmeʒə]	messen, vermessen
	to **strip** [strɪp]	abziehen, abmanteln
	to **tighten** [ˈtaɪtn]	*(Schraube)* anziehen, festziehen
	to **loosen** [ˈluːsn]	lockern, lösen
	bolt [bəʊlt]	Schraube, Bolzen
	hole [həʊl]	Loch
	nut [nʌt]	Mutter
	screw [skruː]	Schraube
	water pump pliers *pl* [ˈwɔːtə pʌmp plaɪəz]	Wasserpumpenzange
	order [ˈɔːdə]	Bestellung, Auftrag
	to **place an order** [ˌpleɪs ən ˈɔːdə]	eine Bestellung aufgeben, einen Auftrag erteilen
	order [ˈɔːdə]	Reihenfolge
	delivery [dɪˈlɪvəri]	Lieferung
	cash on delivery (COD) [ˌkæʃ ɒn dɪˈlɪvəri]	zahlbar bei Lieferung, per Nachnahme
	in stock [ɪn ˈstɒk]	am/auf Lager, vorrätig, lieferbar
	handle [ˈhændl]	Griff
	invoice [ˈɪnvɔɪs]	Rechnung
	bench [bentʃ]	Werkbank, Arbeitstisch
P	**serial number** [ˈsɪəriəl nʌmbə]	Seriennummer
	manufacturer [ˌmænjuˈfæktʃərə]	Hersteller
	payment [ˈpeɪmənt]	Zahlung
	payment terms *pl* [ˈpeɪmənt tɜːmz]	Zahlungsbedingungen
22	**trade** [treɪd]	Beruf, Handwerk, Metier
	fully equipped [ˌfʊli ɪˈkwɪpt]	voll ausgestattet
	not … until [nɒt ənˈtɪl]	erst
	work experience placement *BE* [ˈwɜːk ɪkspɪəriəns pleɪsmənt]	Praktikum
	apprenticeship [əˈprentɪʃɪp]	Lehre, Ausbildung
	to **attend sth** [əˈtend]	etw besuchen, an etw teilnehmen
	college [ˈkɒlɪdʒ]	Berufsfachschule, Fachhochschule
	trainee [treɪˈniː]	Auszubildende/r
	supervisor [ˈsuːpəvaɪzə]	Vorgesetzte/r
	to **mention** [ˈmenʃn]	erwähnen, nennen
T	**concrete flooring** [ˈkɒŋkriːt flɔːrɪŋ]	Betonfußboden
	trench [trentʃ]	Graben
	to **reckon** [ˈrekən]	vermuten, glauben, schätzen
	angle grinder [ˈæŋgl graɪndə]	Winkelschleifer, Trennschleifer

	wall chaser ['wɔ:l tʃeɪsə]	Schlitzfräse
	cutting blade ['kʌtɪŋ bleɪd]	Sägeblatt
	to **position** [pə'zɪʃn]	anordnen
	neat [ni:t]	sauber
	to **knock sth out** [ˌnɒk 'aʊt]	etw herausschlagen
	chisel ['tʃɪzl]	Meißel
	mallet ['mælɪt]	Schlegel, Hammer
	this lot [ðɪs 'lɒt]	*etwa: diese Sachen*
	extension cable [ɪk'stenʃn keɪbl]	Verlängerungskabel
	junction box ['dʒʌŋkʃn bɒks]	Verteilerdose, -kasten
	to **turn sth into sth** ['tɜ:n ɪntə]	etw zu etw machen, etw in etw umwandeln/umbauen
	storage room ['stɔ:rɪdʒ ru:m]	Lagerraum
	to **mark** [mɑ:k]	kennzeichnen, markieren
	measurements *pl* ['meʒəmənts]	Maße
	to **plug (in)** [plʌg]	(ein-)stecken
	to **line sth up with sth** [ˌlaɪn 'ʌp]	etw an etw ausrichten
	marking ['mɑ:kɪŋ]	Markierung
	to **press** [pres]	drücken
	trigger ['trɪgə]	Auslöser, Schalter, Knopf
	hardly ['hɑ:dli]	kaum
	to **rotate** [rəʊ'teɪt]	sich drehen, rotieren
	smell [smel]	Geruch
	smoke [sməʊk]	Rauch
	annoying [ə'nɔɪɪŋ]	ärgerlich, nervend
	to **pick sb/sth up** [ˌpɪk 'ʌp]	jdn/etw abholen, etw holen
	lad [læd]	Junge, Kumpel
	warranty ['wɒrənti]	Garantie, Gewährleistung
	void [vɔɪd]	unwirksam, ungültig
	likely ['laɪkli]	wahrscheinlich
	worthwhile [ˌwɜ:θ'waɪl]	lohnenswert, den Aufwand wert
23	**suitable** ['su:təbl]	passend, geeignet
	suited ['su:tɪd]	geeignet
	to **suggest** [sə'dʒest]	vorschlagen
24	**design** [dɪ'zaɪn]	Konstruktion, Entwurf, Design
	to **care for sth** ['keə fə]	*hier:* etw warten
	use [ju:s]	Gebrauch, Benutzung
	meter ['mi:tə]	Messgerät
	dry [draɪ]	trocken
	at all times [ət ɔ:l 'taɪmz]	stets, jederzeit
	liquid ['lɪkwɪd]	Flüssigkeit
	to **contain** [kən'teɪn]	enthalten
	minerals *pl* ['mɪnərəlz]	Mineralstoffe, Mineralien
	to **corrode sth** [kə'rəʊd]	etw zersetzen, etw angreifen
	delicate ['delɪkət]	empfindlich
	to **wipe** [waɪp]	wischen, reiben
	moisture ['mɔɪstʃə]	Feuchtigkeit
	environment [ɪn'vaɪrənmənt]	Umgebung, Umfeld
	temperature ['temprətʃə]	Temperatur
	to **crack** [kræk]	platzen, reißen, springen
	to **deplete** [dɪ'pli:t]	leeren, entladen
	battery ['bætəri]	Akku, Batterie
	to **shorten** ['ʃɔ:tn]	kürzen, verkürzen
	condition [kən'dɪʃn]	Zustand
	damp [dæmp]	feucht
	cloth [klɒθ]	Tuch
	including [ɪn'klu:dɪŋ]	einschließlich
	harsh [hɑ:ʃ]	*hier:* scharf, aggressiv
	solvent ['sɒlvənt]	Lösungsmittel
	detergent [dɪ'tɜ:dʒənt]	Reinigungsmittel
	to **avoid** [ə'vɔɪd]	vermeiden
	to **attempt** [ə'tempt]	versuchen
	to **cause** [kɔ:z]	verursachen, bewirken, dazu führen
	to **invalidate** [ɪn'vælɪdeɪt]	außer Kraft setzen, ungültig machen, aufheben
	along with [ə'lɒŋ wɪð]	zusammen mit
	receipt [rɪ'si:t]	Quittung, Beleg
	purchase ['pɜ:tʃəs]	Kauf
	retailer ['ri:teɪlə]	Einzelhändler/in
	Caution! ['kɔ:ʃn]	Achtung!, Vorsicht!
	electric shock [ɪˌlektrɪk 'ʃɒk]	elektrischer Schlag
	test probe ['test prəʊb]	Prüfspitze
	removal [rɪ'mu:vl]	Entfernung, Entnahme, Ausbau
	user-servicable parts *pl* [ˌju:zə sɜ:vɪsəbl 'pɑ:ts]	vom Anwender zu wartende Teile
	service ['sɜ:vɪs]	Wartung
	qualified ['kwɒlɪfaɪd]	qualifiziert, ausgebildet, mit Abschluss
	personnel [ˌpɜ:sə'nel]	Personal
	spare [speə]	Ersatz-
	to **be located (in/at ...)** [bi ləʊ'keɪtɪd]	sich (in/am ...) befinden
	compartment [kəm'pɑ:tmənt]	Fach
	lead [li:d]	Leitung, Zuleitung

	test lead ['test li:d]	Prüfleitung
	to **turn on/off** [ˌtɜ:n 'ɒn/'ɒf]	ein-/ausschalten
	cover ['kʌvə]	Deckel, Klappe
	to **pull** [pʊl]	ziehen
	ribbon ['rɪbən]	Band
	to **eject** [i'dʒekt]	auswerfen, ausgeworfen werden
	to **insert** [ɪn'sɜ:t]	einsetzen, einbauen
	replacement [rɪ'pleɪsmənt]	Ersatz
	fuse rating ['fju:z reɪtɪŋ]	Sicherungswert, Sicherungsleistung
	to **snap sth closed** [ˌsnæp 'kləʊzd]	etw einrasten lassen
25	**electrotechnical** [ɪˌlektrəʊ'teknɪkl]	elektrotechnisch
	careers adviser [kə'rɪəz ədvaɪzə]	Berufsberater/in
	to **apply for sth** [ə'plaɪ fə]	sich für/um etw bewerben
	varied ['veərid]	abwechslungsreich
	even though ['i:vn ðəʊ]	obwohl
	not yet [nɒt 'jet]	noch nicht
	responsibility [rɪˌspɒnsə'bɪləti]	Verantwortung
	day release ['deɪ rɪli:s]	ausbildungsbegleitender Berufsschultag
	past [pɑ:st]	Vergangenheit
	level ['levl]	Niveau, Ebene, Höhe
	skill [skɪl]	Fähigkeit, Fertigkeit, Kenntnis
	functional skills *pl* [ˌfʌŋkʃənl 'skɪlz]	Fachkenntnisse
	maths *pl* [mæθs]	Mathe(matik)
	physics *pl* ['fɪzɪks]	Physik
	knowledge ['nɒlɪdʒ]	Wissen
	definitely ['defɪnətli]	ganz bestimmt
	financial(ly) [faɪ'nænʃl]	finanziell
	as well as [əz 'wel əz]	ebenso wie
	to **take sb on** [ˌteɪk 'ɒn]	jdn einstellen
	permanent ['pɜ:mənənt]	dauerhaft, unbefristet
	confident ['kɒnfɪdənt]	zuversichtlich, überzeugt
	demand [dɪ'mɑ:nd]	Nachfrage
	in demand [ɪn dɪ'mɑ:nd]	gefragt, begehrt
	sparky *BE* ['spɑ:ki]	*ugs Elektriker/in*
	to **compare** [kəm'peə]	vergleichen

UNIT 3

26	**house wiring** ['haʊs waɪərɪŋ]	Hausinstallation
	consumer unit [kən'sju:mə ju:nɪt]	Hausverteilung, Sicherungskasten
	earth [ɜ:θ]	Erde
	earth terminal ['ɜ:θ tɜ:mɪnl]	Erdklemme, Masseklemme
	electricity meter [ɪˌlek'trɪsəti mi:tə]	Stromzähler
	flex [fleks]	flexibles Netzkabel, Anschlussleitung
	light switch ['laɪt swɪtʃ]	Lichtschalter
	plug [plʌg]	Stecker
	RCD (Residual Current Device) [ˌɑ: si: 'di:/ rɪˌzɪdjuəl 'kʌrənt dɪvaɪs]	FI-Schalter, Fehlerstrom-Schutzeinrichtung
	service entrance ['sɜ:vɪs entrəns]	Hauseinführung
	translation [træns'leɪʃn]	Übersetzung
	to **conduct** [kən'dʌkt]	leiten
	to **house** [haʊs]	unterbringen
	to **protect** [prə'tekt]	schützen
27	to **expand** [ɪk'spænd]	expandieren, *(den Geschäftsbereich)* erweitern
	rapid ['ræpɪd]	rasch, schnell
	Pleased to meet you. [ˌpli:zd tə 'mi:t ju]	Schön, Sie/dich/euch kennen zu lernen.
	storey ['stɔ:ri]	Stock, Etage
	three-storey [ˌθri: 'stɔ:ri]	dreistöckig
	conventional [kən'venʃənl]	herkömmlich, konventionell
	to **program** ['prəʊgræm]	programmieren
	consumer [kən'sju:mə]	Verbraucher
	blinds *pl* [blaɪndz]	Jalousie(n), Rolladen
	central heating [ˌsentrəl 'hi:tɪŋ]	Zentralheizung
	amazing [ə'meɪzɪŋ]	erstaunlich, verblüffend
	actuator ['æktʃueɪtə]	Aktor
	planning permission ['plænɪŋ pəmɪʃn]	Baugenehmigung
	ordinary ['ɔ:dnri]	normal, gewöhnlich
	principle ['prɪnsəpl]	Grundlage, Prinzip
	remotely [rɪ'məʊtli]	aus der Ferne, fern-, entfernt
28	**wire** ['waɪə]	Draht
	stranded wire [ˌstrændɪd 'waɪə]	Litze
	insulation [ˌɪnsju'leɪʃn]	Isolierung, Isolation
	insulated ['ɪnsjuleɪtɪd]	isoliert
	uninsulated [ˌʌn'ɪnsjuleɪtɪd]	unisoliert
	two-way switch [ˌtu: weɪ 'swɪtʃ]	Zweiwegeschalter, Wechselschalter
	hint [hɪnt]	Hinweis, Tipp
	conductor [kən'dʌktə]	Ader *(eines Kabels)*, Leiter

	terminal ['tɜ:mɪnl]	Anschluss, Anschlussklemme
	to **lock** [lɒk]	verriegeln, sperren
	to **tag** [tæg]	kennzeichnen, etikettieren
	mounting box ['maʊntɪŋ bɒks]	Einbaudose, Unterputzdose
	recess [rɪ'ses]	Aussparung, Vertiefung
	to **select** [sɪ'lekt]	auswählen, wählen
	rocker ['rɒkə]	Kippschalter
29	**spur circuit** ['spɜ: sɜ:kɪt]	Stichleitung
	amp [æmp]	Ampere
	ring circuit ['rɪŋ sɜ:kɪt]	Ringleitung
	to **power sth** ['paʊə]	etw mit Strom versorgen
	dishwasher ['dɪʃwɒʃə]	Geschirrspüler, Spülmaschine
	lighting circuit ['laɪtɪŋ sɜ:kɪt]	Lichtstromkreis
	spur [spɜ:]	Stichleitung
	switched and fused [ˌswɪtʃt ənd 'fju:zd]	geschaltet und abgesichert
	connection [kə'nekʃn]	Verbindung
	shower ['ʃaʊə]	Dusche
	cartridge fuse ['kɑ:trɪdʒ fju:z]	Patronensicherung
	to **blow** [bləʊ]	durchbrennen
	to **overload** ['əʊvələʊd]	überlasten
	ceiling ['si:lɪŋ]	(Zimmer-)Decke
	cooker ['kʊkə]	Herd
	heater ['hi:tə]	Heizlüfter
30	to **label** ['leɪbl]	beschriften, etikettieren
	protective earth [prəˌtektɪv 'ɜ:θ]	Schutzerde
	pipe [paɪp]	Röhre, Rohr
	to **escape** [ɪ'skeɪp]	entkommen, entweichen
	bathroom ['bɑ:θru:m]	Badezimmer, Bad
	to **pass through sth** ['pɑ:s θru:]	durch etw hindurchgehen/-fließen
	explanation [ˌeksplə'neɪʃn]	Erläuterung, Erklärung
	field [fi:ld]	Feld
	in contrast to [ɪn 'kɒntrɑ:st tə]	im Gegensatz zu
	direction [də'rekʃn]	Richtung
	distributor [dɪ'strɪbjətə]	Verteiler
	valve [vælv]	Ventil
T	to **turn** [tɜ:n]	sich drehen
	to **lower** ['ləʊə]	herunterlassen, senken
	to **raise** [reɪz]	hochfahren, heben
	to **imagine sth** [ɪ'mædʒɪn]	sich etw vorstellen
	video projector ['vɪdiəʊ prədʒektə]	Beamer
	to **dim** [dɪm]	dämpfen, dimmen
	to **adjust** [ə'dʒʌst]	anpassen, einstellen, regeln
	flick [flɪk]	Drücken *(eines Schalters)*
	command [kə'mɑ:nd]	Befehl, Steuerbefehl
	to **wonder** ['wʌndə]	sich fragen
	to **reprogram** [ˌri:'prəʊgræm]	umprogrammieren
	front door [ˌfrʌnt 'dɔ:]	Haustür
	in the first place [ɪn ðə 'fɜ:st pleɪs]	zuerst, gleich
	brilliant ['brɪliənt]	genial, super, toll
31	**feature** ['fi:tʃə]	Merkmal, Eigenschaft
	to **recommend** [ˌrekə'mend]	empfehlen
	to **make sense** [ˌmeɪk 'sens]	sinnvoll sein, vernünftig sein
	security [sɪ'kjʊərəti]	Sicherheit
	perimeter fence [pə'rɪmɪtə fens]	Umzäunung
	sliding gate [ˌslaɪdɪŋ 'geɪt]	Schiebetor
	break area ['breɪk eəriə]	Pausenbereich
	entrance hall ['entrəns hɔ:l]	Eingangsbereich
	stairs *pl* [steəz]	Treppenhaus
	ground floor [ˌgraʊnd 'flɔ:]	Erdgeschoss
	motion ['məʊʃn]	Bewegung
	motion detector ['məʊʃn dɪtektə]	Bewegungsmelder
	lighting outlet ['laɪtɪŋ aʊtlet]	Lichtauslass, Lichtanschluss
	spotlight ['spɒtlaɪt]	Strahler, Spot
	arc lamp ['ɑ:k læmp]	Bogenlampe, Spot
	dimmable ['dɪməbl]	dimmbar
	flower bed ['flaʊə bed]	Blumenbeet
T	to **finish sth off** [ˌfɪnɪʃ 'ɒf]	etw fertig machen, etw abschließen
	to **record** [re'kɔ:d]	aufzeichnen
	receptionist [rɪ'sepʃənɪst]	Empfangsmitarbeiter/in
	to **think of sth** ['θɪŋk əv]	an etw denken
	reception [rɪ'sepʃn]	Rezeption, Empfang
	side door ['saɪd dɔ:]	Nebeneingang
	to **cut sth** [kʌt]	etw streichen, etw kürzen
	to **plant** [plɑ:nt]	pflanzen
32	**screen** [skri:n]	Bildschirm, Leinwand
	surface ['sɜ:fɪs]	Oberfläche

	to attach sth to sth [ə'tætʃ tə]	etw an etw befestigen, etw an etw anbringen
	right-/left-hand ['raɪt/'left hænd]	rechte/r/s, linke/r/s
	corner ['kɔ:nə]	Ecke
33	**live** [lɪv]	stromführend, unter Spannung stehend
	to hurt oneself [hɜ:t]	sich wehtun
	warning ['wɔ:nɪŋ]	Hinweis, Warnung
	workman ['wɜ:kmən]	Arbeiter
	overhead cable [əʊvə^ˌhed 'keɪbl]	Freileitung
	ladder ['lædə]	Leiter
	to kill [kɪl]	umbringen, töten
	nasty ['nɑ:sti]	böse, übel
	accident ['æksɪdənt]	Unfall
	to tie [taɪ]	binden
	to drill [drɪl]	bohren
	to trip [trɪp]	ansprechen, auslösen
	cellar ['selə]	Keller
	to electrocute sb [ɪ'lektrəkju:t]	jdn durch Stromschlag töten
	microwave ['maɪkrəweɪv]	Mikrowelle
34	**to take a message** [ˌteɪk ə 'mesɪdʒ]	etw ausrichten T
	to be located in … [bi ləʊ'keɪtɪd ɪn]	seinen Sitz in … haben
	to leave a message [ˌli:v ə 'mesɪdʒ]	eine Nachricht hinterlassen
	straight [streɪt]	direkt, sofort
	to examine [ɪg'zæmɪn]	untersuchen, überprüfen
	to pass on a message [pɑ:s ˌɒn ə 'mesɪdʒ]	etw ausrichten
35	**square foot** [ˌskweə 'fʊt]	Quadratfuß
	failure ['feɪljə]	Ausfall, Versagen
	full-time [ˌfʊl 'taɪm]	Vollzeit-, hauptberuflich
	interface ['ɪntəfeɪs]	Schnittstelle
	unidirectional [ˌju:nidə'rekʃənl]	in eine Richtung wirkend
	ballast ['bæləst]	Vorschaltgerät
	to receive [rɪ'si:v]	erhalten, empfangen, bekommen
	physical ['fɪzɪkl]	physisch, real
	reliable [rɪ'laɪəbl]	zuverlässig, verlässlich
	bidirectional [ˌbaɪdə'rekʃənl]	in beide Richtungen
	feedback ['fi:dbæk]	Reaktion, Rückmeldung
	to indicate ['ɪndɪkeɪt]	anzeigen
	to enable [ɪ'neɪbl]	erlauben
	creation [kri'eɪʃn]	Erstellung, Gestaltung
	pre-defined [ˌpri: dɪ'faɪnd]	vorher festgelegt
	lighting scenario ['laɪtɪŋ sənɑ:riəʊ]	Lichtszene, Lichtstimmung
	mouse [maʊs]	Maus
	to convert [kən'vɜ:t]	umwandeln, verwandeln, umfunktionieren
	venue ['venju:]	Veranstaltungsort
	concert hall ['kɒnsət hɔ:l]	Konzertsaal
	consumption [kən'sʌmpʃn]	Verbrauch
	particular [pə'tɪkjələ]	bestimmte/r/s
	peak [pi:k]	Spitze, Spitzenwert, Spitzen-
	savings *pl* ['seɪvɪŋz]	Einsparung(en)
	to achieve [ə'tʃi:v]	erzielen, erreichen
	to consist of sth [kən'sɪst əv]	aus etw bestehen
	loop [lu:p]	Kreislauf, Schleife
	to interlink [ˌɪntə'lɪŋk]	koppeln, verknüpfen, vernetzen
	retrofit ['retrəʊfɪt]	Nachrüstung, nachträglicher Einbau
	electrical fixture [ɪˌlektrɪkl 'fɪkstʃə]	Elektroinstallation
	e.g. [ˌi: 'dʒi:]	z.B.
	semi-skilled worker [ˌsemiskɪld 'wɜ:kə]	angelernte Arbeitskraft
	to confirm [kən'fɜ:m]	bestätigen
	driver ['draɪvə]	Treiber
	colour-coding ['kʌlə kəʊdɪŋ]	Farbkodierung

UNIT 4

36	**wiring diagram** ['waɪərɪŋ daɪəgræm]	Schaltplan
	safety rules *pl* ['seɪfti ru:lz]	Sicherheitsvorschriften
	to make sure [ˌmeɪk 'ʃʊə]	sich vergewissern
	seriously ['sɪəriəsli]	ernsthaft, schwer
	to injure ['ɪndʒə]	verletzen
	to be electrocuted [bi ɪ'lektrəkju:tɪd]	einen Stromschlag erleiden, durch Stromschlag getötet werden
	blade fuse ['bleɪd fju:z]	Flachsicherung, Stecksicherung
	to expect [ɪk'spekt]	erwarten, annehmen
37	**mixed up** [ˌmɪkst 'ʌp]	durcheinander
	three phase junction box [ˌθri: feɪz 'dʒʌŋkʃn bɒks]	Drehstromsteckdose
	door opener ['dɔ:r əʊpənə]	Türöffner

	double/triple/fourfold socket [dʌbl/trɪpl/fɔ:fəʊld 'sɒkɪt]	Doppel-/Dreifach-/Vierfachsteckdose
	one-way switch [ˌwʌn weɪ 'swɪtʃ]	Ausschalter
	double switch [ˌdʌbl 'swɪtʃ]	Wechselschalter
	earthed socket outlet [ˌɜ:θt 'sɒkɪt aʊtlet]	geerdete Steckdose, Schutzsteckdose
	push button ['pʊʃ bʌtn]	Taster
	TV socket [ˌti: 'vi: sɒkɪt]	Fernsehanschlussdose
	to **draw** [drɔ:]	ziehen, zeichnen
	close to ['kləʊs tə]	nahe bei, in der Nähe von, neben
P	to **swap** [swɒp]	tauschen
38	**kitchen appliance** ['kɪtʃɪn əplaɪəns]	Küchengerät
T	**eye-level** ['aɪ levl]	auf Augenhöhe
	oven ['ʌvn]	Backofen
	ceramic hob [səˌræmɪk 'hɒb]	Glaskeramik-Kochfeld
	cooker hood ['kʊkə hʊd]	Dunstabzugshaube
	extractor fan ['ekstræktə fæn]	Sauglüfter, Abzugsgebläse
	to **extract** ['ekstrækt]	absaugen
	cooking fumes *pl* ['kʊkɪŋ fju:mz]	Kochdämpfe, Wrasen
	cable TV ['keɪbl ti: vi:]	Kabelfernsehen
	husband ['hʌzbənd]	(Ehe-)Mann
	fridge [frɪdʒ]	Kühlschrank
	freezer ['fri:zə]	Tiefkühler
	to **block** [blɒk]	blockieren, verstellen
	buzzer ['bʌzə]	Summer, Türöffner
	to **buzz sb in** [ˌbʌz 'ɪn]	jdm (mit dem Türöffner) hereinlassen
	intercom ['ɪntəkɒm]	Gegensprechanlage
39	**face** [feɪs]	Gesicht
	separately ['seprətli]	einzeln
	burglar ['bɜ:glə]	Einbrecher, Dieb
	to **break in** [ˌbreɪk 'ɪn]	einbrechen
	security company [sɪ'kjʊərəti kʌmpəni]	Wachschutzfirma
	immediately [ɪ'mi:diətli]	unmittelbar, sofort
	chain reaction ['tʃeɪn rækʃn]	Kettenreaktion
	to **melt** [melt]	schmelzen
	to **be annoyed** [bi ə'nɔɪd]	sich ärgern
	to **get into trouble** [ˌget ɪntə 'trʌbl]	Ärger bekommen
40	**technical text** [ˌteknɪkl 'tekst]	Fachtext
	... times [taɪmz]	-fach
	nominal current [ˌnɒmɪnl 'kʌrənt]	Nennstrom
	bimetallic strip [baɪməˌtælɪk 'strɪp]	Bimetallstreifen
	to **break** [breɪk]	unterbrechen
	solenoid ['sɒlənɔɪd]	Spule, Magnetspule
	to **react** [ri'ækt]	reagieren
	to **rise** [raɪz]	steigen, ansteigen
	unacceptable [ˌʌnək'septəbl]	inakzeptabel, unzumutbar
	thermal-magnetic [ˌθɜ:ml mæg'netɪk]	thermomagnetisch
	thermal ['θɜ:ml]	thermisch, Thermo-
	to **expand** [ɪk'spænd]	sich ausdehnen
	rate [reɪt]	Geschwindigkeit
	to **heat** [hi:t]	erhitzen
	straight [streɪt]	gerade
	heat [hi:t]	Hitze
	figure ['fɪgə]	Abbildung
	electromagnetic [ɪˌlektrəʊmæg'netɪk]	elektromagnetisch
	combination [ˌkɒmbɪ'neɪʃn]	Zusammenstellung, Verbindung, Kombination
	sudden ['sʌdn]	plötzlich, abrupt, unerwartet
	surge [sɜ:dʒ]	starker Anstieg, starker Strom-/Spannungsstoß
	long-term [ˌlɒŋ'tɜ:m]	langfristig
	overload [əʊvə'ləʊd]	Überlast, Überlastung
41	**residual current** [ˌrɪzɪdjuəl 'kʌrənt]	Fehlerstrom, Reststrom
	fault current ['fɔ:lt kʌrənt]	Fehlerstrom
	load [ləʊd]	Last
	load current ['ləʊd kʌrənt]	Laststrom
	magnetic circuit [mægˌnetɪk 'sɜ:kɪt]	Magnetkreis
	resistor [rɪ'zɪstə]	Widerstand
	test resistor ['test rɪzɪstə]	Testwiderstand
	coil [kɔɪl]	Spule
	magnetic flux [mægˌnetɪk 'flʌks]	magnetischer Fluss, Induktionsfluss
	sensing coil ['sensɪŋ kɔɪl]	Sensorspule
	source [sɔ:s]	Quelle
	neutral ['nju:trəl]	neutral, Neutralleiter
	neutral current [ˌnju:trəl 'kʌrənt]	Neutralleiter(strom)
	identical [aɪ'dentɪkl]	identisch
	to **wind** [waɪnd]	wickeln
	opposite ['ɒpəzɪt]	entgegengesetzt

	to **cancel out** [ˌkænsl 'aʊt]	auslöschen, sich aufheben
	to **pick sth up** [ˌpɪk 'ʌp]	etw erkennen
	to **trigger** ['trɪɡə]	auslösen
42	**power station** ['paʊə steɪʃn]	Elektrizitätswerk
	hot wire [ˌhɒt 'waɪə]	Phase
	to **act (as sth)** [ækt]	als etw fungieren
	resistance [rɪ'zɪstəns]	Widerstand
	uncontrolled [ˌʌnkən'trəʊld]	unkontrolliert, ungeregelt
	to **short-circuit** [ˌʃɔːt 'sɜːkɪt]	kurzschließen
	massive ['mæsɪv]	riesig, gewaltig
	extra ['ekstrə]	zusätzlich, überschüssig
	fire ['faɪə]	Brand, Feuer
	whereas [ˌweər'æz]	während, wogegen
	current leakage ['kʌrənt liːkɪdʒ]	Leckstrom
	ground fault ['ɡraʊnd fɔːlt]	Erdschluss
43	**work placement** ['wɜːk pleɪsmənt]	Praktikum
	notice ['nəʊtɪs]	Hinweis, Aushang
	piece of equipment [ˌpiːs əv ɪ'kwɪpmənt]	Gerät
	to **bother** ['bɒðə]	stören, belästigen
	to **get the wrong end of the stick** [get ðə ˌrɒŋ end əv ðə 'stɪk]	etw völlig falsch verstehen
	to **cover sth up** [ˌkʌvər 'ʌp]	etw abdecken
	to **fence sth off** [ˌfens 'ɒf]	etw abschranken, etw abzäunen
	nearby ['nɪəbaɪ]	in der Nähe, benachbart
	to **make a note of sth** [ˌmeɪk ə 'nəʊt əv]	sich etw merken, sich etw aufschreiben
	reading ['riːdɪŋ]	Messwert
	workmate ['wɜːkmeɪt]	Arbeitskollege/-in
45	**death** [deθ]	Todesfall, Tod
	to **result from sth** [rɪ'zʌlt frəm]	sich aus etw ergeben, aus etw resultieren
	chest [tʃest]	Brust
	strength [streŋθ]	Stärke
	amperage ['æmpərədʒ]	Stromstärke
	duration [dju'reɪʃn]	Dauer
	painful ['peɪnfl]	schmerzhaft
	slight [slaɪt]	leicht, sanft
	tingle ['tɪŋɡl]	Kribbeln
	if anything [ɪf 'eniθɪŋ]	wenn überhaupt
	unpleasant [ʌn'pleznt]	unangenehm
	slightly ['slaɪtli]	etwas, geringfügig, leicht
	muscle ['mʌsl]	Muskel
	to **freeze** [friːz]	erstarren
	to **let go of sth** [ˌlet 'ɡəʊ əv]	etw loslassen
	reaction [rɪ'ækʃn]	Reaktion
	greatly ['ɡreɪtli]	sehr, massiv, in hohem Maße
	to **increase** [ɪn'kriːs]	steigern, erhöhen
	value ['væljuː]	Wert
	rhythm ['rɪðəm]	Rhythmus
	heartbeat ['hɑːtbiːt]	Herzschlag
	ventricular febrillation [venˌtrɪkjələ febrɪ'leɪʃn]	Herzkammerflimmern
	uncoordinated [ˌʌnkəʊ'ɔːdɪneɪtɪd]	unkoordiniert
	nerve [nɜːv]	Nerv
	cardiac arrest [ˌkɑːdɪək ə'rest]	Herzstillstand
	burns *pl* [bɜːnz]	Verbrennung(en)
	mild [maɪld]	leicht
	severe [sɪ'vɪə]	schwer
	tingling ['tɪŋɡlɪŋ]	Kribbeln
	first aid [ˌfɜːst 'eɪd]	Erste Hilfe

UNIT 5

46	**appointment** [ə'pɔɪntmənt]	Termin
	instruction manual [ɪn'strʌkʃn mænjuəl]	Bedienungsanleitung, Betriebsanweisung
	process ['prəʊses]	Vorgang
	sliding door ['slaɪdɪŋ dɔː]	Schiebetür, Schiebetor
	small-scale business [ˌsmɔːl skeɪl 'bɪznəs]	Kleinbetrieb
	salesperson ['seɪlzpɜːsn]	Vertriebsmitarbeiter/in, Verkäufer/in
	passage ['pæsɪdʒ]	Gang, Durchgang
	to **maintain** [meɪn'teɪn]	aufrechterhalten
	forklift truck [ˌfɔːklɪft 'trʌk]	Gabelstapler
	driver ['draɪvə]	Fahrer/in
	to **signal** ['sɪɡnəl]	melden, mitteilen
	concerned [kən'sɜːnd]	besorgt
47	**old-fashioned** [ˌəʊld-'fæʃənd]	altmodisch, unmodern
	self-coiling door [ˌself kɔɪlɪŋ 'dɔː]	Rolltor
	constant ['kɒnstənt]	konstant
	fresh [freʃ]	frisch
	to **roll sth up/down** [ˌrəʊl 'ʌp/'daʊn]	etw hoch-/herunterrollen
	to **automate** ['ɔːtəmeɪt]	automatisieren
	automatic(ally) [ˌɔːtə'mætɪk]	automatisch
	set [set]	Satz
	pretty ['prɪti]	ziemlich

	complicated ['kɒmplɪkeɪtɪd]	kompliziert
	to **be dedicated to do sth** [bi 'dedɪkeɪtɪd te du:]	speziell dafür vorgesehen sein, etw zu tun
	to **fit sth** [fɪt]	etw einbauen
	to **afford sth** [ə'fɔ:d]	sich etw leisten können
	to **worry about sth** ['wʌri əbaʊt]	sich um etw Sorgen machen, sich über etw Gedanken machen
	to **fit** [fɪt]	passen
48	**guide** [gaɪd]	Führer
	automation [,ɔ:tə'meɪʃn]	Automatisierung
	these days [ðiːz 'deɪz]	heutzutage
	to **encounter sth** [ɪn'kaʊntə]	einer Sache begegnen, auf etw treffen
	clever ['klevə]	intelligent, klug, schlau
	to **continue to do sth** [kən'tɪnju:]	etw weiterhin tun
	central ['sentrəl]	wesentlich, zentral
	to **issue sth** ['ɪʃu:]	etw ausgeben, (Befehl) erteilen
	to **power sth** ['paʊə]	etw antreiben
	hydraulic cylinder [haɪ,drɔ:lɪk 'sɪlɪndə]	Hydraulikzylinder
	pneumatic cylinder [nju:,mætɪk 'sɪlɪndə]	Pneumatikzylinder
	to **perform sth** [pə'fɔ:m]	etw ausführen
	via ['vaɪə]	über, mittels
	depending on [dɪ'pendɪŋ ɒn]	je nachdem, abhängig von
	to **require** [rɪ'kwaɪə]	wünschen, benötigen, erfordern
	variety [və'raɪəti]	Vielfalt, Auswahl, Vielzahl
	for instance [fə'r ɪnstəns]	zum Beispiel, beispielsweise
	speed [spi:d]	Geschwindigkeit
	input ['ɪnpʊt]	Eingabe, Eingang
	output ['aʊtpʊt]	Ausgabe, Ausgang
	either … or [,aɪðə 'ɔ:]	entweder … oder
	analogue *BE* ['ænəlɒg]	analog
	to **activate** ['æktɪveɪt]	aktivieren
	cost-effective(ly) [,kɒst ɪ'fektɪv]	kostengünstig
	additional [ə'dɪʃənl]	zusätzlich
49	to **invite** [ɪn'vaɪt]	einladen
	to **follow up on sth** [,fɒləʊ 'ʌp ɒn]	auf etw zurückkommen, etw weiterverfolgen, nachhaken
	to **drive** [draɪv]	antreiben
	therefore ['ðeəfɔ:]	daher, folglich
	to **consider** [kən'sɪdə]	in Erwägung ziehen, in Betracht ziehen
	to **notice** ['nəʊtɪs]	bemerken, (jdm) auffallen
	dark [dɑ:k]	dunkel
	further ['fɜ:ðə]	weitere/r/s
	stable ['steɪbl]	stabil, gleichbleibend
	fan [fæn]	Lüfter, Ventilator
	to **blow** [bləʊ]	blasen
	to **attach sth** [ə'tætʃ]	*(E-Mail:)* etw anhängen
	the costs involved [,kɒsts ɪn'vɒlvd]	die damit verbundenen Kosten
	to **be of assistance** [bi əv ə'sɪstəns]	behilflich sein
	Best regards, [,best rɪ'gɑ:dz]	Mit freundlichen Grüßen
T	**obviously** ['ɒbviəsli]	natürlich, selbstverständlich
	to **go ahead** [,gəʊ ə'hed]	vorgehen, verfahren, loslegen
	to **go for sth** ['gəʊ fə]	etw nehmen
	to **propose** [prə'pəʊz]	vorschlagen
	schedule ['ʃedju:l]	Terminkalender
	first thing ['fɜ:st θɪŋ]	als erstes, früh
	to **slow down** [,sləʊ 'daʊn]	verlangsamen, bremsen
	splendid ['splendɪd]	großartig
	pleasure ['pleʒə]	Vergnügen
	My pleasure. [,maɪ 'pleʒə]	Gern geschehen.
	convection [kən'vekʃn]	Konvektion
50	**sensible** ['sensəbl]	vernünftig
	to **reject** [rɪ'dʒekt]	ablehnen, zurückweisen
51	**extension module** [ɪk'stenʃn mɒdju:l]	Erweiterungsmodul
	workload ['wɜ:kləʊd]	Arbeitspensum
	to **mount** [maʊnt]	montieren, anbringen
	spot [spɒt]	Punkt, Platz, Ort
	to **invest** [ɪn'vest]	investieren
	process memory ['prəʊses meməri]	Prozessspeicher
52	**operating speed** ['ɒpəreɪtɪŋ spi:d]	Arbeitsgeschwindigkeit
	port [pɔ:t]	Anschluss
	length [leŋθ]	Länge
	width [wɪdθ]	Breite
	to **accommodate** [ə'kɒmədeɪt]	unterbringen
	clearance ['klɪərəns]	Abstand
	to **cool** [ku:l]	kühlen
	vertical(ly) ['vɜ:tɪkl]	senkrecht, vertikal
	natural ['nætʃrəl]	natürlich
	effective [ɪ'fektɪv]	effektiv, wirkungsvoll
	cooling ['ku:lɪŋ]	Kühlung

	horizontal(ly) [ˌhɒrɪ'zɒntl]	waagrecht, horizontal
	to **allow for sth** [ə'laʊ fə]	etw einkalkulieren, etw berücksichtigen, etw vorsehen
	to **intend to do sth** [ɪn'tend tə]	vorhaben/beabsichtigen, etw zu tun
	sufficient [sə'fɪʃnt]	ausreichend, genügend
	space [speɪs]	Raum, Platz, Abstand
	removal [rɪ'mu:vl]	Demontage, Aus-/Abbau
	mounting plan ['maʊntɪŋ plæn]	Montageanleitung
	eye lug ['aɪ lʌg]	Ösenanker
	to **ground** [graʊnd]	erden
	wiring route ['waɪərɪŋ ru:t]	Kabelstrecke
	close [kləʊs]	eng
53	**failure** ['feɪljə]	Versäumen, Versäumnis
	guideline ['gaɪdlaɪn]	Richtlinie
	ground terminal ['graʊnd tɜ:mɪnl]	Erdklemme, Masseklemme
	single point ground terminal [ˌsɪŋgl pɔɪnt 'graʊnd tɜ:mɪnl]	Einfach-Erdungspunkt
	impedance [ɪm'pi:dəns]	Impedanz
	to **attach** [ə'tætʃ]	anbringen
	by means of [baɪ 'mi:nz əv]	mittels, durch
	crimping ['krɪmpɪŋ]	Bördeln, Crimpen
	to **solder** ['səʊldə]	löten
	ground [graʊnd]	Masse, Erdung
	bus bar ['bʌs bɑ:]	Sammelschiene, Stromschiene
	ground return ['graʊnd rɪtɜ:n]	Erdungsanschluss/-leitung
	earth ground ['ɜ:θ graʊnd]	Erdung
	panel ground termination ['pænl graʊnd tɜ:mɪ'neɪʃn]	Erdanschluss im Schaltschrank
	common ['kɒmən]	gemeinsam
	ground reference ['graʊnd refərəns]	Bezugsmasse
	essential [ɪ'senʃl]	unerlässlich, wesentlich
	operation [ˌɒpə'reɪʃn]	Betrieb, Funktion
	ground lead ['graʊnd li:d]	Masseleitung
	flexible ['fleksəbl]	biegsam, flexibel
	shielded cable [ˌʃi:ldɪd 'keɪbl]	armiertes Kabel
	several ['sevrəl]	mehrere
	method ['meθəd]	Art, Methode

	adequate ['ædɪkwət]	angemessen, ausreichend
	ground rod ['graʊnd rɒd]	Staberder
	incoming power system ground [ˌɪnkʌmɪŋ 'paʊə sɪstəm graʊnd]	Systemerdung nach dem Übergabepunkt
	isolation transformer [ˌaɪsə'leɪʃn trænsfɔ:mə]	Trenntransformator
	to **eliminate** [ɪ'lɪmɪneɪt]	beseitigen, eliminieren
	to **reduce** [rɪ'dju:s]	verringern, reduzieren
	suspected [sə'spektɪd]	mutmaßlich, vermutet
	to **exceed** [ɪk'si:d]	überschreiten, hinausgehen über
	capacity [kə'pæsəti]	Kapazität
	continuous [kən'tɪnjuəs]	ununterbrochen, kontinuierlich
	cable tray ['keɪbl treɪ]	Kabelkanal, Kabelrinne
	cable routing ['keɪbl ru:tɪŋ]	Kabelführung
	voltage drop ['vəʊltɪdʒ drɒp]	Spannungsabfall
	distance ['dɪstəns]	Strecke
	multiple ['mʌltɪpl]	vielfach, mehrfach
	return line [rɪ'tɜ:n laɪn]	Rücklaufleitung
	in close proximity [ɪn ˌkləʊs prɒk'sɪməti]	in unmittelbarer Nähe
	sharp(ly) ['ʃɑ:p]	scharf
54	to **be about** [bi ə'baʊt]	in der Nähe sein, da sein T
	in person [ɪn 'pɜ:sn]	persönlich
	instead [ɪn'sted]	stattdessen
	point of view [ˌpɔɪnt əv 'vju:]	Standpunkt
	grateful ['greɪtfl]	dankbar
55	**ladder logic** ['lædə lɒdʒɪk]	Leiterlogik, Kontaktplan
	the basics *pl* [ðə 'beɪsɪks]	die Grundlagen
	common ['kɒmən]	(weit) verbreitet
	graphic ['græfɪk]	bildlich, grafisch
	rail [reɪl]	Schiene
	series ['sɪəri:z]	Reihe
	rung [rʌŋ]	Sprosse
	schematic [ski:'mætik]	Schaltbild
	relay circuit ['ri:leɪ sɜ:kɪt]	Relaisschaltung
	similarity [ˌsɪmə'lærəti]	Ähnlichkeit
	sequential control [sɪˌkwenʃl kən'trəʊl]	Ablaufsteuerung, Folgeschaltung
	real-time [ˌri:əl 'taɪm]	Echtzeit-
	critical ['krɪtɪkl]	entscheidend
	to **rework** [ˌri:'wɜ:k]	überarbeiten
	hardwired [ˌhɑ:d'waɪəd]	festverdrahtet

	sophisticated [sə'fɪstɪkeɪtɪd]	hoch entwickelt, raffiniert
	closely related [ˌkləʊsli rɪ'leɪtɪd]	eng verwandt
	compatible [kəm'pætəbl]	austauschbar, kompatibel
	ladder notification ['lædə nəʊtɪfɪkeɪʃn]	Programmablaufplan
	seamless(ly) ['si:mləs]	nahtlos
	to **interchange** ['ɪntətʃeɪndʒ]	untereinander austauschen
	tricky ['trɪki]	schwierig
	range [reɪndʒ]	Bandbreite, Reihe, Auswahl

UNIT 6

56	**environment** [ɪn'vaɪrənmənt]	Umwelt
	biomass ['baɪəʊmæs]	Biomasse
	fossil ['fɒsl]	fossil
	fuel ['fju:əl]	Brennstoff, Kraftstoff, Treibstoff
	geothermal energy [dʒi:əʊˌθɜ:ml 'enədʒi]	Erdwärme
	hydro-electric energy [haɪdrəʊɪˌlektrɪk 'enədʒi]	Wasserkraft
	methane ['mi:θeɪn]	Methan
	nuclear energy [ˌnju:kliə 'enədʒi]	Kernkraft
	solar energy [ˌsəʊlər 'enədʒi]	Sonnenenergie, Solarenergie
	tidal energy [ˌtaɪdl 'enədʒi]	Gezeitenenergie
	alternative [ɔ:l'tɜ:nətɪv]	alternativ
	to **generate** ['dʒenəreɪt]	erzeugen, gewinnen
	if so [ɪf 'səʊ]	falls ja
	PV system [ˌpi: 'vi: sɪstəm]	Photovoltaikanlage
	worth [wɜ:θ]	wert
	investment [ɪn'vestmənt]	Investition
	solar thermal collector [ˌsəʊlə 'θɜ:ml kəlektə]	thermischer Solarkollektor
	photovoltaic [ˌfəʊtəʊvəl'tejɪk]	Photovoltaik
57	**reliance (on sth)** [rɪ'laɪəns]	Abhängigkeit (von etw)
	public utilities *pl* [ˌpʌblɪk ju:'tɪlətiz]	öffentliche Versorgungsbetriebe
	to **cut** [kʌt]	verringern, abbauen, senken
	environmental [ɪnˌvaɪrən'mentl]	Umwelt-
	pollution [pə'lu:ʃn]	Verschmutzung
	free [fri:]	kostenlos
	to **capture** ['kæptʃə]	einfangen
	to **trap** [træp]	einfangen, speichern
	infrared~ (IR) [ˌɪnfrə'red]	infrarot, Infrarot(-)
	radiation [ˌreɪdi'eɪʃn]	Strahlung
	glass panel ['glɑ:s pænl]	Glasscheibe
	housing ['haʊzɪŋ]	Gehäuse
	fluid ['flu:ɪd]	Flüssigkeit
	to **pipe sth** [paɪp]	etw (durch ein Rohr) leiten
	radiator ['reɪdieɪtə]	Heizkörper
	silicon ['sɪlɪkən]	Silizium
	cell [sel]	Zelle
	sunlight ['sʌnlaɪt]	Sonnenlicht
	to **strike sth** [straɪk]	auf etw treffen
	electron [ɪ'lektrɒn]	Elektron
	to **release** [rɪ'li:s]	freisetzen
	pros and cons [ˌprəʊz ənd 'kɒnz]	Für und Wider
	in favour of sth [ɪn 'feɪvər əv]	für etw
	durable ['djʊərəbl]	langlebig, robust
	to **preserve** [prɪ'zɜ:v]	erhalten
	renewable [rɪ'nju:əbl]	erneuerbar
	downside ['daʊnsaɪd]	Nachteil, Kehrseite
	on the downside [ɒn ðə 'daʊnsaɪd]	andererseits
	fairly ['feəli]	ziemlich
	to **shine** [ʃaɪn]	scheinen
	cloudy ['klaʊdi]	bewölkt
	to **draw sth** [drɔ:]	etw beziehen
58	**wave power** ['weɪv paʊə]	Wellenenergie
	to **exploit** [ɪk'splɔɪt]	nutzen, ausbeuten
	antifreeze solution ['æntɪˌfri:z səlu:ʃn]	Frostschutzmittel
	rain [reɪn]	Regen
	tough [tʌf]	strapazierfähig, robust
	in the short term [ɪn ðə ˌʃɔ:t 'tɜ:m]	kurzfristig
	catastrophic [ˌkætə'strɒfɪk]	katastrophal
	impact ['ɪmpækt]	Auswirkung(en), Folgen
	to **pollute** [pə'lu:t]	verschmutzen
	stage [steɪdʒ]	Phase, Etappe, Stufe
59	**lunchtime** ['lʌntʃtaɪm]	Mittagszeit
	orientation [ˌɔ:riən'teɪʃn]	Ausrichtung, Orientierung
	roof [ru:f]	Dach
	inclination [ˌɪnklɪ'neɪʃn]	Neigung
	to **face** [feɪs]	*(in eine Richtung)* ausgerichtet sein
	angle ['æŋgl]	Winkel

	to **cover** ['kʌvə]	decken
	household ['haʊshəʊld]	Haushalt
	demand [dɪ'mɑ:nd]	Bedarf
	regarding [rɪ'gɑ:dɪŋ]	bezüglich, betreffend
	scaffolding ['skæfəldɪŋ]	Baugerüst
	platform ['plætfɔ:m]	Plattform
	roof anchor ['ru:f æŋkə]	Deckenanker
	chalk [tʃɔ:k]	Kreide
	to **rain** [reɪn]	regnen
	to **wash off** [ˌwɒʃ 'ɒf]	etw (von etw) abwaschen
	to **fix** [fɪks]	befestigen
	roof tile ['ru:f taɪl]	Dachziegel
	in place [ɪn 'pleɪs]	an Ort und Stelle, bereit, fertig
	bar [bɑ:]	Leiste, Stange
	to **make sth up** [ˌmeɪk 'ʌp]	etw ausmachen
	to **screw** [skru:]	schrauben
	array [ə'reɪ]	Anordnung
	frame [freɪm]	Rahmen
	to **secure** [sɪ'kjuə]	sichern, befestigen
	watertight ['wɔ:tətaɪt]	wasserdicht
	sealant ['si:lənt]	Dichtungsmittel
	Thank goodness. [ˌθæŋk 'gʊdnəs]	Gott sei Dank!
	in the meantime [ɪn ðə 'mi:ntaɪm]	in der Zwischenzeit
	inverter [ɪn'vɜ:tə]	Wechselrichter, Inverter
	direct current (DC) [dəˌrekt 'kʌrənt]	Gleichstrom
	to **power up** [ˌpaʊər 'ʌp]	einschalten, starten
	to **function** ['fʌŋkʃn]	funktionieren
	efficiency [ɪ'fɪʃnsi]	Wirkungsgrad, Effizienz
	energy efficiency [ˌenədʒi ɪ'fɪʃnsi]	Energieeffizienz
60	to **erect** [ɪ'rekt]	errichten, aufbauen
	nought *BE* [nɔ:t]	null
	zero *AE* ['zɪərəʊ]	null
	point [pɔɪnt]	Komma
	trillion ['trɪljən]	Billion
P	**mathematical** [ˌmæθə'mætɪkl]	mathematisch
61	**subtraction** [səb'trækʃn]	Subtraktion
	multiplication [ˌmʌltɪplɪ'keɪʃn]	Multiplikation
	times [taɪmz]	mal
	to **multiply** ['mʌltɪplaɪ]	multiplizieren, malnehmen
	over ['əʊvə]	geteilt durch
	to **divide (by)** [dɪ'vaɪd]	teilen (durch)
	equal ['i:kwəl]	gleich
	equals ['i:kwəlz]	ist gleich
	squared [skweəd]	im Quadrat, hoch zwei
	cubed [kju:bd]	hoch drei
	to the power of [tə ðə 'paʊər əv]	*(Exponent:)* hoch
	square metre ['skweə mi:tə]	Quadratmeter
	cubic metre ['kju:bɪk mi:tə]	Kubikmeter
	fraction ['frækʃn]	Bruch
	to **determine** [dɪ'tɜ:mɪn]	bestimmen, ermitteln
	solar module ['səʊlə mɒdju:l]	Solarmodul
	kilowatt hour ['kɪləwɒt aʊə]	Kilowattstunde
	on average [ɒn 'ævərɪdʒ]	durchschnittlich
	electricity bill [ɪˌlek'trɪsəti bɪl]	Stromrechnung
	watt hour ['wɒt aʊə]	Wattstunde
	to **calculate** ['kælkjuleɪt]	ausrechnen, berechnen
	saving ['seɪvɪŋ]	Ersparnis
	percentage [pə'sentɪdʒ]	Prozentsatz
	inefficiency [ˌɪnɪ'fɪʃnsi]	Ineffizienz, Unwirtschaftlichkeit
	wattage ['wɒtɪdʒ]	Leistung, Stromverbrauch
	to **round up** [ˌraʊnd 'ʌp]	aufrunden
62	**meter** ['mi:tə]	Zähler
T	to **run through sth** ['rʌn θru:]	etw durchgehen
	at all [ət 'ɔ:l]	überhaupt
	charge [tʃɑ:dʒ]	Ladung
	to **regulate** ['regjuleɪt]	regeln, regulieren
	charge controller ['tʃɑ:dʒ kəntrəʊlə]	Laderegler
	to **feed into** ['fi:d ɪntə]	einspeisen
	electricity provider [ɪˌlek'trɪsəti prəvaɪdə]	Stromversorger
	Remind me. [rɪ'maɪnd mi:]	Erklär's mir nochmal.
	domestic [də'mestɪk]	häuslich, Haus-
	wind turbine ['wɪnd tɜ:baɪn]	Windrad, Windanlage
	electrochemical [ɪˌlektrəʊ'kemɪkl]	elektrochemisch
	hydrogen ['haɪdrədʒən]	Wasserstoff
	rotation [rəʊ'teɪʃn]	Umdrehung, Rotation
	miles per hour (mph) [ˌmaɪlz pər 'aʊə]	Meilen pro Stunde
	emission [ɪ'mɪʃn]	Ausstoß, Emission
	significant(ly) [sɪg'nɪfɪkənt]	beträchtlich, bedeutsam, erheblich
	fuel cell ['fju:əl sel]	Brennstoffzelle

	noise [nɔɪz]	Lärm
	vibration [vaɪ'breɪʃn]	Vibration(en), Erschütterung(en)
	generation [ˌdʒenə'reɪʃn]	Erzeugung
	mechanism ['mekənɪzəm]	Mechanismus
	blade [bleɪd]	(Rotor-)Blatt, (Turbinen-)Schaufel
	tip [tɪp]	Spitze
	proton exchange membrane [ˌprəʊtɒn ɪks'tʃeɪndʒ membreɪn]	Protonenaustauschmembran
T	**disappointing** [ˌdɪsə'pɔɪntɪŋ]	enttäuschend
	dramatic(ally) [drə'mætɪk]	dramatisch
	noisy ['nɔɪzi]	laut
	CHP unit [ˌsiː eɪtʃ 'piː juːnɪt]	Blockheizkraftwerk
	to **burn** [bɜːn]	verbrennen
	cut [kʌt]	Reduzierung, Senkung, Abbau
63	to **waste** [weɪst]	verschwenden, vergeuden
	standby ['stændbaɪ]	Bereitschaft
	mode [məʊd]	Modus
	waste [weɪst]	Verschwendung, Vergeudung
	no wonder [nəʊ 'wʌndə]	kein Wunder(, dass)
	target ['tɑːɡɪt]	Ziel
	disaster [dɪ'zɑːstə]	Katastrophe
	scientist ['saɪəntɪst]	Naturwissenschaftler/in
	to **take sth seriously** [ˌteɪk 'sɪəriəsli]	etw ernst nehmen
64	**war** [wɔː]	Krieg
	well-enough-known [ˌwel ɪnʌf 'nəʊn]	nur allzu bekannt
	contest ['kɒntest]	Wettstreit
	century ['sentʃəri]	Jahrhundert
	to **transport** [træn'spɔːt]	befördern, transportieren
	large-scale ['lɑːdʒskeɪl]	groß angelegt, ausgedehnt
	to **challenge** ['tʃælɪndʒ]	herausfordern
	to **suffer** ['sʌfə]	leiden, erleiden
	loss [lɒs]	Verlust
	of a lower order [əv ə ˌləʊə 'ɔːdə]	nachrangig, niedriger
	to amount to sth [ə'maʊnt tə]	sich auf etw belaufen
	result [rɪ'zʌlt]	Folge, Auswirkung
	cash [kæʃ]	Geld, Bargeld

	in terms of … [ɪn 'tɜːmz əv]	was … betrifft
	to **be set to do sth** [bi 'set tə]	darauf eingestellt sein, etw zu tun
	to **result in sth** [rɪ'zʌlt ɪn]	etw zur Folge haben
	far-reaching [ˌfɑː 'riːtʃɪŋ]	folgenschwer, weitreichend, tiefgreifend
	to **experience** [ɪk'spɪəriəns]	erleben, durchmachen
	to **isolate** ['aɪsəleɪt]	isolieren, absondern
	to **clear the way for sth** [ˌklɪə ðə 'weɪ fə]	den Weg für etw bereiten
	harnessing ['hɑːnɪsɪŋ]	Nutzbarmachung, Nutzung
	truly ['truːli]	wirklich
	grand [ɡrænd]	groß, gewaltig, eindrucksvoll
	scale [skeɪl]	Umfang
	according to [ə'kɔːdɪŋ tə]	gemäß, laut, nach
	analyst ['ænəlɪst]	Analyst/in
	consultancy [kən'sʌltənsi]	Beratungsfirma
	development [dɪ'veləpmənt]	*(Immobilie:)* Erschließung
	enormous [ɪ'nɔːməs]	enorm, riesig
	isolated ['aɪsəleɪtɪd]	*(Ort:)* abgeschieden, abgelegen
	far-flung [ˌfɑː 'flʌŋ]	abgelegen
	region ['riːdʒən]	Region, Gegend, Gebiet
	practicable ['præktɪkəbl]	durchführbar, machbar, praktikabel
	technologist [tek'nɒlədʒɪst]	Technologe/-in
	up until now [ʌp ənˌtɪl 'naʊ]	bislang, bis jetzt
	potential [pə'tenʃl]	potenziell
	reality [ri'æləti]	Wirklichkeit, Realität
	wastes *pl* [weɪsts]	Einöde, Wüste
	desert ['dezət]	Wüste
	gigantic [dʒaɪ'ɡæntɪk]	gigantisch, ungeheuer
	realizable ['rɪəlaɪzəbl]	umsetzbar, realisierbar
	thanks to ['θæŋks tə]	dank
	beyond [bɪ'jɒnd]	jenseits
	optimism ['ɒptɪmɪzəm]	Zuversicht, Optimismus
65	**smart** [smɑːt]	intelligent
	government ['ɡʌvənmənt]	Regierung
	across … [ə'krɒs]	in ganz …
	by 2020 [baɪ]	bis 2020
	to **come in for sth** [ˌkʌm 'ɪn fə]	etw *(Kritik usw.)* abbekommen

	simultaneous [ˌsɪml'teɪniəs]	gleichzeitig
	praise [preɪz]	Lob
	criticism ['krɪtɪsɪzəm]	Kritik
	roll-out ['rəʊlaʊt]	Einführung
	attempt [ə'tempt]	Versuch, Bestreben
	to **emit** [ɪ'mɪt]	ausstoßen, emittieren
	move [mu:v]	Maßnahme, Schritt
	to **welcome** ['welkəm]	begrüßen
	watchdog ['wɒtʃdɒg]	Wachhund
	watchdog organization ['wɒtʃdɒg ɔ:gənaɪzeɪʃn]	*hier:* Verbraucherschutzorganisation
	to **promote sth** [prə'məʊt]	etw *(Interessen usw.)* vertreten
	spokesperson ['spəʊkspɜ:sn]	Sprecher/in
	widespread ['waɪdspred]	großflächig, umfassend
	implementation [ˌɪmplɪmen'teɪʃn]	Einführung, Umsetzung, Anwendung
	overall [ˌəʊvər'ɔ:l]	gesamt, allgemein
	benefit ['benɪfɪt]	Nutzen, Vorteil
	to **estimate** ['estɪmeɪt]	schätzen
	to **read a meter** [ˌri:d ə 'mi:tə]	einen Zähler ablesen
	to **be required to do sth** [bi rɪ'kwaɪəd tə]	verpflichtet sein, etw zu tun; etw tun müssen
	to **leave sb in the dark** [ˌli:v ɪn ðə 'dɑ:k]	jdn im Unklaren lassen
	to **cut sth back** [ˌkʌt 'bæk]	etw zurückschrauben, etw verringern
	odd [ɒd]	seltsam, merkwürdig, sonderbar
	given that ['gɪvn ðət]	angesichts
	to **call on sb to do sth** [ˌkɔ:l ɒn]	jdn auffordern, etw zu tun
	integrated ['ɪntɪgreɪtɪd]	integriert
	usage ['ju:sɪdʒ]	Verbrauch
	use [ju:s]	Verwendung, Verbrauch
	to **identify** [aɪ'dentɪfaɪ]	herausfinden, identifizieren
	to **consume** [kən'sju:m]	verbrauchen
	appropriate [ə'prəʊpriət]	angemessen, geeignet
	to **take steps** [ˌteɪk 'steps]	Schritte unternehmen, Maßnahmen ergreifen
	to **claim** [kleɪm]	behaupten
	so far [ˌsəʊ 'fɑ:]	bisher, bislang
	to **be dismissive of sth** [bi dɪs'mɪsɪv əv]	einer Sache ablehnend gegenüberstehen
	to **check up on sth** [ˌtʃek 'ʌp ɒn]	etw nachsehen, etw überprüfen
	to **encourage** [ɪn'kʌrɪdʒ]	ermutigen, ermuntern, auffordern
	to **think again** [ˌθɪŋk ə'gen]	umdenken, seine Meinung ändern
	measure ['meʒə]	Maßnahme
	objection [əb'dʒekʃn]	Einwand
	member ['membə]	Mitglied
	to **report to sb (on sth)** [rɪ'pɔ:t tə]	jdm (über etw) Bericht erstatten

UNIT 7

66	to **trace** [treɪs]	ausfindig machen, aufspüren
	data sheet ['deɪtə ʃi:t]	Datenblatt
	capacitor [kə'pæsɪtə]	Kondensator
	diode ['daɪəʊd]	Diode
	bridge rectifier ['brɪdʒ rektɪfaɪə]	Brückengleichrichter
	full-wave bridge rectifier [ˌfʊl weɪv 'brɪdʒ rektɪfaɪə]	Vollwellenbrückengleichrichter
	glass fuse ['glɑ:s fju:z]	Glassicherung
	integrated voltage stabilizer [ˌɪntɪgreɪtɪd 'vəʊltɪdʒ steɪbəlaɪzə]	integrierter Spannungsstabilisator
	mains input socket [ˌmeɪnz 'ɪnpʊt sɒkɪt]	Netzanschlussbuchse
	transistor [træn'zɪstə]	Transistor
	(vacuum) tube *AE* [tju:b]	(Elektronen-)Röhre
67	**radio ham** ['reɪdiəʊ hæm]	Amateurfunker/in
	call sign ['kɔ:l saɪn]	Rufzeichen
	ham radio ['hæm reɪdiəʊ]	Amateurfunk
	enthusiast [ɪn'θju:ziæzt]	Liebhaber/in, Enthusiast
	to **communicate** [kə'mju:nɪkeɪt]	kommunizieren
	means [mi:nz]	Mittel
	to **fail** [feɪl]	versagen, ausfallen
	earthquake ['ɜ:θkweɪk]	Erdbeben
	licence ['laɪsns]	Genehmigung, Lizenz
	examination [ɪgˌzæmɪ'neɪʃn]	Prüfung
	to **take an examination** [ˌteɪk ən ɪgzæmɪ'neɪʃn]	eine Prüfung ablegen
	to **obtain** [əb'teɪn]	erlangen, erhalten, bekommen
T	**loud** [laʊd]	laut
	to **spare** [speə]	erübrigen
	to **be glad to do sth** [bi 'glæd tə]	etw gern tun
	guitar [gɪ'tɑ:]	Gitarre
	amp(lifier) ['æmplɪfaɪə]	Verstärker

	radio shack ['reɪdiəʊ ʃæk]	Funkbude, Elektrowerkstatt
	guitarist [gɪ'tɑːrɪst]	Gitarrist/in
	gig [gɪg]	*(Pop, Rock, Jazz:)* Konzert
	dead [ded]	stromlos, tot
	to **go dead** [ˌgəʊ 'ded]	ausgehen, ausfallen
	control light [kən'trəʊl laɪt]	Kontrolllampe
	to **come on** [ˌkʌm 'ɒn]	angehen
	to **illuminate** [ɪ'luːmɪneɪt]	beleuchten
	sensory ['sensəri]	sensorisch
	charred [tʃɑːd]	verkohlt
	burning ['bɜːnɪŋ]	Verbrennung, Brand
	to **rectify** ['rektɪfaɪ]	gleichrichten
	semi-conductor [ˌsemi kən'dʌktə]	Halbleiter
	You're welcome. [jɔː 'welkəm]	Bitte, Gern geschehen.
	pleased [pliːzd]	froh, erfreut
	power supply ['pauə səplaɪ]	Netzteil
68	**square** [skweə]	Quadrat, Feld
	cause [kɔːz]	Ursache, Grund
	paper clip ['peɪpə klɪp]	Büroklammer
	dry solder joint [ˌdraɪ 'səʊldə dʒɔɪnt]	kalte Lötstelle
	circuit board ['sɜːkɪt bɔːd]	Leiterplatte
	loose [luːs]	locker, lose
	to **come loose** [ˌkʌm 'luːs]	sich lockern
69	**troubleshooting** ['trʌblʃuːtɪŋ]	Fehlersuche
	to **appreciate** [ə'priːʃieɪt]	schätzen, zu schätzen wissen
	Cheers! [tʃɪəz]	Tschüs!, Danke!
	obvious ['ɒbviəs]	offensichtlich, offenbar, klar
	mains input ['meɪnz ɪnpʊt]	Netzeingang, Netzanschluss
	smoothing circuit ['smuːðɪŋ sɜːkɪt]	Glättungskreis
	to **take a close/r look at sth** [teɪk ə ˌkləʊs/'kləʊsə 'lʊk ət]	sich etw genau/er ansehen
	discoloured [ˌdɪs'kʌləd]	verfärbt, entfärbt
	base [beɪs]	Sockel, Unterlage, Träger, Basis
	to **unsolder** [ˌʌn'səʊldə]	entlöten
	outlet ['aʊtlet]	Ausgang
	desoldering pump [ˌdiː'səʊldərɪŋ pʌmp]	Entlötpumpe
	to **suck sth off** [ˌsʌk 'ɒf]	etw absaugen
	solder ['səʊldə]	Lot, Lötzinn
	consequently ['kɒnsɪkwəntli]	folglich, demzufolge
	forward current [ˌfɔːwəd 'kʌrənt]	Durchlassstrom
	reverse current [rɪˌvɜːs 'kʌrənt]	Sperrstrom, Strom in Sperrrichtung
70	**previous** ['priːviəs]	vorige/r/s, vorherige/r/s
	battery-operated ['bætəri ɒpəreɪtɪd]	batteriebetrieben
	to **break down** [ˌbreɪk 'daʊn]	kaputtgehen
	to **take sth apart** [ˌteɪk ə'pɑːt]	etw auseinanderbauen
	test point ['test pɔɪnt]	Prüfpunkt, Messstelle
	to **remove** [rɪ'muːv]	entfernen, ausbauen
	birthday ['bɜːθdeɪ]	Geburtstag
71	**album** ['ælbəm]	Schallplatte, CD
	tour [tʊə]	Tournee
	concert ['kɒnsət]	Konzert
	follow-up ['fɒləʊ ʌp]	Folge-, Anschluss-
72	to **handle sth** ['hændl]	etw erledigen, etw handhaben, etw bewältigen T
73	**avalanche** ['ævəlɑːnʃ]	Lawine
	avanlanche diode ['ævəlɑːnʃ daɪəʊd]	Lawinendiode
	sinterglass ['sɪntəglɑːs]	Sinterglas
	characteristics *pl* [ˌkærəktə'rɪstɪks]	Charakteristika
	glass passivated ['glɑːs pæsɪveɪtɪd]	glaspassiviert
	junction ['dʒʌŋkʃn]	P-N-Übergang (in Halbleitern)
	hermetically sealed [hɜːˌmetɪkli 'siːld]	hermetisch abgedichtet
	package ['pækɪdʒ]	*hier:* Gehäuse
	surge current loading ['sɜːdʒ kʌrənt ləʊdɪŋ]	Stoßstrom-Grenzwert
	application [ˌæplɪ'keɪʃn]	Anwendung
	case [keɪs]	Gehäuse
	sintered glass [ˌsɪntəd 'glɑːs]	Sinterglas
	plated ['pleɪtɪd]	metallüberzogen
	axial ['æksiəl]	axial
	solderable ['səʊldərəbl]	lötbar
	polarity [pə'lærəti]	Polung, Polarität
	color band *AE* ['kʌlə bænd]	Farbring
	to **denote** [dɪ'nəʊt]	bezeichnen, kennzeichnen
	cathode ['kæθəʊd]	Kathode
	weight [weɪt]	Gewicht
	absolute ['æbsəluːt]	absolut

test condition ['test kəndɪʃn] Testbedingung
repetitive peak reverse voltage [rɪˌpetətɪv ˌpi:k rɪvɜ:s 'vəʊltɪdʒ] wiederkehrende Spitzensperrspannung
peak forward surge current [ˌpi:k ˌfɔ:wəd 'sɜ:dʒ kʌrənt] Spitzendurchlassstrom
repetitive peak forward current [rɪˌpetətɪv ˌpi:k fɔ:wəd 'vəʊltɪdʒ] wiederkehrender Spitzendurchlassstrom
pulse avalanche peak power [ˌpʌls ævəlɑ:nʃ 'pi:k paʊə] Spitzenleistung bei Pulsbelastung
sine wave ['saɪn weɪv] Sinuskurve, Sinuswelle
74 **fault-tolerant** ['fɔ:lt tɒlərənt] fehlertolerant
redundant [rɪ'dʌndənt] redundant
driving motor ['draɪvɪŋ məʊtə] Antriebsmotor
conveyor [kən'veɪə] Förderband
spare part [ˌspeə 'pɑ:t] Ersatzteil
convenient [kən'vi:niənt] günstig, praktisch
to **demonstrate** ['demənstreɪt] vorführen, beweisen, demonstrieren
to **hit sth** [hɪt] auf etw treffen
gulf [gʌlf] Golf
coast [kəʊst] Küste
television station ['telɪvɪʒn steɪʃn] Fernsehsender
to **interview** ['ɪntəvju:] befragen, interviewen
telecom carrier ['telɪkɒm kærɪə] Telefongesellschaft
operational [ˌɒpə'reɪʃənl] einsatzbereit, betriebsfähig
to **lose service** [ˌlu:z 'sɜ:vɪs] *hier:* den Betrieb einstellen (müssen)
to **reply (to)** [rɪ'plaɪ] antworten (auf)
industrial complex [ɪnˌdʌstriəl 'kɒmpleks] Industriekomplex
backup system ['bækʌp sɪstəm] Notfallsystem, Reservesystem
battery bank ['bætəri bæŋk] Batteriebank
uninterruptible [ˌʌnˌɪntə'rʌptəbl] unterbrechungsfrei, ausfallsicher
frequently ['fri:kwəntli] häufig, oft
terminology [ˌtɜ:mɪ'nɒlədʒi] Terminologie, Begriffe
to **hot-swap** ['hɒt swɒp] im laufenden Betrieb wechseln
to **swap** [swɒp] austauschen, auswechseln
disruption [dɪs'rʌpʃn] Unterbrechung, Störung
rare event [ˌreər ɪ'vent] seltener Fall
shorted ['ʃɔ:tɪd] kurzgeschlossen
short [ʃɔ:t] Kurzschluss
to **bring down** [ˌbrɪŋ 'daʊn] senken, herunterfahren
to **flag sth up** [ˌflæg 'ʌp] etw anzeigen
alarm relay [ə'lɑ:m ri:leɪ] Alarmrelais
to **prevent** [prɪ'vent] verhindern
to **go unnoticed** [ˌgəʊ ʌn'nəʊtɪst] unbemerkt bleiben
75 **high-power** [ˌhaɪ 'paʊə] Hochleistungs-
radio frequency (RF) [ˌreɪdiəʊ 'fri:kwənsi] Hochfrequenz (HF)
radio station ['reɪdiəʊ steɪʃn] Radiosender
power tube ['paʊə tju:b] Leistungsröhre
ultra high frequency (UHF) [ˌʌltrə haɪ 'fri:kwənsi] Ultrahochfrequenz
frequency modulation (FM) ['fri:kwənsi mɒdjuleɪʃn] Frequenzmodulation, UKW
broadcast station ['brɔ:dkɑ:st steɪʃn] (Radio-/TV-)Sender
exclusive(ly) [ɪk'sklu:sɪv] ausschließlich
solid-state [ˌsɒlɪd 'steɪt] Halbleiter-
transmitter [træns'mɪtə] Sender
power transistor ['paʊə trænzɪstə] Leistungstransistor
heat-sink ['hi:t sɪŋk] Kühlkörper
equivalent [ɪ'kwɪvələnt] entsprechend
economic [ˌi:kə'nɒmɪk] wirtschaftlich, kostengünstig
tone [təʊn] Klang, Ton
musician [mju:'zɪʃn] Musiker/in
speaker ['spi:kə] Lautsprecher
musical instrument [ˌmju:zɪkl 'ɪnstrəmənt] Musikinstrument
distortion [dɪ'stɔ:ʃn] Verzerrung
output transformer ['aʊtpʊt trænsfɔ:mə] Ausgangsübertrager, -transformator
unique [ju'ni:k] einzigartig
to **simulate** ['sɪmjuleɪt] nachahmen, nachbilden
conservative [kən'sɜ:vətɪv] konservativ
to **insist on sth** [ɪn'sɪst ɒn] auf etw bestehen
valve *BE* [vælv] (Elektronen-)Röhre
oscillation [ˌɒsɪ'leɪʃn] Schwingung
wave [weɪv] Welle

	range [reɪndʒ]	Bereich, (Frequenz-) Band
	wavelength ['weɪvleŋθ]	Wellenlänge
	to **vary** ['veəri]	verändern, variieren
	approximately [ə'prɒksɪmətli]	ungefähr, zirka

UNIT 8

76	**ammeter** ['æmmi:tə]	Amperemeter
	capacitance meter [kə'pæsɪtəns mi:tə]	Kapazitätsmessgerät
	mains tester ['meɪnz testə]	Phasenprüfer
	ohmmeter ['əummi:tə]	Ohmmeter
	oscilloscope [ə'sɪləskəʊp]	Oszilloskop, Oszillograph
	test light ['test laɪt]	Prüflicht
	voltmeter ['vəʊltmi:tə]	Voltmeter
77	**root mean square (RMS)** [ˌru:t mi:n 'skweə]	Quadratmittel, Effektivwert
	peak voltage (PV) [ˌpi:k 'vəʊltɪdʒ]	Spitzenspannung
	square root ['skweə ru:t]	Quadratwurzel
	calculator ['kælkjuleɪtə]	Taschenrechner
78	**axis** ['æksɪs]	Achse
	to **display** [dɪ'spleɪ]	darstellen, zeigen
	waveform ['weɪvfɔ:m]	Kurve, Stromverlauf
	to **alternate** ['ɔ:ltɜ:neɪt]	wechseln, alternieren
	input socket ['ɪnpʊt sɒkɪt]	Eingangsbuchse
	voltage per division [ˌvəʊltɪdʒ pɜ: dɪ'vɪʒn]	Volt pro Einheit/Strich
	control [kən'trəʊl]	Regler
	knob [nɒb]	(Dreh-)Knopf
	intensity [ɪn'tensəti]	Intensität
	brightness ['braɪtnəs]	Helligkeit
	to **focus** ['fəʊkəs]	scharf stellen, fokussieren
	trace [treɪs]	Kurve
	button ['bʌtn]	(Druck-)Knopf, Taste
	sinusoidal [ˌsaɪnə'sɔɪdl]	sinusförmig, Sinus-
	rectified waveform [ˌrektɪfaɪd 'weɪvfɔ:m]	Form der gleichgerichteten Spannung/ Welle
	brief [bri:f]	kurz, knapp
79	**battery charger** ['bætəri tʃɑ:dʒə]	Akku-/Batterie-Ladegerät
	exchange student [ɪks'tʃeɪndʒ stju:dnt]	Austauschschüler/in/-student/in
	to **charge** [tʃɑ:dʒ]	laden, aufladen
T	**otherwise** ['ʌðəwaɪz]	sonst
	to **miss sth** [mɪs]	etw übersehen, etw verfehlen
	electrolytic capacitor [ɪlektrəˌlɪtɪk kə'pæsɪtə]	Elektrolytkondensator
	writing ['raɪtɪŋ]	Schrift
	adjustable [ə'dʒʌstəbl]	regelbar, einstellbar
	integrated voltage regulator [ˌɪntɪgreɪtɪd 'vəʊltɪdʒ regjuleɪtə]	integrierter Spannungsregler
	colour-coded ['kʌlə kəʊdɪd]	farbkodiert
	potentiometer [pəˌtenʃi'ɒmɪtə]	Potentiometer
	to **get started** [ˌget 'stɑ:tɪd]	anfangen, loslegen
	assignment [ə'saɪnmənt]	Aufgabe, Auftrag
80	to **let sth through** [ˌlet 'θru:]	etw durchlassen
	to **limit** ['lɪmɪt]	begrenzen
	to **decrease** [dɪ'kri:s]	senken
	to **join** [dʒɔɪn]	(miteinander) verbinden
81	to **write up** [ˌraɪt 'ʌp]	ausarbeiten, erstellen
	training officer ['treɪnɪŋ ɒfɪsə]	Ausbildungsleiter/in
	to **refer to sth** [rɪ'fɜ: tə]	sich auf etw beziehen
	pulsating [pʌl'seɪtɪŋ]	pulsierend
	to **smooth** [smu:ð]	glätten
	ripple ['rɪpl]	Kräuseln, Welligkeit
82	**smoothing capacitor** ['smu:ðɪŋ kəpæsɪtə]	Glättungskondensator
83	**terrible** ['terəbl]	furchtbar, schrecklich
	to **go crazy** [ˌgəʊ 'kreɪzi]	durchdrehen, ausrasten
84	**remote control** [rɪˌməʊt kən'trəʊl]	Fernbedienung
	blocker ['blɒkə]	Blockierer
	to **point sth to sth** ['pɔɪnt tə]	etw auf etw richten
	to **jam** [dʒæm]	lahmlegen, blockieren
	self-explanatory [ˌself ɪk'splænətri]	selbsterklärend
	astable multivibrator [ˌæstəbl ˌmʌltɪvaɪ'breɪtə]	astabiler Multivibrator
	beam [bi:m]	Strahl
	roughly ['rʌfli]	ungefähr
	range [reɪndʒ]	Reichweite
	ray [reɪ]	Strahl
	trial and error [ˌtraɪəl ənd 'erə]	Versuch und Irrtum, Ausprobieren
	to **respond** [rɪ'spɒnd]	reagieren
	indicator ['ɪndɪkeɪtə]	Anzeige, Anzeiger
	to **employ** [ɪm'plɔɪ]	verwenden
	to **feed** [fi:d]	zuführen
	to **sound an alarm** [ˌsaʊnd ən ə'lɑ:m]	einen Warnton erklingen lassen

	reasonable ['ri:znəbl]	sinnvoll, angemessen
	to **calibrate** ['kælɪbreɪt]	kalibrieren
	base (of a transistor) [beɪs]	Basis (eines Transistors)
	to **pull sth low** [ˌpʊl 'ləʊ]	etw *(z.B. Spannung)* herunterziehen
	to **saturate** ['sætʃəreɪt]	sättigen
85	**in excess of** [ɪn 'ekses əv]	(von) mehr als, über
	floating operation [ˌfləʊtɪŋ ɒpə'reɪʃn]	erdfreier Betrieb
	current limiting ['kʌrənt lɪmɪtɪŋ]	Strombegrenzung
	thermal shutdown [ˌθɜ:ml 'ʃʌtdaʊn]	Überhitzungsschutz
	safe operation area (SOA) [ˌseɪf ɒpə'reɪʃn eəriə]	sicherer Arbeitsbereich, Sicherheitsbereich
	integrated circuit [ˌɪntɪgreɪtɪd 'sɜ:kɪt]	integrierter Schaltkreis
	monolithic integrated circuit [mɒnəˌlɪθɪk ˌɪntɪgreɪtɪd 'sɜ:kɪt]	Festkörperschaltkreis, monolithischer Schaltkreis
	intended for sth [ɪn'tendɪd fə]	für etw gedacht, für etw geeignet
	resistive divide [rɪˌzɪstɪv dɪ'vaɪd]	Widerstandsspannungsteiler
	exceptional(ly) [ɪk'sepʃənl]	außergewöhnlich
	stocking ['stɒkɪŋ]	Lagerhaltung
	fixed [fɪkst]	fest, unveränderlich
	desired [dɪ'zaɪəd]	gewünscht
	to **heat up** [ˌhi:t 'ʌp]	sich erhitzen

UNIT 9

86	**electric motor** [ɪˌlektrɪk 'məʊtə]	Elektromotor
	hair dryer ['heə draɪə]	Fön
	car seat positioning device [ˌkɑ: si:t pə'zɪʃnɪŋ dɪvaɪs]	Sitzeinstellungsvorrichtung (im Auto)
	cordless drill [ˌkɔ:dləs 'drɪl]	Akkuschrauber
	conveyor belt [kən'veɪə belt]	Förderband
	food mixer ['fu:d mɪksə]	Küchenmaschine
87	**fantastic(ally)** [fæn'tæstɪk]	ungeheuer
	versatile ['vɜ:sətaɪl]	vielseitig
	science ['saɪəns]	(Natur-)Wissenschaft
	adaptable [ə'dæptəbl]	anpassungsfähig, flexibel
	straightforward [ˌstreɪt'fɔ:wəd]	einfach
	to **put** [pʊt]	formulieren, sagen
	like [laɪk]	gleich
	to **repel** [rɪ'pel]	sich abstoßen
	unlike [ˌʌn'laɪk]	unähnlich
	to **attract** [ə'trækt]	sich anziehen
	magnetic field [mægˌnetɪk 'fi:ld]	Magnetfeld
	to **be comprised of sth** [bi kəm'praɪzd əv]	aus etw bestehen
	to **put sth to work** [ˌpʊt tə 'wɜ:k]	etw einsetzen
	three-phase AC motor [ˌθri: feɪz eɪ 'si: məʊtə]	Drehstrommotor
	to **take advantage of sth** [ˌteɪk əd'vɑ:ntɪdʒ əv]	etw ausnutzen
	stator ['steɪtə]	Ständer, Stator
	rotor ['rəʊtə]	Läufer, Rotor
	due to the fact that [ˌdju: tə ðə 'fækt ðət]	aufgrund der Tatsache, dass
	circular ['sɜ:kjələ]	kreisförmig
	network ['netwɜ:k]	Geflecht, Verbund
	cage [keɪdʒ]	Käfig
	squirrel ['skwɪrəl]	Eichhörnchen
	to **space sth** [speɪs]	etw in (regelmäßigen) Abständen anordnen
	evenly ['i:vnli]	gleichmäßig
	to **hook sth up** [ˌhʊk 'ʌp]	etw anschließen
	out of phase [aʊt əf ˌfeɪz]	phasenverschoben
	in turn [ɪn 'tɜ:n]	wiederum
	to **spin** [spɪn]	sich drehen, rotieren
	universal motor [ju:nɪˌvɜ:sl 'məʊtə]	Universalmotor
	electromagnet [ɪˌlektrəʊ'mægnɪt]	Elektromagnet
	cycle ['saɪkl]	Phase, Zyklus, Periode
	to **reverse** [rɪ'vɜ:s]	umkehren
	torque [tɔ:k]	Drehmoment
	starting torque ['stɑ:tɪŋ tɔ:k]	Anlauf(dreh)moment
	compact ['kɒmpækt]	kompakt
	speed [spi:d]	Drehzahl
	to **demand** [dɪ'mɑ:nd]	erfordern
	bearing ['beərɪŋ]	(Kugel-, Wälz-)Lager
	commutator ['kɒmjuteɪtə]	Kommutator, Kollektor, Stromwender
88	**nameplate** ['neɪmpleɪt]	Typenschild
	rated ['reɪtɪd]	Nenn-
	full-load [ˌfʊl 'ləʊd]	Volllast-
	rated full-load speed [ˌreɪtɪd ˌfʊl ləʊd 'spi:d]	Nenndrehzahl bei Volllast
	insulation class [ˌɪnsju'leɪʃn klɑ:s]	Isolationsklasse, Schutzgrad

	ambient temperature [ˌæmbiənt 'temprətʃə]	Umgebungstemperatur
	horsepower (HP) ['hɔːspaʊə]	Pferdestärke(n) (PS)
	rated horsepower [ˌreɪtɪd 'hɔːspaʊə]	Nennleistung (in PS)
	service factor ['sɜːvɪs fæktə]	Wartungsfaktor, Betriebsfaktor
	revolutions per minute (RPM) [revəˌluːʃnz pə 'mɪnɪt]	Umdrehungen pro Minute (U/min)
	continuous duty [kənˌtɪnjuəs 'djuːti]	Dauerbetrieb
	National Electrical Manufacturers Association (NEMA) [ˌnæʃnəl ɪˌlektrɪkl mænju'fæktʃərəz əsəʊsieɪʃn]	*Berufsverband der elektrotechnischen Industrie Nordamerikas*
	nominal ['nɒmɪnl]	nominell, Nenn-
	induction motor [ɪn'dʌkʃn məʊtə]	Induktionsmotor
	excerpt ['eksɜːpt]	Ausschnitt
	engine ['endʒɪn]	Motor
T	to **blot sth out** [ˌblɒt 'aʊt]	etw verdecken, etw auslöschen
	to **deal with sth** ['diːl wɪð]	mit etw zu tun haben
89	to **grab** [græb]	greifen, packen
	aooooo ['œlkooo]	Zugang
	difficulty ['dɪfɪkəlti]	Schwierigkeit, Problem
	continuity [ˌkɒntɪn'juːəti]	Durchgang, Durchgangsprüfung
	moderate ['mɒdrət]	mäßig, mittelmäßig
	time-consuming ['taɪm kənsjuːmɪŋ]	zeitraubend, langwierig
	inexpensive [ˌɪnɪk'spensɪv]	preisgünstig, nicht teuer
	the latter [ðə 'lætə]	letztere/r/s
	power rating ['paʊə reɪtɪŋ]	Nennleistung
90	**light engineering** [ˌlaɪt endʒɪ'nɪərɪŋ]	Feinmechanik
	technical support service [ˌteknɪkl sə'pɔːt sɜːvɪs]	technischer Kundendienst
	to **mind** [maɪnd]	etw dagegen haben
	to **get to the bottom of sth** [ˌget tə ðə 'bɒtəm əv]	einer Sache auf den Grund gehen
	to **occur** [ə'kɜː]	sich ereignen, auftreten
	to **vibrate** ['vaɪbreɪt]	vibrieren
	to **rattle** ['rætl]	klappern, rasseln
	to **hum** [hʌm]	summen
	to **be hot to the touch** [bi ˌhɒt tə ðə 'tʌtʃ]	sich heiß anfühlen, heiß sein
	to **be getting on** [bi ˌgetɪŋ 'ɒn]	alt werden
	to **wear out** [ˌweər 'aʊt]	sich abnutzen, sich verschleißen
91	to **role-play** ['rəʊl pleɪ]	(in einem Rollenspiel) spielen
	to **fix** [fɪks]	reparieren
92	to **note sth** [nəʊt]	etw beachten
	to **equip** [ɪ'kwɪp]	ausrüsten, ausstatten
	in accordance with [ɪn ə'kɔːdəns wɪð]	in Übereinstimmung mit, entsprechend
	load factor ['ləʊd fæktə]	Auslastungsgrad
	improper [ɪm'prɒpə]	unsachgemäß, unvorschriftsmäßig
	open winding [ˌəʊpən 'waɪndɪŋ]	offene Wicklung
	omission [ə'mɪʃn]	Ausbleiben
	to **reset** [ˌriː'set]	zurücksetzen
	to **accelerate** [ək'seləreɪt]	beschleunigen
	otherwise ['ʌðəwaɪz]	anderweitig
	wear and tear [ˌweər ən 'teə]	Verschleiß
	worn [wɔːn]	abgenutzt, verschlissen
93	to **pay** [peɪ]	sich auszahlen
	patient ['peɪʃnt]	geduldig
	to **treat** [triːt]	behandeln
	polite [pə'laɪt]	höflich
	to **confuse sb** [kən'fjuːz]	jdn verwirren
	to **care for sth** ['keə fə]	am Herzen liegen
	to **value** ['væljuː]	wertschätzen, schätzen
	honest ['ɒnɪst]	ehrlich, aufrichtig
95	to **speculate** ['spekjuleɪt]	spekulieren
	possibility [ˌpɒsə'bɪləti]	Möglichkeit
	improvement [ɪm'pruːvmənt]	Verbesserung
	petrol ['petrəl]	Benzin
	increasing [ɪn'kriːsɪŋ]	zunehmend, steigend
	configuration [kənˌfɪgə'reɪʃn]	Ausstattung, Konfigurierung
	to **range (from … to)** [reɪndʒ]	sich erstrecken (von … bis)
	pure [pjʊə]	rein
	solely ['səʊlli]	allein, einzig, nur
	whatever [wɒt'evə]	was (auch immer)
	noise pollution ['nɔɪz pəluːʃn]	Lärmverschmutzung
	interrelated [ˌɪntərɪ'leɪtɪd]	(damit) zusammenhängend
	to **stand in the way of sth** [ˌstænd ɪn ðə 'weɪ əv]	einer Sache im Wege stehen

	increase ['ɪŋkriːs]	Zunahme
	heavy ['hevi]	schwer
	to **tend to do sth** ['tend tə]	dazu neigen, etw zu tun
	related to [rɪ'leɪtɪd tə]	verwandt mit
	recharging station [ˌriː'tʃɑːdʒɪŋ steɪʃn]	Ladestation
	motorist *BE* ['məʊtərɪst]	Autofahrer/in
	to **recharge** [ˌriː'tʃɑːdʒ]	aufladen
	to **standardize** ['stændədaɪz]	normen
	trip [trɪp]	Fahrt
	experience [ɪk'spɪəriəns]	Erfahrung(en)
	full-scale ['fʊl skeɪl]	in vollem Umfang, in großem Stil
	subheading ['sʌbhedɪŋ]	Zwischenüberschrift
	limitation [ˌlɪmɪ'teɪʃn]	Beschränkung, Einschränkung
	remaining [rɪ'meɪnɪŋ]	übrig

UNIT 10

96	**trade** [treɪd]	Handel, Gewerbe, Branche
	trade fair ['treɪd feə]	Handelsmesse, Branchenmesse
	to **make a point** [ˌmeɪk ə 'pɔɪnt]	auf etw hinauswollen, etw sagen wollen
	caption ['kæpʃn]	Bildunterschrift
	to **vote on sth** ['vəʊt ɒn]	über etw abstimmen
	item ['aɪtəm]	Artikel, Gegenstand
	to **rank** [ræŋk]	einstufen, ordnen
	importance [ɪm'pɔːtns]	Bedeutung, Wichtigkeit
97	**aim** [eɪm]	Ziel, Zweck (T)
	to **brainstorm** ['breɪnstɔːm]	Ideen sammeln
	abroad [ə'brɔːd]	im/ins Ausland
	to **arise** [ə'raɪz]	*(Probleme usw.:)* auftreten, auftauchen
	to **come in (on sth)** [ˌkʌm 'ɪn]	etw (zu etw) sagen
	as far as I am concerned [əz fɑːr əz ˌaɪ əm kən'sɜːnd]	was mich betrifft, meines Erachtens
	documentation [ˌdɒkjumen'teɪʃn]	Unterlagen, Dokumente
	routinely [ruː'tiːnli]	regelmäßig
	paperwork ['peɪpəwɜːk]	Unterlagen
	expenses *pl* [ɪk'spensɪz]	Kosten, Ausgaben, Spesen
	sound [saʊnd]	vernünftig, gut, solide
	to **pack** [pæk]	packen, einpacken
	to **leave sth behind** [ˌliːv bɪ'haɪnd]	etw zurücklassen
	to **team up with sb** [ˌtiːm 'ʌp wɪð]	mit jdm zusammenarbeiten, sich mit jdm zusammentun
	to **invite sth** [ɪn'vaɪt]	etw erbitten
98	to **represent** [ˌreprɪ'zent]	vertreten, darstellen
	to **enquire about sth** [ɪn'kwaɪər əbaʊt]	sich nach etw erkundigen
	representative [ˌreprɪ'zentətɪv]	Vertreter/in, Repräsentant/in
	to **rewrite** [ˌriː'raɪt]	umformulieren
	brochure ['brəʊʃə]	Prospekt
	leaflet ['liːflət]	Informationsblatt, Faltblatt
	business card ['bɪznəs kɑːd]	Visitenkarte
	impolite [ˌɪmpə'laɪt]	unhöflich
	politeness [pə'laɪtnəs]	Höflichkeit
	native speaker [ˌneɪtɪv 'spiːkə]	Muttersprachler/in
	abrupt [ə'brʌpt]	brüsk, schroff, abrupt
P	**trade show** ['treɪd ʃəʊ]	Fachmesse, Branchenmesse
	stand [stænd]	(Messe-)Stand
	to **approach sb** [ə'prəʊtʃ]	an jdn herantreten, auf jdn zugehen
	to **decline** [dɪ'klaɪn]	*(Angebot etc.)* ablehnen
	to **get in touch with sb** [ˌget ɪn 'tʌtʃ wɪð]	sich bei jdm melden
99	**attitude** ['ætɪtjuːd]	Einstellung, Haltung
	to **be willing to do sth** [bi 'wɪlɪŋ tə duː]	bereit/willens sein, etw zu tun
	standardization [ˌstændədaɪ'zeɪʃn]	Normierung, Normung
	challenge ['tʃælɪndʒ]	Herausforderung
	to **face sth** [feɪs]	vor etw stehen, sich einer Sache gegenübersehen
	property ['prɒpəti]	Eigentum
	trade standards *pl* ['treɪd stændədz]	Branchennormen, Handelsstandards
	to **take sth as given** [ˌteɪk əz 'gɪvn]	etw als gegeben voraussetzen
	to **set up** [ˌset 'ʌp]	gründen
	consensus [kən'sensəs]	Übereinstimmung, Einigung, Konsens
	to **recognize** ['rekəgnaɪz]	erkennen
	voluntary ['vɒləntri]	freiwillig
	rigid ['rɪdʒɪd]	starr
	directive [də'rektɪv]	Anweisung, Anordnung, Richtlinie
	compromise ['kɒmprəmaɪz]	Kompromiss
	commission [kə'mɪʃn]	Kommission

	creation [kri'eɪʃn]	*hier:* Gründung
	to **harmonize** ['hɑ:mənaɪz]	angleichen, harmonisieren
	particularly [pə'tɪkjələli]	besonders, insbesondere
	to **keep up with sth** [ˌki:p 'ʌp wɪð]	mit etw Schritt halten
	compatibility [kəmˌpætə'bɪləti]	Austauschbarkeit, Kompatibilität
	convergence [kən'vɜ:dʒəns]	Annäherung, Konvergenz
	telephony [tɪ'lefni]	Fernsprechwesen, Telefonie
	jungle ['dʒʌŋgl]	Dschungel, Urwald
100	**gift** [gɪft]	Geschenk
	uncompromising [ˌʌn'kɒmprəmaɪzɪŋ]	unnachgiebig, kompromisslos
	free choice [ˌfri: 'tʃɔɪs]	freie Entscheidung
	to **apply** [ə'plaɪ]	anwenden
	to **pick** [pɪk]	(sich) etw aussuchen
101	to **serve as sth** ['sɜ:v əz]	als etw dienen
	measuring tool ['meʒərɪŋ tu:l]	Messinstrument
	inch [ɪntʃ]	Zoll *(= 2,54 cm)*
	relative clause ['relətɪv klɔ:z]	Relativsatz
	relative pronoun [ˌrelətɪv 'prəʊnaʊn]	Relativpronomen
102	**adaptor** [ə'dæptə]	Adapter
	plug adaptor ['plʌg ədæptə]	Adapterstecker
	to **blow up** [ˌbləʊ 'ʌp]	in die Luft fliegen, explodieren
	mains voltage ['meɪnz vəʊltɪdʒ]	Netzspannung
	disparity [dɪs'pærəti]	Unterschied, Verschiedenheit
	to **go up in smoke** [gəʊ ˌʌp ɪn 'sməʊk]	in Rauch aufgehen
	recharger [ˌri:'tʃɑ:dʒə]	Ladegerät
	to **differ** ['dɪfə]	sich unterscheiden
	switched-mode power supply [ˌswɪtʃt məʊd 'paʊə səplaɪ]	Schaltnetzteil
103	to **adopt** [ə'dɒpt]	übernehmen, annehmen
	wall outlet ['wɔ:l aʊtlet]	Wandsteckdose
	variety [və'raɪəti]	Sorte, Art
	ungrounded [ʌn'graʊndɪd]	nicht geerdet
	prong [prɒŋ]	Stift, Kontakt (eines Steckers)
	pin [pɪn]	Stift, Kontakt (eines Steckers)
	grounding contact ['graʊndɪŋ kɒntækt]	Massekontakt, Erdungskontakt
	rectangular [rek'tæŋgjələ]	rechteckig
	to **form** [fɔ:m]	bilden
	triangle ['traɪæŋgl]	Dreieck
	to **arrange** [ə'reɪndʒ]	anordnen
	offset ['ɒfset]	versetzt
	phew! [fju:]	Puh!
	thread [θred]	Faden, Thema
104	**pal** [pæl]	Kumpel
	pocket ['pɒkɪt]	(Hosen-, Jacken-) Tasche
	to **slide in/out** [ˌslaɪd 'ɪn/'aʊt]	hinein-/herausschieben
	to **adapt** [ə'dæpt]	(sich) anpassen
	release button [rɪ'li:s bʌtn]	Entriegelungsknopf
	consumer electronics [kənˌsju:mər ˌɪlek'trɒnɪks]	Unterhaltungselektronik
	to **weigh** [weɪ]	wiegen
	gram [græm]	Gramm
	to **back** [bæk]	unterstützen, absichern
	iron ['aɪən]	Bügeleisen
	top marks *pl* [ˌtɒp 'mɑ:ks]	Bestnoten
	luggage ['lʌgɪdʒ]	(Reise-)Gepäck
	to **be a bit of a pain** [bi ə ˌbɪt əf ɪ 'peɪn]	lästig sein
	mate [meɪt]	Kumpel, Freund
	to **drop sth** [drɒp]	etw fallen lassen
	carpeted floor [ˌkɑ:pɪtɪd 'flɔ:]	Teppichboden
	casing ['keɪsɪŋ]	Gehäuse
	refund ['ri:fʌnd]	Kostenerstattung
	terms *pl* [tɜ:mz]	Bedingungen, Konditionen
	enemy ['enəmi]	Feind
	to **fall apart** [ˌfɔ:l ə'pɑ:t]	auseinanderfallen
105	**cross-cultural** [ˌkrɒs'kʌltʃərəl]	kulturübergreifend
	understanding [ˌʌndə'stændɪŋ]	Verständnis, Verständigung
	issue ['ɪʃu:]	Frage, Problem, (Streit-)Punkt
	at length [ət 'leŋθ]	ausführlich
	decision [dɪ'sɪʒn]	Entscheidung, Beschluss
	junior to sb ['dʒu:niə tə]	jdm unterstellt
	respect [rɪ'spekt]	Respekt, Achtung
	embarrassed [ɪm'bærəst]	verlegen, beschämt
	to **flirt** [flɜ:t]	flirten
	to **refuse** [rɪ'fju:z]	sich weigern, (es) ablehnen
	to **say sorry** [ˌseɪ 'sɒri]	sich entschuldigen

	to embarrass sb [ɪm'bærəs]	jdn in Verlegenheit bringen, jdn bloßstellen
	to insist in doing sth [ɪn'sɪst ɪn]	etw beharrlich weiter tun
	to fold [fəʊld]	falten, (Arme) verschränken
	plain [pleɪn]	(ganz) einfach
	toilet ['tɔɪlət]	Toilette
	to pray [preɪ]	beten
	dirty ['dɜ:ti]	schmutzig
	sweaty ['sweti]	verschwitzt, schwitzig
	to smell [smel]	riechen
	lateness ['leɪtnəs]	Verspätung, Zuspätkommen
	to be considered sth [bi kən'sɪdəd]	als etw gelten, als etw angesehen werden
	uneasy [ʌn'i:zi]	unsicher, nervös
	to score [skɔ:]	abschneiden, eine Punktzahl erreichen

UNIT 11

106	**to mediate** ['mi:dieɪt]	vermitteln
	booking ['bʊkɪŋ]	Reservierung, Buchung
T	**to depart** [dɪ'pɑ:t]	abfahren, abfliegen, gehen
	to check in [ˌtʃek 'ɪn]	einchecken
	at least [ət 'li:st]	mindestens
	departure [dɪ'pɑ:tʃə]	Abfahrt, Abflug
	stopover ['stɒpəʊvə]	Zwischenlandung, Aufenthalt
	leg [leg]	Etappe
	journey ['dʒɜ:ni]	Reise
	scheduled ['ʃedju:ld]	planmäßig, geplant
	arrival [ə'raɪvl]	Ankunft
	destination [ˌdestɪ'neɪʃn]	Ziel(ort)
	stay [steɪ]	Aufenthalt
	driving license *AE* ['draɪvɪŋ laɪsns]	Führerschein
	at the latest [ət ðə 'leɪtɪst]	spätestens
	to collect [kə'lekt]	sammeln, aufheben
107	**jacket** ['dʒækɪt]	Jacke
	tray [treɪ]	Schale
	to declare [dɪ'kleə]	deklarieren, verzollen
	alcohol ['ælkəhɒl]	Alkohol, Spirituosen
	cigarette [ˌsɪgə'ret]	Zigarette
	for sale [fə 'seɪl]	zum Verkauf, zu verkaufen
	purpose ['pɜ:pəs]	Zweck, Absicht
	departures area [dɪ'pɑ:tʃəz eəriə]	Abflugbereich
	sign [saɪn]	Schild
	passenger ['pæsɪndʒə]	Passagier
	row [rəʊ]	Reihe
	to board [bɔ:d]	an Bord gehen, einsteigen
	hold [həʊld]	Frachtraum, Laderaum
	boarding card ['bɔ:dɪŋ kɑ:d]	Bordkarte
	straight [streɪt]	gleich, sofort
	security [sɪ'kjʊərəti]	*(Flughafen:)* Sicherheitskontrolle
	clerk [klɑ:k]	Angestellte/r
	check-in counter ['tʃek ɪn kaʊntə]	Abfertigungsschalter
	over-booked [ˌəʊvə 'bʊkt]	überbucht
	delayed [dɪ'leɪd]	verspätet
	seat [si:t]	Sitz, Platz
T	**Never mind.** [ˌnevə 'maɪnd]	Das macht nichts.
	chance [tʃɑ:ns]	Gelegenheit, Möglichkeit
	aircraft ['eəkrɑ:ft]	Flugzeug
	Oh dear. [əʊ 'dɪə]	O je!
	baggage ['bægɪdʒ]	(Reise-)Gepäck
	limit ['lɪmɪt]	Obergrenze, Beschränkung
	case [keɪs]	Koffer
	scale [skeɪl]	Waage
	gate [geɪt]	Flugsteig
108	**complication** [ˌkɒmplɪ'keɪʃn]	Komplikation
	agenda [ə'dʒendə]	Tagesordnung
	minutes *pl* ['mɪnɪts]	Protokoll
	packaging ['pækɪdʒɪŋ]	Verpackung
	chair [tʃeə]	(Sitzungs-)Leiter/in
	attendee [əˌten'di:]	Teilnehmer/in
	objective [əb'dʒektɪv]	Ziel
	status ['steɪtəs]	Stand (der Dinge)
	review [rɪ'vju:]	Bericht, Lagebesprechung, Überprüfung
	responsibility [rɪˌspɒnsə'bɪləti]	Zuständigkeit, Verantwortlichkeit
	schedule ['ʃedju:l]	Terminplan, Zeitplan
	project phase ['prɒdʒekt feɪz]	Projektphase
	preparation [ˌprepə'reɪʃn]	Vorbereitung
	flooring ['flɔ:rɪŋ]	Bodenbelag
	clearance ['klɪərəns]	Räumung
	to clarify ['klærəfaɪ]	klären
	procedure [prə'si:dʒə]	Verfahren, Vorgehen, Ablauf
	shipping ['ʃɪpɪŋ]	Versand
	quality control ['kwɒləti kəntrəʊl]	Qualitätskontrolle

	commissioning [kə'mɪʃnɪŋ]	Inbetriebnahme
	test run ['test rʌn]	Probelauf, Testlauf
	acceptance test [ək'septəns test]	Annahmeprüfung
	key [ki:]	entscheidend, Schlüssel-, Haupt-
	settings *pl* ['setɪŋz]	Einstellungen
109	**past** [pɑ:st]	vergangen
	event [ɪ'vent]	Ereignis
	extract ['ekstrækt]	Auszug
	operational [,ɒpə'reɪʃənl]	im Betrieb, im Einsatz
	independent(ly) [,ɪndɪ'pendənt]	unabhängig
	expert ['ekspɜ:t]	Fachmann/-frau
	budget ['bʌdʒɪt]	Finanzrahmen, Budget
	foundation [faʊn'deɪʃn]	Fundament
	to **reinforce** [,ri:ɪn'fɔ:s]	verstärken
	to **level sth off** [,levl 'ɒf]	etw planieren, etw einebnen
	to **ship** [ʃɪp]	versenden, verschiffen
	to **be scheduled to arrive** [bi ",ʃedju:ld tə ə'raɪv]	planmäßig ankommen
	in addition to [ɪn ə'dɪʃn tə]	zusätzlich zu
	hands-on [,hændz 'ɒn]	praktisch
	knowledge transfer ['nɒlɪdʒ trænsfɜ:]	Wissensvermittlung
	record ['rekɔ:d]	Aufzeichnung
	goal [gəʊl]	Ziel
	to **hold** [həʊld]	*(Sitzung)* abhalten
	subject ['sʌbdʒɪkt]	Thema
110	**port** [pɔ:t]	Hafen
	to **load** [ləʊd]	laden, verladen
	river barge ['rɪvə bɑ:dʒ]	Binnenschiff, Lastkahn
	port supervisor [,pɔ:t 'su:pəvaɪzə]	Hafenaufseher/in
	to **float** [fləʊt]	treiben
	truck [trʌk]	Lastwagen
	in time [ɪn 'taɪm]	rechtzeitig
	to **set sth up** [,set 'ʌp]	etw aufbauen, etw einrichten
111	to **inform sb** [ɪn'fɔ:m]	jdn unterrichten, jdn informieren
	to **warn** [wɔ:n]	warnen, hinweisen
	to **assure sb** [ə'ʃʊə]	jdn beruhigen
T	to **package** ['pækɪdʒ]	verpacken
	to **emphasize** ['emfəsaɪz]	betonen
	to **go about sth** ['gəʊ əbaʊt]	etw angehen, etw anpacken
	performance [pə'fɔ:məns]	Leistung
	preliminary [prɪ'lɪmɪnəri]	vorläufig
	to **appear** [ə'pɪə]	(zu sein) scheinen
	to **conclude** [kən'klu:d]	schließen
	to **get sth up and running** [get ,ʌp ənd 'rʌnɪŋ]	etw zum Laufen bringen
	input ['ɪnpʊt]	*hier:* Diskussionsbeiträge
	audience ['ɔ:diəns]	Publikum
	tone [təʊn]	Tonfall
	formal ['fɔ:ml]	formell, förmlich
	to **suit sb** [su:t]	zu jdm passen
	time slot ['taɪm slɒt]	Zeitfenster
	ideally [aɪ'di:əli]	im Idealfall
112	to **commission** [kə'mɪʃn]	in Betrieb nehmen
	to **progress** [prə'gres]	vorankommen
	likewise ['laɪkwaɪz]	ebenso
	impressed [ɪm'prest]	beeindruckt
	to **bring sb in** [,brɪŋ 'ɪn]	jdn hinzuziehen
	inlet line ['ɪnlet laɪn]	Zuleitung
	cooling water ['ku:lɪŋ wɔ:tə]	Kühlwasser
	to **pump** [pʌmp]	pumpen
	to **overheat** [,əʊvə'hi:t]	sich überhitzen
	pneumatics line [nju:'mætɪks laɪn]	Druckluftleitung
	compressed air [kəm,prest 'eə]	Druckluft
	handover ['hændəʊvə]	Übergabe
	to **sign off on sth** [,saɪn 'ɒf ɒn]	etw abzeichnen
	to **suppose** [sə'pəʊz]	annehmen, vermuten
	production downtime [prə'dʌkʃn daʊntaɪm]	Produktionsausfall(zeiten)
	length [leŋθ]	Dauer
113	**senior** ['si:niə]	leitend, vorgesetzt, höherrangig, älter
	junior ['dʒu:niə]	untergordnet, jünger
	confident ['kɒnfɪdənt]	sicher, souverän
	to **join with sb** ['dʒɔɪn wɪð]	sich mit jdm zusammentun
	pre-installation [,pri: ɪnstə'leɪʃn]	Vorinstallation
	in the event of [ɪn ði ɪ'vent əv]	im Falle einer/s
	to **co-operate** [kəʊ'ɒpəreɪt]	zusammenarbeiten
	upgrade ['ʌpgreɪd]	Verbesserung, Aufrüstung
	satisfied ['sætɪsfaɪd]	zufrieden
115	to **shake sb's hand** [,ʃeɪk 'hænd]	jdm die Hand geben/schütteln
	firm(ly) [fɜ:m]	fest

	handshake ['hændʃeɪk]	Händedruck, Händeschütteln
	somewhat ['sʌmwɒt]	etwas
	to **bow** [baʊ]	sich verbeugen
	to **keep sth in mind** [ˌkiːp ɪn 'maɪnd]	an etw denken, etw im Gedächtnis behalten
	eye contact ['aɪ kɒntækt]	Blickkontakt
	disrespectful [ˌdɪsrɪ'spektfl]	respektlos, unhöflich
	address [ə'dres]	Anrede
	affair [ə'feə]	Angelegenheit
	in advance of [ɪn əd'vɑːns əv]	vor
	to **attend** [ə'tend]	teilnehmen
	counterpart ['kaʊntəpɑːt]	Pendant, Gegenüber
	strict [strɪkt]	streng
	seating arrangement ['siːtɪŋ əreɪndʒmənt]	Sitzordnung
	descending [dɪ'sendɪŋ]	absteigend
	speech [spiːtʃ]	Rede, Ansprache
	introduction [ˌɪntrə'dʌkʃn]	Einführung, Einleitung
	introductory [ˌɪntrə'dʌktəri]	einführend, einleitend
	remark [rɪ'mɑːk]	Bemerkung
	to **be addressed to sb** [bi ə'drest tə]	an jdn gerichtet sein, sich an jdn richten
	host [həʊst]	Gastgeber/in
	reputation [ˌrepju'teɪʃn]	Ruf
	to **lose face** [ˌluːz 'feɪs]	das Gesicht verlieren
	swift [swɪft]	schnell, zügig
	business contact ['bɪznəs kɒntækt]	Geschäftspartner/in
	to **criticize** ['krɪtɪsaɪz]	kritisieren
	present ['preznt]	anwesend
	directness [də'rektnəs]	Direktheit
	response [rɪ'spɒns]	Reaktion, Antwort
	to **be aware of sth** [bi ə'weər əv]	sich einer Sache bewusst sein
	accidentally [ˌæksɪ'dentəli]	unbeabsichtigt, aus Versehen
	to **upset sb** [ˌʌp'set]	jdn verärgern, jdn verstimmen

UNIT 12

116	to **evaluate** [ɪ'væljueɪt]	beurteilen, auswerten
	job advertisment [ˌdʒɒb əd'vɜːtɪsmənt]	Stellenanzeige
	curriculum vitae (CV) *BE* [kəˌrɪkjələm 'viːtaɪ]	Lebenslauf
	cover letter ['kʌvə letə]	Anschreiben, Begleitbrief
	to **interview** ['ɪntəvjuː]	ein Vorstellungsgespräch führen
	to **turn to sb** ['tɜːn tə]	sich an jdn wenden, sich jdm zuwenden
	résumé *AE* ['rezjumeɪ]	Lebenslauf
117	**profile** ['prəʊfaɪl]	Porträt, Profil
	post [pəʊst]	Stelle, Posten
	opportunity [ˌɒpə'tjuːnəti]	Gelegenheit, Möglichkeit
	cable trunking ['keɪbl trʌŋkɪŋ]	Leitungsführung, -kanal
	tray work ['treɪ wɜːk]	Installation in Kabelpritschen
	education [ˌedʒu'keɪʃn]	Bildung, Schuldbildung
	vocational college *BE* [vəʊˌkeɪʃənl 'kɒlɪdʒ]	Berufsschule, Berufskolleg, Gewerbliche Schule
	school leaving certificate [ˌskuːl liːvɪŋ sə'tɪfɪkət]	Schulabgangszeugnis, Schulabschluss
	primary education [ˌpraɪməri edʒu'keɪʃn]	Grundschule, -schulbildung, Primarstufe
	secondary education [ˌsekəndri edʒu'keɪʃn]	weiterführende Schule/Schulbildung, Sekundarstufe
	work experience ['wɜːk ɪkspɪəriəns]	Berufserfahrung
	contractor ['kɒntræktə]	(Handwerks-)Betrieb, (Bau-)Unternehmen
	technical drawing [ˌteknɪkl 'drɔːɪŋ]	technisches Zeichnen
	familiar with sth [fə'mɪliə wɪð]	mit etw vertraut
	word-processing ['wɜːd prəʊsesɪŋ]	Textverarbeitung
	spreadsheet ['spredʃiːt]	Tabellenkalkulation
	certificate [sə'tɪfɪkət]	Zeugnis, Diplom
	rescue service ['reskjuː sɜːvɪs]	Rettungsdienst
	captain ['kæptɪn]	Kapitän
	soccer *AE* ['sɒkə]	Fußball
	active ['æktɪv]	aktiv
	community [kə'mjuːnəti]	Gemeinde, Gemeinschaft
	church community ['tʃɜːtʃ kəmjuːnəti]	Kirchengemeinde
	date of birth [ˌdeɪt əv 'bɜːθ]	Geburtsdatum
	nationality [ˌnæʃə'næləti]	Staatsangehörigkeit, Nationalität
	marital status [ˌmærɪtl 'steɪtəs]	Familienstand
	reference ['refərəns]	Referenz
	on request [ɒn rɪ'kwest]	auf Anfrage, auf Wunsch
118	**vehicle** ['viːəkl]	Fahrzeug
	fluent ['fluːənt]	*(Sprache:)* fließend
	licensed ['laɪsnst]	zugelassen, konzessioniert

	church choir ['tʃɜ:tʃ kwaɪə]	Kirchenchor
	German higher education entrance qualification [ˌdʒɜ:mən haɪər edʒuˌkeɪʃn 'entrəns kwɒlɪfɪkeɪʃn]	Fachhochschulreife
	primary school ['praɪməri sku:l]	Grundschule
	steel [sti:l]	Stahl
	military service [ˌmɪlətri 'sɜ:vɪs]	Wehrdienst
	community service [kə'mju:nəti sɜ:vɪs]	Zivildienst
	vocational school *AE* [vəʊˌkeɪʃənl 'sku:l]	Berufsschule, Berufskolleg, Gewerbliche Schule
	category B (car) driving licence [kætəgəri ˌbi: 'draɪvɪŋ laɪsns]	Führerschein Klasse 3
	German university entrance qualification [ˌdʒɜ:mən ju:nɪˌvɜ:səti 'entrəns kwɒlɪfɪkeɪʃn]	Allgemeine Hochschulreife (Abitur)
	strong [strɒŋ]	stark
	to **invent** [ɪn'vent]	erfinden, sich ausdenken
	to **contribute** [kən'trɪbju:t]	beitragen
	valuable ['væljuəbl]	wertvoll
	personality [ˌpɜ:sə'næləti]	Persönlichkeit, Wesen
	diplomatic [ˌdɪplə'mætɪk]	diplomatisch
	manner ['mænə]	Art
	leadership ['li:dəʃɪp]	Führung
	charity ['tʃærəti]	Wohltätigkeit
	sporting ['spɔ:tɪŋ]	Sport-, sportlich
	achievement [ə'tʃi:vmənt]	Errungenschaft, Leistung
	prize [praɪz]	Preis
	award [ə'wɔ:d]	Auszeichnung, Preis
	performing arts *pl* [pəˌfɔ:mɪŋ 'ɑ:ts]	darstellende Künste
	acting ['æktɪŋ]	Schauspielerei
	painting ['peɪntɪŋ]	Malen
	sculpture ['skʌlptʃə]	Bildhauerei
119	to **earn** [ɜ:n]	verdienen
	overtime ['əʊvətaɪm]	Überstunden
	global(ly) ['gləʊbl]	weltweit
	recruitment [rɪ'kru:tmənt]	Einstellen (von Arbeitskräften), Personalbeschaffung
	rate [reɪt]	Satz, Tarif
	renewable [rɪ'nju:əbl]	verlängerbar
	as soon as possible (ASAP) [əz ˌsu:n əz 'pɒsəbl]	baldmöglichst
	reference ['refərəns]	Kürzel, (Bestell-) Nummer
	leisure ['leʒə]	Freizeit
	library ['laɪbrəri]	Bibliothek
	duty ['dju:ti]	Aufgabe, Pflicht
	fuse board ['fju:z bɔ:d]	Sicherungstafel, -platte
	hard-working [ˌhɑ:d 'wɜ:kɪŋ]	fleißig
	professional [prə'feʃənl]	professionell
	to **register** ['redʒɪstə]	sich anmelden
	to **upload** [ˌʌp'ləʊd]	hochladen
	to **appear** [ə'pɪə]	auftauchen, erscheinen
	extra-curricular [ˌekstrə kə'rɪkjulə]	außerschulisch
	in the course of [ɪn ðə 'kɔ:s əv]	im Lauf von
	to **gain** [geɪn]	gewinnen, erwerben
120	**vacancy** ['veɪkənsi]	freie/offene Stelle
	with reference to [wɪð 'refrəns tə]	bezüglich, mit Bezug auf
	above-mentioned [əˌbʌv 'menʃnd]	oben genannt
	theoretical [ˌθɪə'retɪkl]	theoretisch, Theorie-
	instruction [ɪn'strʌkʃn]	Unterricht
	operating theatre ['ɒpəreɪtɪŋ θɪətə]	Operationssaal
	to **enclose** [ɪn'kləʊz]	beifügen
	at short notice [ət ˌʃɔ:t 'nəʊtɪs]	kurzfristig
	shortly ['ʃɔ:tli]	in Kürze, bald
	to **specify** ['spesɪfaɪ]	angeben, nennen
	command [kə'mɑ:nd]	Beherrschung
	Yours sincerely, [ˌjɔ:z sɪn'sɪəli]	Mit freundlichen Grüßen
	enclosure [ɪn'kləʊʒə]	*(Brief:)* Anlage
121	**advertisment** [əd'vɜ:tɪsmənt]	Anzeige, Annonce
	specifically [spə'sɪfɪkli]	ausdrücklich, speziell
122	**weakness** ['wi:knəs]	Schwäche
	applicant ['æplɪkənt]	Bewerber/in
T	to **take a seat** [ˌteɪk ə 'si:t]	Platz nehmen
	to **train** [treɪn]	trainieren
	Federal Agency for Technical Relief [ˌfedərəl ˌeɪdʒənsi fə ˌteknɪkl rɪ'li:f]	Technisches Hilfswerk
	punctual ['pʌŋktʃuəl]	pünktlich
	supervision [ˌsu:pə'vɪʒn]	Aufsicht, Betreuung, Anleitung

	in particular [ɪn pə'tɪkjələ]	speziell, im Besonderen
	final grade [ˌfaɪnl 'greɪd]	Abschlussnote
P	**headhunter** ['hedhʌntə]	Kopfjäger
	candidate ['kændɪdət]	Bewerber/in, Kandidat/in
	impatient [ɪm'peɪʃnt]	ungeduldig
	debate [dɪ'beɪt]	Debatte, Diskussion
123	**privacy** ['prɪvəsi]	Privatsphäre
	access to sth ['ækses tə]	Zugang, Zugriff auf etw
	account [ə'kaʊnt]	Konto
	admission [əd'mɪʃn]	Zulassung
	officer ['ɒfɪsə]	Beamte/r, Beauftragte/r
	to **log onto sth** [ˌlɒg 'ɒntə]	sich bei etw einloggen
	prison ['prɪzn]	Gefängnis
	coach [kəʊtʃ]	Trainer/in
	athlete ['æθliːt]	Sportler/in
	to **hire sb** ['haɪə]	jdn beauftragen
	to **share** [ʃeə]	teilen, mitteilen
	password ['pɑːswɜːd]	Passwort
	to **endanger** [ɪn'deɪndʒə]	gefährden
	to **invade sth** [ɪn'veɪd]	in etw eindringen
	sphere [sfɪə]	Sphäre
	practices *pl* ['præktɪsɪz]	Praktiken
	violation [ˌvaɪə'leɪʃn]	Verletzung
	statement of rights [ˌsteɪtmənt əv 'raɪts]	Nutzungsbedingungen
	to **state** [steɪt]	erklären
	policy ['pɒləsi]	Verfahren, Regeln, Richtlinie
	to **have sth in place** [həv ɪn 'pleɪs]	vorhanden sein, in Kraft sein
	confidential [ˌkɒnfɪ'denʃl]	vertraulich
	to **hold sb responsible for sth** [ˌhəʊld rɪ'spɒnsəbl fə]	jdn für etw verantwortlich machen
	to **gather** ['gæðə]	sammeln
	guilty ['gɪlti]	schuldig
	proud [praʊd]	stolz
	to **experiment** [ɪk'sperɪmənt]	experimentieren
	straight away [streɪt ə'weɪ]	sofort
124	**motivated** ['məʊtɪveɪtɪd]	motiviert
	to **short-list sb** ['ʃɔːtlɪst]	jdn in die engere Auswahl nehmen
125	**dos and dont's** [ˌduːz ən 'dəʊnts]	Dinge, die man tun und lassen sollte
	price tag ['praɪs tæg]	Preisschild
	neck [nek]	Hals
	to **pick up** [ˌpɪk 'ʌp]	aufheben
	to **shake** [ʃeɪk]	schütteln
	tone [təʊn]	Farbton
	loud [laʊd]	*(Farbe:)* grell
	shiny ['ʃaɪni]	glänzend
	shirt [ʃɜːt]	Hemd
	blouse [blaʊz]	Bluse
	skin [skɪn]	Haut
	sock [sɒk]	Socke
	skirt [skɜːt]	Rock
	light-coloured ['laɪt kʌləd]	*(Farbe:)* hell
	tights *pl* [taɪts]	Strumpfhose
	to **shave** [ʃeɪv]	sich rasieren
	in advance [ɪn əd'vɑːns]	im Voraus
	to **settle** ['setl]	sich beruhigen
	features *pl* ['fiːtʃəz]	Gesichtszüge
	to **hate** [heɪt]	überhaupt nicht mögen, hassen
	perfume ['pɜːfjuːm]	Parfüm
	jewellery ['dʒuːəlri]	Schmuck
	insecurity [ˌɪnsɪ'kjʊərəti]	Unsicherheit
	chunky ['tʃʌŋki]	dick
	necklace ['nekləs]	Halskette
	bracelet ['breɪslət]	Armband
	garlic ['gɑːlɪk]	Knoblauch
	ahead of time [əˌhed əv 'taɪm]	zeitig
	to **allow** [ə'laʊ]	einplanen
	coat [kəʊt]	Mantel
	umbrella [ʌm'brelə]	Regenschirm
	bathroom ['bɑːθruːm]	Toilette
	glasses *pl* ['glɑːsɪz]	Brille
	to **re-polish** [ˌriː 'pɒlɪʃ]	nachpolieren
	to **dry** [draɪ]	trocknen
	thorough(ly) ['θʌrə]	gründlich
	nail [neɪl]	Nagel
	clothing ['kləʊðɪŋ]	Kleidung
	blue collar ['bluː kɒlə]	Arbeiter-
	attire [ə'taɪə]	Kleidung
	white collar ['waɪt kɒlə]	Angestellten-
	findings *pl* ['faɪndɪŋz]	Ergebnisse

Alphabetical word list

Dieses Wörterverzeichnis enthält alle neuen Wörter aus *Electricity Matters – 3rd Edition* in alphabetischer Reihenfolge. Nicht angeführt sind Wörter, die zum Grundwortschatz (*Basic word list*) gehören. Die Zahl nach dem Stichwort bezieht sich auf die Seite, auf der das Wort zum ersten Mal erscheint. Wörter aus den Hörverständnisübungen sind zusätzlich mit einem **T** (Transkript) und Wörter aus den *Partner files* mit einem **P** gekennzeichnet.

A

abbreviation *15* Abkürzung
about, to **be ~** *54T* in der Nähe sein, da sein; to **be out and ~** *17* unterwegs sein
above-mentioned *120* oben genannt
abroad *97T* im/ins Ausland
abrupt *98* brüsk, schroff, abrupt
absolute *73* absolut
AC (alternating current) *9* Wechselstrom; **three-phase ~** *9* Drehstrom
to **accelerate** *92* beschleunigen
acceptance test *108* Annahmeprüfung
access to sth *89* Zugang zu etw, Zugriff auf etw
accident *33* Unfall
accidentally *115* unbeabsichtigt, aus Versehen
to **accommodate** *52* unterbringen
accordance, in ~ with *92* in Übereinstimmung mit, entsprechend
according to *64* gemäß, laut, nach
account *123* Konto
to **achieve** *35* erzielen, erreichen
achievement *118* Errungenschaft, Leistung
across ... *65* in ganz ...
to **act (as sth)** *42* als etw fungieren
acting *118* Schauspielerei
to **activate** *48* aktivieren
active *117* aktiv
actuator *27* Aktor
to **adapt** *104* (sich) anpassen
adaptable *87* anpassungsfähig, flexibel
adaptor *102* Adapter; **plug ~** *102* Adapterstecker
addition, in ~ *14T* außerdem; **in ~ to** *109* zusätzlich zu
additional *48* zusätzlich
address *115* Anrede; **public ~ system** *15* Beschallungsanlage
addressable *15* individuell identifizierbar, adressierbar
addressed, to **be ~ to sb** *115* an jdn gerichtet sein, sich an jdn richten
adequate *53* angemessen, ausreichend
to **adjust** *30T* anpassen, einstellen, regeln
adjustable *79T* regelbar, einstellbar
admission *123* Zulassung
to **adopt** *103* übernehmen, annehmen
advance, in ~ *125* im Voraus; **in ~ of** *115* vor
advantage, to **take ~ of sth** *87* etw ausnutzen
advertisment *121* Anzeige, Annonce; **job ~** *116* Stellenanzeige
to **advise sb** *18* jdn beraten
adviser *15* Berater/in; **careers ~** *25* Berufsberater/in
affair *115* Angelegenheit
to **afford sth** *47* sich etw leisten können
agenda *108* Tagesordnung
ahead of time *125* zeitig
aid, first ~ *45* Erste Hilfe
aim *97T* Ziel, Zweck
air: compressed ~ *112* Druckluft; **~ conditioning** *15* Klimatisierung, Klimaanlage
aircraft *107T* Flugzeug
alarm: ~ relay *74* Alarmrelais; **voice ~ system** *15* elektroakustisches Notfallwarnsystem; to **sound an ~** *84* einen Warnton erklingen lassen
album *71* Schallplatte, CD
alcohol *107* Alkohol, Spirituosen
all, at ~ *62T* überhaupt
Allen key *20* Inbusschlüssel, Innensechskantschlüssel
to **allow** *125* einplanen; **~ for sth** *52* etw einkalkulieren, etw berücksichtigen, etw vorsehen
along with *24* zusammen mit
to **alternate** *78* wechseln, alternieren
alternating current (AC) *9* Wechselstrom
alternative *56* alternativ
amazing *27* erstaunlich, verblüffend
ambient temperature *88* Umgebungstemperatur
ammeter *76* Amperemeter
to **amount to sth** *64* sich auf etw belaufen
amp *29* Ampere
amperage *45* Stromstärke
amp(lifier) *67T* Verstärker
analogue BE *48* analog
analysis *15* Analyse
analyst *64* Analyst/in
anchor, roof ~ *59* Deckenanker
angle *59* Winkel; **~ grinder** *22T* Winkelschleifer, Trennschleifer
annoyed, to **be ~** *39* sich ärgern
annoying *22T* ärgerlich, nervend
annual *19* jährlich
antifreeze solution *58* Frostschutzmittel
apartment block *12T* Mietshaus, Wohnblock
to **appear** *111T* (zu sein) scheinen; *119* auftauchen, erscheinen
appliance *15* (Elektro-/Haushalts-) Gerät; **kitchen ~** *38* Küchengerät
applicant *122* Bewerber/in
application *73* Anwendung
to **apply** *100* anwenden; **~ for sth** *25* sich für/um etw bewerben
appointment *46* Termin
to **appreciate** *69* schätzen, zu schätzen wissen
apprentice *11* Lehrling, Auszubildende/r
apprenticeship *22* Lehre, Ausbildung
to **approach sb** *98P* an jdn herantreten, auf jdn zugehen
appropriate *65* angemessen, geeignet
approximately *75* ungefähr, zirka
arc lamp *31* Bogenlampe, Spot
architect *17* Architekt/in
to **arise** *97T* *(Probleme usw.) auftreten, auftauchen*
to **arrange** *103* anordnen
array *59* Anordnung
arrest, cardiac ~ *45* Herzstillstand
arrival *106T* Ankunft
art, state of the ~ *7* auf dem neuesten Stand der Technik, neueste/r/s; **performing ~s** pl *118* darstellende Künste
to **ask for directions** *13* nach dem Weg fragen
to **assemble** *12T* montieren, zusammenbauen
assembly *12* Montage; **final ~** *12* Endmontage; **~ line** *14T* Fließband, Montageband; **pre-~** *12* Vormontage
assignment *79* Aufgabe, Auftrag
assistance, to **be of ~** *49* behilflich sein
to **assure sb** *111* jdn beruhigen
astable multivibrator *84* astabiler Multivibrator
at all *62T* überhaupt
athlete *123* Sportler/in
to **attach** *53* anbringen; **~ th** *49* *(E-Mail:)* etw anhängen; **~ sth to sth** *32* etw an etw befestigen, etw an etw anbringen
attempt *65* Versuch, Bestreben
to **attempt** *24* versuchen
to **attend** *115* teilnehmen; **~ sth** *22* etw besuchen, an etw teilnehmen
attendee *108* Teilnehmer/in
attire *125* Kleidung
attitude *99* Einstellung, Haltung
to **attract** *87* sich anziehen
audience *111* Publikum
audio-visual *15* audiovisuell
to **automate** *47* automatisieren
automatic(ally) *47* automatisch
automation *48* Automatisierung
available *17* verfügbar, erhältlich
avalanche *73* Lawine; **~ diode** *73* Lawinendiode; **pulse ~ peak power** *73* Spitzenleistung bei Pulsbelastung
average *19* Durchschnitt, durchschnittlich; **on ~** *61* durchschnittlich
to **avoid** *24* vermeiden
award *118* Auszeichnung, Preis
aware, to **be ~ of sth** *115* sich einer Sache bewusst sein
axial *73* axial
axis *78* Achse

B

to **back** *104* unterstützen, absichern
back of house *15* Verwaltungsbereich, Back of House
backbone *18* Rückgrat
backup system *74* Notfallsystem, Reservesystem
baggage *107T* (Reise-)Gepäck
ballast *35* Vorschaltgerät
band, color ~ AE *73* Farbring
bar *59* Leiste, Stange
barge, river ~ *110* Binnenschiff, Lastkahn
base *69* Sockel, Unterlage, Träger, Basis; *84* Basis (eines Transistors)
based, to **be ~ in** *16* seinen Sitz in ... haben, in ... wohnen
the basics pl *55* die Grundlagen
bathroom *30* Badezimmer, Bad; *125* Toilette
battery *24* Akku, Batterie; **~ bank** *74* Batteriebank; **~ charger** *79* Akku-/Batterie-Ladegerät; **~ -operated** *70* batteriebetrieben
beam *84* Strahl
bearing *87* (Kugel-, Wälz-)Lager
bench *21* Werkbank, Arbeitstisch
to **bend** *12T* biegen
bending machine *13* Biegemaschine

benefit 65 Nutzen, Vorteil
Best regards, 49 Mit freundlichen Grüßen
beyond 64 jenseits
bidirectional 35 in beide Richtungen
billion 14T Milliarde
bimetallic strip 40 Bimetallstreifen
biomass 56 Biomasse
birth, date of ~ 117 Geburtsdatum
birthday 70 Geburtstag
blade 62 (Rotor-)Blatt, (Turbinen-) Schaufel; cutting ~ 22T Sägeblatt; ~ fuse 36 Flachsicherung, Stecksicherung
blade, cutting ~ 22T Sägeblatt
blinds pl 27 Jalousie(n), Rolladen
to block 38T blockieren, verstellen
block of flats BE 17 Mietshaus, Wohnblock
blocker 84 Blockierer
to blot sth out 88T etw verdecken, etw auslöschen
blouse 125 Bluse
to blow 29 durchbrennen; 49 blasen; ~ up 102 in die Luft fliegen, explodieren
blue collar 125 Arbeiter-
board 15 Gremium, Kommission, Amt
to board 107 an Bord gehen, einsteigen
boarding card 107 Bordkarte
bolt 21 Schraube, Bolzen
booking 106 Reservierung, Buchung
to bother 43 stören, belästigen
bottom, to get to the ~ of sth 90 einer Sache auf den Grund gehen
to bow 115 sich verbeugen
box cutter 20 Teppichmesser
bracelet 125 Armband
to brainstorm 97T Ideen sammeln
break 12 Pause; ~ area 31 Pausenbereich
to break 40 unterbrechen; ~ down 70 kaputtgehen; ~ in 39 einbrechen
breakdown 17 Panne
breakthrough 14T bahnbrechend
bridge rectifier 66 Brückengleichrichter
brief 78 kurz, knapp
brightness 78 Helligkeit
brilliant 30T genial, super, toll
to bring: ~ down 74 senken, herunterfahren; ~ sb in 112 jdn hinzuziehen
broadcast station 75 (Radio-/TV-) Sender
brochure 98 Prospekt
broken 9 defekt, kaputt
budget 109 Finanzrahmen, Budget
to build 17 bauen
building 6 Gebäude; ~ site 6 Baustelle
burglar 39 Einbrecher, Dieb
to burn 62T verbrennen
burning 67T Verbrennung, Brand
burns pl 45 Verbrennung(en)
bus bar 53 Sammelschiene, Stromschiene
business: ~ card 98 Visitenkarte; ~ contact 115 Geschäftspartner/in
button 78 (Druck-)Knopf, Taste; push ~ 37 Taster; release ~ 104 Entriegelungsknopf
to buzz sb in 38T jdm (mit dem Türöffner) hereinlassen
buzzer 38T Summer, Türöffner
by 2020 65 bis 2020

C

cable 14T (fest installiertes) Kabel, Leitung; flat ~ 14T Flachkabel; overhead ~ 33 Freileitung; shielded ~ 53 armiertes Kabel; ~ routing 53 Kabelführung; ~ tray 53 Kabelkanal, Kabelrinne; ~ trunking 117 Leitungsführung, -kanal; ~ TV 38T Kabelfernsehen; to lay ~s 17 Kabel verlegen
cabling 15 Leitungen, Verkabelung
cage 87 Käfig
cake 14T Torte, Kuchen; a piece of ~ 14T ein Kinderspiel
to calculate 61 ausrechnen, berechnen
calculator 77 Taschenrechner
to calibrate 84 kalibrieren
call, on ~ 18 in Bereitschaft; ~ sign 67 Rufzeichen
to call on sb to do sth 65 jdn auffordern, etw zu tun
to cancel out 41 auslöschen, sich aufheben
candidate 122P Bewerber/in, Kandidat/in
capacitance meter 76 Kapazitätsmessgerät
capacitor 66 Kondensator; electrolytic ~ 79T Elektrolytkondensator; smoothing ~ 82 Glättungskondensator
capacity 53 Kapazität
captain 117 Kapitän
caption 96 Bildunterschrift
to capture 57 einfangen
car seat positioning device 86 Sitzeinstellungsvorrichtung (im Auto)
cardiac arrest 45 Herzstillstand
to care for sth 24 etw warten; 93 am Herzen liegen
careers adviser 25 Berufsberater/in
carpeted floor 104 Teppichboden
carrier, telecom ~ 74 Telefongesellschaft
to carry sth out 6 etw ausführen, etw durchführen
cartridge fuse 29 Patronensicherung
case 73 Gehäuse; 107T Koffer; ~ study 15 Fallbeispiel, Fallstudie
cash 64 Geld, Bargeld; ~ on delivery (COD) 21 zahlbar bei Lieferung, per Nachnahme
casing 104 Gehäuse
catastrophic 58 katastrophal
category B (car) driving licence 118 Führerschein Klasse 3
cathode 73 Kathode
cause 68 Ursache, Grund
to cause 24 verursachen, bewirken, dazu führen
Caution! 24 Achtung!, Vorsicht!
CCTV 15 Videoüberwachung
ceiling 29 (Zimmer-)Decke
cell 57 Zelle
cellar 33 Keller
central 48 wesentlich, zentral; ~ heating 27 Zentralheizung
century 64 Jahrhundert
CEO (Chief Executive Officer) 11 Geschäftsführer/in, Vorstandsvorsitzende/r
ceramic hob 38T Glaskeramik-Kochfeld
certainly 8T gewiss, natürlich, selbstverständlich
certificate 117 Zeugnis, Diplom; school leaving ~ 117 Schulabgangszeugnis, Schulabschluss
chain 9 Kette; ~ reaction 39 Kettenreaktion
chair 108 (Sitzungs-)Leiter/in
chalk 59 Kreide
challenge 99 Herausforderung
to challenge 64 herausfordern
chance 107T Gelegenheit, Möglichkeit
change of scenery 17 Tapetenwechsel
characteristics pl 73 Charakteristika
charge 62T Ladung; ~ controller 62T Laderegler
to charge 79 laden, aufladen
charity 118 Wohltätigkeit
charred 67T verkohlt
to check: ~ in 106T einchecken; ~ sth out 15 sich etw ansehen; ~ up on sth 65 etw nachsehen, etw überprüfen
check-in counter 107 Abfertigungsschalter
Cheers! 69 Tschüs!, Danke!
chest 45 Brust
Chief Executive Officer (CEO) 11 Geschäftsführer/in, Vorstandsvorsitzende/r
chisel 22T Meißel
choice, free ~ 100 freie Entscheidung
CHP unit 62T Blockheizkraftwerk
chunky 125 dick
church: ~ choir 118 Kirchenchor; ~ community 117 Kirchengemeinde
cigarette 107 Zigarette
circuit 6 Stromkreis, Schaltkreis; integrated ~ 85 integrierter Schaltkreis; lighting ~ 29 Lichtstromkreis; magnetic ~ 41 Magnetkreis; monolithic integrated ~ 85 Festkörperschaltkreis, monolithischer Schaltkreis; relay ~ 55 Relaisschaltung; ring ~ 29 Ringleitung; smoothing ~ 69 Glättungskreis; spur ~ 29 Stichleitung; ~ board 68 Leiterplatte; ~ breaker 17 Leistungsschutzschalter, Sicherungsautomat
circular 87 kreisförmig
to claim 65 behaupten
to clarify 108 klären
to clear the way for sth 64 den Weg für etw bereiten
clearance 52 Abstand; 108 Räumung
clerk 107 Angestellte/r
clever 48 intelligent, klug, schlau
client 15 Kunde/Kundin
close 52 eng; ~ to 37 nahe bei, in der Nähe von, neben; in ~ proximity 53 in unmittelbarer Nähe; to take a ~ look at sth 69 sich etw genau ansehen; ~ly related 55 eng verwandt
cloth 24 Tuch
clothing 125 Kleidung
cloudy 57 bewölkt
coach 123 Trainer/in
coast 74 Küste
coat 125 Mantel
coil 41 Spule; sensing ~ 41 Sensorspule
collar 125 Kragen; blue ~ 125 Arbeiter-; white ~ 125 Angestellten-
colleague 17 Kollege, Kollegin
to collect 106T sammeln, aufheben
college 22 Berufsfachschule, Fachhochschule
colour: ~ band 73 Farbring; ~-coded 79T farbkodiert; ~-coding 35 Farbkodierung
combination 40 Zusammenstellung, Verbindung, Kombination
comfortable 7 angenehm, komfortabel
command 30T Befehl, Steuerbefehl; 120 Beherrschung
to come: ~ in for sth 65 etw *(Kritik usw.)* abbekommen; ~ in on sth 97T etw (zu etw) sagen; ~ on 67T angehen; ~ loose 68 sich lockern
commercial 6 Gewerbe-, gewerblich
commission 99 Kommission
to commission 112 in Betrieb nehmen
commissioning 108 Inbetriebnahme
common 53 gemeinsam; 55 (weit) verbreitet
to communicate 67 kommunizieren

community 117 Gemeinde, Gemeinschaft; ~ service 118 Zivildienst
commutator 87 Kommutator, Kollektor, Stromwender
compact 87 kompakt
to compare 25 vergleichen
compartment 24 Fach
compatibility 99 Austauschbarkeit, Kompatibilität
compatible 55 austauschbar, kompatibel
competition 12T Konkurrenz
complex 17 komplex, aufwändig; industrial ~ 74 Industriekomplex
complicated 47 kompliziert
complication 108 Komplikation
component 6 Bauteil
compressed air 112 Druckluft
comprised, to be ~ of sth 87 aus etw bestehen
compromise 99 Kompromiss
concerned 46 besorgt; as far as I am ~ 97T was mich betrifft, meines Erachtens
concert 71 Konzert; ~ hall 35 Konzertsaal
concession 15 Lizenz, Konzession
to conclude 111T schließen
concrete flooring 22T Betonfußboden
condition 16 Bedingung; 24 Zustand
to conduct 26 leiten
conductor 28 Ader *(eines Kabels)*, Leiter; semi-~ 67T Halbleiter
conduit 17 Rohrleitung, Kabelkanal, Leerrohr
conference room 12 Tagungsraum, Besprechungsraum
confident 25 zuversichtlich, überzeugt; 113 sicher, souverän
confidential 123 vertraulich
configuration 95 Ausstattung, Konfigurierung
to confirm 35 bestätigen
to confuse sb 93 jdn verwirren
to connect 15 verbinden
connection 29 Verbindung; in ~ with 15 in Zusammenhang mit, bezüglich
consensus 99 Übereinstimmung, Einigung, Konsens
consequently 69 folglich, demzufolge
conservative 75 konservativ
to consider 49 in Erwägung ziehen, in Betracht ziehen
considered, to be ~ sth 105 als etw gelten, als etw angesehen werden
to consist of sth 35 aus etw bestehen
constant 47 konstant
construction: plant ~ 11 Anlagenbau; ~ industry 15 Baugewerbe
consultancy 64 Beratungsfirma
to consume 65 verbrauchen
consumer 27 Verbraucher; ~ electronics 104 Unterhaltungselektronik; ~ unit 26 Hausverteilung, Sicherungskasten
consumption 35 Verbrauch
to contact sb 8 sich an jdn wenden, mit jdm Kontakt aufnehmen
contactor 14T Schütz, Schaltschütz; three-phase oil ~ 14T Drehstrom-Ölschütz
to contain 24 enthalten
contest 64 Wettstreit
to continue to do sth 48 etw weiterhin tun
continuity 89 Durchgang, Durchgangsprüfung
continuous 53 ununterbrochen, kontinuierlich; ~ duty 88 Dauerbetrieb
contract 11 Vertrag
contracting services pl 15 Dienstleistungen
contractor 117 (Handwerks-)Betrieb, (Bau-)Unternehmen; sub~ 11 Nachunternehmer, Subunternehmer
contrast, in ~ to 30 im Gegensatz zu
to contribute 118 beitragen
control 78 Regler; sequential ~ 55 Ablaufsteuerung, Folgeschaltung; ~ light 67T Kontrolllampe; ~ panel 17 Steuerkonsole, Schaltschrank; ~ system 12T Steuerung, Steuer-/Regelsystem; ~ systems technology 11 Steuer-/Regel-/Leittechnik
to control 14T steuern, regeln
controller, charge ~ 62T Laderegler; programmable logic ~ (PLC) 14T speicherprogrammierbare Steuerung (SPS)
convection 49 Konvektion
convenient 74 günstig, praktisch
conventional 27 herkömmlich, konventionell
convergence 99 Annäherung, Konvergenz
conversation 12 Gespräch, Unterhaltung
to convert 35 umwandeln, verwandeln, umfunktionieren
converter, frequency ~ 9 Frequenzumrichter
conveyor (belt) 74 Förderband
cooker 29 Herd; ~ hood 38T Dunstabzugshaube
cooking fumes pl 38T Kochdämpfe, Wrasen
to cool 52 kühlen
cooling 52 Kühlung; ~ water 112 Kühlwasser
to co-operate 113 zusammenarbeiten
copper 12 Kupfer
cordless drill 86 Akkuschrauber
corner 32 Ecke
corporation 14T Unternehmen, Konzern
to correspond to sth 11 einer Sache entsprechen
corridor 12T Flur, Gang
to corrode sth 24 etw zersetzen, etw angreifen
cost, the ~s involved 49 die damit verbundenen Kosten; ~-effective(ly) 48 kostengünstig
counter, check-in ~ 107 Abfertigungsschalter
counterpart 115 Pendant, Gegenüber
course, in the ~ of 119 im Lauf von
cover 24 Deckel, Klappe; ~ letter 116 Anschreiben, Begleitbrief
to cover 59 decken; ~ sth up 43 etw abdecken
to crack 24 platzen, reißen, springen
crazy, to go ~ 83 durchdrehen, ausrasten
creation 35 Erstellung, Gestaltung; 99 Gründung
crimping 53 Bördeln, Crimpen
critical 55 entscheidend
criticism 65 Kritik
to criticize 115 kritisieren
cross-cultural 105 kulturübergreifend
cubed 61 hoch drei
cubic metre 61 Kubikmeter
current 9 Strom; 17 aktuell, gegenwärtig; direct ~ (DC) 59 Gleichstrom; forward ~ 69 Durchlassstrom; load ~ 41 Laststrom; neutral ~ 41 Neutralleiter(strom); nominal ~ 40 Nennstrom; peak forward surge ~ 73 Spitzendurchlassstrom; phase ~ 9 Phasenstrom; repetitive peak forward ~ 73 wiederkehrender Spitzendurchlassstrom; residual ~ 41 Fehlerstrom, Reststrom; reverse ~ 69 Sperrstrom, Strom in Sperrrichtung; ~ leakage 42 Leckstrom; ~ limiting 85 Strombegrenzung; surge ~ loading 73 Stoßstrom-Grenzwert; RCD (Residual C~ Device) 26 FI-Schalter, Fehlerstrom-Schutzeinrichtung
currently 8 im Moment, momentan, aktuell
curriculum vitae (CV) BE 116 Lebenslauf
customer 6 Kunde, Kundin
cut 62T Reduzierung, Senkung, Abbau
to cut 57 verringern, abbauen, senken; ~ out 8 ausgehen, (sich) abschalten; ~ sth 31T etw streichen, etw kürzen; ~ sth back 65 etw zurückschrauben, etw verringern
cutter, box ~ 20 Teppichmesser; meat ~ 8 Fleischwolf, Fleischkutter
cutting blade 22T Sägeblatt
cutting room 8 *(Fleischverarbeitung:)* Zerlegeraum
cycle 87 Phase, Zyklus, Periode
cylinder, hydraulic ~ 48 Hydraulikzylinder; pneumatic ~ 48 Pneumatikzylinder

D

damp 24 feucht
dark 49 dunkel; to leave sb in the ~ 65 jdn im Unklaren lassen
data pl 15 Daten; ~ sheet 66 Datenblatt
date of birth 117 Geburtsdatum
day: these ~s 48 heutzutage; ~ release 25 ausbildungsbegleitender Berufsschultag
DC (direct current) 59 Gleichstrom
dead 67T stromlos, tot; to go ~ 67T ausgehen, ausfallen
to deal with sth 8 etw bearbeiten, etw erledigen, sich um etw kümmern; 88T mit etw zu tun haben
dear, Oh ~. 107T O je!
death 45 Todesfall, Tod
debate 122 Debatte, Diskussion
decision 105 Entscheidung, Beschluss
to declare 107 deklarieren, verzollen
to decline 98P *(Angebot usw.)* ablehnen
to decrease 80 senken
dedicated, to be ~ to do sth 47 speziell dafür vorgesehen sein, etw zu tun
defect 16 Schaden, Defekt
defective 7 schadhaft, defekt
definitely 25 ganz bestimmt
delayed 107 verspätet
delicate 24 empfindlich
delivery 21 Lieferung
demand 25 Nachfrage; 59 Bedarf; in ~ 25 gefragt, begehrt
to demand 87 erfordern
to demonstrate 74 vorführen, beweisen, demonstrieren
to denote 73 bezeichnen, kennzeichnen
to depart 106T abfahren, abfliegen, gehen
department 11 Abteilung
departure 106T Abfahrt, Abflug; ~s area 107 Abflugbereich
depending on 48 je nachdem, abhängig von
to deplete 24 leeren, entladen
descending 115 absteigend
desert 64 Wüste
design 12 Konstruktion; 24 Konstruktion, Entwurf, Design; electrical ~ 12 Elektroplanung

exchange student *79* Austauschschüler/in/-student/in
exclusive(ly) *75* ausschließlich
to **expand** *27* expandieren, (den Geschäftsbereich) erweitern; *40* sich ausdehnen
to **expect** *36* erwarten, annehmen
expenses pl *97T* Kosten, Ausgaben, Spesen
experience *95* Erfahrung(en)
to **experience** *64* erleben, durchmachen
to **experiment** *123* experimentieren
expert *109* Fachmann/-frau
explanation *30* Erläuterung, Erklärung
to **explain** *8* erläutern, erklären
to **exploit** *58* nutzen, ausbeuten
expression *13* Ausdruck
extension: ~ **cable** *22T* Verlängerungskabel; ~ **module** *51* Erweiterungsmodul
external *12T* extern, von außen
extra *42* zusätzlich, überschüssig
extract *109* Auszug
to **extract** *38T* absaugen
extractor fan *38T* Sauglüfter, Abzugsgebläse
extra-curricular *119* außerschulisch
eye: ~ **contact** *115* Blickkontakt; ~ **lug** *52* Ösenanker; ~**-level** *38T* auf Augenhöhe

F

face *39* Gesicht; to **lose** ~ *115* das Gesicht verlieren
to **face** *59* *(in eine Richtung)* ausgerichtet sein; ~ **sth** *99* vor etw stehen, sich einer Sache gegenübersehen
to **fail** *67* versagen, ausfallen
fail-safe *7* ausfallsicher, betriebssicher
failure *35* Ausfall, Versagen; *53* Versäumen, Versäumnis
fair, trade ~ *96* Handelsmesse, Branchenmesse
fairly *57* ziemlich
to **fall apart** *104* auseinanderfallen
familiar with sth *117* mit etw vertraut
fan *49* Lüfter, Ventilator; **extractor** ~ *38T* Sauglüfter, Abzugsgebläse
fantastic(ally) *87* ungeheuer
far, so ~ *65* bisher, bislang
far-flung *64* abgelegen
far-reaching *64* folgenschwer, weitreichend, tiefgreifend
fault *17* Fehler, Defekt; **ground** ~ *42* Erdschluss; ~ **current** *41* Fehlerstrom; ~**-tolerant** *74* fehlertolerant
faulty *18* defekt, fehlerhaft, schadhaft
favour, in ~ **of sth** *57* für etw
favourite *17* Lieblings-
feature *31* Merkmal, Eigenschaft; ~**s** pl *125* Gesichtszüge
to **feed** *84* zuführen; ~ **into** *62T* einspeisen
feedback *35* Reaktion, Rückmeldung
fence, perimeter ~ *31* Umzäunung
to **fence sth off** *43* etw abschranken, etw abzäunen
field *30* Feld
figure *40* Abbildung
final *12* letzte/r/s, End-; ~ **assembly** *12* Endmontage; ~ **grade** *122T* Abschlussnote
Finance (Department) *11* Rechnungswesen, Finanzressort
financial(ly) *25* finanziell
to **find one's way around** *13* sich zurechtfinden
findings pl *125* Ergebnisse
to **finish sth off** *31T* etw fertig machen, etw abschließen
fire *42* Brand, Feuer
firm(ly) *115* fest
first: ~ **aid** *45* Erste Hilfe; ~ **thing** *49T* als erstes, früh; **at** ~ *17* zunächst, zuerst; **in the** ~ **place** *30T* zuerst, gleich; **the** ~ **ever** *14T* der/die/das allererste
to **fit** *47* passen; ~ **sth** *47* etw einbauen
fitting *16* Einbau; **electrical** ~**s** pl *6* Elektroinstallation, elektrische Betriebsmittel
to **fix** *17* einbauen, installieren; *59* befestigen; *91* reparieren
fixed *85* fest, unveränderlich; ~ **hours** *18* feste Arbeitszeiten
fixture, electrical ~ *35* Elektroinstallation
to **flag sth up** *74* etw anzeigen
flashlight *20* Taschenlampe
flat *16* Wohnung BE; **block of** ~**s** BE *17* Mietshaus, Wohnblock; ~ **cable** *14T* Flachkabel; ~**-bladed screwdriver** *20* Schlitzschraubenzieher/-dreher
fleet *11* Fuhrpark
flex *26* flexibles Netzkabel, Anschlussleitung
flexible *53* biegsam, flexibel
flick *30T* Drücken (eines Schalters)
flight *9* Flug
to **flirt** *105* flirten
to **float** *110* treiben
floating operation *85* erdfreier Betrieb
flooring *108* Bodenbelag
to **flow** *17* fließen
flower bed *31* Blumenbeet
fluent *118* *(Sprache:) fließend*
fluid *57* Flüssigkeit
flux, magnetic ~ *41* magnetischer Fluss, Induktionsfluss
to **focus** *78* scharf stellen, fokussieren
to **fold** *105* falten, (Arme) verschränken
folding rule *20* Zollstock
to **follow up on sth** *49* auf etw zurückkommen, etw weiterverfolgen, nachhaken
follow-up *71* Folge-, Anschluss-
food mixer *86* Küchenmaschine
forklift truck *46* Gabelstapler
to **form** *103* bilden
formal *111* formell, förmlich
forward current *69* Durchlassstrom; **repetitive peak** ~ *73* wiederkehrender Spitzendurchlassstrom
fossil *56* fossil
to **found** *14T* gründen
foundation *109* Fundament
fraction *61* Bruch
frame *59* Rahmen
free *57* kostenlos
to **freeze** *45* erstarren
freezer *38T* Tiefkühler
frequency *9* Frequenz; **ultra high** ~ **(UHF)** *75* Ultrahochfrequenz; ~ **converter** *9* Frequenzumrichter; ~ **frequency (RF)** *75* Hochfrequenz (HF); ~ **modulation (FM)** *75* Frequenzmodulation, UKW
frequently *74* häufig, oft
fresh *47* frisch
fridge *38T* Kühlschrank
front door *30T* Haustür
fuel *56* Brennstoff, Kraftstoff, Treibstoff; ~ **cell** *62* Brennstoffzelle
full-load *88* Volllast-
full-scale *95* in vollem Umfang, in großem Stil
full-time *35* Vollzeit-
full-wave bridge rectifier *66* Vollwellenbrückengleichrichter
fully *14T* vollständig; ~ **equipped** *22* voll ausgestattet
fumes, cooking ~ pl *38T* Kochdämpfe, Wrasen
to **function** *59* funktionieren
functional skills pl *25* Fachkenntnisse
further *49* weitere/r/s
fuse *17* Sicherung; **cartridge** ~ *29* Patronensicherung; **glass** ~ *66* Glassicherung; **blade** ~ *36* Flachsicherung, Stecksicherung; ~ **board** *119* Sicherungstafel, -platte; ~ **rating** *24* Sicherungswert, Sicherungsleistung

G

to **gain** *119* gewinnen, erwerben
garlic *125* Knoblauch
gate *107T* Flugsteig
to **gather** *123* sammeln
to **generate** *56* erzeugen, gewinnen
generation *62* Erzeugung
geothermal energy *56* Erdwärme
German higher education entrance qualification *118* Fachhochschulreife
German university entrance qualification *118* Allgemeine Hochschulreife (Abitur)
getting on, to **be** ~ *90* alt werden
gift *100* Geschenk
gig *67T* *(Pop, Rock, Jazz:) Konzert*
gigantic *64* gigantisch, ungeheuer
to **give reasons for sth** *19* etw begründen
given: ~ **that** *65* angesichts; to **take sth as** ~ *99* etw als gegeben voraussetzen
glad, to **be** ~ **to do sth** *67T* etw gern tun
glass: sintered ~ *73* Sinterglas; ~ **fuse** *66* Glassicherung; ~ **panel** *57* Glasscheibe; ~ **passivated** *73* glaspassiviert
glasses pl *125* Brille
global(ly) *119* weltweit
to **go:** ~ **about sth** *111T* etw angehen, etw anpacken; ~ **ahead** *49T* vorgehen, verfahren, loslegen; ~ **crazy** *83* durchdrehen, ausrasten; ~ **dead** *67T* ausgehen, ausfallen; ~ **for sth** *49T* etw nehmen
goal *109* Ziel
goodness, Thank ~**.** *59* Gott sei Dank!
goods pl *12* Ware(n), Güter; ~ **inwards examination** *12* Wareneingangskontrolle
government *65* Regierung
to **grab** *89* greifen, packen
grade, final ~ *122T* Abschlussnote
graduate engineer *8* Diplom-Ingenieur/in
gram *104* Gramm
grand *64* groß, gewaltig, eindrucksvoll
graph *9* Kurve, Diagramm
graphic *55* bildlich, grafisch
grateful *54T* dankbar
greatly *45* sehr, massiv, in hohem Maße
grid *15* Stromnetz
to **grip** *21* greifen, packen
to **ground** *52* erden
ground *17* Erde, Erdboden; *53* Masse, Erdung; **earth** ~ *53* Erdung; ~ **fault** *42* Erdschluss; ~ **fault circuit interrupter** *14T* Fehlerstromschutzschalter; ~ **floor** *31* Erdgeschoss; ~ **lead** *53* Masseleitung; ~ **reference** *53* Bezugsmasse; ~ **return** *53* Erdungsanschluss/-leitung; ~ **rod** *53* Staberder; ~ **terminal** *53* Erdklemme, Masseklemme; **incoming power system** ~ *53* Systemerdung nach dem Übergabepunkt; **panel** ~ **termination**

53 Erdanschluss im Schaltschrank; **single point ~ terminal** 53 Einfach-Erdungspunkt
grounding contact 103 Massekontakt, Erdungskontakt
to **guarantee** 7 garantieren
guide 48 Führer
guided tour 12 Führung
guideline 53 Richtlinie
guilty 123 schuldig
guitar 67T Gitarre
guitarist 67T Gitarrist/in
gulf 74 Golf

H
hacksaw 20 Bügelsäge
hair dryer 86 Fön
hall 13 Saal, Halle, Flur
ham: ~ radio 67 Amateurfunk; **radio ~** 67 Amateurfunker/in
hand, right-/left-~ 32 rechte/r/s, linke/r/s; to **shake sb's ~** 115 jdm die Hand geben/schütteln
handle 21 Griff
to **handle sth** 110 etw erledigen, etw handhaben, etw bewältigen
to **hand over** 19 übergeben
handover 112 Übergabe
handshake 115 Händedruck, Händeschütteln
hands-on 109 praktisch
hardly 22T kaum
hardwired 55 festverdrahtet
hard-working 119 fleißig
to **harmonize** 99 angleichen, harmonisieren
harness 18 Klettergurt
harnessing 64 Nutzbarmachung, Nutzung
harsh 24 *hier:* scharf, aggressiv
to **hate** 125 überhaupt nicht mögen, hassen
head 10 Leiter/in, Chef/in; **H~ of Finance** 11 Leiter/in Finanzen
headhunter 122P Kopfjäger
heading 6 Überschrift
headquarters pl 14T Firmensitz, Zentrale
health 15 Gesundheit; **~ and safety** 15 Arbeitssicherheit
heartbeat 45 Herzschlag
heat 40 Hitze
to **heat** 40 erhitzen; **~ up** 85 sich erhitzen
heater 29 Heizlüfter
heating 15 Heizung; **central ~** 27 Zentralheizung
heat-sink 75 Kühlkörper
heavy 95 schwer; **~-duty** 7 Hochleistungs-
height 17 Höhe
hermetically sealed 73 hermetisch abgedichtet
to **hesitate** 14T zögern
to **highlight** 18 hervorheben, markieren
high-power 75 Hochleistungs-
hint 28 Hinweis, Tipp
to **hire sb** 123 jdn beauftragen
to **hit sth** 74 auf etw treffen
hob, ceramic ~ 38T Glaskeramik-Kochfeld
hold 107 Frachtraum, Laderaum
to **hold** 109 *(Sitzung) abhalten*
hole 21 Loch
holidays pl, **paid ~** 19 (bezahlte) Urlaubstage
honest 93 ehrlich, aufrichtig
to **hook sth up** 87 etw anschließen
horizontal(ly) 52 waagrecht, horizontal
horsepower (HP) 88 Pferdestärke(n) (PS); **rated ~** 88 Nennleistung (in PS)
hospital 7 Krankenhaus
host 115 Gastgeber/in
hot: ~ wire 42 Phase; to **be ~ to the touch** 90 sich heiß anfühlen, heiß sein
to **hot-swap** 74 im laufenden Betrieb wechseln
hours pl 16 Arbeitszeit(en); **fixed ~** 18 feste Arbeitszeiten
to **house** 26 unterbringen
house wiring 26 Hausinstallation
household 59 Haushalt
housing 57 Gehäuse
to **hum** 90 summen
Human Resources (HR) 11 Personal(abteilung)
to **hurt oneself** 33 sich wehtun
husband 38T (Ehe-)Mann
hydraulic cylinder 48 Hydraulikzylinder
hydro-electric energy 56 Wasserkraft
hydrogen 62 Wasserstoff

I
ideally 111 im Idealfall
identical 41 identisch
to **identify** 65 herausfinden, identifizieren
if: ~ anything 45 wenn überhaupt; **~ so** 56 falls ja
to **illuminate** 67T beleuchten
to **imagine sth** 30T sich etw vorstellen
immediately 39 unmittelbar, sofort
impact 58 Auswirkung(en), Folgen
impatient 122P ungeduldig
impedance 53 Impedanz
to **implement** 7 *(Ideen usw.)* umsetzen
implementation 65 Einführung, Umsetzung, Anwendung
impolite 98 unhöflich
importance 96 Bedeutung, Wichtigkeit
impressed 112 beeindruckt
impressive 12T beeindruckend
improper 92 unsachgemäß, unvorschriftsmäßig
to **improve** 8 verbessern
improvement 95 Verbesserung
inch 101 Zoll *(= 2,54 cm)*
inclination 59 Neigung
to **include** 14T einschließen, einbeziehen
including 24 einschließlich
incoming power system ground 53 Systemerdung nach dem Übergabepunkt
increase 95 Zunahme
to **increase** 45 steigern, erhöhen
increasing 95 zunehmend, steigend
independent(ly) 109 unabhängig
to **indicate** 35 anzeigen
indicator 84 Anzeige, Anzeiger
induction motor 88 Induktionsmotor
industrial 6 Industrie-, industriell; **~ complex** 74 Industriekomplex; **~ plant** 17 Industrieanlage, Werk
inefficiency 61 Ineffizienz, Unwirtschaftlichkeit
inexpensive 89 preisgünstig, nicht teuer
to **inform sb** 111 jdn unterrichten, jdn informieren
infrared (IR) 57 infrarot, Infrarot(-)
to **injure** 36 verletzen
inlet line 112 Zuleitung
input 48 Eingabe, Eingang; 111 Diskussionsbeiträge; **mains ~** 69 Netzeingang, Netzanschluss; **~ socket** 78 Eingangsbuchse
insecurity 125 Unsicherheit
to **insert** 24 einsetzen, einbauen
to **insist: ~ in doing sth** 105 etw beharrlich weiter tun; **~ on sth** 75 auf etw bestehen
to **inspect** 16 überprüfen
inspection 15 Prüfung, Kontrolle, Abnahme
to **install** 6 installieren, einbauen
installation: ~ board 12T Installationsplatte; **~ electrician** 16 Elektroinstallateur/in; **~ technology** 11 Installationstechnik
instance, for ~ 48 zum Beispiel, beispielsweise
instead 54T stattdessen
instruction 7 Anweisung; 120 Unterricht; **~ manual** 46 Bedienungsanleitung, Betriebsanweisung
insulated 28 isoliert
insulation 28 Isolierung, Isolation; **~ class** 88 Isolationsklasse, Schutzgrad
integrated 65 integriert; **~ circuit** 85 integrierter Schaltkreis; **~ voltage regulator** 79T integrierter Spannungsregler; **~ voltage stabilizer** 66 integrierter Spannungsstabilisator; **monolithic ~ circuit** 85 Festkörperschaltkreis, monolithischer Schaltkreis
to **intend to do sth** 52 vorhaben/beabsichtigen, etw zu tun
intended for sth 85 für etw gedacht, für etw geeignet
intensity 78 Intensität
to **interchange** 55 untereinander austauschen
intercom 38T Gegensprechanlage
to **interconnect** 14T miteinander verbinden
interface 35 Schnittstelle
to **interlink** 35 koppeln, verknüpfen, vernetzen
internal 15 intern
interrelated 95 (damit) zusammenhängend
to **interrupt** 19 (jdn) unterbrechen
to **interview** 74 befragen, interviewen; 116 ein Vorstellungsgespräch führen
introduction 115 Einführung, Einleitung
introductory 115 einführend, einleitend
to **invade sth** 123 in etw eindringen
to **invalidate** 24 außer Kraft setzen, ungültig machen, aufheben
to **invent** 118 erfinden, sich ausdenken
inverter 59 Wechselrichter, Inverter
to **invest** 51 investieren
investment 56 Investition
to **invite** 49 einladen; **~ sth** 97 etw erbitten
invoice 21 Rechnung
to **involve** 16 beinhalten, mit sich bringen, einbeziehen
involved, the costs ~ 49 die damit verbundenen Kosten
inwards, goods ~ examination 12 Wareneingangskontrolle
iron 104 Bügeleisen; **soldering ~** 20 Lötkolben
irregular 9 unregelmäßig
to **isolate** 64 isolieren, absondern
isolated 64 *(Ort:)* abgeschieden, abgelegen
isolation transformer 53 Trenntransformator
issue 105 Frage, Problem, (Streit-)Punkt
to **issue sth** 48 etw ausgeben, (Befehl) erteilen
item 96 Artikel, Gegenstand

J
jacket 107 Jacke
to **jam** 84 lahmlegen, blockieren
jewellery 125 Schmuck

job: ~ advertisment 116 Stellenanzeige; **~ title** 16 Berufsbezeichnung, Stellenbezeichnung

to **join** 80 (miteinander) verbinden; **~ with sb** 113 sich mit jdm zusammentun

joint, dry solder ~ 68 kalte Lötstelle

journey 106T Reise

junction 73 P-N-Übergang (in Halbleitern); **three-phase ~ box** 37 Drehstromsteckdose; **~ box** 22T Verteilerdose, -kasten

jungle 99 Dschungel, Urwald

junior 113 untergeordnet, jünger; **~ to sb** 105 jdm unterstellt

K

to **keep: ~ up with sth** 99 mit etw Schritt halten; **~ sth in mind** 115 an etw denken, etw im Gedächtnis behalten

key 108 entscheidend, Schlüssel-, Haupt-

to **kill** 33 umbringen, töten

kilowatt hour 61 Kilowattstunde

kitchen appliance 38 Küchengerät

knob 78 (Dreh-)Knopf

to **knock sth out** 22T etw herausschlagen

knowledge 25 Wissen; **~ transfer** 109 Wissensvermittlung

known, well-enough-~ 64 nur allzu bekannt

L

to **label** 30 beschriften, etikettieren

lad 22T Junge, Kumpel

ladder 33 Leiter; **~ logic** 55 Leiterlogik, Kontaktplan; **~ notification** 55 Programmablaufplan

large-scale 64 groß angelegt, ausgedehnt

lateness 105 Verspätung, Zuspätkommen

latest 15 neueste/r/s; **at the ~** 106T spätestens

lathe 12 Drehbank, Drehmaschine

the latter 89 letztere/r/s

to **lay cables** 17 Kabel verlegen

lead 24 Leitung, Zuleitung; **ground ~** 53 Masseleitung; **test ~** 24 Prüfleitung

leadership 118 Führung

leaflet 98 Informationsblatt, Faltblatt

leakage, current ~ 42 Leckstrom

least, at ~ 106T mindestens

to **leave sth behind** 97 etw zurücklassen

leg 106T Etappe

leisure 119 Freizeit

length 52 Länge; 112 Dauer; **at ~** 105 ausführlich

to **let: ~ sth through** 80 etw durchlassen; **~ go of sth** 45 etw loslassen

level 25 Niveau, Ebene, Höhe; **spirit ~** 20 Wasserwaage

to **level sth off** 109 etw planieren, etw einebnen

library 119 Bibliothek

licence 67 Genehmigung, Lizenz; **driving ~** 106T Führerschein

licensed 118 zugelassen, konzessioniert

light: test ~ 76 Prüflicht; **~-coloured** 125 *(Farbe:)* hell; **~ engineering** 90 Feinmechanik; **~ switch** 26 Lichtschalter

lighting 8 Beleuchtung, Licht; **~ circuit** 29 Lichtstromkreis; **~ outlet** 31 Lichtauslass, Lichtanschluss; **~ scenario** 35 Lichtszene, Lichtstimmung; **~ scheme** 15 Beleuchtungskonzept

like 87 gleich

likely 22T wahrscheinlich

likewise 112 ebenso

limit 107T Obergrenze, Beschränkung

to **limit** 80 begrenzen

limiting, current ~ 85 Strombegrenzung

limitation 95 Beschränkung, Einschränkung

line, production ~ 18 Fertigungsstraße; **inlet ~** 112 Zuleitung; **pneumatics ~** 112 Druckluftleitung; **return ~** 53 Rücklaufleitung

to **line sth up with sth** 22T etw an etw ausrichten

lineworker 16 *Elektriker/in, der/die am öffentlichen Stromnetz arbeitet*

to **link (up)** 7 verbinden, anschließen

liquid 24 Flüssigkeit

live 33 stromführend, unter Spannung stehend

load 41 Last; **full-~** 88 Volllast-; **~ current** 41 Laststrom; **~ factor** 92 Auslastungsgrad

to **load** 110 laden, verladen

loading, surge current ~ 73 Stoßstrom-Grenzwert

to **locate** 17 aufspüren, ausfindig machen

located, to **be ~ in …** 6 in … sein/liegen; 24 sich (in/am ...) befinden; 34T seinen Sitz in … haben

location 6 Standort

to **lock** 28 verriegeln, sperren

to **log onto sth** 123 sich bei etw einloggen

long-term 40 langfristig

look, to **take a close ~ at sth** 69 sich etw genau ansehen

loop 35 Kreislauf, Schleife

loose 68 locker, lose; to **come ~** 68 sich lockern

to **loosen** 21 lockern, lösen

loss 64 Verlust

lot, this ~ 22T *etwa:* diese Sachen

loud 67T laut; 125 *(Farbe:)* grell

low voltage 7 Niederspannung

to **lower** 30T herunterlassen, senken

lug, eye ~ 52 Ösenanker

luggage 104 (Reise-)Gepäck

lunchtime 59 Mittagszeit

M

machine 7 Gerät, Maschine; **electrical ~ repairer** 16 Elektriker/in für Maschinen/Motoren

machinery 16 Maschinen, Maschinenanlagen

magnetic: ~ circuit 41 Magnetkreis; **~ field** 87 Magnetfeld; **~ flux** 41 magnetischer Fluss, Induktionsfluss

mains pl 15 (Versorgungs-)Netz, Stromnetz, Netzstrom; **~ distribution** 15 Hauptverteiler; **~ input** 69 Netzeingang, Netzanschluss; **~ input socket** 66 Netzanschlussbuchse; **~ tester** 76 Phasenprüfer; **~ voltage** 102 Netzspannung; **sub ~ distribution** 15 Unterverteiler

to **maintain** 6 warten, instandhalten; 46 aufrechterhalten

maintenance 15 Wartung, Instandhaltung

major 6 groß, bedeutend

to **make: ~ sth up** 59 etw ausmachen; **~ sure** 12T sicherstellen, gewährleisten; 36 sich vergewissern

to **malfunction** 17 ausfallen, nicht richtig funktionieren

mallet 22T Schlegel, Hammer

management 11 Geschäftsführung

manual, instruction ~ 46 Bedienungsanleitung, Betriebsanweisung

manner 118 Art

manufacture 7 Herstellung, Fertigung, Bau

to **manufacture** 6 herstellen, fertigen

manufacturer 21P Hersteller

marital status 117 Familienstand

to **mark** 22T kennzeichnen, markieren

mark, top ~s pl 104 Bestnoten

market Markt

marking 22T Markierung

massive 42 riesig, gewaltig

master electrician 11 Elektromeister/in

mate 104 Kumpel, Freund

mathematical 60P mathematisch

maths pl 25 Mathe(matik)

meaning 18 Bedeutung

means 67 Mittel; **by ~ of** 53 mittels, durch

meantime, in the ~ 59 in der Zwischenzeit

message, to **leave a ~** 34T eine Nachricht hinterlassen; to **pass on a ~** 34T etw ausrichten; to **take a ~** 34T etw ausrichten

measure 65 Maßnahme

to **measure** 21 messen, vermessen

measurements pl 22T Maße

measuring tool 101 Messinstrument

meat 8 Fleisch; **~ cutter** 8 Fleischwolf, Fleischkutter; **~ processing** 8 Fleischverarbeitung

mechanical 7 mechanisch; **~ engineering** 7 Maschinenbau

mechanism 62 Mechanismus

mechatronics pl 7 Mechatronik

to **mediate** 106 vermitteln

medium voltage 7 Mittelspannung

to **melt** 39 schmelzen

member 65 Mitglied

memory, process ~ 51 Prozessspeicher

to **mention** 22 erwähnen, nennen

meter 24 Messgerät; 62 Zähler; to **read a ~** 65 einen Zähler ablesen

methane 56 Methan

method 53 Art, Methode

microwave 33 Mikrowelle

middle, in the ~ of sth 17 mitten in etw

mild 45 leicht

miles per hour (mph) 62 Meilen pro Stunde

military service 118 Wehrdienst

mind, to **keep sth in ~** 115 an etw denken, etw im Gedächtnis behalten

to **mind** 90 etw dagegen haben; **Never ~.** 107T Das macht nichts.

minerals pl 24 Mineralstoffe, Mineralien

minutes pl 108 Protokoll

to **miss sth** 79T etw übersehen, etw verfehlen

mixed up 37 durcheinander; to **get ~** 7 durcheinander geraten

mobile 6 mobil, beweglich, fahrbar

mode 63 Modus

model 12 Vorlage

moderate 89 mäßig, mittelmäßig

moisture 24 Feuchtigkeit

to **monitor** 15 überwachen

monolithic integrated circuit 85 Festkörperschaltkreis, monolithischer Schaltkreis

motion 31 Bewegung; **~ detector** 31 Bewegungsmelder

motivated 124 motiviert

motor, driving ~ 74 Antriebsmotor; **induction ~** 88 Induktionsmotor;

three-phase AC ~ 87 Drehstrommotor; universal ~ 87 Universalmotor
motorist BE 95 Autofahrer/in
to mount 51 montieren, anbringen
mounting: ~ box 28 Einbaudose, Unterputzdose; ~ plan 52 Montageanleitung
mouse 35 Maus
move 65 Maßnahme, Schritt
movement 15 Bewegung
multimeter 20 Mehrfachmessgerät
to multiply 61 multiplizieren, malnehmen
multivibrator, astable ~ 84 astabiler Multivibrator
multiple 53 vielfach, mehrfach
multiplication 61 Multiplikation
muscle 45 Muskel
musical instrument 75 Musikinstrument
musician 75 Musiker/in

N

nail 125 Nagel
nameplate 88 Typenschild
nasty 33 böse, übel
national grid 15 Stromnetz
nationality 117 Staatsangehörigkeit, Nationalität
native speaker 98 Muttersprachler/in
natural 52 natürlich
nearby 43 in der Nähe, benachbart
neat 22T sauber
necessary 15 nötig, notwendig, erforderlich
neck 125 Hals
necklace 125 Halskette
needle nose pliers pl 20 Spitzzange
neighbourhood 7 Stadtteil, Wohngegend
nerve 45 Nerv
nervous 17 aufgeregt, nervös
network 15 Netz, Netzwerk; 87 Geflecht, Verbund
neutral 41 neutral, Neutralleiter; ~ current 41 Neutralleiter(strom)
Never mind. 107T Das macht nichts.
next door to 12T neben
noise 62 Lärm; ~ pollution 95 Lärmverschmutzung
noisy 62T laut
nominal 88 nominell, Nenn-; ~ current 40 Nennstrom
note, to make a ~ of sth 43 sich etw merken, sich etw aufschreiben
to note sth 92 etw beachten
notice 43 Hinweis, Aushang; at short ~ 120 kurzfristig
to notice 49 bemerken, (jdm) auffallen
notification, ladder ~ 55 Programmablaufplan
nought BE 60 null
nuclear energy 56 Kernkraft
nut 21 Mutter

O

objection 65 Einwand
objective 108 Ziel
to obtain 67 erlangen, erhalten, bekommen
obvious 69 offensichtlich, offenbar, klar
obviously 49T natürlich, selbstverständlich
occasional(ly) 16 gelegentlich
to occur 90 sich ereignen, auftreten
odd 65 seltsam, merkwürdig, sonderbar
offering 15 Angebot
officer 123 Beamte/r, Beauftragte/r
offset 103 versetzt
ohmmeter 76 Ohmmeter
old-fashioned 47 altmodisch, unmodern
omission 92 Ausbleiben
one-way switch 37 Ausschalter
open, in the ~ 18 im Freien; ~ winding 92 offene Wicklung
to operate 17 in Betrieb sein, laufen, funktionieren; ~ sth 9 etw betreiben, etw bedienen, etw steuern
operating speed 52 Arbeitsgeschwindigkeit
operating theatre 120 Operationssaal
operation 53 Betrieb, Funktion; floating ~ 85 erdfreier Betrieb
operational 74 einsatzbereit, betriebsfähig; 109 im Betrieb, im Einsatz
opinion 19 Meinung, Ansicht
opportunity 117 Gelegenheit, Möglichkeit
opposite 41 entgegengesetzt
optimism 64 Zuversicht, Optimismus
order 21 Bestellung, Auftrag; 21 Reihenfolge; in ~ 9 in Ordnung; of a lower ~ 64 nachrangig, niedriger; to place an ~ 21 eine Bestellung aufgeben, einen Auftrag erteilen
ordinary 27 normal, gewöhnlich
organization chart 10 Organigramm
orientation 59 Ausrichtung, Orientierung
oscillation 75 Schwingung
oscilloscope 76 Oszilloskop, Oszillograph
otherwise 79T sonst; 92 anderweitig
out, to be ~ and about 17 unterwegs sein; ~ of phase 87 phasenverschoben
outage, power ~ 7 Stromausfall
outdoors 17 draußen, im Freien
outlet 69 Ausgang; earthed socket ~ 37 geerdete Steckdose, Schutzsteckdose; lighting ~ 31 Lichtauslass, Lichtanschluss; wall ~ 103 Wandsteckdose
output 48 Ausgabe, Ausgang; ~ transformer 75 Ausgangsübertrager, -transformator
oven 38T Backofen
over 61 geteilt durch
overall 65 gesamt, allgemein
over-booked 107 überbucht
overhead cable 33 Freileitung
to overheat 112 sich überhitzen
overload 40 Überlast, Überlastung
to overload 29 überlasten
overtime 119 Überstunden; to work ~ 17 Überstunden machen

P

to pack 97 packen, einpacken
package 73 *hier:* Gehäuse
to package 111T verpacken
packaging 108 Verpackung
paid holidays pl 19 (bezahlte) Urlaubstage
pain, to be a bit of a ~ 104 lästig sein
painful 45 schmerzhaft
painting 118 Malen
pal 104 Kumpel
palm switch 14T Handballenschalter, Grobhandtaster
panel 12T Blech, Tafel; 16 Schalttafel, Schaltschrank, Schaltpult, Steuerpult; control ~ 17 Steuerkonsole, Schaltschrank; glass ~ 57 Glasscheibe; ~ building electrician 16 Schalttafelbauer, Schaltschrankbauer; ~ ground termination 53 Erdanschluss im Schaltschrank
paper clip 68 Büroklammer
paperwork 97T Unterlagen
part, spare ~ 74 Ersatzteil; user-servicable ~s pl 24 vom Anwender zu wartende Teile
particular 35 bestimmte/r/s; in ~ 122T speziell, im Besonderen
particularly 99 besonders, insbesondere
partnership 14T Partnerschaft
to pass through sth 30 durch etw hindurchgehen/-fließen
passage 46 Gang, Durchgang
passenger 107 Passagier
passivated, glass ~ 73 glaspassiviert
password 123 Passwort
past 25 Vergangenheit; 109 vergangen; ~ sth 12T an etw vorbei
patient 93 geduldig
to pay 93 sich auszahlen
payment 21P Zahlung; ~ terms pl 21P Zahlungsbedingungen
peak 35 Spitze, Spitzenwert, Spitzen-; ~ forward surge current 73 Spitzendurchlassstrom; ~ voltage (PV) 77 Spitzenspannung; pulse avalanche ~ power 73 Spitzenleistung bei Pulsbelastung; repetitive ~ forward current 73 wiederkehrender Spitzendurchlassstrom; repetitive ~ reverse voltage 73 wiederkehrende Spitzensperrspannung
percentage 61 Prozentsatz
to perform sth 48 etw ausführen
performance 111T Leistung
performing arts pl 118 darstellende Künste
perfume 125 Parfüm
perimeter fence 31 Umzäunung
permanent 25 dauerhaft, unbefristet
permission, planning ~ 27 Baugenehmigung
person, in ~ 54T persönlich
personality 118 Persönlichkeit, Wesen
personnel 24 Personal
petrol 95 Benzin
phase 9 Phase; out of ~ 87 phasenverschoben; ~ current 9 Phasenstrom
phew! 103 Puh!
Phillips screwdriver 20 Kreuzschlitzschraubenzieher/-dreher
photovoltaic 56 Photovoltaik
physical 35 physisch, real
physics pl 25 Physik
to pick 100 (sich) etw aussuchen; ~ sth up 41 etw erkennen; 125 aufheben; ~ sb/sth up 22T jdn/etw abholen, etw holen
picture, to put sb in the ~ 12 jdn informieren, jdn ins Bild setzen
piece of equipment 43 Gerät
pin 103 Stift, Kontakt (eines Steckers)
pipe 30 Röhre, Rohr; ~ wrench 20 Wasserpumpenzange
to pipe sth 57 etw durch ein Rohr leiten
place, in ~ 59 an Ort und Stelle, bereit, fertig; to have sth in ~ 123 vorhanden sein, in Kraft sein; in the first ~ 30T zuerst, gleich
to place an order 21 eine Bestellung aufgeben, einen Auftrag erteilen
plain 105 (ganz) einfach
planning permission 27 Baugenehmigung
plant 8 Werk, Betrieb, Anlage; industrial ~ 17 Industrieanlage, Werk; ~ construction 11 Anlagenbau
to plant 31T pflanzen
plated 73 metallüberzogen
platform 59 Plattform

pleased 67 froh, erfreut; **P~ to meet you.** 27 Schön, Sie/dich/euch kennen zu lernen.
pleasure 49T Vergnügen; **My ~.** 49T Gern geschehen.
pliers pl 20 Zange; **round nose ~** 20 Rundzange; **side-cutting ~** 20 Seitenschneider; **water pump ~** 21 Wasserpumpenzange; **needle nose ~** 20 Spitzzange
to **plot** 9 aufzeichnen, grafisch darstellen, plotten
plug 26 Stecker; **~ adaptor** 102 Adapterstecker
to **plug (in)** 22T (ein-)stecken
pneumatic cylinder 48 Pneumatikzylinder
pneumatics line 112 Druckluftleitung
pocket 104 (Hosen-, Jacken-)Tasche
point 60 Komma; **~ of view** 54T Standpunkt; to **make a ~** 96 auf etw hinauswollen, etw sagen wollen
to **point: ~ sth to sth** 84 etw auf etw richten; **~ out** 13 hinweisen auf
polarity 73 Polung, Polarität
pole 14T Pol
policy 123 Verfahren, Regeln, Richtlinie
polite 93 höflich
politeness 98 Höflichkeit
to **pollute** 58 verschmutzen
pollution 57 Verschmutzung; **noise ~** 95 Lärmverschmutzung
port 52 Anschluss; 110 Hafen; **~ supervisor** 110 Hafenaufseher/in
portable 15 tragbar
to **position** 22T anordnen
positioning, car seat ~ device 86 Sitzeinstellungsvorrichtung (im Auto)
possibility 95 Möglichkeit
post 117 Stelle, Posten
potential 64 potenziell
potentiometer 79T Potentiometer
power: high-~ 75 Hochleistungs-; **small ~** 15 Kleinleistung; **pulse avalanche peak ~** 73 Spitzenleistung bei Pulsbelastung; **wave ~** 58 Wellenenergie; **to the ~ of** 61 *(Exponent:)* hoch; **~ drill** 20 Bohrmaschine; **~ outage** 7 Stromausfall; **~ rating** 89 Nennleistung; **~ station** 42 Elektrizitätswerk; **~ supply** 8 Stromversorgung, Stromzufuhr; 67 Netzteil; **switched-mode ~ supply** 102 Schaltnetzteil; **~ transistor** 75 Leistungstransistor; **~ tube** 75 Leistungsröhre
to **power: ~ sth** 29 etw mit Strom versorgen; 48 etw antreiben; **~ up** 59 einschalten, starten
practicable 64 durchführbar, machbar, praktikabel
practices pl 123 Praktiken
praise 65 Lob
to **pray** 105 beten
pre-assembly 12 Vormontage
pre-defined 35 vorher festgelegt
pre-installation 113 Vorinstallation
preliminary 111T vorläufig
premises pl 7 Räumlichkeiten, (Betriebs-)Gelände
preparation 108 Vorbereitung
to **prepare** 19 (sich) vorbereiten, erstellen
present 115 anwesend
presentation 11 Präsentation
to **preserve** 57 erhalten
to **press** 22T drücken
pretty 47 ziemlich
to **prevent** 74 verhindern
previous 70 vorige/r/s, vorherige/r/s
to **price sth** 7 einen Preis festsetzen
price tag 125 Preisschild
primary: ~ education 117 Grundschule, -schulbildung, Primarstufe; **~ school** 118 Grundschule
principle 27 Grundlage, Prinzip
prison 123 Gefängnis
privacy 123 Privatsphäre
prize 118 Preis
probable 9 wahrscheinlich
procedure 108 Verfahren, Vorgehen, Ablauf
process 46 Vorgang: **~ memory** 51 Prozessspeicher
production: ~ downtime 112 Produktionsausfall(zeiten); **~ line** 18 Fertigungsstraße; **~ robot** 17 Fertigungsroboter
productivity 19 Produktivität
professional 119 professionell
profile 117 Porträt, Profil
to **program** 27 programmieren
programmable logic controller (PLC) 14T speicherprogrammierbare Steuerung (SPS)
to **progress** 112 vorankommen
project 6 Projekt, Auftrag; **~ phase** 108 Projektphase
to **promote sth** 65 etw *(Interessen usw.)* vertreten
prong 103 Stift, Kontakt (eines Steckers)
property 99 Eigentum
to **propose** 49T vorschlagen
proprietor 11 Eigentümer/in
pros and cons 57 Für und Wider
to **protect** 26 schützen
protection 11 Schutz
protective earth 30 Schutzerde
proton exchange membrane 62 Protonenaustauschmembran
proud 123 stolz
proximity, in close ~ 53 in unmittelbarer Nähe
public: ~ address system 15 Beschallungsanlage; **~ utilities** pl 57 öffentliche Versorgungsbetriebe
to **pull** 24 ziehen; **~ sth low** 84 etw *(z.B. Spannung)* herunterziehen
pulsating 81 pulsierend
pulse avalanche peak power 73 Spitzenleistung bei Pulsbelastung
to **pump** 112 pumpen
punching machine 13 Stanzmaschine
punctual 122T pünktlich
purchase 24 Kauf
Purchasing (Department) 11 Einkauf(sabteilung)
pure 95 rein
purpose 107 Zweck, Absicht
push button 37 Taster
to **put** 87 formulieren, sagen; **~ sb through** 8T jdn durchstellen, verbinden
PV system 56 Photovoltaikanlage

Q

qualification 11 Abschluss, Qualifikation; **German higher education entrance ~** 118 Fachhochschulreife; **German university entrance ~** 118 Allgemeine Hochschulreife (Abitur)
qualified 24 qualifiziert, ausgebildet, mit Abschluss
quality: ~ control 108 Qualitätskontrolle; **~ management** 11 Qualitätssicherung

R

radiation 57 Strahlung
radiator 57 Heizkörper
radio: ~ frequency (RF) 75 Hochfrequenz (HF); **~ ham** 67 Amateurfunker/in; **~ shack** 67T Funkbude, Elektrowerkstatt; **~ station** 75 Radiosender
radio, ham ~ 67 Amateurfunk
rail 55 Schiene
rain 58 Regen
to **rain** 59 regnen
to **raise** 30T hochfahren, heben
range 14T Angebot(spalette), Sortiment; 55 Bandbreite, Reihe, Auswahl; 75 Bereich, (Frequenz-)Band; 84 Reichweite
to **range (from … to)** 95 sich erstrecken (von … bis)
to **rank** 96 einstufen, ordnen
ranking 19 Rangliste, Platz
rapid 27 rasch, schnell
rare event 74 seltener Fall
rate 40 Geschwindigkeit; 119 Satz, Tarif
rated 88 Nenn-; **~ full-load speed** 88 Nenndrehzahl bei Volllast; **~ horsepower** 88 Nennleistung (in PS)
rating, fuse ~ 24 Sicherungswert, Sicherungsleistung; **power ~** 89 Nennleistung
to **rattle** 90 klappern, rasseln
ray 84 Strahl
RCD (Residual Current Device) 26 FI-Schalter, Fehlerstrom-Schutzeinrichtung
to **react** 40 reagieren
reaction 45 Reaktion; **chain ~** 39 Kettenreaktion
to **read a meter** 65 einen Zähler ablesen
reading 43 Messwert
reality 64 Wirklichkeit, Realität
realizable 64 umsetzbar, realisierbar
real-time 55 Echtzeit-
reasonable 84 sinnvoll, angemessen
receipt 24 Quittung, Beleg
reception 31T Rezeption, Empfang
receptionist 31T Empfangsmitarbeiter/in
to **receive** 35 erhalten, empfangen, bekommen
recess 28 Aussparung, Vertiefung
to **recharge** 95 aufladen
recharger 102 Ladegerät
recharging station 95 Ladestation
to **reckon** 22T vermuten, glauben, schätzen
to **recognize** 99 erkennen
to **recommend** 31 empfehlen
record 109 Aufzeichnung
to **record** 31T aufzeichnen
recruitment 119 Einstellen (von Arbeitskräften), Personalbeschaffung
rectangular 103 rechteckig
rectified waveform 78 Form der gleichgerichteten Spannung/Welle
rectifier, full-wave bridge ~ 66 Vollwellenbrückengleichrichter
to **rectify** 67T gleichrichten
to **reduce** 53 verringern, reduzieren
redundant 74 redundant
to **refer to sth** 81 sich auf etw beziehen
reference 117 Referenz; 119 Kürzel, (Bestell-)Nummer; **ground ~** 53 Bezugsmasse; **with ~ to** 120 bezüglich, mit Bezug auf
refit 15 Überholung, Instandsetzung, Umbau
refund 104 Kostenerstattung
refurbishment 15 Instandsetzung, Sanierung, Modernisierung, Renovierung
to **refuse** 105 sich weigern, (es) ablehnen

regard, Best ~s, *49* Mit freundlichen Grüßen
regarding *59* bezüglich, betreffend
region *64* Region, Gegend, Gebiet
to **register** *119* sich anmelden
to **regulate** *62T* regeln, regulieren
regulation *15* Vorschrift, Regelung
regulator, integrated voltage ~ *79T* integrierter Spannungsregler
to **reinforce** *109* verstärken
to **reject** *50* ablehnen, zurückweisen
related to *95* verwandt mit; **closely ~** *55* eng verwandt mit
relative: ~ clause *101* Relativsatz; **~ pronoun** *101* Relativpronomen
relay *14T* Relais; **alarm ~** *74* Alarmrelais; **~ circuit** *55* Relaisschaltung
to **release** *57* freisetzen
release, day ~ *25* ausbildungsbegleitender Berufsschultag; **~ button** *104* Entriegelungsknopf
reliable *35* zuverlässig, verlässlich
reliance (on sth) *57* Abhängigkeit (von etw)
remaining *95* übrig
remark *115* Bemerkung
Remind me. *62T* Erklär's mir nochmal.
remote control *84* Fernbedienung
remotely *27* aus der Ferne, fern-, entfernt
removal *24* Entfernung, Entnahme, Ausbau; *52* Demontage, Abbau
to **remove** *70* entfernen, ausbauen
renewable *57* erneuerbar; *119* verlängerbar
repairer, electrical machine ~ *16* Elektriker/in für Maschinen/Motoren
to **repel** *87* sich abstoßen
repetitive: ~ peak forward current *73* wiederkehrender Spitzendurchlassstrom; **~ peak reverse voltage** *73* wiederkehrende Spitzensperrspannung
to **replace** *6* ersetzen, austauschen
replacement *24* Ersatz
to **reply (to)** *74* antworten (auf)
to **re-polish** *125* nachpolieren
report *15* Bericht, Prüfbericht
to **report to sb** *11* jdm unterstellt sein; *65* jdm Bericht erstatten
to **represent** *98* vertreten, darstellen
representative *98* Vertreter/in, Repräsentant/in
to **reprogram** *30T* umprogrammieren
reputation *115* Ruf
request, on ~ *117* auf Anfrage, auf Wunsch
to **require** *48* wünschen, benötigen, erfordern
required, to **be ~ to do sth** *65* verpflichtet sein, etw zu tun; etw tun müssen
requirement *15* Vorschrift, Anforderung
to **research sth** *15* etw recherchieren, über eine Sache Nachforschungen anstellen
rescue service *117* Rettungsdienst
to **reset** *92* zurücksetzen
residual current *41* Fehlerstrom, Reststrom; **R~ Device (RCD)** *26* FI-Schalter, Fehlerstrom-Schutzeinrichtung
resistance *42* Widerstand
resistive divide *85* Widerstandsspannungsteiler
resistor *41* Widerstand; **test ~** *41* Testwiderstand
respect *105* Respekt, Achtung
to **respond** *84* reagieren
response *115* Reaktion, Antwort
responsibility *25* Verantwortung; *108* Zuständigkeit, Verantwortlichkeit
responsible *10* verantwortlich, zuständig; to **hold sb ~ for sth** *123* jdn für etw verantwortlich machen
result *7* Ergebnis; *64* Folge, Auswirkung
to **result: ~ from sth** *45* sich aus etw ergeben, aus etw resultieren; **~ in sth** *64* etw zur Folge haben
résumé AE *116* Lebenslauf
retail *15* Einzelhandel
retailer *24* Einzelhändler/in
retrofit *35* Nachrüstung, nachträglicher Einbau
return: ground ~ *53* Erdungsanschluss/-leitung; **~ line** *53* Rücklaufleitung
reverse: ~ current *69* Sperrstrom, Strom in Sperrrichtung; **repetitive peak ~ voltage** *73* wiederkehrende Spitzensperrspannung
to **reverse** *87* umkehren
review *15* Rezension, Kritik; *108* Bericht, Lagebesprechung, Überprüfung
revolutions per minute (RPM) *88* Umdrehungen pro Minute (U/min)
to **rewire** *15* neu verkabeln, eine neue Elektoinstallation einbauen
to **rework** *55* überarbeiten
to **rewrite** *98* umformulieren
rhythm *45* Rhythmus
ribbon *24* Band
rigid *99* starr
ring circuit *29* Ringleitung
ripple *81* Kräuseln, Welligkeit
to **rise** *40* steigen, ansteigen
risk, to **put sth at ~** *7* etw gefährden
river barge *110* Binnenschiff, Lastkahn
robot, production ~ *17* Fertigungsroboter
rocker *28* Kippschalter
rod, ground ~ *53* Staberder
to **role-play** *91* (in einem Rollenspiel) spielen
to **roll sth up/down** *47* etw hoch-/herunterrollen
roll-out *65* Einführung
roof *59* Dach; **~ anchor** *59* Deckenanker; **~ tile** *59* Dachziegel
root mean square (RMS) *77* Quadratmittel, Effektivwert
to **rotate** *22T* sich drehen, rotieren
rotation *62* Umdrehung, Rotation
rotor *87* Läufer, Rotor
roughly *84* ungefähr
round nose pliers pl *20* Rundzange
to **round up** *61* aufrunden
routinely *97T* regelmäßig
routing, cable ~ *53* Kabelführung
row *107* Reihe
rule, folding ~ *20* Zollstock; **safety ~s** pl *36* Sicherheitsvorschriften
to **run: ~ sth** *17* etw betreiben; **~ through sth** *62T* etw durchgehen
rung *55* Sprosse

S

safe operation area (SOA) *85* sicherer Arbeitsbereich, Sicherheitsbereich
safety *11* Sicherheit; **~ rules** pl *36* Sicherheitsvorschriften
sale, for ~ *107* zum Verkauf, zu verkaufen
sales pl: **S~ (Department)** *12* Verkauf(sabteilung), Vertrieb; **~ floor** *15* Verkaufsraum, -fläche
salesperson *46* Vertriebsmitarbeiter/in, Verkäufer/in
satisfied *113* zufrieden
to **saturate** *84* sättigen
savings pl *35* Einsparung(en); *61* Ersparnis(se)
to **say sorry** *105* sich entschuldigen
scaffolding *59* Baugerüst
scale *64* Umfang; *107T* Waage; **full-~** *95* in vollem Umfang, in großem Stil; **large-~** *64* groß angelegt, ausgedehnt; **small-~ business** *46* Kleinbetrieb
scenario, lighting ~ *35* Lichtszene, Lichtstimmung
scenery *17* Kulisse, Landschaft; **change of ~** *17* Tapetenwechsel
schedule *49T* Terminkalender; *108* Terminplan, Zeitplan
scheduled *106T* planmäßig, geplant; to **be ~ to arrive** *109* planmäßig ankommen
schematic *55* Schaltbild
scheme *15* Programm, Plan; **lighting ~** *15* Beleuchtungskonzept
school leaving certificate *117* Schulabgangszeugnis, Schulabschluss
science *87* (Natur-)Wissenschaft
scientist *63* Naturwissenschaftler/in
to **score** *105* abschneiden, eine Punktzahl erreichen
screen *32* Bildschirm, Leinwand
screw *21* Schraube
to **screw** *59* schrauben
screwdriver, flat-bladed ~ *20* Schlitzschraubenzieher/-dreher; **Phillips ~** *20* Kreuzschlitzschraubenzieher/-dreher
sculpture *118* Bildhauerei
sealant *59* Dichtungsmittel
sealed, hermetically ~ *73* hermetisch abgedichtet
seamless(ly) *55* nahtlos
seat *107* Sitz, Platz; to **take a ~** *122T* Platz nehmen
seating arrangement *115* Sitzordnung
secondary education *117* weiterführende Schule/Schulbildung, Sekundarstufe
secretariat *11* Sekretariat
section *12T* Abteilung, Abschnitt
to **secure** *59* sichern, befestigen
security *31* Sicherheit; *107 (Flughafen:)* Sicherheitskontrolle; **~ company** *39* Wachschutzfirma
to **see for oneself** *9* sich selbst ein Bild machen
to **select** *28* auswählen, wählen
self-coiling door *47* Rolltor
self-explanatory *84* selbsterklärend
semi-conductor *67T* Halbleiter
semi-skilled worker *35* angelernte Arbeitskraft
senior *113* leitend, vorgesetzt, höherrangig, älter
sense, to **make ~** *31* sinnvoll sein, vernünftig sein
sensible *50* vernünftig
sensing coil *41* Sensorspule
sensory *67T* sensorisch
separate *12T* getrennt, eigen
separately *39* einzeln
sequential control *55* Ablaufsteuerung, Folgeschaltung
serial number *21P* Seriennummer
series *55* Reihe
seriously *36* ernsthaft, schwer; to **take sth ~** *63* etw ernst nehmen
to **serve as sth** *101* als etw dienen
service *24* Wartung; **~ entrance** *26* Hauseinführung; **~ factor** *88* Wartungsfaktor, Betriebsfaktor; to **lose ~** *74 hier:* den Betrieb einstellen (müssen)
set *47* Satz; to **be ~ to do sth** *64* darauf eingestellt sein, etw zu tun

Alphabetical word list

to set up 99 gründen; 110 aufbauen, einrichten
settings pl 108 Einstellungen
to settle 125 sich beruhigen
several 53 mehrere
severe 45 schwer
shack, radio ~ 67T Funkbude, Elektrowerkstatt
to shake 125 schütteln; ~ sb's hand 115 jdm die Hand geben/schütteln
to share 123 teilen, mitteilen
sharp(ly) 53 scharf
to shave 125 sich rasieren
shielded cable 53 armiertes Kabel
shift 17 Schicht
to shine 57 scheinen
shiny 125 glänzend
to ship 109 versenden, verschiffen
shipping 108 Versand
shirt 125 Hemd
short 74 Kurzschluss
to short-circuit 42 kurzschließen
shorted 74 kurzgeschlossen
to shorten 24 kürzen, verkürzen
to short-list sb 124 jdn in die engere Auswahl nehmen
shortly 120 in Kürze, bald
to show sb around 12 jdn herumführen, jdm etw zeigen
shower 29 Dusche
showroom 12 Ausstellungsraum
shutdown, thermal ~ 85 Überhitzungsschutz
side door 31T Nebeneingang
side-cutting pliers pl 20 Seitenschneider
sign 107 Schild
to sign off on sth 112 etw abzeichnen
to signal 46 melden, mitteilen
significant(ly) 62 beträchtlich, bedeutsam, erheblich
silicon 57 Silizium
similar 12 ähnlich
similarity 55 Ähnlichkeit
to simulate 75 nachahmen, nachbilden
simultaneous 65 gleichzeitig
sincerely, Yours ~, 120 Mit freundlichen Grüßen
sine wave 73 Sinuskurve, Sinuswelle
single point ground terminal 53 Einfach-Erdungspunkt
sintered glass 73 Sinterglas
sinterglass 73 Sinterglas
sinusoidal 78 sinusförmig, Sinus-
site 10 Ort, Standort, Anlage; on ~ 10 vor Ort
skill 25 Fähigkeit, Fertigkeit, Kenntnis; functional ~s pl 25 Fachkenntnisse
skin 125 Haut
skirt 125 Rock
to slide in/out 104 hinein-/herausschieben
sliding: ~ door 46 Schiebetür, Schiebetor; ~ gate 31 Schiebetor
slight 45 leicht, sanft
slightly 45 etwas, geringfügig, leicht
to slow down 49T verlangsamen, bremsen
small power 15 Kleinleistung
small-scale business 46 Kleinbetrieb
smart 65 intelligent
smell 22T Geruch
to smell 105 riechen
smoke 22T Rauch; to go up in ~ 102 in Rauch aufgehen
to smooth 81 glätten
smoothing: ~ capacitor 82 Glättungskondensator; ~ circuit 69 Glättungskreis
to snap sth closed 24 etw einrasten lassen
so far 65 bisher, bislang
soccer AE 117 Fußball
sock 125 Socke
socket 7 Steckdose; input ~ 78 Eingangsbuchse; mains input ~ 66 Netzanschlussbuchse; TV ~ 37 Fernsehanschlussdose; double/triple/fourfold ~ 37 Doppel-/Dreifach-/Vierfachsteckdose; earthed ~ outlet 37 geerdete Steckdose, Schutzsteckdose
solar: ~ energy 56 Sonnenenergie, Solarenergie; ~ module 61 Solarmodul; ~ thermal collector 56 thermischer Solarkollektor
to solder 53 löten
solder 69 Lot, Lötzinn; dry ~ joint 68 kalte Lötstelle
solderable 73 lötbar
soldering iron 20 Lötkolben
solely 95 allein, einzig, nur
solenoid 40 Spule, Magnetspule
solid-state 75 Halbleiter-
solution 8 Lösung; antifreeze ~ 58 Frostschutzmittel
to solve 6 lösen
solvent 24 Lösungsmittel
somewhat 115 etwas
soon, as ~ as possible (ASAP) 119 baldmöglichst
sophisticated 55 hoch entwickelt, raffiniert
sorry, to say ~ 105 sich entschuldigen
sort 9 Art
sound 97T vernünftig, gut, solide
to sound an alarm 84 einen Warnton erklingen lassen
source 41 Quelle
space 52 Raum, Platz, Abstand
to space sth 87 etw in (regelmäßigen) Abständen anordnen
spanner 20 Schraubenschlüssel
spare 24 Ersatz-; ~ part 74 Ersatzteil
to spare 67T erübrigen
sparky BE 25 ugs Elektriker/in
speaker 75 Lautsprecher
to specialize in sth 17 sich auf etw spezialisieren
specifically 121 ausdrücklich, speziell
specifications pl 12T Spezifikationen, technische Daten
to specify 120 angeben, nennen
to speculate 95 spekulieren
speech 115 Rede, Ansprache
speed 48 Geschwindigkeit; 87 Drehzahl; operating ~ 52 Arbeitsgeschwindigkeit; rated full-load ~ 88 Nenndrehzahl bei Volllast
sphere 123 Sphäre
to spin 87 sich drehen, rotieren
spirit level 20 Wasserwaage
splendid 49T großartig
spokesperson 65 Sprecher/in
sporadic(ally) 8 sporadisch, vereinzelt
sporting 118 Sport-, sportlich
spot 51 Punkt, Platz, Ort
spotlight 31 Strahler, Spot
spreadsheet 117 Tabellenkalkulation
spur (circuit) 29 Stichleitung
square 68 Quadrat, Feld; ~ foot 35 Quadratfuß; ~ metre 61 Quadratmeter; ~ root 77 Quadratwurzel; root mean ~ (RMS) 77 Quadratmittel, Effektivwert
squared 61 im Quadrat, hoch zwei
squirrel 87 Eichhörnchen
stabilizer, integrated voltage ~ 66 integrierter Spannungsstabilisator
stable 49 stabil, gleichbleibend
staff 10 Personal
stage 58 Phase, Etappe, Stufe
stairs pl 31 Treppenhaus
stand 98P (Messe-)Stand
to stand in the way of sth 95 einer Sache im Wege stehen
standard 17 Norm, normal
standardization 99 Normierung, Normung
to standardize 95 normen
standby 63 Bereitschaft; on ~ 17 auf Abruf
standstill 7 Stillstand
started, to get ~ 79T anfangen, loslegen
starting torque 87 Anlauf(dreh)moment
to state 123 erklären
state of the art 7 auf dem neuesten Stand der Technik, neueste/r/s
statement of rights 123 Nutzungsbedingungen
stator 87 Ständer, Stator
status 108 Stand (der Dinge)
stay 106T Aufenthalt
steel 118 Stahl
to step: ~ down 7 (Spannung) senken, heruntertransformieren; ~ up 7 (Spannung) erhöhen, hochtransformieren
step, to take ~s 65 Schritte unternehmen, Maßnahmen ergreifen
stereotype 115 Klischee
stick, to get the wrong end of the ~ 43 etw völlig falsch verstehen
stock, in ~ 21 am/auf Lager, vorrätig, lieferbar
stocking 85 Lagerhaltung
stop 12T Halt
stopover 106T Zwischenlandung, Aufenthalt
storage room 22T Lagerraum
store 15 Geschäft, Laden
to store 11 lagern, speichern
storeroom 12 Lagerraum
storey 27 Stock, Etage; three-~ 27 dreistöckig
straight 34T direkt; 40 gerade; 107 gleich, sofort
straight away 123 sofort
straightforward 87 einfach
stranded wire 28 Litze
strength 45 Stärke
strict 115 streng
to strike sth 57 auf etw treffen
to strip 21 abziehen, abmanteln; ~ sth out 17 etw herausreißen
strippers pl, wire ~ 20 Abisolierzange
strong 118 stark
sub mains distribution 15 Unterverteiler
subcontractor 11 Nachunternehmer, Subunternehmer
subheading 95 Zwischenüberschrift
subject 109 Thema
substation 17 Umspannwerk, Transformatorenstation
subtraction 61 Subtraktion
to suck sth off 69 etw absaugen
sudden 40 plötzlich, abrupt, unerwartet
to suffer 64 leiden, erleiden
sufficient 52 ausreichend, genügend
to suggest 23 vorschlagen
suggestion 19 Vorschlag
to suit sb 111 zu jdm passen
suitable 23 passend, geeignet
suited 23 geeignet
to summarize 19 zusammenfassen
summary 8 Zusammenfassung
sunlight 57 Sonnenlicht
to supervise sb 11 jdm vorgesetzt sein
supervision 122T Aufsicht, Betreuung, Anleitung
supervisor 22 Vorgesetzte/r; port ~ 110 Hafenaufseher/in
supplier 8 Lieferant

Alphabetical word list

supplies pl 9 Vorräte, Nachschub, Lieferungen
support, technical ~ service 90 technischer Kundendienst
to suppose 112 annehmen, vermuten
supply 15 Lieferung, Bereitstellung
to supply (sb with sth) 7 (jdm etw) liefern, (jdn mit etw) versorgen
sure, to make ~ 12T sicherstellen, gewährleisten; 36 sich vergewissern
surface 32 Oberfläche
surge 40 starker Anstieg, starker Strom-/Spannungsstoß; ~ current loading 73 Stoßstrom-Grenzwert; peak forward ~ current 73 Spitzendurchlassstrom
survey 15 Studie
suspected 53 mutmaßlich, vermutet
to swap 37P tauschen; 74 austauschen, auswechseln
sweaty 105 verschwitzt, schwitzig
swift 115 schnell, zügig
switch 7 Schalter; double ~ 37 Wechselschalter; light ~ 26 Lichtschalter; one-way ~ 37 Ausschalter; two-way 28 Zweiwegeschalter, Wechselschalter
to switch on/off 8 ein-/ausschalten
switched and fused 29 geschaltet und abgesichert
switched-mode power supply 102 Schaltnetzteil
switchgear 7 Schaltanlage
switching system 7 Schaltanlage, Schaltsystem

T

to tag 28 kennzeichnen, etikettieren
tag, price ~ 125 Preisschild
to take: ~ sb on 25 jdn einstellen; ~ sth apart 70 etw auseinanderbauen
target 63 Ziel
to team up with sb 97 mit jdm zusammenarbeiten, sich mit jdm zusammentun
technical 7 technisch, Fach-; ~ building equipment 7 technische Gebäudeausrüstung; ~ drawing 117 technisches Zeichnen; ~ support service 90 technischer Kundendienst; ~ text 40 Fachtext
technician 7 Techniker/in
technologist 64 Technologe/-in
telecom carrier 74 Telefongesellschaft
telecommunications 7 Telekommunikation
teleconference 7 Konferenzschaltung
telephony 99 Fernsprechwesen, Telefonie
television station 74 Fernsehsender
temperature 24 Temperatur; ambient ~ 88 Umgebungstemperatur
to tend to do sth 95 dazu neigen, etw zu tun
term 6 Begriff; in ~s of ... 64 was ... betrifft; in the short ~ 58 kurzfristig; long-~ 40 langfristig
terms pl 104 Bedingungen, Konditionen; payment ~s 21P Zahlungsbedingungen
terminal 28 Anschluss, Anschlussklemme; earth ~ 26 Erdklemme, Masseklemme; ground ~ 53 Erdklemme, Masseklemme; single point ground ~ 53 Einfach-Erdungspunkt
termination, panel ground ~ 53 Erdanschluss im Schaltschrank
terminology 74 Terminologie, Begriffe
terrible 83 furchtbar, schrecklich
test: ~ condition 73 Testbedingung; ~ lead 24 Prüfleitung; ~ light 76 Prüflicht; ~ point 70 Prüfpunkt, Messstelle; ~ probe 24 Prüfspitze; ~ resistor 41 Testwiderstand; ~ run 108 Probelauf, Testlauf
testing 12 Prüfung
text, technical ~ 40 Fachtext
thanks to 64 dank
theatre, operating ~ 120 Operationssaal
theoretical 120 theoretisch, Theorie-
therefore 49 daher, folglich
thermal 40 thermisch, Thermo-; ~ shutdown 85 Überhitzungsschutz; ~-magnetic 40 thermomagnetisch
thing, first ~ 49T als erstes, früh
to think: ~ again 65 umdenken, seine Meinung ändern; ~ of sth 31T an etw denken
thorough(ly) 125 gründlich
thread 103 Faden, Thema
three-phase: ~ AC 9 Drehstrom; ~ AC motor 87 Drehstrommotor; ~ junction box 37 Drehstromsteckdose; ~ oil contactor 14T Drehstrom-Ölschütz
tidal energy 56 Gezeitenenergie
to tie 33 binden
to tighten 21 *(Schraube)* anziehen, festziehen
tights pl 125 Strumpfhose
tile, roof ~ 59 Dachziegel
time: ahead of ~ 125 zeitig; in ~ 110 rechtzeitig; on ~ 7 pünktlich; at all ~s 24 stets, jederzeit; full-~ 35 Vollzeit-, hauptberuflich; real-~ 55 Echtzeit-; ~-consuming 89 zeitraubend, langwierig; ~ slot 111 Zeitfenster
times 61 mal; ... ~ 40 -fach
tingle 45 Kribbeln
tingling 45 Kribbeln
tip 62 Spitze
toilet 105 Toilette
tone 75 Klang, Ton; 111 Tonfall; 125 Farbton
tool 6 Werkzeug, Instrument, Gerät
top marks pl 104 Bestnoten
torque 87 Drehmoment; starting ~ 87 Anlauf(dreh)moment
touch, to get in ~ with sb 98P sich bei jdm melden
tough 12T hart; 58 strapazierfähig, robust
tour 6 Rundgang; 71 Tournee; guided ~ 12 Führung
trace 78 Kurve
to trace 66 ausfindig machen, aufspüren
trade 22 Beruf, Handwerk, Metier; 96 Handel, Gewerbe, Branche; ~ fair 96 Handelsmesse, Branchenmesse; ~ show 98P Fachmesse, Branchenmesse; ~ standards pl 99 Branchennormen, Handelsstandards
to train 12T ausbilden, schulen; 122T trainieren
trainee 22 Auszubildende/r
training 10 Ausbildung, Schulung; ~ officer 81 Ausbildungsleiter/in
transformer 7 Transformator, Trafo; isolation ~ 53 Trenntransformator; output ~ 75 Ausgangsübertrager, -transformator; power ~ 75 Leistungstransistor
transistor 66 Transistor
to translate 6 übersetzen
translation 26 Übersetzung
transmission tower 17 Hochspannungsmast
transmitter 75 Sender
to transport 64 befördern, transportieren
to trap 57 einfangen, speichern
tray 107 Schale; cable ~ 53 Kabelkanal, Kabelrinne; ~ work 117 Installation in Kabelpritschen
to treat 93 behandeln
trench 22T Graben
trial and error 84 Versuch und Irrtum, Ausprobieren
triangle 103 Dreieck
tricky 55 schwierig
trigger 22T Auslöser, Schalter, Knopf
to trigger 41 auslösen
trillion 60 Billion
trip 95 Fahrt
to trip 33 ansprechen, auslösen
trouble, to get into ~ 39 Ärger bekommen
to troubleshoot sth 17 die Fehler bei etw suchen, die Störung von etw beheben
troubleshooting 69 Fehlersuche
truck 110 Lastwagen
truly 64 wirklich
trunking, cable ~ 117 Leitungsführung, -kanal
tube AE 66 (Elektronen-)Röhre; power ~ 75 Leistungsröhre
turn, in ~ 87 wiederum; to take ~s 16 sich abwechseln
to turn 30T sich drehen; ~ to sb 116 sich an jdn wenden, sich jdm zuwenden; ~ sth into sth 22T etw zu etw machen, etw in etw umwandeln/umbauen; ~ left/right 13 links/rechts abbiegen; ~ on/off 24 ein-/ausschalten
turnover 14T Umsatz
TV socket 37 Fernsehanschlussdose
two-way switch 28 Zweiwegeschalter, Wechselschalter

U

ultra high frequency (UHF) 75 Ultrahochfrequenz
umbrella 125 Regenschirm
unacceptable 40 inakzeptabel, unzumutbar
uncompromising 100 unnachgiebig, kompromisslos
uncontrolled 42 unkontrolliert, ungeregelt
uncoordinated 45 unkoordiniert
understanding 105 Verständnis, Verständigung
uneasy 105 unsicher, nervös
unfortunately 7 leider
ungrounded 103 nicht geerdet
unidirectional 35 in eine Richtung wirkend
uninsulated 28 unisoliert
uninterruptible 74 unterbrechungsfrei, ausfallsicher
unique 75 einzigartig
unit 12T Gerät, Einheit
universal motor 87 Universalmotor
unlike 87 unähnlich
unnoticed, to go ~ 74 unbemerkt bleiben
unpleasant 45 unangenehm
to unsolder 69 entlöten
unusual 16 ungewöhnlich, unüblich
until, not ... ~ 22 erst
up, ~ until now 64 bislang, bis jetzt; to get sth ~ and running 111T etw zum Laufen bringen
upgrade 113 Verbesserung, Aufrüstung
to upload 119 hochladen
to upset sb 115 jdn verärgern, jdn verstimmen
usage 65 Verbrauch
use 24 Gebrauch, Benutzung; 65 Verwendung, Verbrauch

user-servicable parts pl *24* vom Anwender zu wartende Teile
utilities pl, **public ~** *57* öffentliche Versorgungsbetriebe

V
vacancy *120* freie/offene Stelle
vacuum tube AE *66* (Elektronen-)Röhre
valuable *118* wertvoll
value *45* Wert; **~ for money** *7* Preis-Leistungs-Verhältnis
to **value** *93* wertschätzen, schätzen
valve *30* Ventil; *75* (Elektronen-)Röhre BE
van *6* Lieferwagen
varied *25* abwechslungsreich
variety *17* Abwechslung, Vielfalt; *48* Vielfalt, Auswahl, Vielzahl; *103* Sorte, Art
to **vary** *75* verändern, variieren
vehicle *118* Fahrzeug
ventilation *15* Belüftung
ventricular febrillation *45* Herzkammerflimmern
venue *35* Veranstaltungsort
vernier calliper *20* Messschieber
versatile *87* vielseitig
vertical(ly) *52* senkrecht, vertikal
via *48* über, mittels
to **vibrate** *90* vibrieren
vibration *62* Vibration(en), Erschütterung(en)
video projector *30T* Beamer
to **view sth** *15* sich etw ansehen
violation *123* Verletzung
vocational college BE *117* Berufsschule, Berufskolleg, Gewerbliche Schule
vocational school AE *118* Berufsschule, Berufskolleg, Gewerbliche Schule
voice alarm system *15* elektroakustisches Notfallwarnsystem
void *22T* unwirksam, ungültig
voltage *7* Spannung; **low ~** *7* Niederspannung; **mains ~** *102* Netzspannung; **medium ~** *7* Mittelspannung; **~ drop** *53* Spannungsabfall; **~ per division** *78* Volt pro Einheit/Strich; **integrated ~ regulator** *79T* integrierter Spannungsregler; **integrated ~ stabilizer** *66* integrierter Spannungsstabilisator; **repetitive peak reverse ~** *73* wiederkehrende Spitzensperrspannung
voltmeter *76* Voltmeter
voluntary *99* freiwillig
vote *19* Abstimmung
to **vote on sth** *96* über etw abstimmen

W
wall *12T* Wand; **~ chaser** *22T* Schlitzfräse; **~ outlet** *103* Wandsteckdose
war *64* Krieg
warehouse *8* Lager(halle)
warehouseman *11* Lagerist, Lagerverwalter
to **warn** *111* warnen, hinweisen
warning *33* Hinweis, Warnung
warranty *22T* Garantie, Gewährleistung
to **wash off** *59* etw (von etw) abwaschen
washing machine *7* Waschmaschine
to **waste** *63* verschwenden, vergeuden
waste *63* Verschwendung, Vergeudung
wastes pl *64* Einöde, Wüste
watchdog *65* Wachhund; **~ organization** *65* *hier:* Verbraucherschutzorganisation
water pump pliers pl *21* Wasserpumpenzange
watertight *59* wasserdicht
watt hour *61* Wattstunde
wattage *61* Leistung, Stromverbrauch
wave *75* Welle; **~ power** *58* Wellenenergie
waveform *78* Kurve, Stromverlauf; **rectified ~** *78* Form der gleichgerichteten Spannung/Welle
wavelength *75* Wellenlänge
way, by the ~ *12T* übrigens; **this ~** *12T* hier entlang; to **find one's ~ around** *13* sich zurechtfinden; to **stand in the ~ of sth** *95* einer Sache im Wege stehen; **~ back** *14T* damals
weakness *122* Schwäche
wear and tear *92* Verschleiß
to **wear out** *90* sich abnutzen, sich verschleißen
to **weigh** *104* wiegen
weight *73* Gewicht
to **welcome** *65* begrüßen
welcome, You're ~. *67T* Bitte., Gern geschehen.
welding *12* Schweißen
welding bay *12T* Schweißplatz
well, as ~ as *25* ebenso wie; **~-enough-known** *64* nur allzu bekannt
whatever *95* was (auch immer)
whenever *7* wann (auch) immer, immer wenn, jedesmal wenn
whereas *42* während, wogegen
wherever *7* wo (auch) immer
white collar *125* Angestellten-
wide *14T* groß, breit, weit
widespread *65* großflächig, umfassend
width *52* Breite
willing, to **be ~ to do sth** *99* bereit/willens sein, etw zu tun
to **wind** *41* wickeln
wind turbine *62* Windrad, Windanlage
winding, open ~ *92* offene Wicklung
to **wipe** *24* wischen, reiben
wire *28* Draht; **hot ~** *42* Phase; **stranded ~** *28* Litze; **~ strippers** pl *20* Abisolierzange
wiring *12* Verdrahtung, Beschaltung, Elektroinstallation; **house ~** *26* Hausinstallation; **~ diagram** *36* Schaltplan; **~ plan** *17* Anschlussplan, Verdrahtungsplan; **~ route** *52* Kabelstrecke; **~ system** *16* Leitungsnetz, Elektroinstallation
to **wonder** *30T* sich fragen
wonder, no ~ *63* kein Wunder(, dass)
word-processing *117* Textverarbeitung
work, to **put sth to ~** *87* etw einsetzen
work experience *117* Berufserfahrung; **~ placement** BE *22* Praktikum
work placement *43* Praktikum
workbench *20* Werkbank
workforce *14T* Belegschaft, Arbeitskräfte, Mitarbeiter
working conditions pl *16* Arbeitsbedingungen
workload *51* Arbeitspensum
workman *33* Arbeiter
workmate *43* Arbeitskollege/-in
workplace *6* Arbeitsplatz
workshop *6* Werkstatt
worn *92* abgenutzt, verschlissen
to **worry about sth** *47* sich um etw Sorgen machen, sich über etw Gedanken machen
worth *56* wert
worthwhile *22T* lohnenswert, den Aufwand wert
wrench, pipe ~ *20* Wasserpumpenzange
to **write up** *81* ausarbeiten, erstellen
writing *79T* Schrift

Y
yet, not ~ *25* noch nicht

Z
zero AE *60* null

Beispiel-Europass Lebenslauf

Europass
Curriculum Vitae

Personal Information	
First name(s) / Surname	Sven Meier
Address(es)	Blockstrasse 3, D-78628 Rottweil, Germany
Telephone(s)	+49 741 201 438 Mobile: +49 170 4089101
E-mail	sven.meier97@xmg.de
Nationality	German
Date of birth	24 October 199...
Gender	Male
Desired employment / Occupational Field	Electrician at Blackwells Electrical, Manchester, UK
Work experience	3-year apprenticeship
Dates	06/201... – present
Occupation or position held	Apprentice electrician
Main activities and responsibilities	Installation and maintenance work
Name and address of employer	Elektro Richter GmbH, Oberamteigasse 99, 78628 Rottweil
Type of business sector	Electrical
Education and training	
Dates	06/201... – present
Title of qualification awarded	Qualified electrician as of June 201...
Principal subjects / occupational skills covered	Electrical installation in private, commercial and industrial premises, installation, maintenance and repair of electrical machinery
Name and type of organisation providing education and training	Erich-Hauser-Gewerbeschule Rottweil (Erich Hauser Technical College)
Level in national or international classification	ISCED 06.2
Dates	09/20... – 07/20... Realschule Rottweil (selective secondary school)
Title of qualification awarded	Realschulabschluss (Year 10 School Leaving Certificate)

Personal skills and competences	Life-saving certificate
Mother tongue(s)	German
Other language(s)	

Self-assessment European level (*)	Comprehension		Speaking		Writing
	Listening	Reading	Spoken interaction	Spoken production	
English	B1	B1	B1	B1	B1

(*) Common European Framework of References for Languages

Social skills and competences	Community work with local church Trained mediator for settlement of disputes
Computer skills and competences	MS Excel, MS Word
Artistic skills and competences	Keen amateur photographer. Photographs regularly printed in school magazine
Driving licence	Category B
Additional information	I have taken part in a 2-week exchange visit with students at Park Comprehensive School in Eastbourne, UK.

Conversion tables

Area

English to metric	
1 square inch (in^2)	= 6.452 square centimetres
1 square foot (ft^2)	= 0.0929 square metres
1 acre (ac)	= 4,047 square metres
1 square mile (m^2)	= 2.59 square kilometres

Metric to English	
1 square centimetre	= 0.155 square inches
1 square metre	= 10.764 square feet
1 square kilometre	= 0.3861 square miles

English to English	
1 square foot	= 144 square inches
1 acre	= 43,560 square feet
1 square mile	= 640 acres

Distance

English to metric	
1 inch (in)	= 2.54 centimetres
1 foot (ft)	= 30.48 centimetres
1 yard (yd)	= 0.9144 metres
1 mile (mi)	= 1.609 kilometres

Metric to English	
1 centimetre	= 0.3937 inches (⅜ inch)
1 metre	= 39.37 inches (3 feet, 3 ⅜ inches)
1 kilometre	= 0.62137 miles

English to English	
1 foot	= 12 inches
1 yard	= 3 feet
1 mile	= 5,280 feet

Energy/Force

English to metric	
1 horsepower (hp)	= 0.746 kilowatts
1 ounce-force	= 0.278 newtons
1 pound-force (lbf)	= 4.448 newtons
1 foot pounds (ft-lb)	= 1.355 newtons-metres/joules
1 inch pounds	= 0.112 newtons-metres
1 pounds per foot	= 14.59 newtons-metres
1 British thermal unit (BTU)	= 1055 joules

Metric to English	
1 kilowatt	= 1.341 horsepower
1 newton	= 3.597 ounce-force
1 newton	= 0.224 pound-force
1 newtons-metres / 1 joule	= 0.738 foot pounds
1 kilojoule	= 0.948 British thermal units

Mass/Weight

English to metric	
1 ounce (oz)	= 28.35 grams
1 pound (lb)	= 0.453 kilograms
1 UK ton ('long ton')	= 1,016 kilograms
1 US ton ('short ton')	= 907 kilograms

Metric to English	
1 gram	= 0.035 ounces
1 kilogram	= 2 pounds, 3.3 ounces

English to English	
1 pound	= 16 ounces
1 UK ton ('long ton')	= 2,240 pounds
1 US ton ('short ton')	= 2,000 pounds

Metric to metric	
1 metric tonne (t)	= 1,000 kilograms

Temperature

Fahrenheit (F) to Celsius: subtract 32, then multiply by 5, then divide by 9
Celsius to Fahrenheit: multiply by 9, then divide by 5, then add 2

Volume

English to metric	
1 fluid UK ounce (fl oz)	= 28.41 millilitres
1 UK pint (pt)	= 0.568 litres
1 UK quart (qt)	= 1.137 litres
1 UK gallon (gal)	= 4.546 litres
1 fluid US ounce	= 29.57 millilitres
1 US pint	= 0.473 litres
1 US quart	= 0.946 litres
1 US gallon	= 3.785 litres
1 cubic inch (in^3)	= 16 cubic centimetres
1 cubic foot (ft^3)	= 0.03 cubic metres

Metric to English	
1 litre	= 0.568 UK pints
1 litre	= 0.473 US pints

English to English	
1 pint	= 16 fluid ounces
1 quart	= 2 pints
1 gallon	= 4 quarts

Terms, units and abbreviations

Term		Unit	
English	**German**	**English**	**German**
apparent admittance (*Y*)	Scheinleitwert (*Y*)	siemens (S)	Siemens (S)
capacitance (*C*)	Kapazität (*C*)	farad (F)	Farad (F)
charge (*Q*)	Ladung	coulomb (C) or Ampereseconds (As)	Coulomb (C) Amperesekunden (As)
conductance (*G*)	Leitwert	siemens (S)	Siemens (S)
current (*I*)	Strom	ampere (A)	Ampere (A)
electric field strength (*E*)	Elektrische Feldstärke	volt per metre (V/m)	Volt pro Meter (V/m
electromotive force (*E*)	Spannung, Elektromotorische Kraft (*U*)	volt (V)	Volt (V)
frequency (*f*)	Frequenz (*f*)	cycles per second (cps)	Hertz (Hz)
frequency (*f*)	Frequenz (*f*)	hertz (Hz),	Hertz (Hz)
angular frequency (ω)	Kreisfrequenz (ω)	radian per second (rad/s)	1/s
resonant frequency (*fr*)	Resonanzfrequenz	hertz (Hz)	Hertz (Hz)
gain (G)	Verstärkung, Gewinn	Dezibel (dB)	Dezibel (dB)
inductance (*L*)	Induktivität (*L*)	henry (H)	Henry (H)
magnetic field strength (*H*)	Magnetische Feldstärke (*H*)	ampere turn per metre (At/m)	Ampere pro meter (A/m)
magnetic flux density (*B*)	Magnetische Flußdichte (*B*)	tesla (T)	Tesla (T)
phase angle (φ)	Phasenwinkel (φ)	degree	Grad
apparent power (*S*)	Scheinleistung (*S*)	volt-ampere (VA)	Voltampere (VA)
reactive power(*Q*)	Blindleistung (*Q*)	Volt-ampere-reactive (var)	Var
reactance (*X*)	Blindwiderstand (*X*)	ohm (Ω)	Ohm (Ω)
capacitive reactance (X_C)	Kapzitiver Blindwiderstand (X_C)	ohm (Ω)	Ohm (Ω)
inductive reactance(X_L)	Iduktiver Blindwiderstand (X_L)	ohm (Ω)	Ohm (Ω)
resistance (*R*)	Widerstand	ohm (Ω)	Ohm (Ω)
rotational speed	Drehzahl	revolutions per minute (rpm)	1/s
susceptance (*B*)	Blindleitwert (*B*)	siemens (S)	Siemens (S)
voltage (*V*)	Spannung (*U*)	volt (V)	Volt (V)

For numerical expressions see pp. 60–61.

Acknowledgements

Bilder
S. 6/1/Corbis/© Monty Rakusen/cultura/Corbis (RF), S. 6/2/© Don Mason/Blend Images/Corbis (RF), S. 6/3/mauritius images/ib/ Olaf Döhring, S. 6/4/shutterstock/auremar; S. 8/Alamy/© Vasiliy Vishnevskiy; S. 12/Sebastian Horr; S. 14/1/Eaton.com, S. 14/2/Eaton.com, S. 14/3/AKG/Ria Nowosti, S. 14/4/Eaton.com, S. 14/5/Wikipedia gemeinfrei/Stehfun; S. 15/shutterstock/TonyV3112; S. 16/1/shutterstock/Matee Nuserm; S. 16/2/Alamy © Juice Images (RF), S. 16/3/shutterstock/michaeljung, S. 16/4/shutterstock/Lighthunter; S. 17/1/ shutterstock/Dmitry Kalinovsky, S. 17/2/shutterstock/ auremar, S. 17/3/shutterstock/ Kekyalyaynen, S. 17/4/shutterstock/ auremar; S. 20/1/CBB Redaktion, S. 20/1/CBB Redaktion, S. 20/1/CBB Redaktion, S. 20/2/CBB Redaktion, S. 20/3/ shutterstock/nuttapong, S. 20/4/CBB Redaktion, S. 20/5/CBB Redaktion, S. 20/6/CBB Redaktion, S. 20/7/CBB Redaktion, S. 20/8/CBB Redaktion, S. 20/9/CBB Redaktion, S. 20/10/CBB Redaktion, S. 20/11/shutterstock/ Prapann, S. 20/12/CBB Redaktion, S. 20/13/CBB Redaktion, S. 20/14/CBB Redaktion, S. 20/15/CBB Redaktion, S. 20/16/CBB Redaktion, S. 20/17/CBB Redaktion, S. 20/18/shutterstock/lenestan, S. 20/19/CBB Redaktion, S. 22/1/Sebastian Horr, S. 22/2/shutterstock/Chepe Nicoli, S. 22/3/shutterstock/auremar; S. 23/1/GDI, S. 23/2/ shutterstock/Tompet, S. 23/3/shutterstock/Taigi, S. 23/4/shutterstock/ Andrzej Tokarski S. 23/5/shutterstock/Abel Tumik; S. 25/shutterstock/ Goodluz; S. 28/1/shutterstock/ Bauer Alexander, S. 28/2/shutterstock/cosma; S. 28/3/ shutterstock/idea for life, S. 28/4/shutterstock/fexel, S. 28/5/Sebastian Horr; S. 34/shutterstock/visivastudio; S. 36/shutterstock/dcwcreations; S. 38/1/iStock/ MaksymBondarchuk S. 38/2/iStock/ OkatayOrtakcioglu S. 38/3/ shutterstock/ TetiunaYurchenko, S. 38/4/shutterstock/Kjpargeter, S. 38/5/shutterstock/kavione, S. 38/6/shutterstock/Andrey Eremin, S. 38/7/iStock/Andrey Eremin, S. 38/8/iStock/ kizilkayaphotos, S. 38/9/iStock/ scphoto, S. 38/10/shutterstock/AndrewBuckin; S. 42/1/CBB Redaktion, S42/2/CBB Redaktion; S. 44/1/Micheal Benford, S. 44/2/Michael Benford; S. 45/shutterstock/Vronska; S. 46/1/Alamy/© Q-Images (RM), S. 46/2/shutterstock/ Luiz Rocha, S. 46/3/shutterstock/Nagel Photography, S. 46/4/shutterstock/nikkytok; S. 47/1/shutterstock/Dmitry Kalinovsky S. 47/2/Alamy/© moodboard; S. 54/shutterstock/Aliance; S. 55/1/shutterstock/derter, S. 55/2/shutterstock/dedMazay; S. 57/shutterstock/art4all; S. 59/shutterstock/Tyler Olson; S. 62/1/Vaillant, S. 62/2/Honeywell; S. 66/1-10/Wolf-Rainer Windisch; S. 67/shutterstock/Ron Leishman; S. 72/Corbis/ © Jim Sugar; S. 75/ shutterstock/Dmitry Popov; S. 76/1/shutterstock/Krasowit, S. 76/2/Wolf-Rainer Windisch, S. 76/3/shutterstock/ Madarakis S. 76/4/shutterstock/Boris Sosnovyy S. 76/5/shutterstock/Boltenkoff, S. 76/6/Wolf-Rainer Windisch, S.76/7/shutterstock/Swapan Photography, S. 76/8/Benning – duspol 1000V; S. 77/1/Wolf-Rainer Windisch, S. 77/2/Max Walter; S. 78/ Wolf-Rainer Windisch; S. 79/Corbis/ © Ian Lishman/Juice Images/Corbis (RF); S. 82/ Wolf-Rainer Windisch; S. 86/1/shutterstock/OZaiachin, S. 86/2/shutterstock/ pukach, S. 86/3/shutterstock/ Tom Wang S. 86/4/shutterstock/dekede, S. 86/5/shutterstock/cynoclub S. 86/6/shutterstock/Richard Lyons S. 86/7/shutterstock/ Oleg GawriloFF, S. 86/8/shutterstock/Carsten Reisinger; S. 87/1-2/Michael Benford; S. 96/ shutterstock/Rafa Irusta; S. 98/Vaillant; S. 100/1/shutterstock/Nataliya Hora, S. 100/2/shutterstock/BestPhotoStudio, S. 100/3/shutterstock/isak55, S. 100/4/shutterstock/MaxyM; S. 102/1/shutterstock/Moneca, S. 102/2/ shutterstock/ S.P., S. 102/3/shutterstock/dedMazay; S.110/shutterstock/cozyta; S. 111/Corbis/ © Jade/Blend Images/Corbis (RF); S. 114/shutterstock/Zurijeta; S.115/shutterstock/ Aelius Aaron; S. 120/shutterstock/Ammentorp Photography; S. 122/shutterstock/ Monkey Business Images; S. 124/shutterstock/amorfati.art; S. 135/firefly solar; S.136/shutterstock/Emily Taner; S. 137/firefly solar; S. 138/shutterstock/johnbraid

Mit freundlicher Unterstützung folgender Unternehmen: Ritter Starkstromtechnik GmbH & Co. KG, Dortmund; Vaillant Deutschland GmbH & Co. KG; Firefly Solar Generators Limited; BENNING GmbH & Co.KG

Common irregular verbs

be – was/were – been	sein
become – became – become	werden
begin – began – begun	anfangen, beginnen
break – broke – broken	brechen
bring – brought – brought	bringen
build – built – built	bauen
buy – bought – bought	kaufen
catch – caught – caught	fangen
choose – chose – chosen	wählen
come – came – come	kommen
cost – cost – cost	kosten
cut – cut – cut	schneiden
do – did – done	tun, machen
draw – drew – drawn	zeichnen
dream – dreamt – dreamt	träumen
drink – drank – drunk	trinken
drive – drove – driven	fahren
eat – ate – eaten	essen
fall – fell – fallen	fallen
feed – fed – fed	füttern, ernähren
feel – felt – felt	(sich) fühlen, empfinden
fight – fought – fought	kämpfen
find – found – found	finden
fit – fit/fitted – fit/fitted	passen
fly – flew – flown	fliegen
forget – forgot – forgotten	vergessen
get – got – got (*AE* gotten)	bekommen
give – gave – given	geben
go – went – gone	gehen, fahren
grow – grew – grown	wachsen
hang – hung – hung	hängen
have – had – had	haben
hear – heard – heard	hören
hide – hid – hidden	(sich) verstecken
hit – hit – hit	schlagen
hold – held – held	halten, festhalten
keep – kept – kept	behalten
know – knew – known	kennen, wissen
lay – laid – laid	legen
learn – learnt/learned – learnt/learned	lernen
leave – left – left	abfahren, verlassen, weggehen
let – let – let	lassen
lose – lost – lost	verlieren
make – made – made	machen
mean – meant – meant	meinen, bedeuten
meet – met – met	treffen
pay – paid – paid	bezahlen
put – put – put	setzen, stellen, legen
read – read – read	lesen
ride – rode – ridden	reiten, fahren
ring – rang – rung	klingeln, anrufen
rise – rose – risen	(an)steigen
run – ran – run	laufen, rennen
say – said – said	sagen
see – saw – seen	sehen
sell – sold – sold	verkaufen
send – sent – sent	senden, schicken
set – set – set	setzen, stellen
show – showed – shown	zeigen
shut – shut – shut	schließen
sing – sang – sung	singen
sit – sat – sat	sitzen
sleep – slept – slept	schlafen
smell – smelt/smelled – smelt/smelled	riechen
speak – spoke – spoken	sprechen
spell – spelt/spelled – spelt/spelled	buchstabieren
spend – spent – spent	ausgeben, verbringen
stand – stood – stood	stehen
steal – stole – stolen	stehlen
swim – swam – swum	schwimmen
take – took – taken	nehmen
teach – taught – taught	unterrichten, beibringen
tell – told – told	sagen, erzählen
think – thought – thought	denken
throw – threw – thrown	werfen
understand – understood – understood	verstehen
wake – woke – woken	wecken
wear – wore – worn	tragen (Kleidung)
win – won – won	gewinnen
write – wrote – written	schreiben